LETTERKENNY

Where the Winding Swilly Flows

KIERAN KELLY

First printed in 2014 by
Browne Printers Ltd.
Port Road,
Letterkenny,
Co. Donegal

Designed by Louise O'Grady
Front Cover designed by Michael Eaton
Illustrations by John Ruddy
© Kieran Kelly 2014

All rights resserved. No part of this publication may be reprinted or reproduced or utilised in electronic, mechanical or other means, now known or hereafter invented, including photocopying and recording, or otherwise without the prior written permission of both the copyright owner and the publisher of this book.

Hardback: 978 0 9930630 0 8
Paperback: 978 0 9930630 1 5

Kieran Kelly
Email: windingswilly@gmail.com

For Olivia

The publication of this book would not have been possible without the generous assistance from the people and companies listed below:

Platinum Sponsor: Letterkenny Shopping Centre

Gold Sponsors:
Dr. Philip Boyce, Bishop of Raphoe
Letterkenny Town Council
Cllr. Ciaran Brogan
Old Letterkenny Reunion
John Watson, Watson Hire
Leonard Watson, Watson Menswear
Richard McNamara, McDonald's Letterkenny
Patrick Tinney & Sons
J.P. McCloskey, Evolve Menswear
Lawrence Harrigan, Highland Motors
Cllr. Gerry McMonagle
Letterkenny Community Heritage Group
Paudge & Anne McGowan

Silver Sponsors:

Cllr. Jimmy Kavannagh
Cllr. Jim Lynch
Cllr. Dessie Larkin
Cllr. Lisa Culbert
Cllr. Tom Crossan
Brian Gallagher, Station House Hotel
Mark Doherty, Century Cinemas

J.J. Reid Motors
Martin Kelly, Kelly's Centra
Jason Black, Black's Centra
Paul Foley, Donnelly & Foley
Bernie Lapsley, Donegal Stationery Company
Enda Nicholls, Arena 7
Eunan MacIntyre, Mac's Mace

Patrick Gildea Hairdressing
Alfie Greene, Greene's Shoes
Brendan McGlynn, The Quiet Moment
Letterkenny Music & Drama Group
Workhouse Theatre Co.
An Grianán Theatre
Gerard McCormick, Magees Chemist
Brian McCormick Sports & Leisure

LETTERKENNY
SHOPPING CENTRE

Proud to be the Platinum Sponsor of
Letterkenny: Where the Winding Swilly **Flows**

Contents

Acknowledgements

Introduction	13
1: Leitir Ceanainn	19
2: Plantation & Early Development	36
3: The Battle of Scarrifhollis 1650	52
4: The 'Established Church' and Presbyterianism	57
5: The Letterkenny Ascendancy and the Era of the 'Big House'	71
6: Was Wolfe Tone Really Arrested in Letterkenny?	91
7: Nineteenth Century Change	97
8: Hiring Fairs & the Workhouse	106
9: The Derryveagh Evictions 1861 and Tenant Rights	116
10: The Growth of Catholic Confidence	125
11: The Cathedral of Saints Eunan and Columba	131
12: Educational Establishments in Letterkenny	143
13: World War 1 & Letterkenny	160
14: The Growth of Nationalism	179
15: Independence and Civil War	188
16: The Port and Railway	198
17: Twentieth Century Development	209
18: Sports Clubs in Letterkenny	225
19: Theatre and the Arts	249
20: Boom, Bust and the Future	265
Conclusion	270

Chronology

Appendices

Further Reading

Acknowledgements

I first got the idea of writing a history of my hometown of Letterkenny in 2007. I had recently returned home from living in London for a number of years and my cousin, Brighdín Carr, a teacher in Lurgybrack N.S., approached me and asked if I had any local history ideas that her 6th Class could work on for a project called "The Fire Within". I was immediately reminded of a story about the original town of Letterkenny being located at Conwal before being destroyed by a cat knocking over a lantern and setting the town ablaze, therefore forcing the townspeople to move to where the current town is located today. A 'fire within', I told her, was therefore the origins of Letterkenny.

As I had to take this class on a tour of Letterkenny, I immediately set about refreshing my knowledge on the history of my hometown. I went to the attic and found some old books and Christmas Annuals; I went to the Library and found even more; I also shamelessly resorted to the use of one of the banes of accurate historical research, Wikipedia. I soon discovered though that putting together the information became quite difficult as I would glean bits of information about one aspect of the town in one book, another bit in another book, and so on and the thought occurred to me – wouldn't it be so much easier if all the information available on the town from its origins right up to the present day were together in one place? What you hold now in your hand is my attempt to do just that.

However, as I went through the several history books and guides relating to Letterkenny over the years, rather than just wanting to regurgitate the facts and figures from these previously recorded histories of the town, I found myself going deeper and deeper in the research and as a result, sometimes arriving at vastly different conclusions to local events than what I had previously accepted. For example, I had always believed that the settlement at Conwal, founded by St. Fiachra, was destroyed in a fire caused by that cat; that Letterkenny was named after the O'Cannon Clan of ancient Ireland; that Wolfe Tone was captured at the Market Square and that the Ulster Plantation had only a minor part to play in the town's history. After years of careful research, I now believe differently.

That is not to say that previous historians of Letterkenny were deliberately inaccurate in their recording of events, far from it. That was merely the local history that they had been taught by those that came before them and who were they to doubt their teachers of history? So much of local history has been handed down orally over the years from generation to generation that somewhere along the line accuracy becomes lost. Where possible, this book attempts at all times to rely on primary sources of events, rather than oral history to avoid any distortion of facts. Primary sources on local history tend to be more accurate the closer you get to the modern day and therefore for much older events, secondary sources are, of course, required and very much necessary.

Using these previous recorded histories of Letterkenny as a springboard for research, this book attempts to cover all aspects of Letterkenny's rich history and heritage - from early settlement patterns and the naming of the area, through decisive battles in its hinterland and the effects of the arrival of Scottish and English planters in the seventeenth century, right up to the recent industrial and commercial growth of the town and the present day.

While sometimes disagreeing with the opinions of events by previous local historians, this book would not be possible were it not for their extensive research and perseverance in the preservation of local history over the years and this attempt by myself humbly stands on the vast shoulders of these giants of local heritage.

Canon Edward Maguire wrote the first known extensive recording of the town's history in 1917 entitled *"Letterkenny: Past and Present"* and my book owes more than just a salutary nod to this detailed examination of our town. Without his book, many details in the town's past would have not been preserved and for that reason above all, local historians of Letterkenny owe him a huge debt. Canon Maguire was a former Principal of the 'Old Seminary' and was the first Principal of the new St. Eunan's College in 1906 as well as being to the forefront of the early GAA in the county, so much so that the Senior County Championship Cup was named after him. A keen local historian, he also wrote two detailed volumes on the history of the Diocese of Raphoe.

Sam Fleming of Windyhall also wrote a book entitled *"Letterkenny: Past and Present"* in 1979 as well as a pamphlet on *"Redmond O'Hanlon"* detailing his assertion that the famous rapparree of seventeenth century Ireland is buried in Conwal Parish Church, an event that we shall look at in this book. Fleming was involved in the Macra na Feirme movement, as well as voluntarily taking people on historic walks through graveyards in the town, pointing out the graves of prominent members of the town's past. Sam treasured his inheritance of local historical knowledge and he gladly passed it on to others.

Former Urban District Councilor May McClintock has recorded the history of Letterkenny and its surrounding hinterland through many articles in the Donegal Annual and the Letterkenny Christmas Annual over the years as well as publishing her own books *"Seed-time & Harvest"* (1994) and *"After the Battering Ram"* (1991).

Niall McGinley, the son of former TD Dr. J.P. McGinley, has contributed enormously to the preservation of the knowledge of our town's history also, most notably through his publications of *"Dr. McGinley And His Times"* (1985), *"Donegal, Ireland and the First World War"* (1984) and *"Our Town: Letterkenny and hinterland"* (1994).

Recently, Liam O'Duibhir has undertaken invaluable research into the role played by County Donegal, and by consequence the town of Letterkenny, in the War of Independence, (*"The Donegal Awakening: Donegal & the War of Independence"*, 2010) and the Civil War (*"Donegal and the Civil War: the Untold Story"*, 2011).

Retired Colonel from the Irish Army and former President of the Donegal Historical Society, Declan O'Carroll has written accounts on Rockhill House (1998) and Letterkenny Golf Club (2012) as well as contributing to studies on the Battle of Scarrifhollis (2001).

Many guides and pamphlets for tourists have also been written over the years and they serve as a useful stepping-stone in researching the town's history. The *"Letterkenny Official Guide 1952"* and the *"An Tostal Festival Guide 1954"* both give valuable insights into the town at that time while *"A Local History of Letterkenny"* was compiled by the Letterkenny Guild of the ICA (Irish Countrywomen's Association) in the early 1980s.

Since 1982, of course, the Letterkenny & District Christmas Annual has been instrumental in preserving the knowledge of our town's past through contributions from many local historians as well as interviews with some of the town's oldest residents who gladly shared their memories of experiences in growing up in the town. While there are too many contributors over the years to name everyone, the work of several local historians stand out – namely Cllr. Patsy O'Donnell, Sean Curran, Dick Duffy (football), Sean O'Boyle (GAA), Paddy Curran and Rory Delap (Railways) as well as so many others through the years. Edited since 1987 by Cllr. Jim Lynch, the Christmas Annual remains a stalwart of the preservation of the town's history and a seasonal treat for all 'townies'.

These are just some of the influences that have guided me in my research on the history of the town of Letterkenny, without whom none of this would have been possible. I am also indebted to the staff of the Donegal County Library who assisted me in my research with patience and warmth. Being able to access the primary sources of the *Derry Journal* and the *Donegal News* newspapers was like taking a step back in time.

I would especially like to thank those that read various early drafts and chapters of the book and who provided invaluable feedback as regards content and readability – namely Declan O'Carroll, Liam O'Duibhir, May McClintock, Niall McGinley, Ciaran O'Donnell, Pluincead O'Fearraigh, Canon Stewart Wright, Fr. Frank McHugh, Sarah Craig, Davin Doherty, Iarla McGowan, Billy Patterson, Anne McGowan and, especially, Jamie Murphy. Susan Daly also very kindly provided me with several local history books that belonged to her late husband Benny while Connie Maguire let me read the original minutes of St. Eunan's GAA club, which helped fill in a lot of gaps. Of course I have to mention Paul Doherty and Caoimhe Callaghan for listening to me rabbit on as various drafts were continuously tweaked.

The multi-talented actor and illustrator John Ruddy has brought many of the stories in the book to life beautifully and I am delighted to have him associated with this work while Louise O'Grady has performed a beautiful job on the overall design.

The Rev. Raymond Blair has kindly supplied me with archive newspaper reports, while my talks with William Harris of the Gospel Hall were both illuminating and delightful. Robin Roddie, archivist with the Methodist Historical Society of Ireland was most helpful as was Brother Donatus Brazil of the Presentation Brothers Archives. Rev. Tommy Bruce very kindly met with me over a coffee and assisted with dates and names of former ministers of Trinity Presbyterian Church. Anne Foxe, Doreen Sheridan, John Haran, Odhran McGowan and Maire Nic Ghairbhe shared their time with me also, providing me with details of their schools and I am very thankful to them.

In 2011, Stanley White of Beechwood Road gave me a copy of the original poem of 'Letterkenny Town' that had been preserved by his mother, Mary. The poem most likely predates the well-known local song, as you'll notice that certain words are different, so we can only conclud e that the lyrics were later formatted to fit the tune. I am most grateful to Stanley, who sadly is no longer with us, for providing me with the poem.

For those individuals and businesses that assisted with the funding of the book's costs, I am very grateful. There is a separate list with each generous group, business or individual listed and to each of them I owe a huge thank you, the publication of this book would not have been possible without their assistance.

My mother, Brigid Kelly, was naturally the one reader I wanted to impress the most and she offered me great insight and feedback along the way and for that (and of course many other things!) I am eternally grateful. Of course, my father Hugh, and brothers and sisters Patrick, Mary, Brian, Michael and Cathy have always been supportive in this project, each assisting me in different ways and I am very thankful. My aunts Mary Mansfield and Anna Shiels and my uncle Barney McDaid have always been generous with their time for me, helping me fill in little details along the way.

I would like to thank my beautiful fiancée, Olivia Wilson, for her unwavering support and understanding for me throughout this project. She has had to listen to a lot of annoying '*Did you know…*' trivia as we walked past different buildings in the town over the last couple of years and for displaying the patience of a saint, I am forever thankful.

Lastly, I would like to thank you, the reader, for taking the time to read my opinion of events of the past regarding our town of Letterkenny. If it contradicts your own opinions and provokes a lively debate then I will be absolutely delighted! History is meant to stimulate and if we merely agree with each other all the time then we will never be able to properly question our role in history. And as an old history teacher of mine once told me, if we don't ask the questions, then we'll never know the answers!

Kieran Kelly
2014

Letterkenny Town

My name is Pat McCready, I'll have you all to know
I come from dear old Donegal where the winding Swilly flows
You may search this wide world over but no equal can be found
To the spot where I was born in sweet Letterkenny Town.

When the gold and purple sun sets over Sentry Hill
It illumes the earth from sky to sea from Crocanar to Knockybrin
And old Manor o'er the Swilly glistens brightly in the sun
Twas then I loved best of all Sweet Letterkenny Town.

My Mother's tears were falling that sad morning long ago
When I left that wee thatched cottage in the bounds of Ballyboe
Saying my buachaill save your money and old Ireland don't turn down
But be sure that you return again to Letterkenny Town.

Many times I've wandered and many miles afar
But still I think on the good old days I spent up through Glencar
With my little Irish Colleen and her lovely eyes of brown
But alas today she's gone away from Letterkenny Town.

Now since I've returned again many changes I have found.
My mother she is slumbering in Conwal's holy ground
And my little dark haired colleen, o God knows where she has flown
For all are strangers now to me in Letterkenny Town.

Where are the boys that gathered when the evening tide would fall
To meet and chat the hours away around the old stone wall.
And the country boys would linger till the old town clock struck ten
Then the gay old lights went lowering in sweet Letterkenny Town.

Here's to Letterkenny, the Pride of Donegal
May peace and plenty warm each heart within it's white washed walls
May the sun shine brightly o'er you and may fortune overflow
On the good old boys and girls I knew in Letterkenny Town

An aerial view of Letterkenny in 2013

Introduction

    Amongst the rocks and the heather of Meenaroy, a small trickle of water bursts forth from a spring and gently flows down the side of a hill. From this inauspicious beginning, the trickle flows slowly eastwards, with nearby tributaries and streams joining up to make the flow of water stronger and more purposeful. With each additional tributary joining, the stream widens out to become a river, gathering pace as it moves ever gradually through the surrounding glens and valleys. Eventually, the river meets a town, meandering through it as it continues on its journey out into a much larger lough before finally reaching its destination of the North Sea. This is the River Swilly, and the town it flows through, is Letterkenny.

    A lot of history has occurred along the banks of this river over many centuries - events that have helped shape the destiny of the entire region. Early hunter-gatherers of Neolithic times made shelters along its banks, availing of the rich supply of fresh salmon and trout that the river had in abundance. The river acted as a territory boundary for several ancient Gaelic clans when ferocious battles took place at the crossings as they made advances into each other's lands. In the early seventeenth century, Presbyterian and Anglican settlers from Scotland and England made their homes on the northern hillside, and availing of the constant supply of fresh running water, they laid the foundations for the new market town of Letterkenny. As trade and commerce grew in the subsequent centuries, large ships from all over the world sailed up this river to dock at Ballyraine and the Thorn to deliver shipments of corn, coal and other goods for businesses in the ever-developing market town.

Letterkenny - Where the Winding Swilly Flows

As centuries of history occurred around it, the river kept on flowing; a constant amidst all the change. The gentle flow of the meandering Swilly River and the history of the town of Letterkenny and its immediate hinterland are forever linked, bonded by a sense of mutual appreciation and necessity. Sadly, in recent times, the river appears to have lost its relevance to the modern town. Boats no longer sail upon it; goods are no longer unloaded at its ports. Today the waters of the Swilly River remain still and calm, save for the gentle movement of its graceful flow.

However, the town through which the river flows stands proudly today as the commercial and industrial hub of County Donegal. Its population of almost 20,000 people makes it not only the largest town in the county but also the largest town in any of the three Ulster counties in the Republic of Ireland. It has been transformed in recent years into a multi-cultural, multi-denominational metropolis of the northwest with its most recent residents originating from Poland, Ghana, Nigeria and many other countries from across the world. Despite its Ulster Plantation roots, today it is predominately a town made up of Roman Catholics and serves as the ecclesiastical centre of the Diocese of Raphoe, home to the only Roman Catholic Cathedral in the county. Descendants of the original Plantation settlers still live here of course, worshipping in either the Church of Ireland, situated opposite the Cathedral, or at Trinity Presbyterian meeting house on the Main Street, while many other religions practice their faith in the multidenominational town today such as Baptists, Methodists, Christian Brethren, Hindus and Muslims.

There are currently ten primary schools and four secondary schools while the Letterkenny Institute of Technology has welcomed thousands of third level students each year since its formation in 1971. New residential housing estates and apartments have expanded the town outwards rapidly since the boom of the Celtic Tiger in the late twentieth and early twenty first centuries while many sports clubs and amenities are available for the social interaction of its residents. In the Arts, An Grianán Theatre and the Regional Cultural Centre play host to dramatic and musical talent of the highest order while from a commercial viewpoint, large retail parks bring thousands of shoppers each week. Numerous pubs, hotels, restaurants and nightclubs have transformed the town into a hub of entertainment in recent years with many arriving at weekends to revel in the vibrant Letterkenny nightlife. It is, in short, a rapidly developing town with much to offer any visitor or settler.

This then, is the Letterkenny that we know today - a rapidly growing and expanding modern urban centre. However, as residents of this large town, have you ever stopped for a moment to wonder how we got here? Why, for example, has Letterkenny's population risen so dramatically in the last fifty years at the expense of other towns in the county? If it was simply due to an urban expansion that was commonplace as part of the Celtic Tiger era, why did other towns such as Donegal Town and Ballyshannon not experience the same rapid rate of expansion? As can be seen from the graph, this surge in population in Letterkenny began in the 1950s. This was due, in no small part, to increased activity from the

Introduction

Industrial Development Authority while the Urban District Council redrew the urban boundary at this time and offered incentives for large industries to expand into the town. Aided by these incentives, investments in new businesses led to a slow and steady growth, with, for example, the county's first supermarket (Dillon Bros.) opening in the late 1960s, soon followed by Bests and Dunnes Stores.

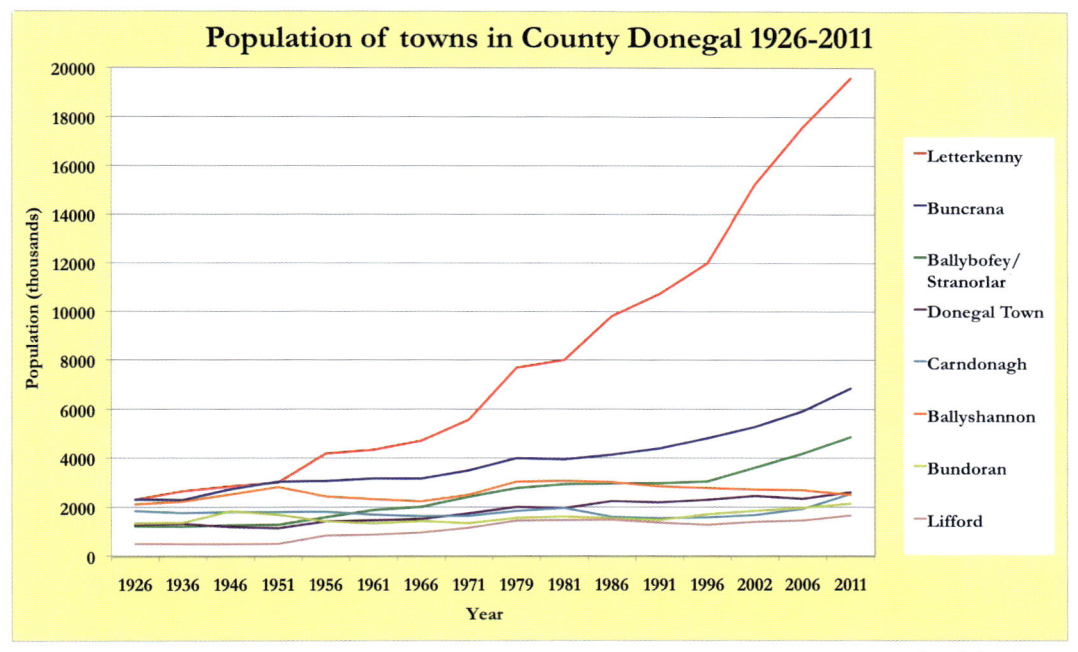

Population changes of the major towns in Donegal between 1926 and 2011. Source: www.census.ie

The 1970s heralded the arrival of the Courtald's (later Unifi) factory and the opening of the Regional Technical College (later LYIT) bringing to the town a skilled workforce and a readymade supply of freshly trained graduates. Industrial development continued into the 1980s and 1990s while, at the same time, the one-time parochial market town slowly transformed into the commercial centre of the county with many large chain stores opening their businesses in new retail parks and shopping centres. With each new influx of people that arrived for work in these new businesses, the town gradually expanded outwards from its original epicentre of the Main Street with new suburban housing estates and apartments springing up in the hinterland to cater for this new demand for settlement.

So if this is 'how' Letterkenny has expanded, 'why' Letterkenny grew at the expense of the other towns of the county is simply down to its location. In 2002, Letterkenny was officially designated a 'Gateway Town', linking it primarily to the city of Derry, and acting as a gateway into the northwest of the County. It can be argued though that the town has always been a 'gateway' with people

Letterkenny - Where the Winding Swilly Flows

passing through it in both directions, either from the west into the east, or vice versa.

The Plantation town of Letterkenny was built in the western most part of the area known as the Laggan. The town consequently became the 'gateway' between this low lying fertile region of East Donegal and the more mountainous and rocky regions to the northwest of the county - benefiting most notably with the growth of the weekly markets and the Hiring Fairs. Children and adults attending the 'Rabble Days' in the town from the eighteenth and nineteenth centuries arrived from these poorer regions of the northwest hoping to find seasonal employment on the bigger farms in the east. The market town of Letterkenny acted as the conduit for this to occur and benefited as a result.

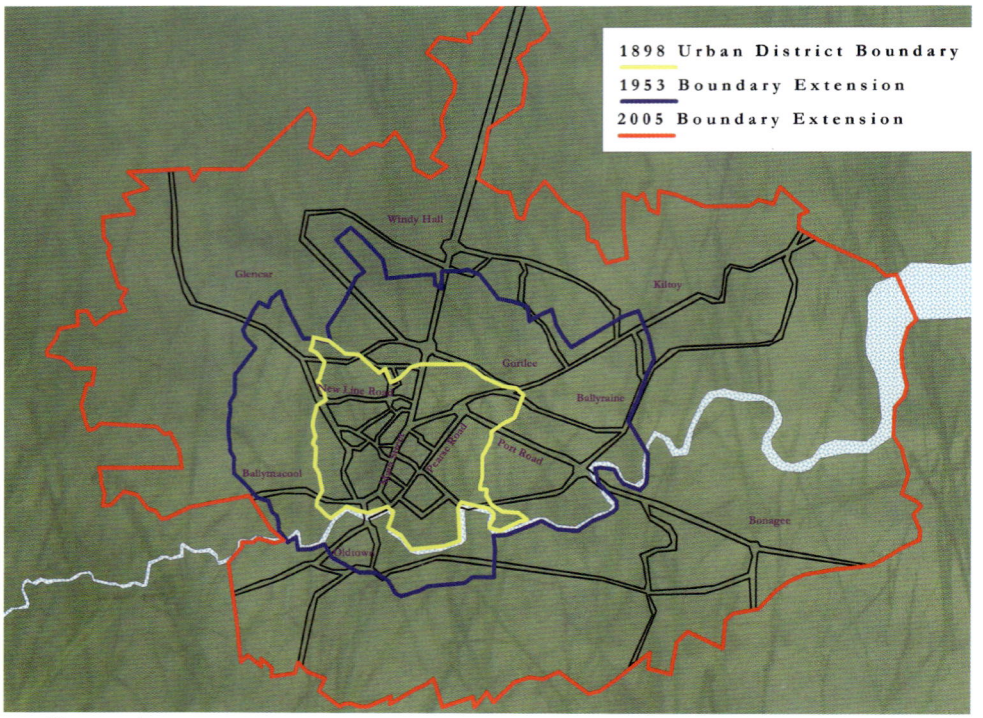

The expansion of Letterkenny outwards is indicated by the redrawing of the Urban Boundary over 100 years. Courtesy of Letterkenny Town Council

As the weekly and seasonal markets continued to develop and expand, railways were built connecting the city of Derry and West Donegal, passing through the town. In the heyday of the railways in County Donegal, Letterkenny was the only town in the county to house both rival rail companies (the CDR and the L&LSR), again principally because of its location. When large factories and retail giants opened premises in the late twentieth century, it was for the very same reasons. The location of the town almost in the centre of the county offered both a trained workforce and of course willing customers in the immediate vicinity. With each person that passed through this 'gateway', the town grew accordingly.

Introduction

However, aside from this, one of the main reasons that Letterkenny has developed so dramatically to become the largest town of the county is without doubt simply due to one crucial factor – its people. The determination and zeal of countless men and women throughout its history made the town succeed. The enthusiasm and drive of many shopkeepers, businessmen and local residents over the centuries have left an indelible mark on the town's landscape, both structurally and socially. The history of the town would be nothing without the people that helped shape it, and it is these people that we shall look at primarily through the course of this book. We shall meet many of these individuals – men and women who have each played a crucial role in shaping and defining what the town of Letterkenny would eventually become.

People such as:

- Captain Patrick Crawford, the original lease holder for the building of the town as part of the Ulster Plantation
- Lady Johanna Everard and Sir George Marbury, who initially developed the small Market Town
- Sir William Sempill who created the district of Manor Sempill with Letterkenny at its centre
- John Boyd of Ballymacool House and his many descendants
- Rev. John Kinnear, MP and champion of Tenant Rights
- Bishop Patrick O'Donnell who organized the building of the Cathedral, St. Eunan's College and other schools
- James Duffy, a Victoria Cross medal recipient for bravery in World War 1
- Charles Kelly, William McKinney, the Dillon Brothers and other large employers
- John Storey and John G. Larkin, former town clerks in local government

These men and women, and many, many more, each contributed to and defined what the town of Letterkenny would become. As the dust seems to have settled on the almost uncontrollable expansion that took place in the latter half of the twentieth century and with the Celtic Tiger having gone into hibernation, there is no better time to ask ourselves who we are and where we have come from. Many old buildings so synonymous with the town are now gone, lost under the wrecking ball of development, the most recent of these being the locally cherished Oatfield Sweet Factory, demolished in April 2014. However, we must remember that Letterkenny is so much more than just its buildings. Peel back the outer layers of what you might perceive the town to be and you come across something much more rich and satisfying - the people of Letterkenny.

I consider myself very privileged to come from the town. I was born in the General Hospital, attended Scoil Cholmcille Primary School and later

Letterkenny - Where the Winding Swilly Flows

St. Eunan's College Secondary School. I have played football for Letterkenny Rovers F.C. and St. Eunan's GAA club and have appeared on stage several times with the Letterkenny Music & Drama Group. My grandmother, Cassie McDaid, ran a second hand clothes shop at 'the foot of the town' for many years in the former premises of Ward's Bakery opposite the Devlin Hall, rearing me on stories of various notable 'townies' and their exploits. Each December, I grew up devouring the seasonal treat of the Letterkenny & District Christmas Annual published by the Community Centre, pouring over the memories and recollections of many older residents, informing us of what is what like to grow up in the Letterkenny of old. I am the very definition of a 'townie', and I am very proud of that.

Come with me then as we now take a step into Letterkenny's past and meet some of the colourful people along the way who have helped define the town through the years and have made Letterkenny what it is today. Indeed, just as the River Swilly's large and determined flow into the expanses of the North Sea begins rather more humbly with a small trickle of water, so then the vibrant and bustling town of Letterkenny has rather more modest origins all of its own, the balliboe of Leitir Ceanainn, which is our first stop on our journey together into the past.

Chapter One: Leitir Ceanainn

The history of the town of Letterkenny officially begins with the Plantation of Ulster in the early seventeenth century. No evidence of any kind can be found of a place called 'Letterkenny' in any document or map prior to 1611, the year in which '*Letterkevin*' is recorded as part of the 1000-acre land grant to Captain Patrick Crawford. Up until then, the land on which the town would be built was covered with large trees and bushes that over time were cleared away with the continuous construction of the market town. Of course, many important and crucial events took place within the immediate hinterland prior to the development of the market town, forming a part of the area's '*pre-history*', if you will. If the town of Letterkenny then is to be our 'story', the history of the surrounding region prior to the construction of the town is certainly our 'prologue'.

Prior to the arrival of English and Scottish settlers who built the market towns of the Plantation, the Gaelic Irish lived in divisions of land generally called 'balliboes' (from *baile bó* meaning 'cow-land') - divisions that we correspond more or less to the boundaries of our townlands today. The balliboe would generally take the name of some physical feature associated with the area or sometimes in connection with a local leader of great importance. The balliboe of *Leitir Ceanainn* was one such place.

The boundaries of the balliboe of Leitir Ceanainn with today's road network

The name of 'Letterkenny' comes from an anglicisation of the Gaelic '*Leitir Ceanainn*'. As can be seen from the map, this balliboe was located approximately where the centre of the town is today (and would later form the boundary for the first Urban District Council of 1898). Of course, there is no

Letterkenny - Where the Winding Swilly Flows

way to accurately identify the exact origins of how the balliboe got its name, but we can look at various possibilities and determine which is the most likely.

Leitir Canannan - "The Hillside of the O'Cannons"

Leitir comes from the old Irish word for a 'hillside', and anyone walking up or down the Main Street of the town today can easily testify to the accuracy of that part of the name! From the second part – *Ceanainn* – many people have associated the area with the ancient O'Cannon rulers of Tír Chonaill. This O'Cannon clan (or to give them their proper Gaelic title, Ua Canannáin) are recorded as being the chieftains of the kingdoms of Tír Chonaill from the 9th to the 13th centuries. Many believe that this clan governed their territories from a fort located at nearby Conwal, an area 2.5 km to the west of the modern town, naming the adjacent balliboe "*Leitir Ceanainn*" or "**Hillside of the Ua Canannáins**".

The belief that the Ua Canannáins ruled from Conwal comes from the location of a large ringfort in the area. In his 1917 account of the history of the town entitled *Letterkenny: Past and Present*, pre-eminent local historian Canon Edward Maguire stated that:

"At Conwal Glebe we discover a charming old fort or dun…That the O'Canannan kings of Tir Chonaill here lived and feasted in their royal palace, from time to time, both the topography and indisputable tradition furnish convincing evidence…Thus we see that, as kings of Tirconaill, the O'Canannains lived and reigned at Conwal."[1]

However, there is no convincing evidence that connects this fort at Conwal with the Ua Canannáin clan. None of the historical annals, such as the Annals of the Four Masters or Annals of Ulster, record any evidence of them reigning at Conwal at all. There are several ringforts in the vicinity of Conwal but there is nothing to suggest that any of these were once the property of the kings of Tír Chonaill. In fact, the 12th century text *Ceart Uí Néill* actually designated the Ua Canannáins' territory as being Mag nÉne, Es Ruaid and Mag Sereth, three areas collectively known as *Trí Saorthuatha Mhuinntire Chanannáin* or the Three Free Territories of Muintir Chanannáin, located near modern day Donegal Town and Ballyshannon.[2]

Generally, if an area were to be named after a person or a clan, it would tend to have the prefix of '*Dún*', '*Ráth*' or '*Líos*' (all variations for the term 'fort') implying a position of strength. Various examples in the immediate area of Letterkenny include:

Dooen – Dún – fort
Dunlewey – Dún Lughaidh – the fort of Lughaidh (Lámhfhada)
Rathdonnell - Ráth Domhnaill – the fort of Donnell
Rathsedoge - Ráth Sedoige – the fort of Sedoige
Ramelton – Ráth Mealtain – the fort of Mealtain
Rathmullan – Ráth Maoláin – the fort of Maoláin
Lismonaghan - Líos Mongain – the fort of Mongan
Lisnenan - Líos nÉnán – the fort of Énán

Chapter One: Leitir Ceanainn

So if the balliboe was named after the Ua Canannáin clan, the area would most likely have been called Dún Canannain, Líos Canannain or Rath Canannain, to signify their dominance, rather than using the softer 'Leitir' (hillside). As in Lettermacaward (*Leitir Mhac A Bhaird*, the Hillside of the Sons of the Bards) the designation of 'Leitir' would have been used for clans of significantly smaller stature than any proud rulers of Tír Chonaill.

However, even taking all of that into account, if a hillside were to be named after the Ua Canannáins in this area, would it not have been located in Conwal or Tullygay, where they supposedly ruled, rather than a balliboe 2.5km east of this?

Leitir Ceann Fhionn – "The Fair-Headed Hillside"

A more likely translation of Leitir Ceanainn is that it derives from *Leitir Ceann Fhionn* (with the 'h' softening the letter F giving us the pronunciation *Leitir Ceann-ionn*), meaning the **Fair Headed Hillside**. Distinguished local historian Sam Fleming disagreed with Canon Maguire's description of the name and tells us in his own 1979 history of the town that:

"Letterkenny derived its name from Leitir Ceanann which means "The Fair Headed Hillside", and not as some historical writers would have it "The Hillside of the O Canannan Clan"[3]

Interestingly, in the Plantation land grant of 1611, it is noted that the balliboe is referred as 'Letterkevin', which could possibly have come from translating 'Ceann Fionn', where the 'h' wasn't softened.

Most balliboes tended to be named after a dominant physical feature of its area, such as:

Sallaghgraine – *Salach na Gréine* - Marshy Place Facing the Sun
Gortlee – *Gort Laoigh* - The Calves Field
Glencar – *Gleann Chairthe* – The Stony Glen
Dromore – *Drom Mór* – Large Ridge
Bonagee – *Bun na Gaoithe* – Shelter from the Wind
Aughaninshin – *Ough an Uinseann* – The Slope of the Ash Tree
Illistrin – '*Feileastram*' flower (yellow iris)

The gorse or whin bush still grows in abundance today in several places within the territory of the former balliboe, such as at Sentry Hill. It is not hard to imagine then, that prior to the laying of streets and the erection of buildings of the market town over time, the balliboe of *Leitir Ceanainn* would likely have been resplendent in these bushes, and in the summer time, as the sun beamed down on their bright yellow flowers in full bloom, it would have given the appearance of a 'fair head' of hair, thereby giving the balliboe its name – **Leitir Ceann Fhionn**, the Fair Headed Hillside.

Letterkenny - Where the Winding Swilly Flows

Fionn MacCumhaill

These then are the two most popular possibilities as to how the area got its name. However, we can also consider other possibilities. According to local legend, the River Swilly was named after the *Súileach* monster of many eyes that was killed by **Saint Colmcille** of Gartan. The legend has it that Colmcille and a man called Feadorach went to kill the beast where it resided in a pool in Meenaroy. Following a lengthy battle, the saint stabbed the monster in the eye, whereupon the blood and water gushed forth carving the shape of a river down through the valley. Feadorach fled the battle and Colmcille tracked him down to an area beside Conwal and threatened to kill him. Feadorach pleaded with Colmcille not to kill him with the blood of the monster still on the sword and

Examples of the whin (gorse) bushes growing around the town today

Chapter One: Leitir Ceanainn

so the saint cleaned his weapon in the new river. On doing this, the saint felt his anger leave him and he claimed that anyone who bathed in these waters would be cleansed from all anger. In memory of the beast, Colmcille called this new river after the Súileach monster – *An tSúileach* – the Swilly.

Intriguingly, in Celtic mythology, Balor of the Evil Eye or **Balor na Súile Nímhe** lived on Tory Island and was slain by his son Lughaigh Lámhfhada by the piercing of his eye with a spear. It would appear that the rulers of the territory, the Cinéal Luighdheach tribe, championed their ancestral links to Lughaigh by naming areas in their territories in his honour such as *Dún Lughaidh* (Dunlewey the fort of Lughaidh) and *Gleann na Nímhe* (the Poisoned Glen) where Balor na Súile Nímhe was defeated. It is possible then that the Cinéal Luighdheach named the river that flowed through their territory after the vanquished Balor na Súile Nímhe (*An tSúileach*) as a memory to this great mythical battle also. With the conversion of the tribe to Christianity in later years when they would eventually become the O'Donnell clan, and the more palatable association with a saint born in their territory, this legend would have been reimagined to champion Saint Colmcille instead.

So, if the Súileach River was originally named from Celtic mythology, there is a possibility that the Cinéal Luighdheach decided to name balliboes in their territory after the greatest hero of Celtic mythology, namely Fionn MacCumhaill. Leitir Ceann Fhionn could just as easily be named after this hero of ancient Ireland; a possibility not so outrageous when one looks at the name of the adjoining balliboe - *Béal Átha MacCumhaill* (Ballymacool). The two adjacent balliboes would thus be **Leitir Ceann Fhionn** '*The Hillside of the Head of Fionn*' and the '*Mouth of the Crossing of MacCumhaill*' (or even possibly Bealach MacCumhaill, 'the Path of MacCumhaill'). It's certainly an intriguing thought.

Leitir nÉanáin

A more likely possibility though concerns **Énán**, the husband of Colmcille's sister Mincoleth, who was of sufficient Cinéal Chonaill princely stock to have several areas named after him. *Líos nÉnan* (Lisnenan – the Fort of Énán) and *Maghair Énán* (Magherenan – the Plain of Énán) are two such areas still in existence while *Cill Mhic Réanáin* (Kilmacrennan – the Church of the Sons of Enan) also bears his name.

When translated from Irish to English and then back to Irish again, certain original townland names can get lost along the way. For example, today the Irish name for Kilmacrennan is *Cill Mhic Réanáin* whereas the original Gaelic title was *Cill Mhic nÉanáin*. One might argue that the same could just as easily have happened with **Leitir nÉanáin** and *Leitir Ceanainn*. The fact that *Líos nÉnán* and *Magher Énán* are in such close proximity to *Leitir Ceanainn* certainly lends a weight to this possibility.

Of course, the name of the balliboe could have come from a variety of possibilities and there is no way that we can ever know for sure. Perhaps it simply comes from its location immediately next to the Swilly - "Hillside at the Head of the River" or *Leitir Ceann Abhann*. Owing to the fact that the Ua Canannáins

Letterkenny - Where the Winding Swilly Flows

were known to have ruled in the south of the modern county, and not at Conwal, we can easily discount that the area was named after them. Weighing up each possibility, we can state with some confidence that the name most likely comes from either The Hillside of Énán or the Fair Headed Hillside.

Neolithic Period, Bronze and Iron Age Settlement

After the last Ice Age, over 20,000 years ago, huge glaciers of ice that covered the northern half of Ireland slowly retreated and melted, and valleys were gradually carved out and shaped underneath them, leaving us with the sloping valley between today's opposite heights of Lismonaghan and Carnamuggagh. Over thousands of years thereafter, plants and flowers slowly took root in the fertile soil of the valley and lush green fields began to appear on the banks of the river that winded through it, patiently awaiting human settlement. Megalithic tombs of the Neolithic and Early Bronze Age can be found in nearby Lisnanese

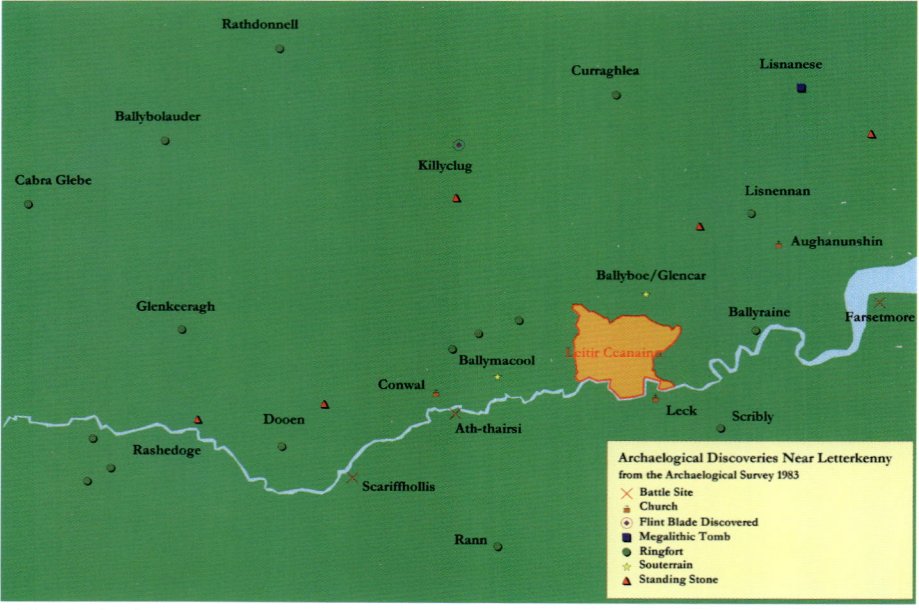

Map showing the main archaeological discoveries in the vicinity of the balliboe of Leitir Ceanainn. Source: Archaeological Survey of County Donegal 1983

and Mondooey, while a gold lunala from this period was also discovered at Gartan and a flint blade was discovered in 2011 in Killyclug[4], indicating ancient settlement patterns near to the balliboe.

Evidence of Iron Age settlements have also been identified with stone built cashels, earthen ring forts, standing stones and souterrains (underground passages) being discovered at Ballymacool, Garrowcarry, Ballymaleel, Killyclug, Curraghlea, Ballyraine and Scribly while forts, raths or cashels can be found at Derrora, Cabra Glebe, Glenkeeragh, Rathdonnell, Seacor, two in Doen Glebe, and three in Ballygawley with others surrounding Letterkenny at Lisnennan (Castlebane) and Rahan.[5] (See Map)

Chapter One: Leitir Ceanainn

Ancient Tribes

Several large tribes governed the large territories of Tír Chonaill, (roughly the area of what we know as Donegal today without Inishowen) and the balliboe of *Leitir Ceanainn* was within one of these territories. The boundaries of the territory of the **Cinéal Luighdheach** tribe, (the 'kindred of Lughaidh'), were described in the Book of Fenagh:

> *"From the same impetuous Dobhar,*
> *The Tricha of Lughaidh, son of Setna,*
> *Extends to the river of clear aspect,*
> *The name of which is Suilidhi"*[6]

This sizeable area was known as *Tír Luighdeach* and roughly corresponds with the barony of Kilmacrennan today. So as the balliboe was situated within this, between the rivers of 'Dobhar' and 'Suilidhi' (Swilly), we can see that Leitir Ceanainn was part of the overall territory of the Cinéal Luighdheach, and two smaller clans within the tribe, the **Clann Snedghile** and **Clann Fhiangusa**, are known to have had forts at Conwal and Tullygay. The Book of Fenagh informs us that both of these clans were named after two brothers, Fiangus and Snedgal, the sons of Airnelach and were descended from Lughaidh, from whom the tribe got its name. The forts in existence near Conwal today belonged to these clans and not as some would contend, the Ua Canannáin clan.

As the River Swilly was once a territorial boundary marker, other tribes appear to have had settlements on the southern banks. Evidence of the Cinéal nEoghain (the 'kindred of Eoghain') and Cinéal nÉanna (the 'kindred of Enda') tribes can be found in various place names south of the river. For example, Mongain was the son of Eoghain, and his fort on the hilltop to the south of the Súileach river was named after him - *Líos Mongain* (Lismonaghan) while Corenna comes from *Corr Éanna*, the 'Rock of Enda'.

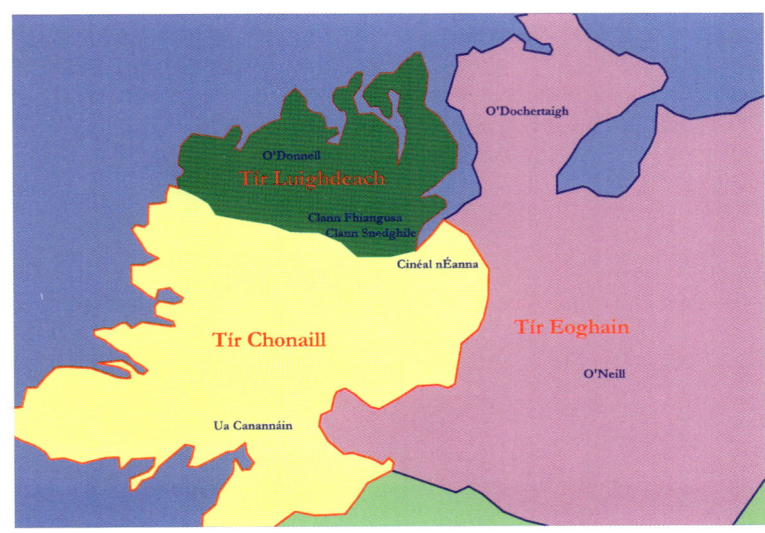

The approximate boundaries of Tír Luighdeach as part of Tír Chonaill

Conwal and the origins of 'the town'

There is a local legend that the town of Letterkenny had its origins at nearby Conwal and after a cat accidently knocked over a lantern, which set fire to the wooden and wattle huts utterly decimating their small hamlet, the people moved east along the river and settled in the area south of the modern day town. According to this legend, these Gaelic locals were the first to create a town in the area and the Scottish planters who arrived in the seventeenth century merely took it over and built their settlement on the opposite side of the River Swilly. Thus, the Gaelic Irish town on the south of the river became 'Oldtown' and the planters had their 'new town' on the opposite hillside. A more plausible explanation for the origins of this dubious legend will be examined later, but for now it is worth noting that the area of Conwal to the west of Letterkenny today is generally accepted as being the nearest ancient Gaelic settlement to the modern town.

Fiachra of Congbhaile

The name Conwal comes from the Gaelic *'Congbhaile'* meaning an 'ecclesiastical habitation' and today we can still see the 12th Century ruins of a church that was built on the site of an original abbey. Reading the sign beside this church, we are told that this is the site of an early ecclesiastical settlement dating from the 7th Century when *"St. Fiachrius was Abbot"*. Thus, it is generally accepted amongst many people that St. Fiachra, the Patron Saint of Gardeners, is the founder of Conwal Abbey. However, under closer inspection, similar to the Ua Canannáins, St. Fiachra actually appears to have no connection to the area at all. It was most likely **Fiachra, son of Ciarán** who was the true founder of the abbey, later becoming confused with a saint of the same name.

The first recording of a place called Conwal comes from the Annals of the Four Masters (AFM) in the year 913 in which a 'herenach' (airchinneach) has died. A herenach was the hereditary keeper of the monastery who had to hold a genealogical connection to the founder:

AFM913

Scannlan, airchinneach of Congbhail-Glinne-Suilighe, died

The next mention we have is from the year 1204, informing us again of the death of a herenach.

AFM1204

Sitric O'Sruithen, Erenagh of Conwal, i.e. head of the Hy-Murtele, and chief man of all the Clann-Snedhgile for his worth, died, after exemplary penance, and was interred in the church which he had himself founded.

Chapter One: Leitir Ceanainn

This church that O'Sruithen founded must be the remains that we see today, built on the site of the earlier abbey.

Fiachra, son of Ciarán, was the nephew of the ruling chief of Tír Chonaill, Aed MicAinmire and he is recorded in the Annals of Tigernach as being the 'other founder' of the monastery at Derry and dying in the year 619.[7] If then, he founded a monastery there, could he have also founded one prior to this in Conwal?

Conwal Abbey believed to date from the twelfth century

To consider this, we would need to connect him to the herenachs (keepers) of the abbey, as they had to be related in some way to the founder. The herenach at Conwal in 1204, Sitric O'Sruithen, was *"chief man of all the Clann-Snedhgile"*. As we have seen, this Clan Snedhgile of Congbhaile were descended from Lughaidh, who was Fiachra's granduncle and given that the keepers of an abbey had to be related to the founder, the significance of this connection becomes clearer. Fiachra, son of Ciarán also holds significant genealogical links both to Colmcille and Eunan as can be seen from the table.

In any research done on the life of St. Fiachra however, no mention is ever made of the Patron Saint of Gardeners spending any time in Donegal. He lived in Kilkenny and later emigrated to France, making a trip north to found a monastery in this local area very unlikely. What is most likely to have happened is that through the passing down of history through the centuries, Fiachra, son of Ciarán became lost in time and became easily misinterpreted as 'Saint Fiachra'.

Letterkenny - Where the Winding Swilly Flows

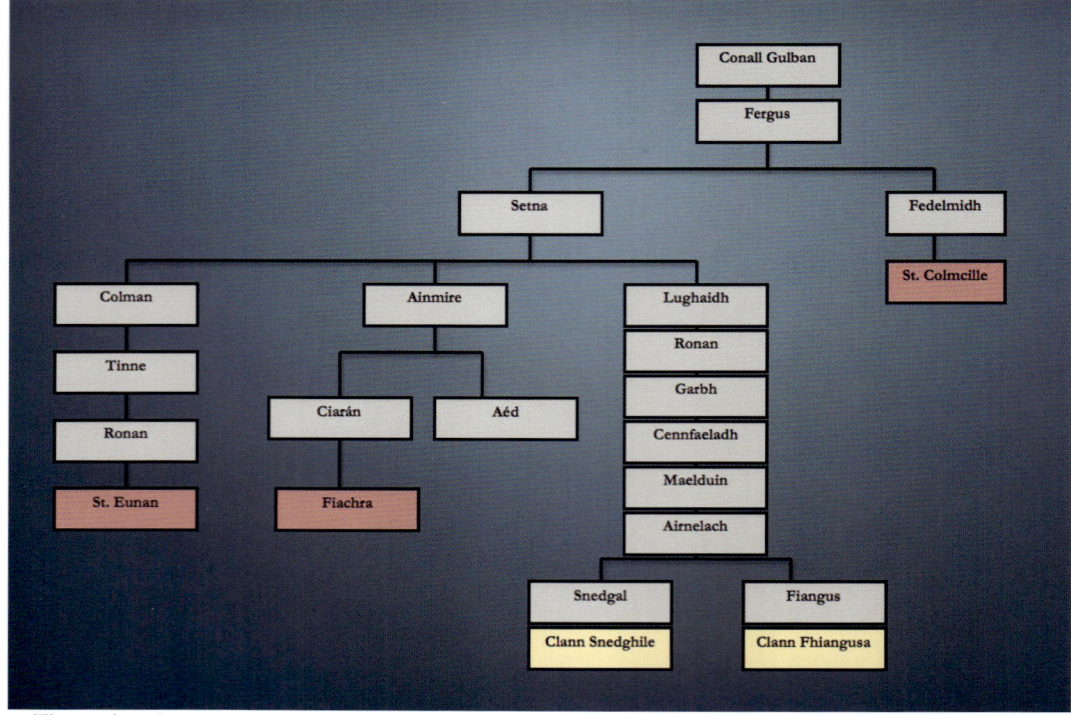

The genealogy of Fiachra, son of Ciarán and his relationship to Colmcille & Eunan

Godfrey O'Donnell and the Battle of Ath Thairsí 1258

Remaining at Conwal, in the graveyard today, near the ruins of the old church of Sitric Ui Sruithin, lies a burial slab with an ancient Celtic cross carving. This simple engraving is believed to mark the final resting place of one of the most famous chiefs of the O'Donnells, the great ruling clan of Tír Chonaill. Following his glorious death in battle at the nearby crossing of Ath-thairsí, **Godfrey O'Donnell** is believed to have been buried here in 1258.

When Niall Óg Ua Canannáin was killed at the hands of the Norman Lord Maurice Fitzgerald in 1248, Godfrey O'Donnell seized power and consolidated his power base within Tír Chonaill. Despite previous Tír Chonaill chiefs residing near Ballyshannon, Godfrey is recorded as having had a crannóg on Lough Bethach (Gartan Lough) where he built a fort closer to his ancestral territories of the Cineal Luighdeach.

Whether due to an offensive into Connacht by Godfrey or by an advance into Tír Chonaill by the Norman Lord, Maurice Fitzgerald, the two armies of Gaelic and

The grave slab at Conwal, supposedly marking the final resting place of Godfrey O'Donnell

Chapter One: Leitir Ceanainn

Norman forces met at Credan Kille, near Drumcliffe in County Sligo in 1257. Godfrey and Fitzgerald met in single combat with Godfrey getting the upper hand and Fitzgerald was carried from the field as the Norman English retreated. Godfrey, however, also received serious injuries in this battle. The Annals tells us:

AFM1257

"A brave battle was fought by Godfrey O'Donnell, Lord of Tirconnell, in defence of his country, with the Lord Justice of Ireland, Maurice Fitzgerald, and the other English nobles of Connaught, at Creadran-Cille in Ros-cede, in the territory of Carbury, to the north of Sligo. A desperate and furious battle was fought between them: bodies were mangled, heroes were disabled, and the senses were stunned on both sides. The field was vigorously maintained by the Kinel-Connell, who made such obstinate and vigorous onsets upon the English that, in the end, they routed them with great slaughter. Godfrey himself, however, was severely wounded; for he met Maurice Fitzgerald face to face in single combat, in which they wounded each other severely. In consequence of the success of this battle, the English and the Geraldines were driven out of Lower Connaught."

Following this Battle at Credan-Kille, Godfrey was borne home with his injuries to die at his crannóg on Lough Bethach. However, hearing that O'Donnell lay stricken, Brian O'Neill, the Cinéal nEoghain ruler of Tír Eoghain, saw his opportunity to demand hostages, pledges of loyalty and submission. Despite his severe injuries, Godfrey rallied all the fighting men of his kingdom and the two armies met near the crossing into his territory at Ath-thairsí, near Conwal. The name Ath–thairsí comes from the Gaelic *Ath Thar Suilí* - The Crossing Over the Swilly.

Godfrey was given his last rites but he gave instructions to his generals and to inspire his troops to victory, knowing that he would not last the battle, he ordered that he be carried on a litter onto the field. When his exhausted troops saw their heroic general they are said to have fought bravely to drive O'Neill and his invading troops away. The Red Hand Army of Tír Eoghain were defeated by the gallant men of Tír Chonaill but their heroic leader died during this bloody battle. His body and those of the other fallen soldiers were laid in the nearby settlement of Congbhaile.

AFM1258

"On the return of the Tirconnelian army from this victory, the bier on which O'Donnell was carried was laid down in the street of Congbhail, and here his soul departed, from the venom of the scars and wounds which he had received in the battle of Creadran. This was not death in cowardice, but the death of a hero, who had at all times triumphed over his enemies"

With such a glorious death, it is no surprise that several poems were written about Godfrey and his battle with O'Neill, painting the picture of the heroic O'Donnell valiantly defending his territory from the invading Cinéal nEoghain. The fierce battle is described as: *"Then rose the roar of battle loud, as clan*

Letterkenny - Where the Winding Swilly Flows

Artist's impression of Godfrey O"Donnell and Maurice Fitzgerald in battle at Credan Kille

Chapter One: Leitir Ceanainn

met clan in fight; The axe and skian grew red with blood, a sad and woeful sight;" with the waters of the Swilly being *"red with blood"*. It was within these poems that the legacy of Godfrey O'Donnell was forever enshrined, one of which can be read in Appendix A. A dominant personality forever associated with Conwal, perhaps the last word on Godfrey O'Donnell is indeed best left to the poets:

> *"Yet died he there all gloriously--a victor in the fight;*
> *A chieftain at his people's head, a warrior in his might;*
> *They dug him there a fitting grave upon that field of pride,*
> *And a lofty cairn they raised above, by fair Lough Swilly's side."*

The Battle of Farsetmore 1567

Fast forward three hundred years from Godfrey O'Donnell's glorious death at Conwal and another famous battle that took place near to modern day Letterkenny between the O'Donnells and the O'Neills was the Battle of Farsetmore in 1567.

Artist's impression of the heroic Godfrey O'Donnell being carried into battle at Ath –Thairsí on his litter 1258

Today, people entering the town from the east or south do so by crossing over the River Swilly at either the Port or Oldtown bridges. However, these crossings only emerged in the seventeenth century with the construction of the new town and the subsequent economic necessity to access its market and trading areas. Prior to this, the principal crossing points of the Súileach river were located at Ath-thairsí, as we have just seen, and Scairbh Sholais to the west and Fearsad

Suilighe Mór to the east.

These entrances into Tír Luighdheach required the building of fortified castles by the O'Donnells at each crossing. Calvagh O'Donnell built a small castle in the 1560s at the western crossing of Scairbh Sholais while another fort was located on a height overlooking the eastern crossing known as **Ard na gCorr Fhiadh** (Height on the Pointed Slope of the Deer), today anglicized as Ardingary. Remains of this fort are evident on the 1836 Ordnance Survey map, located close to the Lisnenan Heights estate in the town today and known as **Castlebane** (from Caisleán Bán, the White Fort).

All of these crossings into Tír Luighdheach were the scenes of ferocious battles over the centuries. We have already seen that Godfrey O'Donnell met his death at the crossing of Aththairsí in 1258 while Scarrifhollis was the location of a decisive battle in 1650 between the Royalist army of Heber MacMahon and the Parliamentary forces of Sir Charles Coote, which we shall look at later.

Canon Maguire states that the name of this western crossing of the Súileach comes from "*scairbh-sholuis, narrow ford of light. It was the custom to place lights at all important and frequented fords.*"[8] However, the name could also have come from *Scairbh Ough Líos* – 'The Narrow Ford at the Slope of the Fort', not unlikely given that it is located opposite the slope of Dooen (Dún – fort).

> **Did you know?**
> A small fort in Ballyraine is evidenced on old OS maps, where the Pitch and Putt course is located today. This small fort or '*Rath-ín*' is most likely how this area got its name – from **Béal Átha an Raithín** (Mouth at the crossing of the small fort) as opposed to previously accepted **Baile Raighin** (the townland of the ferns).

The crossing at **Fearsad Suilighe Mór** also witnessed battles between the O'Donnell and O'Neill clans for centuries prior to its most famous battle in 1567. For example, in the year 1098, the Annals of the Four Masters tells us:

AFM1098.11
"The battle of Fearsat-Suilighe was gained over the Cinel-Conaill by the Cinel-Eoghain, in which Ua Taircheirt, i.e. Eigceartach, was slain, with a number of others"

In the year 1392, peace was brokered between the rival O'Donnell and O'Neill lords at the crossing following a Cinéal nEoghain encroachment into Tír Chonaill territory:

AFM1392.8
"A great army was led by O'Neill (Niall)...they plundered O'Doherty's territory, as well as churches and lay property, and marched on, without once halting, until they reached Fearsat-Mor, intending to give battle to O'Donnell. Here they remained for a long time face to face, but at length they made peace with each other."

Chapter One: Leitir Ceanainn

However, the most famous battle that took place here occurred in 1567 between the forces of Hugh O'Donnell of Tír Chonaill and Shane O'Neill of Tír Eoghain. With his repeated invasions into his neighbouring territories, O'Neill made no secret of his wish to control all of Ulster himself, and was a constant thorn to Queen Elizabeth I. This ambitious and almost Napoleonesque figure of Shane 'The Proud' O'Neill would meet his 'Waterloo' on the banks of the Súileach River on 8 May 1567.

Artist's impression of the Battle of Farsetmore 1567

From the panoramic view of his fort at Ard na gCorr Fhiadh, Hugh O'Donnell observed the approach of Shane O'Neill as he made his invasion into his territory and could determine if he was going to cross at either Fearsad Suilighe Mór, Ath-thairsí or Scarrifhollis. Unsure of the exact number of his opposition, O'Donnell decided to wait for the approach of O'Neill and plan a surprise attack. Assistance arrived in the form of the McSweenys, loyal septs to the O'Donnells. Now greatly strengthened by his allies' arrival, O'Donnell prepared to attack the camp of O'Neill, who had already crossed the river and were now located in a place called *Cluain Áire* (The Meadow of Safety). With this surprise attack, on the 8th May 1567 the **Battle of Fearsad Mór** raged on the eastern banks of the Suileach River:

Letterkenny - Where the Winding Swilly Flows

AFM1567.2
Fierce and desperate were the grim and terrible looks that each cast at the other from their starlike eyes; they raised the battle cry aloud, and their united shouting, when rushing together, was sufficient to strike with dismay and turn to flight the feeble and the unwarlike. They proceeded and continued to strike, mangle, slaughter, and cut down one another for a long time, so that men were soon laid low, heroes wounded, youths slain, and robust heroes mangled in the slaughter

The sheer force and aggression of this attack by O'Donnell, lasting for approximately six hours, caused Shane's troops to pull back and retreat over the crossing of the Suileach. However, by now, the water had risen and concealed the sand banks over which they had so easily crossed only hours previously. In the panic of the retreat, a vast number of O'Neills horses and men drowned

The area of Farsetmore today, to the east of the town

in the river, with a sandbank there still holding the name *Fearsad Eachmharcach* or the "Horseman's bank" in memory of this. In all, O'Neill is said to have lost approximately 1300 men while O'Donnell's losses were said to be much fewer.

Knowing of the other crossing over the Suileach at Ath-thairsi, Shane made an ignominious escape travelling westwards along the banks, accompanied by the former allies of O'Donnell, the O'Gallaghers. From here he managed to cross the river and make his escape back to his own territory of Tír Eoghain.

Bereft of troops and support, Shane approached his one-time enemies, the Antrim Scots, for assistance. The McDonnells of the Glens initially welcomed

Chapter One: Leitir Ceanainn

him but *"after extraordinary drinking, and over-liberall carouses…Shane was set upon, overmastered, and with many wounds slain"* [9] as the McDonnells decided to *"mangle him nimbly, and put him unsparingly to the sword, and bereave him of life."* [10]

The significance of this Battle at Fearsad Suilighe Mór to the east of the modern town of Letterkenny cannot be overstated. Not only was it to prove to be the last significant historical event in the immediate area prior to the construction of the town some forty years later, but it was also to be the last battle between the centuries old competing factions of the O'Neills and O'Donnells prior to their unification in the Nine Years' War (1594-1603). This would set in motion a chain of events that would eventually lead the King of England, James I, to surmise that the only way to deal with this continuously rebellious province of Ulster was through the settlement of loyal English and Scottish subjects. With the arrival of the Plantation of Ulster, the era of the balliboe of *Leitir Ceanainn* was at an end and the dawn of the town of *Letterkenny* was about to take place.

End Notes
1 Maguire, Canon, "Letterkenny: Past and Present", 1917, p28
2 Ó Canann, Thomas, "*Carraig an Dúnáin: Probable Ua Canannáin Inauguration Site*", JRSAI, 133, 2003
3 Fleming, Sam, "Letterkenny: Past and Present", Donegal Democrat, 1979, p29
4 Derry People, 3/6/2011
5 Lacy, Brian (Ed), "Archaeological Survey of County Donegal – A description of the field antiquities of the County from the Mesolithic Period to the 17th century A.D.", Donegal County Council, Lifford, 1983
6 Kelly, D,H , "The Book of Fenagh in Irish and English, Originally Compiled by St. Cailin", Alexander Thom,1875, p397
7 Annals of Tigernach 619.2 available at www.ucc.ie/celt
8 Maguire, Canon, "Letterkenny: Past and Present", 1917, p94
9 Hayes-McCoy, G.A. "Scots Mercenary Forces in Ireland (1565-1603)", Edmund Burke Publisher, 1996 (first ed 1937), p84
10 Annals of the Four Masters 1567.3 available at www.ucc.ie/celt

Chapter Two: Plantation and Early Development

So far, we have seen that the small balliboe of Leitir Ceanainn was once located within the overall territory of Tír Luighdeach, ruled by the O'Donnell clan since their accession to power in the 13th century. This clan was able to repel many attempted advances into their territory by their neighbouring O'Neill clan of Tyrone from Brian in 1258 through to Shane in 1567. At the end of the sixteenth century however, these two rival clans united to fight the common enemy of England and started a domino effect that would eventually lead to the Plantation of Ulster and the subsequent formation of the market town of Letterkenny. To understand why the Plantation occurred, it is worth briefly looking at the events in the build up to it.

The Nine Years War 1594-1603

Fearing his lands would be targeted for English expansion outside of the Pale, the chief of Tir Chonaill, Red Hugh O'Donnell, son of the victor of Farsetmore, joined forces with the Maguires of Fermanagh against the English. Hugh O'Neill of Tir Eoghain soon united with the rebelling lords and the Nine Years War against the Queen of England began.

Initially successful at the Ford of the Biscuits, Clontibret and most notably, Yellow Ford, the combined forces of the Gaelic lords gradually extended their rebellion outside of Ulster, with O'Donnell taking the revolt into Connacht. On various occasions, ocean storms thwarted the arrival of Spanish assistance but one final attempt resulted in the landing of troops under Don Juan del Águila at Kinsale in Cork. A failed attack on Christmas Eve 1601 by the combined forces of O'Donnell and O'Neill to assist the besieged Spanish resulted in catastrophic defeat with the Irish forces scattered and slaughtered. Red Hugh sailed with the retreating Spanish ships and died in Simancas in 1602. The humiliated and defeated forces of the lords of Ulster were left to march humbly northwards again and with the signing of the Treaty of Mellifont in 1603, the Nine Years War was at an end.

Following the death of Elizabeth I, with the accession of James Stuart of Scotland to the throne, O'Neill and Ruadhrí Ua Domhnaill (Red Hugh's successor) met a surprisingly generous monarch, as their lands were restored to them, under restrictions, and they were given titles of the Earls of Tyrone and Tyrconnel respectively.

The Flight of the Earls 1607

Cúchonnacht Maguire of Fermanagh convinced the earls to sail with him to Spain to return with a great army. Fearing that the English had uncovered the plot and that they would be arrested if they stayed, O'Neill and O'Donnell

Chapter Two: Plantation and Early Development

boarded the boat near Rathmullan, 24km north of Leitir Ceanainn, on 14th September 1607 and sailed into history. The earls never returned and died in Rome, O'Donnell in 1608 and O'Neill in 1618.

The Flight of the Earls would prove to be one of the most important events in Irish history. With the nominal leaders of the territories of Ulster departed, their lands were there for the taking by the English. Ideas for plantation of the lands were now widespread at court in London but it would take one more significant event to finally convince the King once and for all that Ulster needed to be planted with loyal British subjects, an event crucial to the origins of the town of Letterkenny.

The Rebellion of Cahir O'Dochertaigh

Sir Cahir O'Dochertaigh of Inishowen had been foreman of the jury that declared that the earls had committed treason against the King and thus their lands were forfeited to the Crown. However, following an altercation with the Governor of Derry, Sir George Paulet, O'Dochertaigh led a rebellion, sacking and burning the city, killing Paulet and also later capturing and burning Strabane. With support from the O'Cahans and O'Hanlons, the rebellion soon spread across the Swilly into Tír Chonaill. To assist in quelling this rebellion, the King authorised the use of Scottish forces under the command of Captain William Stewart and **Captain Patrick Crawford**:

Letter from the Scottish Privy Council 21st June 1608:
"Letter from the Council to the Governor of Knockfergus: Having ressavit directioun from our most sacred Soveraigne, the Mngis Majestie, to send over tua hundreth men of warr for assisting and furthering his Majisteis service in that Kingdome . . . we have accordingly sent thame unto you under the charge of thir two gentilmen, Capitane Patrik Craufurde and Capitane Williame Stewart"[1]

The rebellion was quickly put down before these Scottish captains arrived and O'Dochertaigh was ambushed and killed near Doon Rock, in Kilmacrennan, the inauguration site of the O'Donnells. Following this rebellion, Sir Arthur Chichester claimed all of O'Doherty's lands in Inishowen as his own and the Summer Assizes of 1608 proclaimed that almost all of the counties of Tír Chonaill, Tír Eoghan, Coleraine/Derry, Armagh, Fermanagh and Cavan were now under control of the crown. In arriving to assist in bringing down the rebellion, even though it had been resolved by the time they got there, Captains Crawford and Stewart would be suitably rewarded for their service with Crawford being stationed at Lifford fort until such time as his allocation of land was decided upon.

It was the rebellion of Cahir O'Dochertaigh that finally convinced the King that Plantation was the only answer for Ulster. Garrisoned towns would need to be put into place throughout the province to maintain order. Ulster had very few towns in place prior to the seventeenth century. The new towns would be defended garrison settlements located at strategic places while they would also

Letterkenny - Where the Winding Swilly Flows

act as centres of commerce, with each town connecting and trading with each other creating a self sufficient urban network throughout the province. Thus, the Orders and Conditions of the Plantation decreed that:

"there shall be a convenient number of market towns and corporations erected, for the habitation and settling of tradesmen and artificers…Every undertaker shall within three years… plant or place upon a small proportion, the number of 24 able men of the age of 18 years or upwards, being English or inland Scottish. Every of the said undertakers shall draw their tenants to build houses for themselves and their families, not scattering, but together, near the principal house or bawn, as well for their mutual defence and strength, as for the making of villages and townships" [2]

Plantation Mapping

Shane O'Neill's actions against the English in the 1560s made the government appreciate the need for increased knowledge of the layout of Ulster. Robert Lythe's map of 1567 was the first attempt to understand the cartographical nature of the province and was followed by Francis Jobson's maps of 1590 showing the boundaries of the newly created counties (the territories of Tír Chonaill and Inis Eoghain were amalgamated on 1st September 1585 creating the new County Donegal).

With the arrival of the Plantation though, map-making became even more important in understanding the allocation of land and many other maps of the northwest were subsequently drawn, with more accuracy in their scale with each effort. Maps by John Norden and John Speed, amongst others, give us a valuable insight into the county at this time. From these maps we can see the existence of settlements at Buncrana, Ballyshannon, Lifford and Donegal while the chief areas of fortified settlements in the county are also noted in the Calendar of State Papers as *"the Deny, Lyffor, Ballishanon, Dunegall, Castle Doe, and Culmore."* [3]

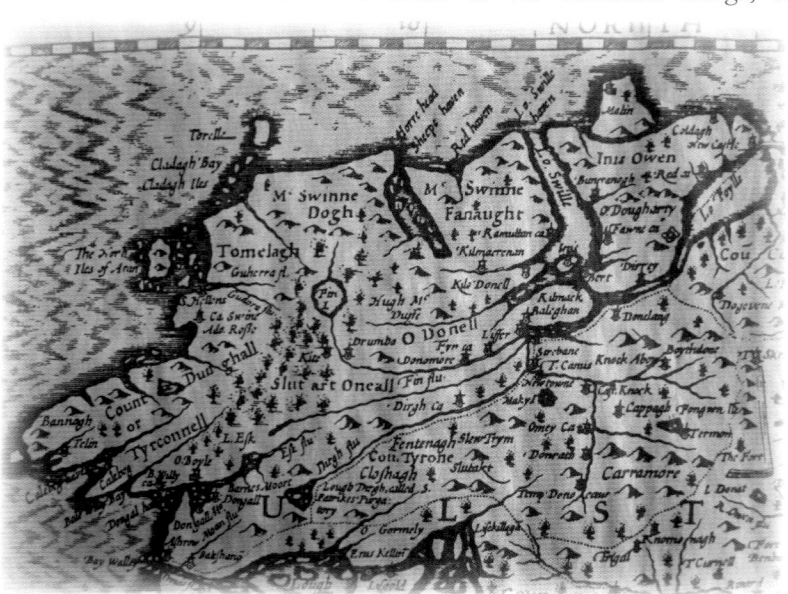

John Speede's map of County Donegal in 1610 – noticeably there is no settlement at Letterkenny

Chapter Two: Plantation and Early Development

Naturally, as it does not yet exist, a settlement at Letterkenny is not mentioned on any of these maps or papers.

Using these maps, the land in the six 'escheated' counties (Antrim, Down and Monaghan being excluded due to previous settlement arrangements) was allocated to different groups of people who would settle and colonise these new territories:

1. **Undertakers** – those that 'undertook' to plant loyal settlers, usually knights and gentlemen from England and Scotland. It was intended that they would not hold any Irish tenants, but rather they would bring over colonists with them to their new lands.
2. **Servitors** – those that served the crown in various capacities and were to be rewarded. Servitors were not compelled to hold British tenants but they got a rebate in rent if they did. Rent was £5-6-8 for British tenants but £8 for Irish tenants. Captain Crawford was considered to be a servitor.
3. **The Native Irish** – also referred to as 'meere Irish', these landowners would hold the lease for the terms of their lives but could not be passed on at their deaths.
4. **The Church** – herenach lands (such as Congbhaile) were to go to the bishops of the Church of Ireland and 'glebe' lands were to be created in each parish. Trinity College also received land in this category.

Baronies

In Donegal, baronies were created into which the different types of landowners could be assigned. The baronies of Raphoe, Boylagh and Banagh, and Kilmacrennan followed the approximate layout of the ancient Gaelic territories. Inishowen was exempt, as it had been given to Sir Arthur Chichester following O'Dochertaigh's rebellion while most of Tirhugh, in the south of the county, was given to Trinity College. The barony of Raphoe was split into two 'precincts' – Portlough being assigned to Scottish undertakers and Lifford being assigned to English undertakers. Boylagh and Banagh went to undertakers from Scotland while the barony of Kilmacrennan was also split into two – the 'precincts' of Doe and Fanad, both being assigned to Servitors and Native Irish. The idea of putting Servitors and Irish together in baronies was that these men of military experience, loyal to the crown, would be able to monitor the native Irish with a close and watchful eye.

Letterkenny - Where the Winding Swilly Flows

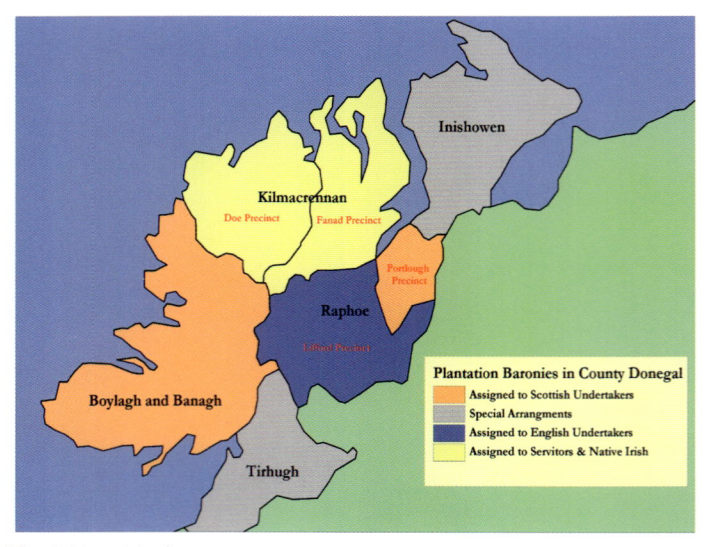

The division of land into baronies and precincts as part of the Plantation

Similar to the ancient territorial markers, natural features tended to be used as boundaries and so the Swilly River divided the baronies of Raphoe and Kilmacrennan. The lands south of the river, including the areas of present day Oldtown, Lismonaghan, Dromore and Lurgybrack were in the barony of Raphoe and therefore were granted to English undertakers whereas the balliboe of Leitir Ceanainn, being on the north of the Swilly was part of the barony of Kilmacrennan in the precinct of Fanad and was therefore part of a land parcel originally granted to the native Irishman **Hugh McHugh Dubh O'Donnell**, Red Hugh's granduncle who held a castle at Ramelton.

"he held an extensive country, l^ing between the rivers Swilly and Lannan…His chief residence was at Ramelton, on the western side of Lough Swilly. By a patent of the year 1610 he had a re-grant of portion of his estates…enclosed between the rivers mentioned, and comprising the parishes of Aughnish, and Aughanunshin, and portions of Conwal and Kilmacrenan."[4]

The territory of Hugh McHugh Dubh O'Donnell. Courtesy of Donegal County Library

The barony of Kilmacrennan was not divided up into parcels of land for servitors until after the undertakers from Scotland and England had received their lands in Raphoe and Boylagh and Banagh. In the barony of Raphoe, most of the present day villages have their origin in the Plantation such as Manorcunningham and Newtowncunningham, named after two of the first undertakers in the area, and also St. Johnston, Castlefin, Killygordon and Stranorlar. This Laggan area held the most fertile ground in the county and would prove to be the area where the Plantation was deemed most successful in Donegal.

In the precinct of Lifford, **Sir Thomas Coach** was granted the lands of Lismonaghan, while **Sir Maurice Barkley** was granted the lands of Dromore and Lurgagh, later selling them to **Sir Ralph Bingley**.

Chapter Two: Plantation and Early Development

John Norden's 1609 map showing parcels of land in the Raphoe barony. Lismonaghan and Dromore are noted south of the river with Leck Church prominent. Courtesy of Donegal County Library

Within each barony and precinct, the land would be divided up into parcels of land of various sizes of 2,000, 1,500 and 1,000 acres. However, these land parcels were very much estimations based on the oral descriptions of the balliboes within each district. Because of this, the land allocations were not always accurate and individual undertakers would often receive far more territory in acreage than was originally intended. A 'quarter' was a unit of measurement that varied in size throughout different parts of Donegal, not to mention the rest of Ulster. For the territories assigned to Captain Patrick Crawford, a quarter equated to approximately 135 acres. Therefore, for example, 2/3 of a quarter would be 2/3 of 135 equaling 90 acres.

Following his arrival to quell the rebellion, Captain Crawford had been stationed at Lifford Fort. For his loyalty, on 5th April 1610 he was chosen as a servitor who would receive land in the Kilmacrennan barony and on the 20th September 1611, Captain Patrick Crawford was allocated the balliboes of Leitir Ceanainn, along with Ballyraine, Sallaghgraine, Gortlee, Glencar, Carnamuggagh, and Killylastin for the purpose of building a new town, as per the conditions of the Plantation of Ulster:

<u>20 September 1611</u>
Grant to Patrick Crawford, of Lifford, Esq. The towns and lands of Ballylirehan and Letterkevin, one quarter each; Salregrean, 2/3 of a quarter; Gortlea, one and ½ quarter; Clancharaha and Carrownamoglagh, one quarter each; Killolosty, ¾ of a quarter; of

Letterkenny - Where the Winding Swilly Flows

Lallessedner, ½ quarter; in all, 1,000 acres, with free fishing in Loughswillie. The premises are created the manor of ballirehan, with 300 acres in demesne, and a court baron. Rent, 8/. English, to commence at Easter, 1614. To hold forever, as of the castle of Dublin, in common socage, and subject to the conditions of the Plantation of Ulster. [5]

The fact that *Ballylirehan* is mentioned ahead of Letterkenny and that the '*manor of ballirehan*' was to be created with a court baron suggest that it was to be this balliboe, near to the ancient crossing of Fearsad Suilighe Mór, that was the original choice for the building of the new town. However, possibly for defence purposes, Crawford chose the balliboe of Leitir Ceanainn instead.

Interestingly, the balliboe of 'Lallessedner' mentioned in the land grant is no longer in existence and most likely refers to the modern areas of Windy Hall and Knocknamona, given that they are not mentioned in the grant but form a part of the overall 1000 acres, as can be seen from the map.

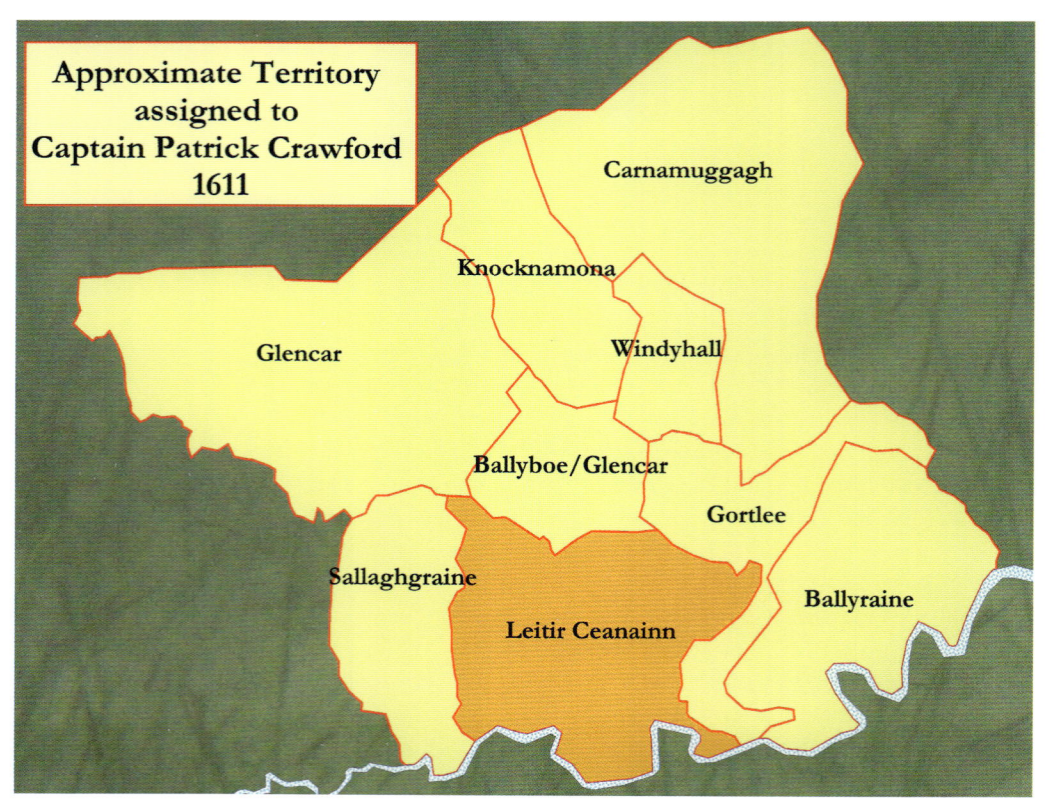

Approximate boundaries of the balliboes assigned to Captain Patrick Crawford in 1611

Unfortunately, very little is known of Captain Patrick Crawford himself. Ulster Plantation historian George Hill claims that he was the son of John (or Owen) Crawford who in 1610 was living near the town of Donegal.[6] Certainly, a Captain John Crawford did come to Ireland at the time of Agnes McDonnell's wedding to Turlough Luineach O'Neill[7] but whether this was Patrick Crawford's father is unclear. A David Crawford is listed as being on board the boat that left from

Chapter Two: Plantation and Early Development

Rathmullan in the Flight of the Earls, being a servant to Rory O'Donnell and Hill claims that this was a brother of Patrick Crawford, but again, proof of this alleged family connection is difficult to attain.

Joanna Everard

Even though very little is known of Captain Crawford, we do know that he was married to **Joanna Everard**, a lady from Belgium who was the daughter of Levimus Everard, Councilor of State to the King of Spain in the Province of Mechlin, and she has proven to be one of the most important figures in the early development of the town of Letterkenny. Previously unmentioned in local history books, it has only recently been discovered that it was through family connections to her that the Ascendancy families of the Boyds, Southwells, Hamiltons and Sempills were able to acquire land in this area, families that we will meet in a later chapter.

Joanna Everard was married four times; Captain Crawford was actually her third marriage. She was married first to John Hamilton, (son of Claud Hamilton, the 1st Lord Paisley) in Scotland. They had one daughter together - Margaret Hamilton - but following her husband's death, she remarried, this time to Robert Sempill, 4th Baron Sempill in 1604, having a son William to him. This marriage lasted only seven years as Robert Sempill died on the 25th March 1611. The 1,000 acres on the Swilly were granted to Captain Crawford six months after this and so a Captain in the Scottish army who had just acquired a sizeable portion of land in Ulster would have been most enticing to the widow Joanna Sempill and so she again remarried a short time after this, this time to Captain Crawford.

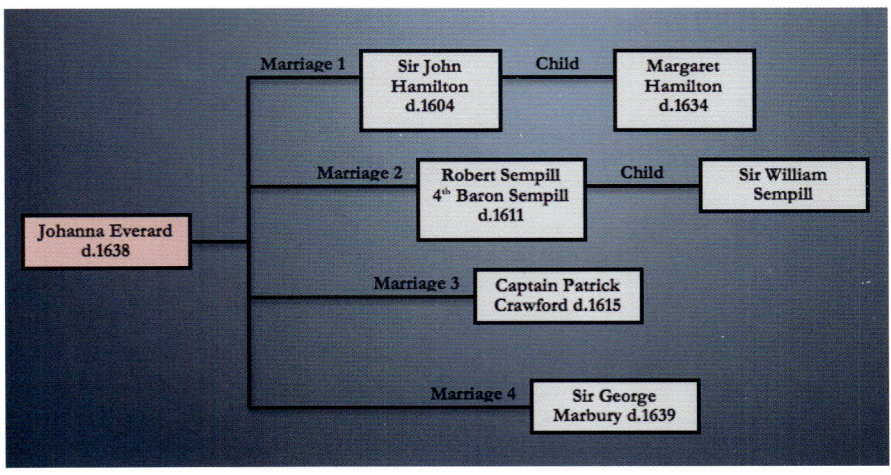

Marriage Chart for Johanna Everard, buried in Conwal Parish Church

By 1612-13, little progress had been made with the development of the towns in the province of Ulster. A suspected conspiracy from the native Irish was declared as the reason for the slow progress, *"and although discovered before it could be sufficiently matured, the excitement in Ulster produced a weakening effect on the new settlements."*[8] Patrick and Joanna Crawford had made some progress though. Following an earlier survey by George Carew, Josias Bodley was sent to Ulster by King James to report on the overall progress of the undertakers. Bodley gave a most unfavourable report to the King for Ulster but for Crawford's estate he noted that at least a start had been made on the construction of a new town, as there was a *"large number of stones collected for building."*[9]

Siege of Dunyveg Castle

Another reason for the initial slow progress in the development of the new town of Letterkenny after 1611 was Captain Crawford's preoccupation with military matters. Serving under Sir Oliver Lambert, he was called to serve in the siege of Dunyveg Castle on the island of Isla off the coast of Scotland. Dunyveg Castle was home to the McDonnells and in 1612 Angus McDonnell had sold the island to Sir John Campbell of Cawdor. Several McDonald chiefs occupied Dunyveg Castle in defiance of this and Campbell laid siege as a result with Captain Crawford summoned to assist with this siege. On the morning of 1st February 1615, Crawford was injured in the leg and died as a result of his wounds soon afterwards.[10] Lambert wrote to the King telling him that: *"Your Majesty has lost, in the death of Captain Craifford, a valiant and painful captain, by whom I was not a little assisted. The fortune of war is not to be resisted."*[11]

Sir George Marbury

Following Captain Crawford's death, Joanna then married for the fourth and final time. Her new husband, **Sir George Marbury** was then granted the 1,000 acres through the marriage and was charged with the task of completing the building of the town of Letterkenny. As stated, Bodley's report had noted that small progress had already been made and to cater for the small number of planters who would have settled in the area already and to attract even more, Marbury was granted a patent for a market on 9th December 1616.[12] Letterkenny's urban development now sprang into action.

Pynnar's Survey 1619

Following the poor reports of Carew and Bodley on the progress of the Plantation, Nicholas Pynnar was charged by the King of inspecting the province, arriving in Ireland in 1618 and delivering his completed report in 1619. Significant progress in the development of the towns across Ulster had been made and in his report, he noted the building of a Market Town of Letterkenny with 40 houses:

"Captain Craifford was the first Patentee. Sir George Marburie hath 1,000 acres called Letterkenny. Upon this there is built a Bawne of lime and stone 60 feet square, with two flankers 12 feet high and standeth waste. Near adjoining to this Bawne there is built a Township wherein there is 40 houses wherein he dwelleth, and all these houses are inhabited with British tenants, being able to make 50 men. It is a great Market Town and standeth very well for the King's service." [13]

A bawne was a concrete enclosure with a yard within and derives from the Gaelic for 'cow barn'. It was another condition of the Plantation that these 12 feet high walls were built for defence purposes against the native Irish. Generally, the market area was built in front of this bawne and the houses of the new town were built quite close to it. From this we can surmise from the location of the Market Square today that this bawne was located approximately were Mount

Chapter Two: Plantation and Early Development

Southwell Place is and the first houses of the town were built in close proximity to it.

So we see that although the land had been granted to Crawford in 1611 for the purpose of the building of a town, due to the slow progress of the Plantation and his death at Dunyveg, Sir George Marbury is usually credited with its actual development. Marbury completed the building of a small castle within the bawne by 1625 but by 1725, it was reported to be in ruins. No trace of the castle is now evident, but today the road leading to where it would have stood is still called Castle Street while 'Castle Gardens' were noted in this area in 1835. A well for water located near to the castle also came to be called 'the Fort Well', whose name is retained today in a housing estate in the town.

Artist's impression of what Letterkenny Castle may have looked like

Cartwright's 1625 Report

By 1625, the town of Letterkenny had grown significantly under Sir George and Lady Joanna Marbury, although it would appear to have been a town of quite ill repute. Marbury appears to have been a stern and authoritive figure, with power solely vested in him. Robert Cartwright, the Donegal Provost Marshall, made a visit to the town and had an altercation with several men who had escaped from jail. In a letter dated 28th January 1625 that gives us an interesting glimpse into the early development of Letterkenny, he refers to Marbury as *"a man of so evill government, and given to drinking as makes himself a laughing stock and scorne to the countreye"*. Cartwright informs us that *"willinglye he will not suffer neither sheriff nor any other officer to exercise any authoritye in that towne."* and proceeds to tell us that he informed Marbury *"lewd fellowes frequented his towne and used to playe thear for 4 or five daies together, whearof some of them had formerly broken jayle"*. When he attempted to arrest these men *"Sr. George took them away from him and set them at liberty, saying that he would discharge as many as I should commit."* [14] This letter is available in more detail in the Appendix.

Manor Sempill

Joanna Marbury died on 14 June 1638 and is stated in official genealogical papers as being buried in the newly built Conwal Parish church near to the castle; Sir George died the following year. A grave map of Conwal Parish Church was

Artist's impression of George Marbury with the family coat of arms

45

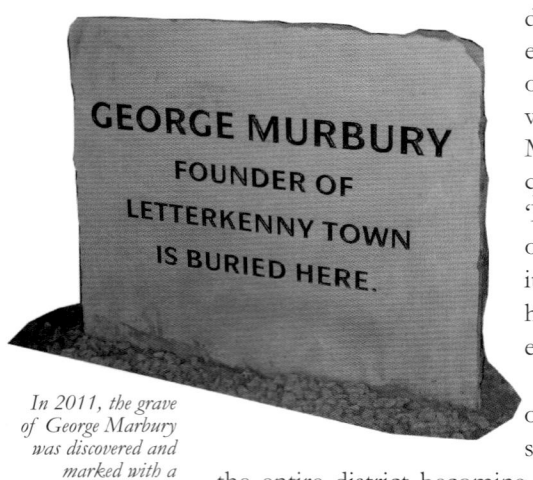

In 2011, the grave of George Marbury was discovered and marked with a monumental stone

discovered in 1983 and gives the location of an early grave by the name of 'Moobery'. The name of Marbury has been reported with many different variants in official documents such as Marburie, Maybury, Malberry, Malburye and Merburries. It is quite conceivable then that this grave, simply entitled 'Moobery' on the map is the grave of the founders of the market town of Letterkenny, especially when it is stated in official records that Joanna was buried here. Upon this discovery in 2011, a plaque was erected at their burial place.

As the Marburys had no children of their own, the estate then passed to **Sir William Sempill**, son to Joanna Marbury by her second husband, with the entire district becoming known as Manor Sempill, with Letterkenny at its centre:

22 June 1639
"To Sir William Sempill, Knt of the Manor of Letterkenny, The Castle, Towns and Lands of Ballyrehan, Letterkenny, Salregrean, Gortlea, alias Gortlett, Glancharha, Golaw, Carrowenamoggagh and Killosty. To hold ye Castle or Capital Mansion house of Letterkenny, the garden and orchard behind ye same, and 12 acres on the N/W side of ye garden in capite. Created the Manor of Manor Sempill with 500 acres in demesne: a grower to create tenures, to hold Courts Leet and Baron, to enjoy all waifes and strayes, to unpark 400 acres with free warren and parke." [15]

Sir William Sempill married **Anne Stewart**, the daughter of Captain William Stewart, who as a servitor like Crawford had been granted land in Ramelton for assisting in the O'Doherty Rebellion of 1608 and later built the town of Newtownstewart in County Tyrone.

Letterkenny in the middle of the seventeenth century was gradually growing and taking its shape with a main street developing that connected the Market Square to the Planter and Gaelic residents of the surrounding areas. Notably, at Glencar, both Scottish planters and native Irish were segregated, with the area divided into 'Glencar Scotch' and 'Glencar Irish'. A bridge was required to cross the River at the bottom of the hillside and connect it with residents in the barony of Raphoe. By 1654, the Civil Survey stated that

"There is a towne called Letterkenny wch hath a Markett every fFryday, and two faires in the yeare with a larg dwelling stone house haveing a Bawne of fower flackers a fair Church And a bridge at the End of the sd. towne over the sd. River of Swolly" [16]

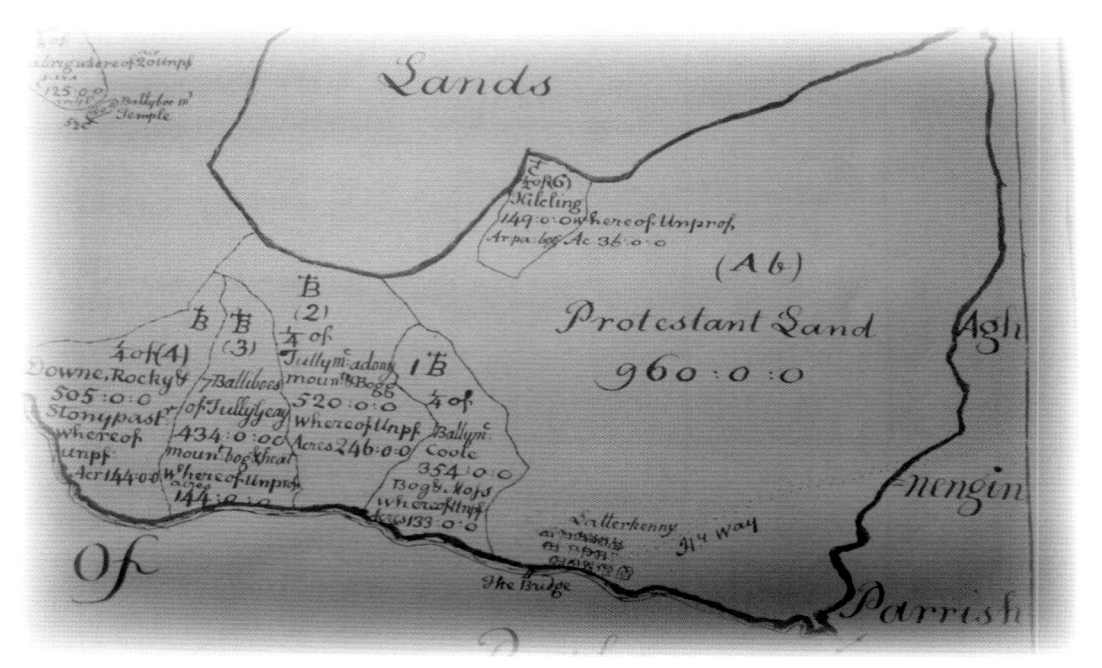

Chapter Two: Plantation and Early Development

1655 map of the area showing the boundaries of the 1000 acres with the new town of Letterkenny evident. Courtesy of Donegal County Library

The first map to show the town of Letterkenny dates from 1655 and clearly shows this new bridge.

The 1659 Census of Donegal

In 1659, a Census of Donegal was performed and it states that the population of the town of Letterkenny at this time was 73 people with 49 English/Scottish and 24 Irish residents. The principal landowners are given as **Alexander Cunningham, James Cunningham, Alexander Ewing, Levinnis Sempill, Gilbert McIlwee, Peter Colhoune, William Jamisone, Walter Buchanan, Will Anderson** and **John Colhoune**. The numbers of the neighbouring areas of Lisnennan, Carnamuggagh, Gortlee, Ballyraine, Glencar, Sallaghraine and Ballyraine are also given in Table 1:

Letterkenny - Where the Winding Swilly Flows

Townland	No. People	English/Scottish	Irish
Letterkenny Town	73	49	24
Lisnanane	4	2	2
Carrongboggagh	5	3	2
Gortleg	6	6	0
Bellireehan	5	0	5
Glencarre	5	3	2
Salarigrean	1	0	1
Bellimacoole	8	6	2

Table 1: Population of areas around Letterkenny.
Source: 1659 Census of Donegal

For the barony of Kilmacrennan as a whole, there were 2,156 people in total recorded with 605 English/Scottish and 1,551 Irish, clearly showing the dominance of the Native Irish in this barony. The only barony in Donegal in which the planters outnumbered the Irish was the barony of Raphoe with 1,825 English/Scottish and 1,330 Irish. The total population of the county of Donegal was given as 12,001 with 3,412 English/Scottish and 8,589 Irish. The size of Letterkenny's population at this time can now be compared with the older Gaelic settlements of Donegal:

Townland	No. People	English/Scottish	Irish
Ballishannon	134	63	71
Rapho Towne	104	80	24
Donegall Towne	95	24	71
Letterkenny Town	73	49	24
Lifford	68	44	24

Table 2: Population of towns in County Donegal.
Source: 1659 Census of Donegal

Although the population appears quite small, Letterkenny's growth in just over 40 years was very impressive, overtaking the older settlement of Lifford quite rapidly, indicating a determination amongst the first settlers to make the town prosper. As we have seen, in 1619, Pynnar's survey stated that in Letterkenny there were "*40 houses…and all these houses are inhabited with British tenants*" whereas by 1659 the Census noted the existence of 24 Irish in the town. This clearly

Chapter Two: Plantation and Early Development

Artist's impression of what Letterkenny would have looked like in the middle of the seventeenth century

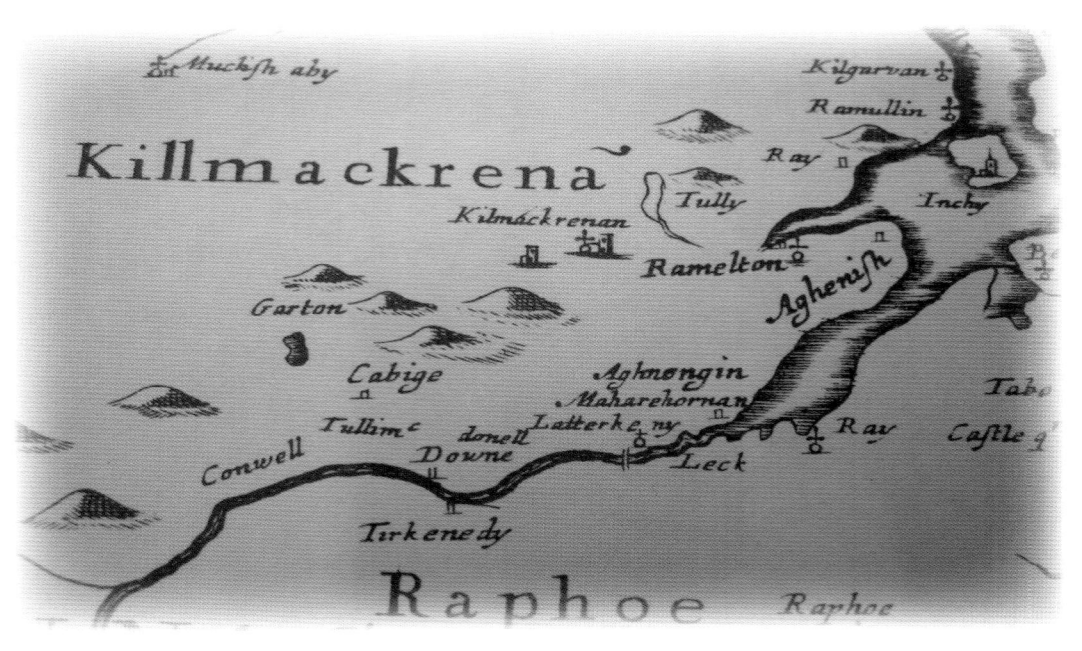

Letterkenny - Where the Winding Swilly Flows

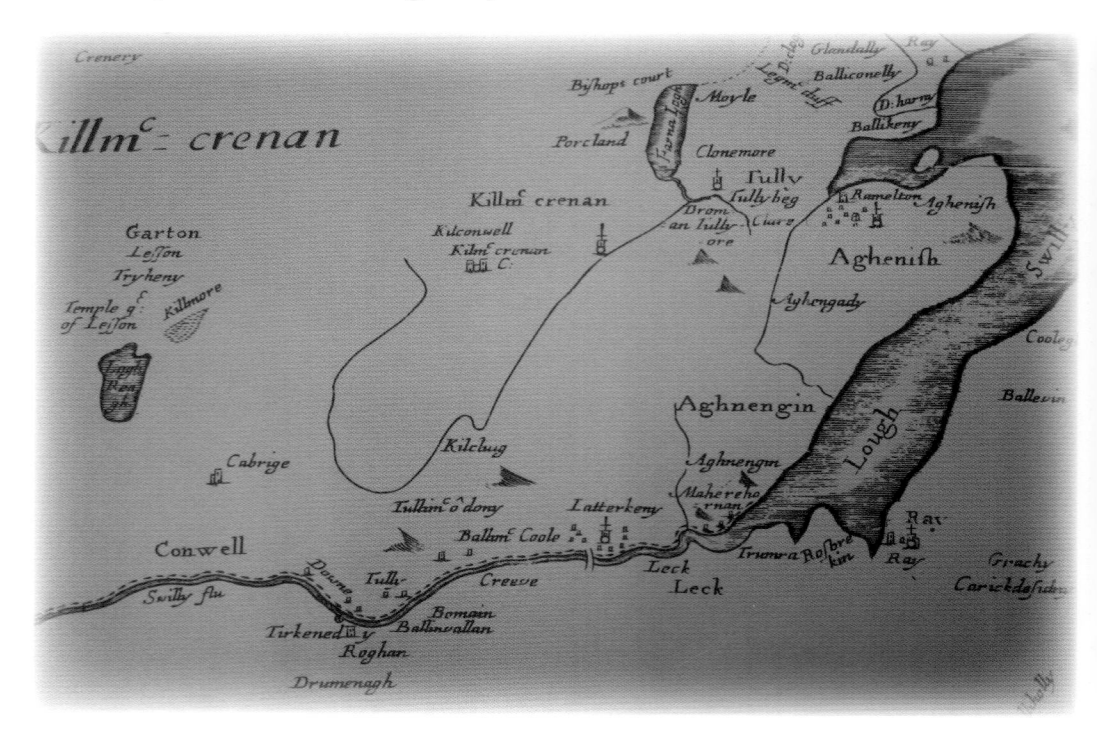

Two maps (above and previous page) from 1685 showing the town of Letterkenny with its bridge, church and the surrounding regions. Courtesy of Donegal County Library

shows that with the development and growth of the Market town, the native Irish began to move from the surrounding areas to the town of Letterkenny and settle there.

Now we can return to the popular local legend of the cat knocking over the lantern at Conwal, which was discussed in the previous chapter. The 1659 Census states that in the townland of Leck there were only 13 people, 9 being English/Scottish and 4 being Irish. Even allowing for possible discrepancies in the data, this number of Irish residents in the area is quite small for any 'Old-town' to be in existence. In all of the areas immediately south of the River Swilly, the largest grouping of Irish in one place is recorded as 13 people, recorded as being located in two separate places at 'Lergee' (Lurgy) and 'Cullen' (Cullion), neither of which correspond to the area of Oldtown today.

This 1659 Census then, along with the 1655 Thomas Betts map, which shows no settlement in the area around modern day Oldtown, certainly seems to disregard the local tradition of the 'original town' being located here. What is most probable is that something occurred between the recording of Nicholas Pynnar's survey in 1619 and the recording of the census forty years later that would necessitate the migration of the Gaelic Irish from Conwal nearer to the new town of Letterkenny. The event that most likely would have caused this migration was not a cat knocking over a lantern at all but rather the savage and bloody Battle of Scarrifhollis, which took place in June 1650.

Chapter Two: Plantation and Early Development

Endnotes

1 This quote was discovered in a forum online and is taken from the **register of the Privy Council of Scotland**: www.mckinneyandstewart.com/genealogy/getperson.php?personID=I0183&tree=McKinneyandStewart

2 Hill, George, "An Historical Account of the Plantation in Ulster at the Commencement of the Seventeenth Century 1608 – 1620", Irish University Press, 1970, First Ed. 1877

3 Calendar of State Papers 1601 A.D.: A dispatch from Sir Robert Cecil to Sir George Carey. Prior to the Plantation, Derry – the Deny – was considered a part of Tír Chonaill

4 From the "Leabhar Chlainne Suibhne : An Account of the Mac Sweeney Families in Ireland, with Pedigrees" available at http://www.archive.org/stream/leabharchlainnes00wals/leabharchlainnes00wals_djvu.txt

5 Hill, George, "An Historical Account of the Plantation in Ulster at the Commencement of the Seventeenth Century 1608 – 1620", Irish University Press, 1970, First Ed. 1877 p323

6 Ibid p323

7 Hayes-McCoy, G.A. "Scots Mercenary Forces in Ireland (1565-1603)", Edmund Burke Publisher, 1996 (first ed 1937), pp130-137

8 Ibid p449

9 Perceval-Maxwell, M., "The Scottish Migration to Ulster in the Reign of James I" Routledge & Kegan Paul, 1973, p359

10 Gregory, Donald, "History Of The Western Highlands and Isles Of Scotland, from A.D. 1493 to A.D. 1625" William Tait, Edinburgh, Longman and Co., London and John Cumming, Dublin, 1836, p363

11 Hill, George, "An Historical Account of the Plantation in Ulster at the Commencement of the Seventeenth Century 1608 – 1620", Irish University Press, 1970, First Ed. 1877, p323

12 McGill, P.J., "Some Old Fairs of Co. Donegal", Donegal Annual, 1960 p228

13 Hill, George, "An Historical Account of the Plantation in Ulster at the Commencement of the Seventeenth Century 1608 – 1620", Irish University Press, 1970, First Ed. 1877, p523

14 Hunter, Robert 'The Settler Population of an Ulster Plantation County', Donegal Annual, 1972, pp 124-54

15 Donegal County Library papers

16 Simmington, Robert, "the Civil Survey, AD 1654-1656", Stationary Office for the Irish Manuscripts Commission, Dublin, 1931-61

Chapter Three: The Battle of Scarrifhollis 1650

The River Swilly was no stranger to brutal and bloody battles throughout its history. The waters ran red with blood in 1258 at Ath Thairsi while Shane O'Neill met the robust forces of Hugh O'Donnell at Farsetmore in 1567. One final major battle was to take place at another of its principal crossing points to the west of the still young town of Letterkenny at Scarrifhollis, near to the village of Newmills today. To understand why this battle took place, we must first examine the build up to it and the tense atmosphere that existed in the recently planted province of Ulster. Following the Plantation, religious tension had been growing steadily with resentment from the Catholic Irish towards the new Protestant settlers intensifying since their arrival from 1609 onwards. By the early 1640s, this tension was now about to erupt into outright rebellion, culminating in the Battle of Scarrifhollis in June 1650.

The 1641 Rebellion

Sir Phelim O'Neill of Dungannon, had been one of the 'deserving Irish' who had received lands in the Ulster Plantation. Now in 1641, deep in debt, and concerned by the growing religious tensions in the country, O'Neill's Ulster rebellion began, quickly taking the strongholds of Charlemont, Armagh, Newry and Dungannon. The long pent up resentment of the native Irish against the new planters now exploded throughout the province as their passions were inflamed by rumours and tales of injustices suffered by the natives since the Plantation. Filled with an insatiable lust for revenge and infused with a religious fervour, the natives plundered town after town throughout the province.

Assistance to those under attack arrived in the guise of Robert Munro, who landed at the Foyle in 1642, while in Donegal in the precinct of Portlough, the Laggan Army had been formed by Sir William Stewart, who had served with Captain Crawford in 1608, to defend their settlements.

Eoghan Rua O'Neill who arrived to assist the Irish in their rebellion. Image courtesy of National Library

Eoghan Rua O'Neill and Oliver Cromwell

Eoghan Rua O'Neill, a nephew of Hugh, returned to Ireland in 1642, landing at Doe Castle to aid the Irish rebellion. Seeing this as an opportunity to reverse the Plantation of Ulster and also restore the status of the Catholic Church in Ireland, Eoghan Rua's

Chapter Three: The Battle of Scarrifhollis 1650

arrival signaled an end to the confused and sporadic nature of the initial uprising and he instigated instead a highly trained and organised offensive against the English crown in Ireland.

Coinciding with the outbreak of the Civil War in England in 1642, leading members of the Catholic hierarchy met in Kilkenny seeking to capitalise on the confusion overseas and to restore order on the island. They formed the Confederation of Kilkenny, which would act as the *de facto* government of Ireland controlling almost the entire island. In January 1649, the Confederacy signed a treaty with the English Royalists but two weeks later, King Charles I was beheaded by the Parliamentarians and the victor in the English Civil War, Oliver Cromwell, could now turn his attention towards Ireland.

Still mindful of the exaggerated tales of the 1641 massacres against the settlers in Ulster, Cromwell made no secret of his primary motive of vengeance against the native Irish. Ruthlessly taking the walled town of Drogheda after a short siege in 1649, tales of Cromwell's barbarous slaughter of the Irish are well recorded with Cromwell himself stating that his viciousness was *"a righteous judgment of God upon these barbarous wretches"*.[1] Cromwell continued his march across the coast of Munster regaining control from the Confederacy, with Kilkenny itself succumbing in April 1650.

Eoghan Rua O'Neill died in November 1649, thus leaving the Ulster Army leaderless. Despite his lack of military experience the young and dynamic clergyman **Bishop Heber MacMahon** was chosen as Eoghan Rua's successor. Following the capture of Charlemont, Dungiven and Ballycastle, MacMahon crossed the Foyle at Clonleigh and led the Ulster Army into the town of Letterkenny in June 1650. The settlers of the town at this time were too few to engage with this large army and so withdrew to Inishowen for protection.[2] The Parliamentarians, under the leadership of **Sir Charles Coote** marched on MacMahon's Ulster Army, crossing into Donegal at Lifford and following them to Letterkenny.

Scarrifhollis

Rather than engage with the Parliamentarians in the town, MacMahon chose the more defensive higher ground of nearby Dooen, near the crossing at Scariffhollis to wait for their arrival. The terrain of this area suited this defensive stance, being rocky and inaccessible to horses.[3] MacMahon, however, then made a fatal mistake while awaiting the arrival of Coote by allowing Col. McSwiney and 1,300 men to march on Doe Castle to secure the fort and return with provisions, depleting his numbers considerably as a result.

And so it was that in the summer of 1650, the opposing forces of the Royalist/Confederate army under Bishop Heber MacMahon and the Parliamentary forces of Sir Charles Coote stood on either side of the shallow ford of Scarrifhollis outside of Letterkenny, ready to engage in battle. On the 20th of June, MacMahon could see Coote's army on the opposite side of the river near Crieve/Rockhill. The Laggan Army had joined forces with the Parliamentarians and aided by reinforcements from Cols. Venables and

53

Letterkenny - Where the Winding Swilly Flows

Fenwick, Coote's army now held approximately 3,000 infantry and 800 horses, outnumbering MacMahon's 2,600 and 400. On the morning of the 21st June 1650, Bishop MacMahon, against the advice of his generals, moved from his defensive position on the hill of Dooen and engaged Coote's army on the flat lands around the river.

The area of Scarriffhollis today. Dooen Rectory can be seen in the bottom right

After about an hour of engagement, the Parliamentary forces utterly routed the Ulster Army. In the mayhem and panic of the Royalists that followed, many drowned in the river or were trapped in the silt of the tidal banks thus making them easy targets for ruthless execution. By sunset, the rout was complete. In a letter to Cromwell, Colonel Coote tells us of the battle:

"we marched up towards the Enemy, that lay near to Letterkenny, where, upon Sight of our Party, they then being encamped on this side of a Mountain, inaccessible to either horse or foot... by the blessing of God, after about an hours' hot dispute, with great Resolution on both sides, we wholly routed them." [4]

For two days, Coote pursued the retreating Irish who had fled in all directions towards Glenfin, Fintown and Glenswilly and he showed no mercy in their capture. Those who had stationed themselves in the safety of the Castle at Scariffhollis were easily captured and executed. Bishop MacMahon escaped however and made his way to Enniskillen but was captured and beheaded six months later with his head being displayed on a pike at Derry's gates. After this resounding defeat, the Ulster Army had been obliterated and the re-conquest of the northwest was complete.

Chapter Three: The Battle of Scarrifhollis 1650

Aftermath

The surrounding Native Irish population in the vicinity felt the ruthless destruction of the Ulster Army at Scarrifhollis very keenly. Local tradition informs us of the names of many areas that come directly from the results of this battle. The townland of Ardahee in which the Castle stood is said to be derived from '*Ard a'Chaion*' or the Hill of Sorrow owing to the wailing and weeping of the dying men as they were executed while Meenaroy is said to come from "*Mín an Fhir Ruaidh*" or the Plain of the Red Haired Man, named from a man who had fled the battle but was hit by a bullet and fell in the area.[5] Today in the town of Letterkenny, the estate of MacMahon Villas on the New Line Road is named after the defeated Bishop while at Scarrifhollis itself a monument to the battle stands, erected in the year 2000 to mark the 350th anniversary.

There are no remains today of the Castle at Scarrifhollis although the site is noted on the 1835 OS map of the area with O'Donovan's memoirs giving us this description:

Artist's impression of the Battle of Scarrifhollis 1650

"*Many leaden bullets have been dug out the earth in the neighbourhood of the Castle which prove it to have been the scene of a mighty struggle between the two parties…The foundation of a Castle, called by the natives Castle Sollus, is shown here and Cahir O'Dogherty, in whose farm it lies, says that about fifteen or twenty feet of the walls were standing not many years ago and says he himself was the very man that tore them down to use the stones for building a barn withal. He pointed out to me some of the corner stones of the Castle in the wall of his barn; they are very large, squared and chiselled, and show that the Castle was well built.*"[6]

Perhaps the most lasting legacy of the Battle of Scarrifhollis though was to the town of Letterkenny itself. In their pursuit of the fleeing Royalists, the Parliamentary forces under Charles Coote destroyed the small Gaelic hamlets of nearby Tullygay and Conwal. We know that settlements in

A monument was erected in 2000 to commemorate the 350th anniversary of the Battle of Scarrifhollis

Letterkenny - Where the Winding Swilly Flows

the area existed up until the sixteenth century at least with the Four Masters telling us that *"the town of Conwall"* was in existence in 1540.[7] The destruction of this settlement in the aftermath of the Battle of Scarrifhollis in 1650 necessitated the relocation of their community up the river to settle in the new town of Letterkenny, as evidenced by the number of Irish in the town in the Census of Donegal nine years after the battle. A new hamlet of 'Old Irish' on the south of the river would eventually adopt the name of 'Old town' to differentiate themselves from the 'New' settler population.

Most likely then, it was not in fact a small black cat knocking over a lantern that destroyed the Gaelic settlement at Conwal at all. The 'Cat' in fact was most likely a 'Coote'. In the aftermath of the Battle of Scarrifhollis, the statement that *'Conwal was destroyed by Coote'* in time became *'Conwal was destroyed by a Cat'* - the true nature for the migration of the Gaelic Irish to Letterkenny getting lost as it was passed down through the generations.

Thus, following the bloody and decisive Battle of Scarrifhollis in the middle of the seventeenth century, having no place else to go to rebuild their livelihoods, the Gaelic Irish moved a short distance east up the river, settling in the new town of Letterkenny with a bridge being built by 1655 that connected those south of the river to the Market area where they would trade and gradually integrate with their new English and Scottish Protestant neighbours.

A black cat overlooks the destruction of the settlement of Congbhaile – but was he responsible?

Endnotes
1 Bardon, Jonathan, "A History of Ireland in 250 Episodes", Gill & Macmillan, 2008, p197
2 McKenny, Kevin, "The Laggan Army in Ireland 1640-1685", Four Courts Press, 2005
3 Ronayne, Liam (ed), "The Battle of Scarrifhollis", Eagrain Dhun na nGall, 2001 pp45-53
4 Ibid p43
5 Ibid pp58-61
6 Maguire, Canon, "Letterkenny Past and Present", 1917, p90
7 Annals of the Four Masters 1540.1 available at www.ucc.ie/celt

Chapter Four: The 'Established Church' and Presbyterianism

According to census statistics, Catholicism is the predominant religion in the town of Letterkenny today. However, given that the town has its origins in the Plantation of Ulster, it is no surprise to learn that many individuals and families of both the Church of Ireland and Presbyterian communities have left a rich imprint on the history of the town – not to mention, of course, Methodists, Baptists and many other religions that still practice their beliefs locally today. Being the oldest of these religions in the town, in this chapter, we shall meet the various rectors of both the Church of Ireland (called the Established Church until 1879) and Presbyterian churches and examine their role in shaping the history of Letterkenny.

Although successful with his Reformation in England, King Henry VIII's Protestantism never really took root in Roman Catholic dominated Ireland in the sixteenth century, apart from areas in and around the Pale. It was difficult enough to gain territory in Ulster, never mind attempt to spread a new religion amongst its Gaelic inhabitants. This all changed with the Plantation of Ulster. Prior to this, church lands in Donegal had been Catholic, and for the areas around *Leitir Ceanainn*, those church lands were Conwal, Leck and Aughananshin.

The church at Conwal has its origins in the seventh century under Fiachra, son of Ciarán, and by 1425, **Nicholas Magmalgaussa** was herenach of the Abbey, being succeeded by **John McGillabride**, **Roger Macungail**, **Godfredus Macdalaidh** and **Eugenius O'Gallagher**.[1] At Leck, the original church remains are believed to date from 1336[2] while a monastery at Aughananshin is thought to have existed from the seventh century as mensal lands of the Muintir Ceallach (or Kellys).

The old church at Leck

However, in the immediate aftermath of Plantation, the churches and lands of Leck, Aughananshin and Conwal and others were transferred to the 'Established Church'. Religious territories were known as 'glebe' lands and their locations near the town are easily located today by their names such as Gartan Glebe, Dooen Glebe and Conwal Glebe.

Phelim O'Doghertie was installed as Rector of Conwal in 1609 and by

Letterkenny - Where the Winding Swilly Flows

1615, **Dougall Campbell** (who '*understandeth the Irish language and is able to preach herein*')³ had succeeded him as Rector. As the ancient site had been badly neglected over the years, it was therefore decided that a new church was needed. One of the stipends of building a new town in the Plantation was to have its own church near to its inhabitants and as the abbey at Conwal was deemed too far away from the new town (while the abbeys of Leck and Aughananshin were in different parishes) work began on the construction of a new church near to the home of the Marburys, completed by 1636.

Conwal Parish Church. The tower of the original church remains as the oldest building in Letterkenny dating from 1636

"*The Ancient Parish Church of Conwal is now ruinated and decayed being situated before in a remote place, and is now fitted to be transported to a market town called Letterkenny, where eighty families of British inhabitants within the midst of the parish…As in many other Parishes the pre-reformation Church building was in ruins through the disorders and neglect of our times. As result of this recommendation a new Parish Church was built in Letterkenny in October 1636*"⁴

This church was constructed within a short walking distance of the Market Square at a junction of two streets – one from the town to the church called Church Street and one leading to the castle of the Marburys called Castle Street. The church was built most likely using stone from the nearby quarry at Sentry Hill, and it was here that Lady Johanna Marbury and her husband Sir George were buried in 1638 and 1639 respectively.

Many renovations took place in the church

Canon Stewart Wright takes visitors to the grave of George Marbury as part of the Letterkenny 400 events in June 2011

Chapter Four: The 'Established Church' and Presbyterianism

itself over the years to the extent that unfortunately very little of the original building remains. **Rev. William Spann** (Rector 1715-1752) had the roof slated in 1733 and he donated a silver chalice and paten to the church in 1744, which the church still has in its possession. In 1776, it was almost entirely demolished when the nave was extended and a chancel was added under the auspices of **Rev. John Whittingham** (Rector 1753-1779) but the original tower was retained while the original date stone from 1636 can still be seen as part of the building. **Rev. Charles Boyton** (Rector 1832-1836) oversaw a new spire being built in 1832 while **Rev. Henry Kingsmill** (Rector 1836-1876) added a south aisle and vestry room in 1865.

In 1809, **Rev. Joseph Stopford** was appointed Rector and it was under him that Glendooen Rectory was built as a residence in 1814. It was here in 1832 that his grandson, Stopford Brooke was born; he would later go on to translate the German carol "*Stille Nacht*" into English. Glendooen Rectory remained as the residence of the rectors until 1913 when Lancelot Eustace Smyth and his wife, Frances Elizabeth Rosalie Smyth, presented their private residence of Murrac A Boo to the parish in memory of her father Major Doyne - **Archdeacon William Hardy Holmes** was the first to occupy this new residence. Following the sale of Murrac A Boo to the Urban District Council in 1979, the rectory was located in Magherenan from 1980 until the present rectory on New Line Road was built in 1998 for the present rector, **Canon Stewart Wright**.

The Irish Church Act of 1869 led to the disestablishment of the Church and the creation of the new 'Church of Ireland'. This came into effect in 1871 and one year later, the parishes of Aughananshin and Leck were formally amalgamated, being further merged with the Parish of Conwal in 1900 creating the Conwal Union. By 1957, Gartan was added to this union while the churches at Leck and Aughananshin were closed down in 1972 with all Church of Ireland parishioners of Letterkenny attending service in Conwal Parish Church. For the record, the twentieth century rectors of Conwal Parish Church were:

The former rectory of Murrac A Boo, later the Urban District Council offices. The Regional Cultural Centre now stands on its site. From Christmas Annual 2002

59

Letterkenny - Where the Winding Swilly Flows

- **Richard Aemilius Baillie** (1876-1902)
- **Joseph Potter** (1903-1904)
- **William Fitzroy Garstin** (1905-1915)
- **William Hardy Holmes** (1916-1918)
- **Henry St. George McClenaghan** (1919-1937)
- **Leslie Robert Lawrenson** (1938-46)
- **Louis Warden Crooks** (1946–80)
- **Peter Graham Cartwright** (1980-84)
- **Peter Francis Barrett** (1985-90)
- **William Wright Morton** (1991-1997)
- **William Charles Stewart Wright** (1998-present)[5]

Richard Aemilius Baillie Rector 1876-1902. Courtesy of Canon Stewart Wright

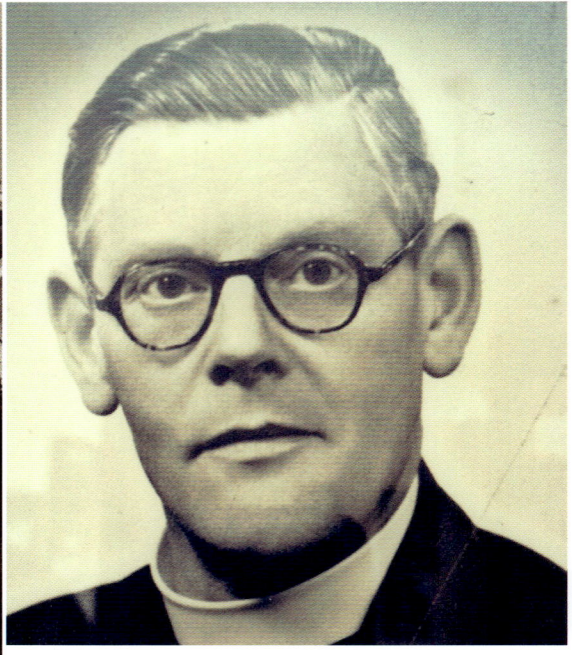

Louis Warden Crooks Rector 1946–80. Courtesy of Canon Stewart Wright

Conwal Parish Church Graveyard & Redmond O'Hanlon

For two hundred years prior to disestablishment, the civil parishes of the Established Church acted almost as a Town Council for each town in Ireland. A Grand Jury of local landlords would look after the general governance of the town but it was the civil parishes of the Established Church that were responsible for the poor relief, graveyards, education, sanitation and the enforcement of law and order amongst the town's inhabitants. They would pay for the upkeep of

Chapter Four: The 'Established Church' and Presbyterianism

these through the collection of the tithe, a sort of tax that was enforced on every citizen regardless of religious denomination.

The graveyard of Conwal Parish Church in Letterkenny was thus used as the graveyard for all inhabitants of the town, regardless of their religion, with many Catholics being buried alongside their Protestant neighbours. As the church was built on an area of almost solid rock, large quantities of soil were brought in and placed around the church to be used as burial areas, which is why today, the whole church and graveyard is raised higher than the areas outside of the walls. Due to the large number of burials of the town's residents over the centuries, many families were buried in plots 'outside the walls', most likely in the land that now holds the car park.

We have seen that one of the earliest graves located in Conwal Parish Church is that of the founders of Letterkenny, the Marburys (marked Moobery on the grave map) while a stone tablet is still visible in the church noting the deaths not long after the church was completed of Henry Wray (11th February 1652), his son Henry (12th August 1656) and his wife Elizabeth (13th May 1674), a noted ascendancy family that will be discussed in a later chapter. Graves of many other Letterkenny men and women are noted on the grave map also with the Boyds, Groves and Stewarts figuring prominently while there are many notable memorials inside the church itself, including a stained glass window to commemorate those parishioners that lost their lives in World War 1 with a brass memorial dedicated to all those from the parish that returned alive.

One of the best-known graves in Conwal Parish Church is said to be that of **Count Redmond O'Hanlon**, the notorious seventeenth century bandit. Originally from County Armagh, O'Hanlon had fought under Eoghan Rua O'Neill at the Battle of Benburb but rose to prominence in the late 1650s following his return from France where he had been made a Count. Operating as a lone highwayman (or rapparee) in his native territory at first, extracting 'protection' money from those that now lived on his former lands, other bandits soon joined him in his exploits.

His crimes soon became common news at London court as he extended his attacks into Down, Leitrim and Roscommon and relentlessly pursued by Dublin Castle, he was eventually shot by his foster brother, Art, on April 25th 1681 and was buried at Ballinabreck in Co. Down.

The grave of Redmond Hanlen, merchant of Letterkenny which many people believe is the final resting place of Count Redmond O'Hanlon

In his 1979 pamphlet, "*Count Redmond O'Hanlon*", local historian Sam Fleming states that following a decree of 1679 which ordered the arrest of family relatives of outlaws, Count Redmond's father, (also called Redmond), left Armagh for the safety of his family and moved to Letterkenny. This, Fleming contends,

Letterkenny - Where the Winding Swilly Flows

is the "**Redmond Hanlen**, Merchant" listed on the gravestone in the graveyard:

The five sons of Redmond Hanlen Merchant in Letterkenny:
John, the firstborn, Alexander, Francis, John and Redmond.
Also here lieth the body of William, son of the afore said Redmond Hanlen,
who departed this life on the 27th…1708 aged 3 years…months and 14 days.
Also the remains of David Conyngham, Gent and Cath,
his wife, daughter of Redmond Hanlen.
They were esteemed more for goodness of heart than for affluence of fortune.
Died lamented here on…December 1752, 72 years old.
She: 21st August 1775 aged 80

Fleming notes that the reason for Redmond Senior choosing Letterkenny at this time was that his daughter was married to David Conyngham, brother to Sir John Conyngham, who was by now the proprietor of Letterkenny Castle. According to legend, Sir John Conyngham sent an escort of swordsmen to the cemetery at Ballinabreck to exhume the body of Count Redmond and reinter his remains in Letterkenny in the family plot, at the request of the O'Hanlons. Fleming surmises from this legend that Count Redmond's final resting place is Letterkenny, buried with his father and brothers.

However, taking the dates on the headstone into account, the numbers do not seem to add up. Count Redmond fought at the Battle of Benburb in 1646 and yet according to the gravestone, he had a son William fifty-nine years later in 1705 (noted on the headstone as having died in 1708 aged 3 years)? Also, the daughter of Redmond Snr., Catherine, who married David Conyngham (and thus was the 'reason' for the family to move to Letterkenny in 1679), is noted on the gravestone as dying in 1775, aged 80, giving her birth as 1695 - sixteen years after the decree which allegedly forced the O'Hanlons to move to the town!

It is quite clear then that this Redmond Hanlen who is buried in Conwal Parish Church is not Count Redmond's father, nor indeed the famous rapparee. That is not to say that they weren't a relation of some kind – possibly cousins who fled the Armagh territory for their own safety and moved to Letterkenny for a new life.

However, there is an actual connection of the rapparee to the town, which could explain the confusion. Prior to his becoming an outlaw, O'Hanlon worked for Sir George Acheson of Markethill in Armagh. Acheson was a grandson of Johanna Marbury, his mother being Margaret Hamilton, the daughter of Johanna and her first husband Sir John Hamilton. In fact, Archibald Acheson, George's father, died at Letterkenny Castle in 1634. This connection to the Achesons then would have made a trip to Letterkenny at some stage very possible for Count Redmond O'Hanlon in his younger years, while owing to their links with the Achesons, perhaps other members of the wider O'Hanlon family moved to the town, changed their name to Hanlen and were then buried in the graveyard, causing the confusion.

This is admittedly speculation. No convincing evidence has ever surfaced

Chapter Four: The 'Established Church' and Presbyterianism

linking the Hanlen grave at Conwal Parish Church with Count Redmond. However, even if there were no family connection, the Redmond Hanlen who is buried in the town is noted to have been quite a prominent merchant and businessman in the eighteenth century market town of Letterkenny, recorded in Presbytery records in 1697 and again in a deed of Indenture of 1711:

"*Windy Hall and six Balliboes of Glencar by Indenture dated 10th August 1711 between Sir Francis Hamelton of Castlehamilton, Co. Cavan Bart to Redmond O'Hanlon of Letterkenny Merchant for the sum of £368=0=0d. paid by Redmond O'Hanlon to Sir Francis Hamilton, together with a house and garden formerly belonging to Robert Ewing, and two gardens adjoining the Churchyard, and other tenement gardens formerly possessed by John Boyd.*"[6]

Presbyterianism

Owing to the predominantly Scottish nature of the new town of Letterkenny in the seventeenth century, the arrival of Presbyterianism was to be expected. The Scottish army who had arrived to assist in quelling the Ulster Rising of 1641 found Church life generally without leadership throughout the province and so in 1642, a new Presbytery was formed in Carrickfergus to restore the church along Scottish lines. Sir William Sempill, son to Johanna Marbury from her second marriage, had been granted the lands around Letterkenny in 1639 and by 1640, a new presbytery was set up in the town with **Rev. Andrew Semple**, brother of Robert Semple of Nether-Walkingshaw near Glasgow, appointed Presbyterian minister for Letterkenny in 1642.[7] Presumably he was some sort of relation to the new titleholder of the lands around Letterkenny (despite the slight difference in name spelling) and was encouraged to come and practice his ministry and build a meetinghouse on the Main Street.

He was succeeded by **Rev. William Semple**, again more than likely another relation, who was born in Glasgow in 1624 and ordained to Letterkenny Presbytery in 1647. Not long after this though, he was forced to leave Ireland for his opposition to the Puritans and he ministered in Scotland until his return to Letterkenny in 1654.

Laws had been passed against Presbyterians throughout the 1640s that restricted their freedom to worship in England and Ireland. As such, it was more politically advantageous to be a member of the Established Church and so the Presbyterian Rev. William Semple, was appointed rector for Conwal Parish Church. Following the Restoration of Charles II to the throne of England, a government act of 1661 declared that all clergymen in

The datestone noting the foundation of the Letterkenny Presbytery in 1640

the Established Church were now to hold an Episcopal ordination and, refusing to conform to this, Rev. William Semple was removed from his position in the Church. He continued to exercise his Presbyterian ministry in the local area but was arrested for this in 1664 (along with John Hart, Thomas Drummond, and Adam White) by Bishop Leslie of Raphoe and held in Lifford gaol for six years. He was released in 1670 and returned to his ministry but due to prolonged ill-health, he died in October 1674.

Rev. William Liston, who arrived in the town in 1675, replaced Rev. Semple as Presbyterian minister in Letterkenny. By now there was a regular Meeting House in the town, which would have been a large thatched barn with an earthen floor and no fixed furnishings. People brought their own benches and stools and sat in areas according to what part of the district they came from. Rev. Liston ministered in both Letterkenny and Ramelton until his death in 1695.

There was an interval of twelve years before the next minister that we know of was ordained to Letterkenny. **Rev. Samuel Dunlop**'s ministry began in August 1707 and lasted for fifty-five years, until he died in 1762 aged eighty-two. Mr. Dunlop is believed to have been a fluent Irish speaker and preached sermons in the native language, thus showing a willingness to converse and assimilate with the Gaelic speaking population of Letterkenny.[8] Under his successor, **Rev. Joseph Lyttle,** a new meetinghouse was erected on the Main Street around 1763 as the roof of the building had collapsed immediately following a meeting. He told his congregation:

"When your old meeting house which was in a ruinous condition, fell, which happened on the Sabbath day, if the congregation then assembled had continued eight minutes longer, they must have been buried in the ruins of it; an instance of Providence that calls for the highest gratitude."[9]

Gortlee Church where Reformed Presbyterians or Covenanters met from 1785.

Chapter Four: The 'Established Church' and Presbyterianism

During Mr. Lyttle's ministry, reformed Presbyterians or Covenanters, were established at Gortlee and built a Meeting House there. **Robert Young** from Scotland came to Donegal in 1779 and linked up with like-minded reformers in the Ramelton and Laggan areas, establishing a ministry at Gortlee in 1785. He was succeeded as minister at Gortlee first by **William Gamble** (1788-1839), followed by **William Henry** (1842-1852), **John Robinson** (1859-1866) and **Joseph Moffett** (1874-1907). Dr. Moffett also opened a classical academy in Letterkenny where he educated the children of his ministry.

On the Main Street, Rev. Lyttle retired in 1803 and died on 7th January 1805. His nephew, also called **Rev. Joseph Lyttle**, succeeded him, being ordained in May 1803. He was a vehement supporter of the crown and declared himself ready to raise "*a thousand men, being two from every family in the congregation, in defence of Protestant principles.*"[10] Due to infirmary, Mr. Lyttle retired in 1839 and died in 1852.

In 1820, there was a split in Mr. Lyttle's ministry, with the Seceders establishing a congregation on the Port Road at Barkhall and becoming known as 'Second' Letterkenny, with the original congregation now known as 'First' Letterkenny. Dissatisfied with the rules and standards of the main Synod of Ulster **Rev. Dr. Andrew Spratt** was ordained in this new ministry in August 1821. Dr. Spratt was described as "*earnest, faithful and painstaking*" who had "*the meekness and constancy of a Christian*" while his "*kindliness of heart and peacefulness of disposition was pleasingly apparent.*"[11] He died in July 1858. His congregation was generally of the poorer class of the district and following his death, the difficulty of continuing their independent existence as a congregation became too much and so was dissolved. Barkhall Meeting House then became a school for Presbyterian children from 1860.

A further split occurred within 'First' Letterkenny in 1840 and a new Meeting House was built in 1841 next to Conwal Parish

Joseph Moffett, Minister at Gortlee from 1874-1907. From Weir, A.J., "Letterkenny Congregations, Ministers & People 1615-1960", 1960

The former church of Barkhall that later became a school on the Port Road. From Weir, A.J., "Letterkenny Congregations, Ministers & People 1615-1960", 1960

Letterkenny - Where the Winding Swilly Flows

Church. This congregation became known as 'Third' Letterkenny, ministered by **Rev. Oliver Leitch** until his death in 1893. Following the death of Dr. Spratt in 1858, this 'Third' congregation at first adopted the name of 'Second Letterkenny' but rather than being confused with the previous church at Barkhall, and also because they didn't want to be seen as 'second' to anybody else, they changed their name to 'Trinity Church'. In 1894 **Rev. Ross Millar** was installed as minister of this congregation and remained there until he retired in 1925.

At First Letterkenny on the Main Street, **Rev. Moses Houston** succeeded

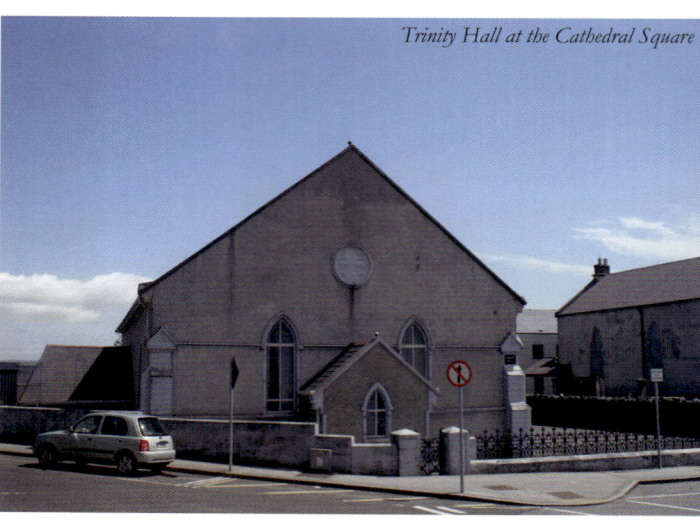

Trinity Hall at the Cathedral Square

Rev. Ross Millar, Minister 1894 – 1925. From Weir, A.J., "Letterkenny Congregations, Ministers & People 1615-1960", 1960

Rev. Lyttle in 1841 and within four years, the Meeting House was extensively repaired. Following his resignation in 1847, **Rev. John Kinnear**, became minister of First Letterkenny in 1848 and served his parish until his retirement in 1899 and his death in 1909. He was elected Liberal MP for Donegal in 1880 and his active work as a politician in Tenant Rights will be explored later. In 1870, the Meeting-house was nearly burned down due to an accidental fire and full renovations of the church interior took place five years later. In 1898, a visitor remarked on the Meetinghouse, describing it as:

"...a quaint old building, situated in the Main Street, built in the form of a letter T, with galleries over the main transepts, and capable of seating 800. Only the walls are intact from the former

Rev. Oliver Leitch, Minister 1841 – 1893. From Weir, A.J., "Letterkenny Congregations, Ministers & People 1615-1960", 1960

Chapter Four: The 'Established Church' and Presbyterianism

building; but the pulpit is more than a century old, of Irish white oak, stained (and backing directly on the Main Street)." [12]

Rev. James Millar Craig succeeded Dr. Kinnear in 1900 and ministered for three years in First Letterkenny, being succeeded by **Rev. William John Logan** in 1904. In 1909 during Rev. Logan's ministry, the Meeting House was completely rebuilt but on 31st August 1921 it was burned down as it was believed to be a possible arms dump for the Ulster Volunteer Force, although no evidence of this was ever found. As this was over a month after the IRA truce, claims that it was burned down as part of the War of Independence appear unfounded. Immediately after this fire, the meeting hall of Trinity Church was used to shelter this homeless congregation, bringing the two separate groups closer together and paving the way for a complete union three years later. From April 1922 until the union, Rev. Logan and Rev. Ross Millar exercised a joint

The former Presbyterian Meeting House on the Main Street. Image courtesy of the National Library of Ireland

The present Presbyterian Meeting House built in 1927

Letterkenny - Where the Winding Swilly Flows

ministry over the combined Letterkenny congregations.

By 1925, under the ministry of **Rev. Alfred McAlpine Dodds**, the union of First, Trinity and Gortlee Reformed Presbyterian congregations formally took place under the united name of Trinity Church with its newly built Meetinghouse on the Main Street from 1927. Rev. Dodds was then succeeded as minister of Trinity Presbyterian Church by:

- **Rev. Samuel James Park** (1931-1942)
- **Rev. John Charles Pedlow** (1942-1952)
- **Rev. Andrew John Weir** (1952-1962)
- **Rev. Frank Russell** (1963 – 1974)
- **Rev. William Ivor Hunter** (1976-1979)
- **Rev. Joseph Kerr McCormick** (1981 – 1997)
- **Rev. William Alexander McCully** (1998-2010)
- **Rev. Thomas John Bruce** (2011 – present)[13]

Today, the Presbyterian congregation of Letterkenny consists of approximately 225 families.

Rev. James Millar Craig, Minister 1900 – 1903. From Weir, A.J., "Letterkenny Congregations, Ministers & People 1615-1960", 1960,

Rev. William John Logan, Minister 1904 – 1925. From Weir, A.J., "Letterkenny Congregations, Ministers & People 1615-1960", 1960

Chapter Four: The 'Established Church' and Presbyterianism

Rev. Alfred McAlpine Dodds Minister 1925 – 1930. From Weir, A.J., "Letterkenny Congregations, Ministers & People 1615-1960", 1960

Rev. John Charles Pedlow (1942-1952). From Weir, A.J., "Letterkenny Congregations, Ministers & People 1615-1960", 1960

Rev. Samuel James Park (1931-1942). From Weir, A.J., "Letterkenny Congregations, Ministers & People 1615-1960", 1960

Rev. Andrew John Weir (1952-1962). From Weir, A.J., "Letterkenny Congregations, Ministers & People 1615-1960", 1960

Letterkenny - Where the Winding Swilly Flows

Endnotes
1 Leslie, Rev. J.B., "Biographical Succession Lists", from "Clergy of Derry and Raphoe", the Ulster Historical Foundation, 1999, p55
2 Day, Angelique and McWilliams, Patrick, "Ordnance Survey Memoirs Of Ireland, Vol 39: County Donegal II, 1835-36" Institute of Irish Studies, 1997 p116
3 Leslie, Rev. J.B., "Biographical Succession Lists", from "Clergy of Derry and Raphoe", the Ulster Historical Foundation, 1999, p55
4 Fleming, Sam, "Letterkenny Past and Present", Donegal Democrat, 1979, p36
5 Leslie, Rev. J.B., "Biographical Succession Lists", from "Clergy of Derry and Raphoe", the Ulster Historical Foundation, 1999
6 Fleming, Sam, "Redmond O'Hanlon", unknown date, p25
7 Seaton Reid, James, "A History of the Presbyterian Church in Ireland" Vol. II, Whitaker & Co. London, 1853, p130
8 McClintock, May, "From Dark Troubled Times to an Ecumenical Politician – Early Presbyterianism in Letterkenny (1642 – 1909), Christmas Annual 1992, p71
9 Fleming, Sam, "Letterkenny Past and Present", Donegal Democrat, 1979, p39
10 Weir, A.J., "Letterkenny Congregations, Ministers & People 1615-1960", 1960, p17
11 Ibid p22
12 Ibid p27
13 Information courtesy of Rev. Thomas Bruce, Trinity Presbyterian Church.

Chapter Five: The Letterkenny Ascendancy and the Era of the 'Big House'

The dispossession of lands from Roman Catholics in Ireland that began with the Ulster Plantation had continued unabated throughout the seventeenth century so that by the time of the Treaty of Limerick in 1691, Catholics in Ireland held only 14 per cent of the land. The introduction of the Penal Laws in the eighteenth century reduced this ownership even more and by the 1770s, only 5 per cent of the land of Ireland was in the possession of Roman Catholics.

Allied with this transfer of land ownership in Ireland, there arose a ruling class of aristocrats, landlords and prosperous lawyers, commonly referred to as 'The Protestant Ascendancy'. Estates characterised by stately mansions and large tended gardens arose around the ever growing town of Letterkenny with several privileged families such as the Wrays of Castleway and Ards, the Mansfields of Oakpark, the Groves of Castlegrove, the Stewarts of Gortlee, the Chambers and Stewarts of Rockhill and the Boyds of Ballymacool creating Letterkenny's very own Ascendancy class between the 17th and 20th Centuries.

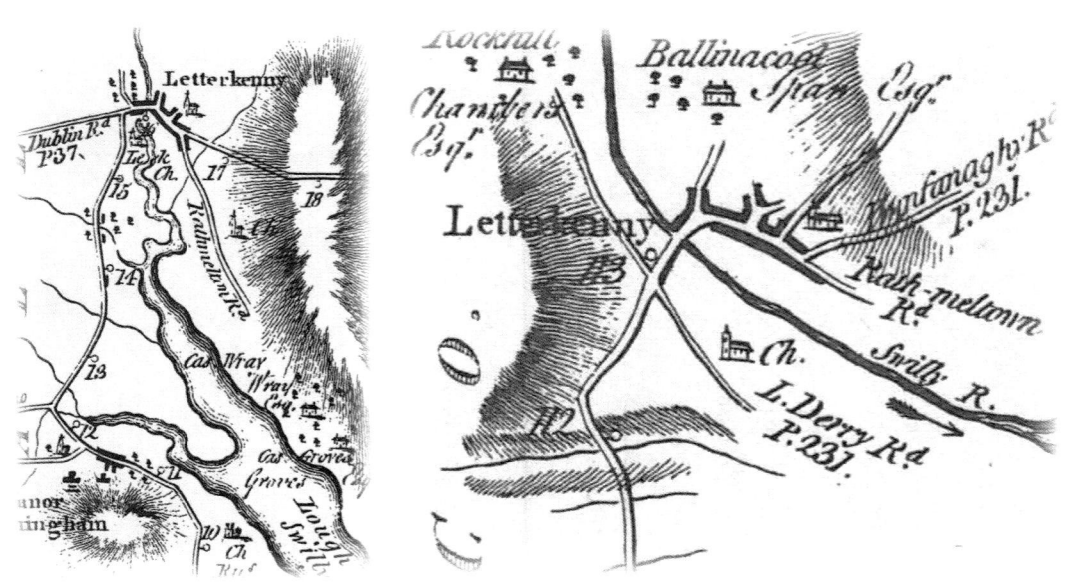

Two eighteenth century maps showing the Ascendancy Houses of the Letterkenny Area. Courtesy of Donegal County Library

The Wrays of Castlewray

The original patentee for the lands around Cornagill in 1611 was **Sir John Vaughan**, a military engineer who supervised the completion of the walls of the new Plantation town of Londonderry in 1618:

19 February (1610-11)
Grant to John Vaughan, Esq. Dogh-iyey, Carnagilly, Lisndise and Dromon, one quarter each; Colleboy, one and 1/3 quarter; Lissanana, one and ½ quarter; half of Ellistran quarter; and half of Ighterosse quarter: in all 1,000 acres, with free fishing in Lough Swilly.

Letterkenny - Where the Winding Swilly Flows

The premises are created the manor of Carnagilly, qith 30 acres in demesne, and a court baron. Rent, 8/. English. To hold forever, as of the castle of Dublin, and subject to the conditions of the plantation of Ulster. [1]

John Wray had come to Ireland in the early 1600s from Richmond, Yorkshire and he was well acquainted with Sir John Vaughan as they are listed together as Aldermen of the City of Londonderry (along with Ralph Bingley, Henry Vaughan, Henry Harte and others who also received lands in Donegal as part of the Plantation). John Wray purchased the grand estate at Cornagill from Vaughan not long before Pynnar's Survey in 1619:

Sir John Vaughan was first Patentee. John Wray, esq. hath 1,000 acres called Carnagilly. Upon this there is a good strong Bawne of Lime and Stone, 40 feet long with four Flankers, in which there is a good Lodgings, being two stories high; also a Stone House of the length of the Bawne, being two Stories high; this is inhabited with an English Gentleman and his Family, who hath some English tenants under him, and this standeth in a good place for the King's Service. [2]

The original "Stone House" listed in Pynnar's Survey was most likely located where Oakpark is located today, near to the golf course. John Wray died in 1624 and his son **Henry Wray**, aged 14, was named as heir to the manor of Cornagill. In 1639, Henry and his family moved from the original home at Oakpark and built a new house at Castleway, receiving a grant from the Crown that created the Manor of Castleway in the process. (In these Ascendancy families, there are several people who share the same first name so to avoid confusion in the text, numbers shall be assigned to each person, who can be seen in the corresponding family tree.) This is the Henry Wray (2) whose memorial tablet adorns the wall in Conwal Parish Church where he is buried along with his wife and son:

A stone tablet commemorating the death of Henry Wray in 1652 on display in Conwal Parish Church

Here lyeth ye body of Henry Wray
Esqr. Who Died J. Fey Anno
Domino 1652
His Son Esqr. Henry Wray died
12 of Aug Anno Dom 1666 Mrs. Elezebeth
Wray Who Died 13 May Anno Dom 1674

Henry's eldest son, **Henry Wray** (3) inherited the estate of Castleway aged ten, upon his father's death in 1652, but he himself died at the rather young age of 24 in 1666. The lands then passed to his younger brother **William Wray** (4) who married Anne Sampson and had a son, **Henry Wray** (5) in 1673. Upon Anne's death in 1678 though, William married for a second time, this time to Angel Galbraith by whom he had another

Chapter Five: The Letterkenny Ascendancy and the Era of the 'Big House'

son, **Humphrey Wray** (6). These two sons caused a split in the family tree as we then have the Wrays of Castlewray and the Wrays of Ards.

The Wrays of Ards

In 1700, Henry Wray (5) married Jane Jackson and his father transferred the lands of Castlewray to his supervision as he decided to move his new wife and family to Dunfanaghy. Upon his death in 1710, William named Henry as heir to Castlewray and Humphrey received lands in Ards that had been acquired through his first wife, Anne Sampson. Deciding that Humphrey should have a grander house than Castlewray, his mother set about building Ards House, which is described by Sir Bernard Burke:

"At Ards, Wray built him a good and large mansion on a sunny bank facing the sweet south, and running down to meet the purple rocks, and white strands, and clear blue waters of Sheephaven; and here he lived in a princely way, amidst his woods and pleasure grounds and many retainers enjoying a climate like that of Italy for softness, where, sheltered from the north and east, the myrtles and geraniums grew richly in the open air, and beds of rhododendrons and fuchsias stretch down to meet the kisses of the salt sea." [3]

Sadly the original Wray mansion at Ards is no longer in existence but the lands that surround it now house the Franciscan monastery and Ards Forest Park. Burke further describes Ards at this time as

"an oasis in a desert; all outside the park gates was mountain heaped upon mountain, stony valleys, huge grey boulders standing up like sentries on the road side" [4]

Humphrey's son, **William Wray** (7) was quite an industrious man and so set about improving the road infrastructure in the area so that the estate at Ards would not be so difficult to reach for his aristocratic visitors.

"At that time there was but one available road from Letterkenny, the frontier town, to Ards, and this had been made by William Wray himself and with such zeal, that he caused his labourers to work at it all night by torch-light." [5]

William Wray (7) also improved the ancient road that had connected Raphoe to Gartan through Mongorry Hill at considerable personal expense:

"A second road he constructed over Mongorry Mountain between Letterkenny and Raphoe, with incredible trouble and cost. No hard whinstone rock, no shaking bog, no hill-side torrent, ever could turn our rectilinear road maker one foot from his straight-forward course. He would blast the first, pave the second and bridge the third; and on the map of the recent Ordnance Survey, the engineer's rule could never draw a straighter line than the delineation of this long road presents. It is now quite forsaken, only cattle drivers make use of 'ould Willie Wray's road", the present generation having discovered that it is wiser, if not shorter, to skirt the base of a hill than to scale the summit." [6]

Letterkenny - Where the Winding Swilly Flows

Through the construction of these roads for visitors to his estate, William Wray built up quite considerable debts and was thus compelled to sell Ards in 1782 to Alexander Stewart of Kilrea, Co. Derry. This Alexander Stewart was the father of John Vandeleur Stewart who would later purchase the estate at Rockhill from the Chambers family.

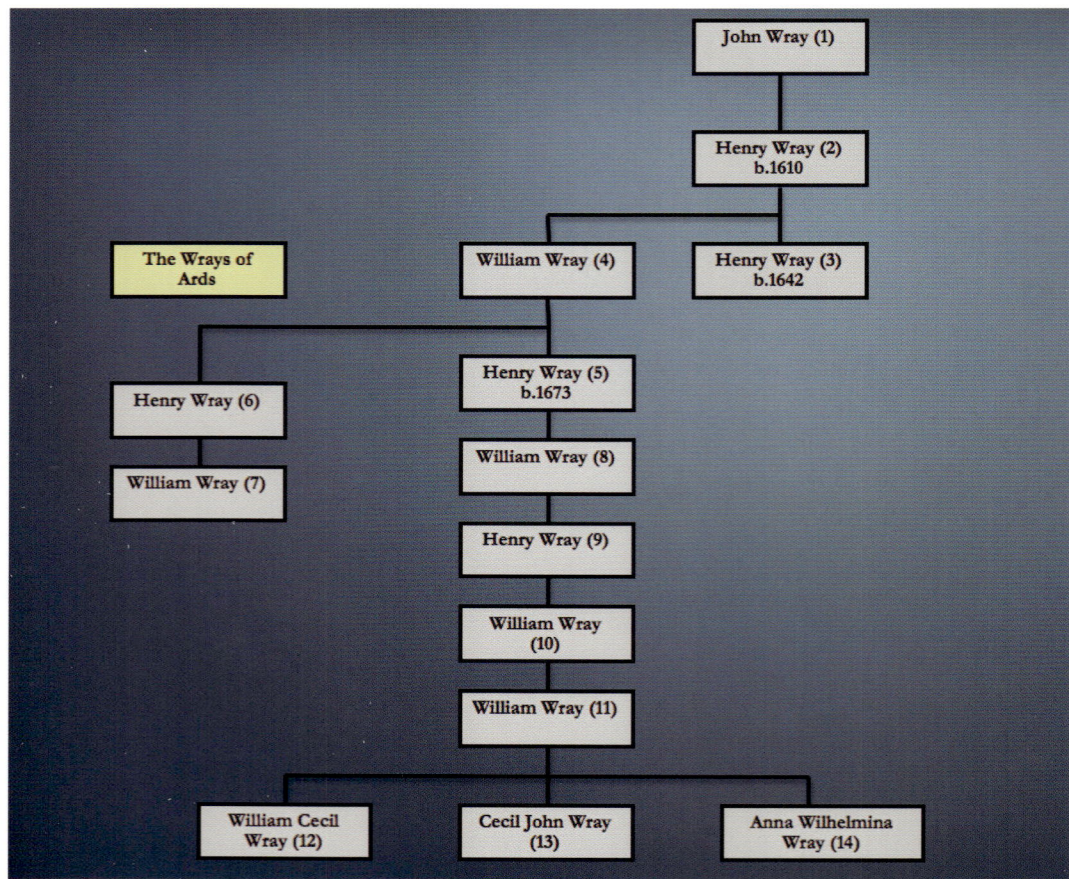

```
                                      John Wray (1)
                                            |
                                      Henry Wray (2)
                                         b.1610
                                   _____|_____
                                  |                 |
                          William Wray (4)    Henry Wray (3)
                                  |              b.1642
   The Wrays of   _____|
      Ards       |                |
                 |           Henry Wray (5)
           Henry Wray (6)      b.1673
                 |                |
          William Wray (7)  William Wray (8)
                                  |
                            Henry Wray (9)
                                  |
                           William Wray (10)
                                  |
                           William Wray (11)
                   _____|_____
                  |               |               |
          William Cecil    Cecil John Wray   Anna Wilhelmina
           Wray (12)           (13)            Wray (14)
```

Family Chart of the Wrays of Castlewray and Ards.

Castlewray

Returning to Castlewray, Henry Wray (4) died in 1737 and the estate passed onto his eldest son, **William Wray** (8). When William died in 1767, the estate passed to his son, **Henry Wray** (9). This Henry, however was quite a poor businessman and owing to a lavish lifestyle and crippling gambling debts, was forced to sell the manor of Castlewray to Francis Mansfield by 1800, although the Wrays continued to live at the original estate of Oakpark with their status in Letterkenny's Ascendency greatly diminished.

Henry's son, **William Wray** (10) married Elizabeth Mansfield, sister to Francis but upon her death he married Anne Jane Johnston by whom he had a son, **William Wray** (11), who took over the estate of Oakpark in 1843. Upon

Chapter Five: The Letterkenny Ascendancy and the Era of the 'Big House'

his death in 1888, the Wrays financial status had been diminished even further. A combination of rapidly declining finances on account of the Famine years, crippling debts (Wray had borrowed upwards of twenty thousand pounds) and two sons, **William Cecil Wray** (12) and **Cecil John Wray** (13), who were not interested in tending to the estate led the last of the Wrays, **Anna Wilhelmina** (14) and her mother to depart Oakpark in 1892 and set sail for California. The Wray estate of Oakpark was then placed in the Encumbered Estates Courts where a local man purchased it for £1,200. This was to be the end of the Wrays of Oakpark and Castlewray.

Charlotte Violet Trench in her book "The Wrays of Donegal" describes the state of the once proud manor of Castlewray when she visited in the 1940s:

"It must have been a very ordinary and ugly square house since the new front was built onto the old 'modern' house of Henry and Jane Jackson's day, but I was hardly prepared for the forlorn tumbledown derelict that is now all that remains. One bow-window had fallen completely out on to the lawn, where stones and rubble lay in heaps, leaving an open view into the rooms on both stories with the ceiling and floor between them sagging down in the centre. The wall round the bow-window on the other side was all cracked and looked ready to fall at any moment. The hall door was boarded up, but in any case it would not have been safe to go inside this crumbling shell of a house."[7]

The Groves of Castlegrove

Another local Ascendancy family of the Letterkenny area are the Groves of Castlegrove. The family were originally residents of Castle Shanaghan in the seventeenth century and only moved to the Castlegrove area around 1730. Castle Shanaghan was originally granted to William Stewart as part of the Plantation in 1610 but was sold to the Grove family sometime before 1654. We know this because the Civic Survey of 1654 lists a Thomas Grove as holding lands in this area while the 1659 census states that "Thomas Groves" was a tituladoe (titleholder) for Castleshanaghan. **Thomas Grove** (1) was Commissioner of Assessments for Donegal in 1655, Collector of Customs in Londonderry from 1643-74, and Sheriff of Donegal in 1664. He was married to Margaret Benson with whom he had a son, **William Grove** (2) in 1662. Upon his death in 1677, Thomas Grove's will bequeathed 40 shillings to be paid to the church wardens of the parish of Conwal towards *'the relief of the poor inhabitants of Letterkenny...English inhabitants of ye town to be preferred.'*[8] His son, William, served through the Siege of Derry of 1688, and married firstly Constance Kingsmill and then Elizabeth Leigh upon his first wife's death in 1687.

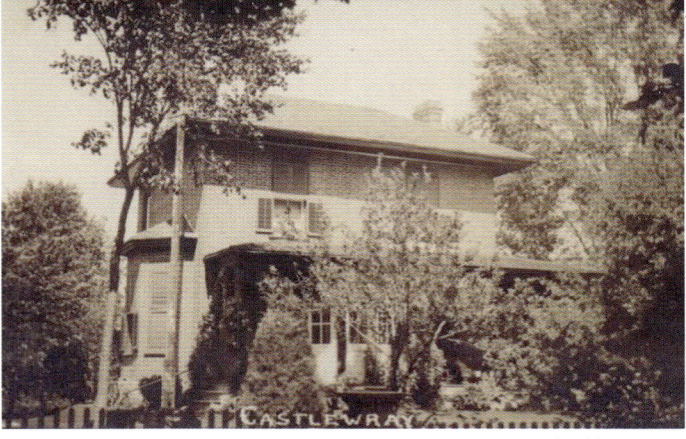

An old photograph of Castlewray House

Letterkenny - Where the Winding Swilly Flows

William's son, **Thomas Grove** (3), inherited the Castle Shanaghan estate upon his father's death in 1697 and served as High Sheriff of County Donegal in 1724. His son, **William Grove** (4) served as High Sheriff of County Donegal between 1727-28 and moved the family estate to Castle Grove, which he built around 1730. He married Susanna Barry and had a son, **Thomas Grove** (5) in 1719, who inherited the estate upon his death in 1742. As Thomas died a bachelor, the estate was transferred to his brother, **James Grove** (6), who married Rose Vaughan Brooke, and died in 1793. His son **Thomas Grove** (7) married his cousin Mary Susanna Grove in 1794 but renounced his surname and took his mother's maiden name of Brooke in 1808. His aunt, **Dorothy Grove** (8) had married John Wood in 1802 and acquired the Grove estate upon Thomas's decision to change his surname to Brooke.

Dorothy's son, **James Grove Wood Grove** (9) succeeded to the estate in 1863 having served as High Sheriff of the County in 1855. In 1843, he married Frances Judith Montgomery of Convoy House and their son **John Montgomery Charles Grove** (10) was born in 1847, serving as Justice of the Peace and Secretary to the Grand Jury of Donegal from 1877-99. He married Lucy Georgina Gabbett and they had one son, **James Robert Wood Grove** (11) who served in the First World War, being wounded in the hand at Gallipoli, and became a Major in 1919. He later joined the Royal Tank Corps in 1924 and married Eileen Edmonstone Kirk. James Robert Wood Grove died in 1969 and the estate passed to a relative, **Commandant Peter Campbell** (12) on the condition that he changed his name to Grove. In 1989, after a period of ill health, Peter Campbell Grove sold the estate to **Raymond** and **Mary Sweeney** who opened the luxurious Castle Grove House Hotel, which is still open today.

The Grove estate lay adjacent to the Wrays estate of Castlewray and were both connected through a small road that ran between the gardens of the two estates. Charlotte Trench describes the Castle Grove gardens in the 1940s as:

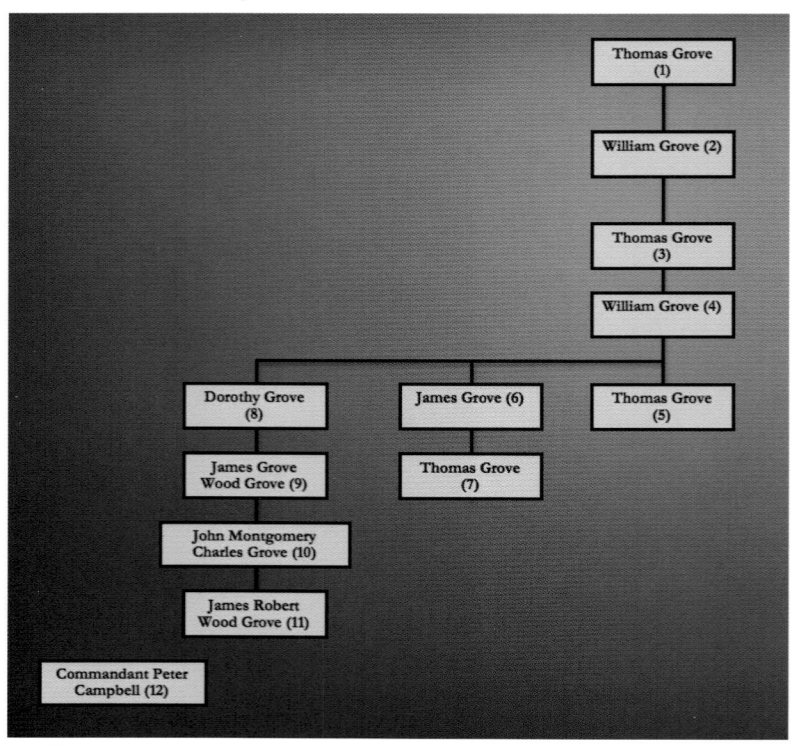

Family chart of the Groves of Castlegrove

Chapter Five: The Letterkenny Ascendancy and the Era of the 'Big House'

"a vast place, enclosed by great high stone walls. It seemed very full of fruit trees and vegetables of all sorts, some parts were rather wild; it would have needed a regiment of gardeners to keep it really in order; but the old-time herbaceous border was a blaze of colour and rich in beauty."[9]

Castlegrove House today

The Stewarts of Gortlee

Gortlee House is built on lands that were originally owned by the Stewarts, who had obtained the lands at the end of the seventeenth century at the end of the Williamite Wars. These Stewarts were quite distinct from another local ascendancy family of the same name, the Stewarts of Rockhill and were the ancestors of Charles Stewart Parnell, the land reform campaigner, champion of Home Rule and the 'uncrowned King of Ireland'.

Charles Stewart (1) was born in 1670 in Scotland and served in the army of King William of Orange in the Battle of the Boyne in 1690. For his gallantry in this decisive battle, Charles Stewart obtained land at Gortlee from the king. In 1695 he married Isabella Weare and died in 1722. Their only child, **Robert Stewart** (2) was born at Gortlee in 1701 and he married first Margaret Stuart in 1723 and then secondly, Martha Ewing in 1727 having five children - Margaret (b. 1725), Charles (1729 - 1800), Robert (1732 - 1787), John (1735 - 1795) and Alexander (1761 - 1785), all born at Gortlee House. Their eldest son, Charles Stewart, moved to America in 1750 and served with distinction under George Washington in the American War of Independence, later becoming Commissary

Letterkenny - Where the Winding Swilly Flows

General and a Representative in the U.S. Congress.

None of these children appear to have had any interest in the Gortlee estate however and so upon Robert Stewart's death around 1770, the family sold the estate to **John Ramsay**. Upon Ramsay's death in 1789, his family sold it to **William Boyd** of Ballymacool (1742 – 1791) who was the Treasurer for County Donegal & Collector of the Port of Ballyraine. The Boyds obtained the lease for Gortlee on 8th December 1789 but William died two years later and in his will he left the estate to his brother, **Alexander Boyd** (1752 – 1825). Upon his death in 1825, as he had no children, he left Gortlee estate to his wife, **Florinda Boyd** who then sold the estate to **Thomas Patterson** in April 1825 for £2,600. The Pattersons sold the Gortlee estate in the early 1830s to **James Cochrane**, whose sons John and David Crawford Cochrane were born at Gortlee in 1834 and 1835 respectively.[10] The Cochrane family later sold the estate to the Robinson family who are the current owners.

The Cochrane family, residents of Gortlee House at the end of the nineteenth century

The connection of the Stewarts of Gortlee and Charles Stewart Parnell

The connection to Charles Stewart Parnell comes through the brother of

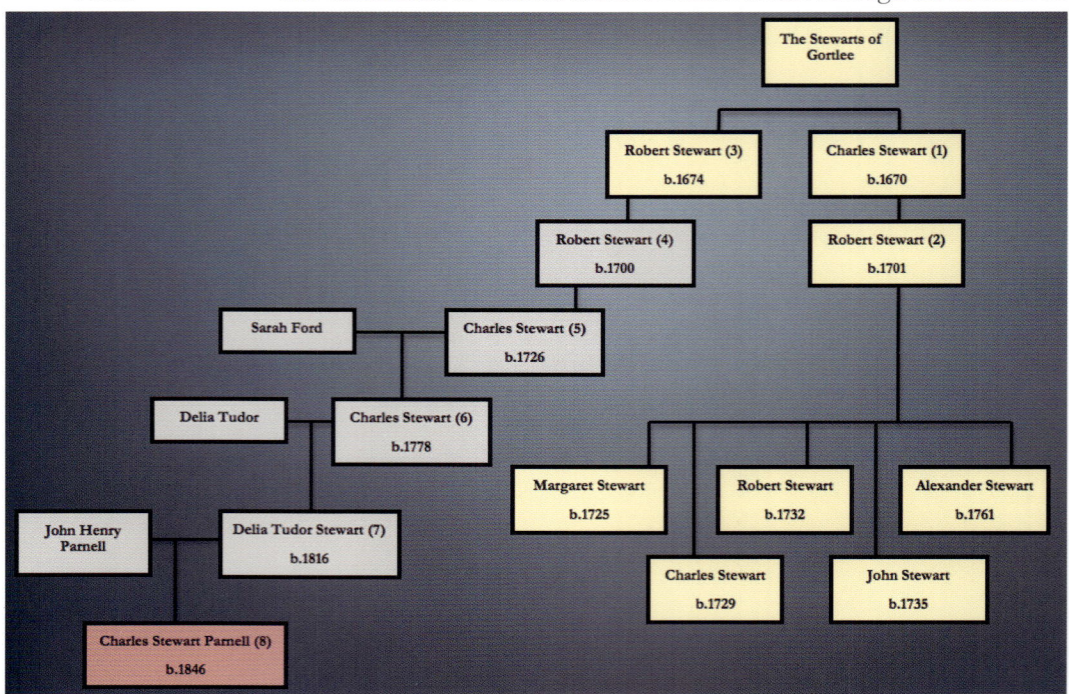

78

Chapter Five: The Letterkenny Ascendancy and the Era of the 'Big House'

the original grantee of the estate of Gortlee, Charles Stewart. **Robert Stewart** (3) was born about 1674 and, like his brother Charles, was also an officer in King William and Mary's army but he was too young to participate in the Battle of the Boyne. Robert had a son, **Robert Stewart** (4), who was born about 1700. Not much is known about him only that he had a son, **Charles Stewart** (5), born in 1726. He was a sea-faring man and after marrying Sarah Ford, they left Belfast for Philadelphia, where he died in 1780. Their youngest son, **Charles Stewart** (6) was born in 1778 and he married Delia Tudor in 1813. Charles rose to become an Admiral in the United States Navy winning fame in American History during the war of 1812. In 1841, he was even considered as a possible candidate for the Presidency of the United States. He died in 1869, aged 91. His daughter **Delia Stewart** (7) married John Henry Parnell, an English gentleman who visited the United States in 1834. Their son was born in Avondale, Co. Wicklow in 1846, and was given the same first name of his ancestors from Gortlee - **Charles Stewart Parnell** (8).

The Chambers of Rockhill

In the Plantation of Ulster, an English Knight **Sir Thomas Coach** was granted 1,500 acres on the south side of the River Swilly called 'Lismongan'. While we might associate that solely with the small area of Lismonaghan today, the land in fact stretched out much further than that to take in the areas of Rockhill and Scarrifhollis also. Pynnar's Survey in 1619 states that

"Sir Thomas Coach, knight, hath 1,500 acres, called Lismongan. Upon this Proportion he hath a Trench cast up with a Hedge upon it, invironed with a small Brook, in which there is a house of Cagework, wherein himself with his Lady and Family are dwelling. There is Brick and Lime, with all other Materials, ready for the building of a Bawne and a House. The place is very convenient for the King's service, and the good of the Country. He hath six good Houses near unto him inhabited with English Families."[11]

Charles Stewart Parnell 1846 - 1891. Image courtesy of the National Library of Ireland.

We know that Coach's lands stretched past Rockhill as in his overall report for the area, Pynnar tells us that:

"Sir Thomas Coache, Knight, 1,500 acres; is a resident, has built a large timber house adjoining to the castle of Skarfollis, and is providing materials for re-edifying the Castle"[12]

Coach's son, **Captain Thomas Coach**, also held lands in Cabra, Co. Cavan and from the 1660s onwards, it would appear that he confined his family business primarily to there. After bequeathing the estate to his son, **Colonel Thomas Coach**, the overall 1,500 acres then came into the possession of the Pratt family through marriage. **Joseph Pratt** was originally married to Frances Coach, sister to the Colonel but in 1686 was re-married to Elizabeth Coach, daughter to the Colonel. Upon Colonel Coach's death in 1699, the lands of Lismonaghan passed to the Pratts who remained in the area right up until the nineteenth century.

Rockhill, or Corr as it was known then, being approximately 240 acres in size, was just a small part of this overall 1,500 acres of the Coach family estate. In a grant of 26 July 1693, **John Chambers** was granted the lands of Rockhill from Thomas Coach, grandson to the original patentee:

"Thomas Coach of Cabra in the County of Cavan Esq. and Madame Catherine Coach, alias Saunderson, his wife, on one part and John Chambers and Anne Chambers, his wife, of the other part, for ever, of that quarter of land by the name of Corr otherwise Rockhill in the Parish of Leck and Country of Donegal"[13]

Thus the Chambers family came to occupy Rockhill at the end of the seventeenth century and they built a manor house on their lands, on the site of the current Rockhill House. These Chambers were descended from **William Chambers** who had been the Curate of Leck in 1633. The succession of the Chambers of Rockhill was as follows: **Thomas Chambers**, brother to John, **William Chambers** (1670 – 1724) Colonel in the Donegal Militia, **Brooke Chambers** (1696 – 1760) Captain in the army, **Daniel Chambers** (1724 – 1811) Captain in the Royal Leck Volunteers, Donegal Regiment of Militia and High Sheriff of the County in 1763, **Brooke Chambers** (1754 – 1805) Captain in Donegal Regiment of Militia and High Sheriff of Donegal 1795, and **Daniel Chambers** (1789 – 1850) Captain of Donegal Militia 1812 and High Sheriff of Donegal 1839.[14]

Daniel Chambers sold the estate at Rockhill to John Vandeleur Stewart of Ards on 21 February 1832 for £900 and retired to Loughveagh House on his other estate at Gartan (where Gartan Outdoor Pursuits centre now stands) but sold that in 1845 and moved to Dublin where he died in 1850.

The Stewarts of Rockhill

As we have seen, Alexander Stewart from Kilrea in Co. Derry had purchased the Wray estate at Ards in 1782. Now, fifty years later, his son **John Vandeleur Stewart** purchased the Chambers estate of Rockhill thus beginning the Stewart ownership of the estate that lasted until 1937.

John Vandeluer Stewart was appointed High Sheriff of Donegal in 1838 and made extensive renovations to the former Chambers house, so closely modeled on the family home of Ards House that they came to be almost 'sister houses'. The Stewart estate stretched from Oldtown to Bomany and up to Letterleauge where the ruins of the former gatehouse can still be seen. Flax, beet, corn and potatoes were cultivated on the estate with a large orchard near to the house while coursing and hunting on the estate was offered for £10 annually. The Rockhill Coursing Club was set up in 1890 with Sir Thomas Lecky as President.

Chapter Five: The Letterkenny Ascendancy and the Era of the 'Big House'

Family Chart of the Chambers and Stewarts of Rockhill

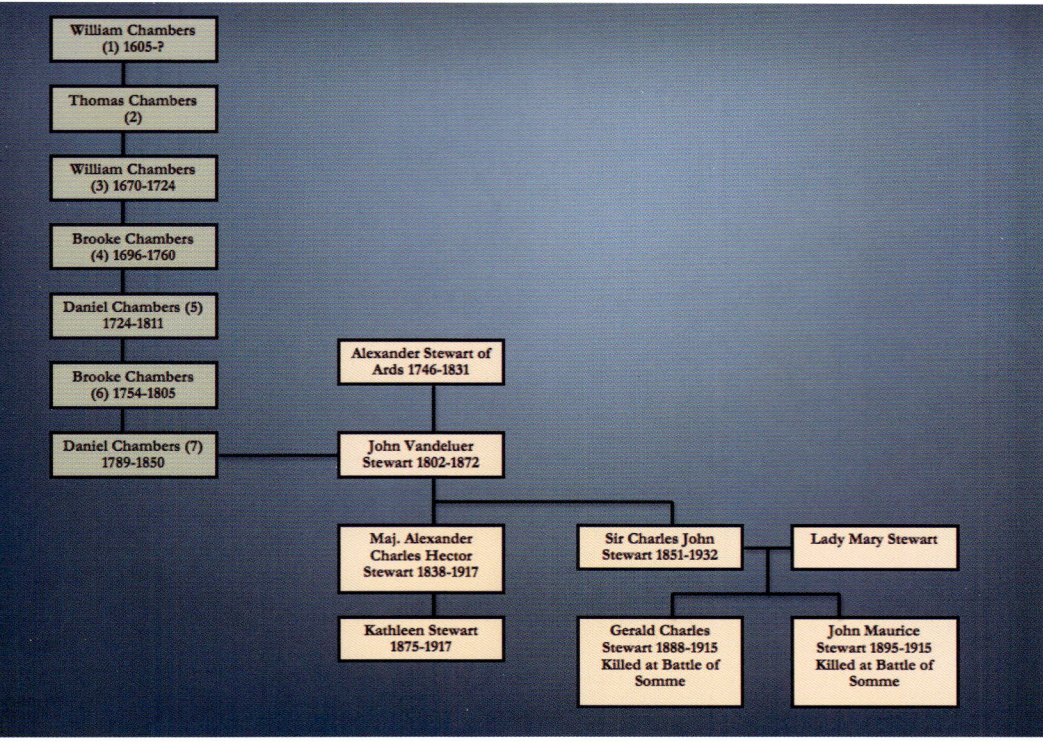

The Rockhill Stakes, The Letterkenny Stakes and The Swilly Stakes were competed for annually at Crieve Meadows, with competitors arriving with their greyhounds from all over the northwest.[15]

John Vandeluer Stewart died in 1872 and the estate passed to his eldest son, **Major General Alexander Charles Hector Stewart**, who was High Sheriff of Donegal in 1881. Upon his death in 1917, the Rockhill estate was left in trust to his daughter **Kathleen Stewart**, but his brother **Sir Charles John Stewart** effectively became the administrator of the estate as she lived in Sussex with her husband Philip Arthur McGregor.

Sir Charles John Stewart and his wife, Lady Mary Stewart had two sons, John and Gerald, who were both killed within six weeks of one another in World War I. Upon their sons' deaths in 1915, they were so heartbroken that they seemed to lose interest in returning to the estate of Rockhill. The land steward **Robert R. Robinson** tended to the management of the estate in Sir Charles John's seasonal absences.

With nobody occupying the estate, Rockhill House was taken over by Anti Treaty IRA troops upon the outbreak of Civil War in Ireland in 1922. Across the river, Ballymacool House was also taken over with the Boyds being forcibly removed from their home. The Pro Treaty forces launched an attack on both houses on 22 June 1922 and removed the insurgents.

Owing to this political unrest in Ireland, the loss of his sons and an overall lack of interest from the family in the estate, Sir Charles John Stewart finally left

Letterkenny - Where the Winding Swilly Flows

Rockhill House, built by the Stewarts. Image courtesy of the National Library of Ireland

Rockhill in 1927 and moved to Scotland. The family home then served as a Preparatory Irish College for student teachers until 1930 but the estate soon fell into decline and was sold in various lots on 19 January 1937 to the Commissioners of Public Works. The Department of Defence then came to occupy the main estate of 29 acres from the 1940s and housed the Army on a permanent basis from 1969 until 2009 when it closed due to government cutbacks on military expenditure.[16]

The Boyds of Ballymacool

The Boyd family of Ballymacool were connected via marriage to Lady Johanna Marbury of Letterkenny Castle who died in 1638. As can be seen from the table, her first husband, Sir John Hamilton was brother in law to Marion Boyd through her marriage to James Hamilton, the Earl of Abercorn. John and James Hamilton were also great, great grandsons to Margaret Boyd, wife to James IV of Scotland and granddaughter to Robert, 1st Lord Boyd of Kilmarnock. Johanna Marbury therefore became connected to the Boyd family through her

The connection of the Boyds to Johanna Everard

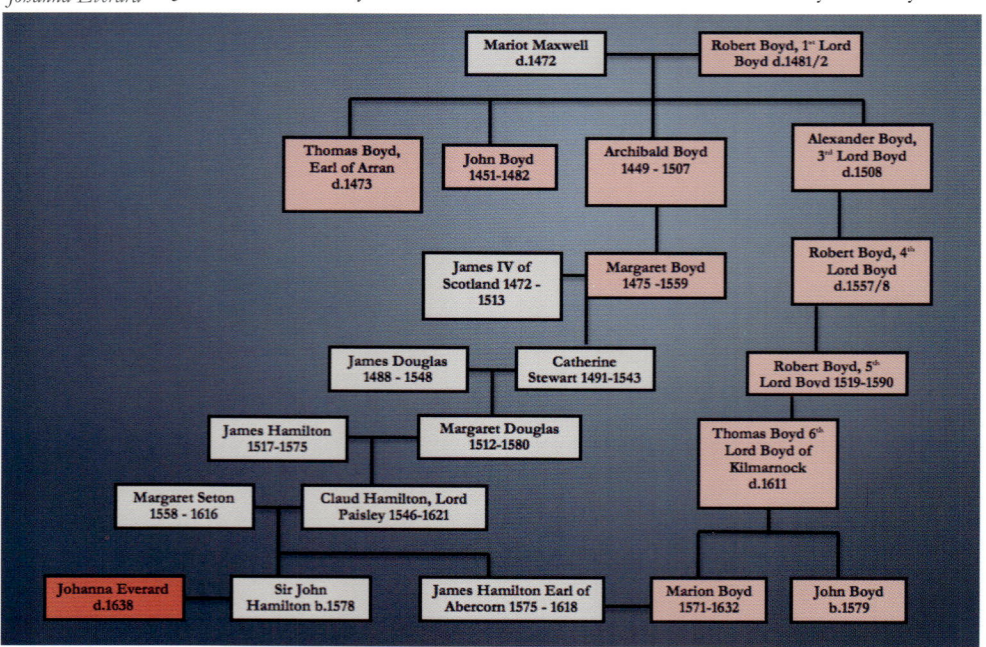

Chapter Five: The Letterkenny Ascendancy and the Era of the 'Big House'

first marriage and this enabled the Scottish brothers John, William and Robert Boyd to arrive in the town in the 1660s and claim a piece of the 'family' lands. Johanna Marbury's son from her second marriage, William Sempill, had inherited the lands and then upon his death, the deeds for Manor Sempill were passed to his daughter Catherine Sempill and her husband Sir Charles Hamilton. Their son and heir to the Manor Sempill, Sir Francis Hamilton had been appointed by King Charles II as one of the commissioners to solve land disputes under the Act of Settlement of 1661. Thus **Sir Francis Hamilton 3rd Baronet** approved the Boyds of Kilmarnock's claims to lands in Letterkenny in the 1660s and John Boyd built the family mansion in the town by 1672, approximately in the area where the former Charles Kelly Hardware shop stands on the Main Street.

John Boyd (1) was married first to Isabel Smith but she died in 1661 and so he married Helena Ewing, daughter of Alexander Ewing of Letterkenny in 1673 and was granted the lease of the Manor, Tolls & Customs of Letterkenny from Sir Francis Hamilton in 1679. He died in 1710 aged 78 and was succeeded by his eldest son, who obtained the grant of the Letterkenny Mills and lands in 1709 and a confirmation of the Manor, Tolls & Customs of Letterkenny in 1711.

John Boyd (2) married Eleanor Orr in 1695 and had a son **John Boyd** (3) who succeeded him as head of the family upon his death in 1722. This John Boyd was a Captain in the Donegal Militia and was High Sheriff for County Donegal in 1740. He married Anne Gamble of Londonderry in 1736 and died in 1764. **John Boyd** (4) was a Major in the Donegal Militia and High Sheriff for County Donegal in 1772. He was a Magistrate for County Donegal and received the family mansion in Letterkenny upon his father's death in 1764. It was this John Boyd that purchased the lands at Ballymacool in 1783.

Following the Plantation of Ulster, Conwal and Ballymacool were glebe lands that were owned by the Established Church but in 1636 John Leslie, the Bishop of Raphoe, sold the lands at Ballymacool to John Cunningham of Letterkenny on a 58-year lease to raise money for a new Bishop's Palace in Raphoe. In 1735, the Bishop of Raphoe, John Oswald, sold the lease of Ballymacool to Rev. William Span, Rector of Conwal, which was passed onto his son Rev. Benjamin Span. When he left Conwal Rectory, the lease passed to John Hamilton of Dublin, but when Rev. Benjamin Span recovered the lease he sold it to his relation, Samuel Span, a merchant of Bristol for £3000 in 1776. Having no time for the upkeep of the estate, Samuel

Ballymacool House in the early twentieth century. Image courtesy of the National Library of Ireland

Letterkenny - Where the Winding Swilly Flows

Span sold the estate in 1783 to John Boyd (4) who built a new palatial mansion on the grounds. Ballymacool was now to be the new official residence of the Boyds as the family mansion on the Main Street was sold to **William McMonagle** who pulled it down and opened livery stables on the site.

The first John Boyd of Ballymacool was apparently quite an industrious man, for as well as building the new family mansion, according to the General Assizes, along with his brother William Boyd of Gortlee, he made a contribution to the modern shape and development of the town of Letterkenny:

General Assizes 8th October 1763
£6=10=0 Paid to John Boyd and Daniel Chambers Esq. whom we appoint overseers therewith together with the sum of four pounds sterling in the hands of John Boyd, to stone and gravel twenty four perches twenty feet wide, between the curtain walls of the Bridge leading from Letterkenny to Old Town, both Market Towns in the County of Donegal, and to repeair four and a half perches of the curtain walls of the said Bridge. The said John Boyd and Daniel Chambers to oversee the said work.

General Assizes 4th April 1783
£31=11=0 Paid to William Boyd, Esq. and William Higgins to have 1370 square yeards in the Street of Letterkenny between Stuarts Corner and William Bonnart at five and a half pence (5 ½) per yard.

General Assizes 29th September 1783
£27=10=0 Paid to William Boyd, Esq. and John McDougal to pave 1302 square yeards in the street of Letterkenny, between William Hanley and Redmond Cunningham on road from Letterkenny to Ramelton.[17]

Family Chart of the Boyds

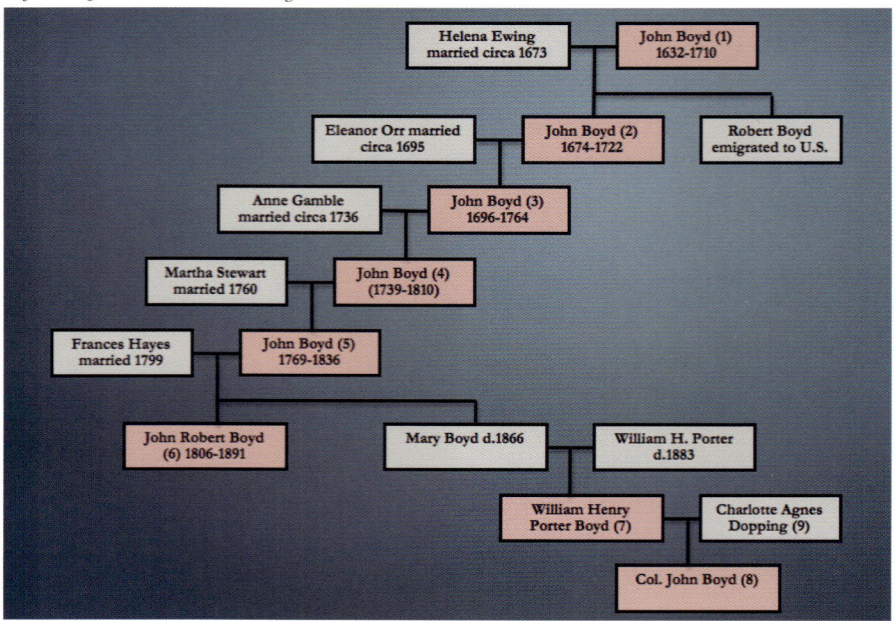

Chapter Five: The Letterkenny Ascendancy and the Era of the 'Big House'

John Boyd had married Martha Stewart in 1766 and had three sons, William, Robert and the eldest, **John Boyd** (5) who inherited the Ballymacool estate upon his father's death in 1810. He served as High Sheriff of County Donegal in 1806 and was a Barrister-at-law. He married Frances Hayes in 1799 and upon his death in 1836, the estate passed to his son, **John Robert Boyd** (6) who was called to the Irish Bar in 1830 and served as High Sheriff of County Donegal in 1846, as well as serving as Chairman of the Town Commissioners of Letterkenny from 1858. He also erected a Town Clock for Letterkenny at the Market Square around this time which stood for almost 100 years. By all accounts however, John Robert Boyd was quite an arrogant man who had no time for the welfare of his tenants and in 1870, a great Tenants Rights Meeting was held at Letterkenny Market Square where *"Mr. J.R. Boyd, J.P., of Ballymacool, a resident landlord, when he was riding up and down the street on a grey horse, was hooted and groaned on two occasions."*[18]

He died in 1891, childless, and so the estate was left to his nephew, **William Henry Porter** (7), under the condition that he assume the surname Boyd, which he did by Royal License in 1891. His daughter, **Mary Rosalie Treharne Boyd** went to South Africa in 1911 and settled in Port Elizabeth where she won three "Bardic Chairs", South Africa's highest literary award, for her poems "The Veldt" (1921), "Drought" (1930) and "Table Mountain" (1931). In 1900, William Henry Boyd sold the Corn Mills to Charles Kelly Ltd., which had been in the family since before 1710 while in 1910 he sold Kiltoy Lodge and the Cornmarket to the Kellys where they built their shop and yard. William Henry Porter Boyd died in 1913 and is buried on the grounds of the estate. Upon his death the estate passed to his eldest son, **Col. John Boyd** (8).

As we have seen with the Stewarts of Rockhill House, a party of Anti Treaty IRA forces occupied Ballymacool House in 1921. The Boyds were ordered to leave the house within a few minutes and told never to return. The graves of family members were opened by these forces, searching for arms that were thought to have been taken from the Meeting House in the town and hidden for safety in Ballymacool. Also during this occupation, a priceless salver was taken which had been in the family since 1467, when Thomas Boyd was married to Mary Stewart, daughter of King James II of Scotland. The salver was never recovered but the Boyds reported receiving several letters from someone in Letterkenny who offered to inform them of its location for a large

Stone tablet showing the death of John Robert Boyd and members of his family in Conwal Parish Church

sum of money, an offer that was never accepted. Following this experience, Col. John Boyd left Ballymacool House and his mother, **Charlotte Agnes Boyd** (9), left for England in 1930. Mrs. Boyd was described as a *"smallish woman with fine eyes and regular features and when she drove into Letterkenny in her carriage and pair, she was dressed with the sober magnificence suitable to a woman of birth and wealth. She had a strait-laced, severe appearance which everybody found intimidating."*[19] In 1938 the Ballymacool Estate was sold to the Kellys for less than £2,000[20] and the era of the Boyds of Ballymacool and Letterkenny was no more.

Did you know?

Patti Boyd, ex-wife of Beatle George Harrison and also Eric Clapton and about whom the songs, *"Something"* and *"Wonderful Tonight"* were composed, is descended from the Boyds of Ballymacool. She is the great-great-great granddaughter of Archibald Boyd, John Boyd's (3) fifth son.

The Southwells

The final family that we shall look at are the Southwells, the pre-eminent Ascendancy family of Letterkenny. As we have seen, when Johanna Marbury died, the estate passed to her son from her second marriage, William Sempill, who in 1639 created the district of Manor Sempill, which included the small market town of Letterkenny and the surrounding townlands of Ballyraine, Glencar, Sallaghgraine etc. Upon his death, the estate passed to his daughter **Catherine Sempill** and her husband, **Sir Charles Hamilton**, 2nd Baronet of Castlehamilton, County Cavan and, coincidentally, grandson to Sir Charles Coote, the victor of Scarrifhollis in 1650. The Hamiltons had no interest in living in Letterkenny though, residing mostly in Cavan, and so John Cunningham leased the Castle and its gardens. This is evidenced by details accompanying the 1655 map of the town in which '*John Keningham and Cha. Hamilton*' are listed as being the owners of 960 acres in the parish of Conwal.

Sir Francis Hamilton 3rd Baronet succeeded to the estate upon his father's death and when he died in 1714 without any children, the estate of Manor Sempill passed to his nephew, the son of his sister Nichola Hamilton from her marriage to Philip Cecil. Thus **Arthur Cecil Hamilton** became the owner of Manor Sempill and when his daughter, Margaret Hamilton married **Thomas George Southwell**, who had been made a Viscount in 1776, the lands passed into the Southwell family of Castle Matrix in County Limerick.

Chapter Five: The Letterkenny Ascendancy and the Era of the 'Big House'

> ### Did you know?
> Robert Boyd, the youngest son of John Boyd (1) emigrated to Franklin County in Pennsylvania in 1734 and founded a township. He decided to call this new township after the town of his birth in County Donegal. Today, the township of Letterkenny is mostly rural, holding small communities encompassing a 70 square mile area with a population of 2,380. It is perhaps most famous for its Army Depot which was founded in 1941, eleven days after the bombing of Pearl Harbour. Letterkenny Army Depot provides ammunition, trucks, parts and other supplies for the U.S. Army. Letterkenny is officially twinned with Elizabethtown in Pennsylvania, (population 11,545), located 70 miles from the Letterkenny Army Depot. Interestingly, there is also a Letter Kenny in South America, in Guyana, next to Suriname and Brazil, founded by Presbyterian missionaries.

Thomas George Southwell, 1st Viscount Southwell (1721-1780) served in the Irish House of Commons for Enniscorthy and also Limerick County. His son, **Thomas Arthur Southwell**, 2nd Viscount Southwell (1742-1796) was an MP for the Irish House of Commons in 1767 and inherited the Manor Sempill lands upon his father's death in 1780. His son, through his marriage to Sophia Maria Josepha Walsh, was **Thomas Anthony Southwell** 3rd Viscount Southwell (1777 – 1860) who built the red-bricked houses at the top of the Market Square in 1837 and after whom Mount Southwell Place is named. By several accounts, Thomas Anthony Southwell was a quite popular landlord. Henry D.Inglis in his "A Journey throughout Donegal" in 1834 tells us *"The town (Letterkenny) is the property of Lord Southwell; and I was glad to hear his lordship everywhere well spoken of."*[21]

The passing of the deed for the 1000 acres (in red) from Johanna Everard Marbury to the Southwells

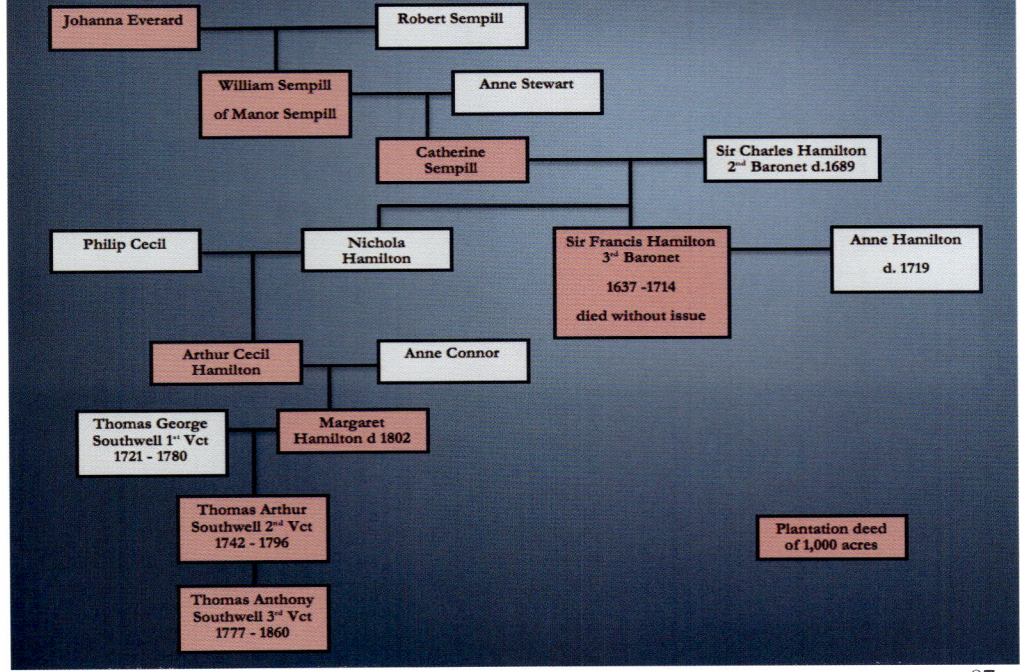

Letterkenny - Where the Winding Swilly Flows

He was succeeded as Viscount by his son **Thomas Arthur Joseph Southwell**, 4th Viscount Southwell (1836–1878), followed by **Arthur Robert Pyers Southwell**, 5th Viscount Southwell (1872–1944), **Robert Arthur William Joseph Southwell**, 6th Viscount Southwell (1898–1960), **Pyers Anthony Joseph Southwell**, 7th Viscount Southwell (b. 1930) and the current heir apparent to the title is the **Hon. Richard Andrew Pyers Southwell** (b. 1956).

From Clockwise: The 1st, 3rd, 4th and 5th Viscount Southwells who held the deeds to Letterkenny

Chapter Five: The Letterkenny Ascendancy and the Era of the 'Big House'

However, by the twentieth century, the Southwell Family grew less and less interested in retaining property in the town. With more and more people gradually being able to purchase their own property through the introduction of various Land Reform Acts, this pre-eminent family of the Letterkenny Ascendancy sold up various leases throughout the town in the twentieth century. Canon Maguire believed that, despite constructing several buildings in the town, due to their prolonged absences and role as absentee landlords, the Southwells never took much interest in the development of Letterkenny as a market town: *"Though the Southwells have done something for the embellishment of the town, neither they nor their predecessors in title did much to promote its material progress."*[22]

Did you know?

The Southwell family had been established in county Limerick since the 16th Century. Following a revolt in 1579, the lands of the Munster Geraldines were divided up amongst Edmund Spenser, Walter Raleigh and Edmund Southwell with Southwell being granted Castle Matrix in County Limerick. Raleigh gave a present to Southwell for his new estate that he had brought back from America. These 'Virginia Tubers' potatoes were planted in the land around Castle Matrix and, in 1610, the crop was distributed throughout the province of Munster, and the potato had 'arrived' in Ireland. Thus, the direct ancestor of Lord Southwell of Letterkenny is credited with introducing the use of the potato crop amongst the people of Ireland!

With this gradual sale of the leases of various plots of land around the town by the Southwells, the original 1,000 acre land grant that had been granted to Captain Patrick Crawford in 1611 and had been passed down through various marriage alliances and their offspring by the Marburys, Sempills, Hamiltons and finally the Southwells, was now at an end. Letterkenny's Ascendancy was no more.

The red brick houses of Mount Southwell Place at the top of the Market Square built in 1837

Letterkenny - Where the Winding Swilly Flows

Endnotes
1 Hill, George, "An Historical Account of the Plantation in Ulster at the Commencement of the Seventeenth Century 1608 – 1620", Irish University Press, 1970, First Ed. 1877, p323
2 Ibid p524
3 Burke, Sir Bernard, "Vicissitudes of Families", London, 1861
4 Ibid p 60
5 Ibid p 63
6 Ibid p 65
7 Trench, Charlotte Violet, "The Wrays of Donegal, Londonderry and Antrim", Oxford University Press, 1945, p205
8 MacDonagh, J.C.T., "A Seventeenth Century Letterkenny Manuscript", Donegal Annual 1956 pp139-142
9 Trench, Charlotte Violet, "The Wrays of Donegal, Londonderry and Antrim", Oxford University Press, 1945, p205
10 Henderson, Dr. Geoffrey H, "The Cochrane Family in Donegal", 2002, p19 & 23
11 Hill, George, "An Historical Account of the Plantation in Ulster at the Commencement of the Seventeenth Century 1608 – 1620", Irish University Press, 1970, First Ed. 1877, p521
12 Ibid p514
13 O'Carroll, Col. Declan, "Rockhill House – A History", Defence Forces Printing Press, 2nd Edition, 1998, p6
14 Ibid p7-8
15 Derry Journal 28/1/1891
16 This is just a short history of Rockhill House. For a more complete history of the Chambers, Stewarts and military occupation, Col. Declan O'Carroll's 62-page book "Rockhill House – A History" is highly recommended
17 Donegal County Library papers
18 Derry Journal 5/2/1870
19 McClintock, May, "Boyd of Ballymacool", Letterkenny Christmas Annual 1991
20 Much of this information on the Boyds has come from the private research undertaken by Brian Brooke-Boyd, a descendant of the Boyds of Ballymacool Estate. His letters are available in the Donegal County Library
21 Inglis, Henry D., "A Journey Throughout Ireland, During the Spring, Summer and Autumn of 1834", Vol. II, London, 1834 p190
22 Maguire, Canon "Letterkenny: Past and Present", 1917, p31

Chapter Six: Was Wolfe Tone Really Arrested in Letterkenny?

One personality long associated with Letterkenny (at least locally) is that of national and Republican icon Theobald Wolfe Tone. In fact, an interesting debate has existed amongst many people for some time concerning his capture following the failed rebellion of 1798. Historians state that after being recognized by an old school friend, Tone was caught and apprehended at Buncrana but many Letterkenny people disagree and argue that the event took place at the Market Square, either at Hegarty's or Laird's Hotel, premises that were located approximately where the Market Centre stands today. We shall now examine where this belief has come from and reveal if there is actually any truth behind it.

Referred today as 'the father of Irish Republicanism', the Dubliner Theobald Wolfe Tone formed the Society of United Irishmen in 1791 in Belfast along with Napper Tandy, Thomas Russell and others with a view to unite all Irish people regardless of religion to achieve parliamentary reform. Inspired by the recent revolutionary actions in France and the United States to overthrow their governments, the United Irishmen planned a rebellion of their own in 1798 to address their grievances. With assistance from the French, who they hoped would land at various parts of Ireland, the United Irishmen planned to overthrow their English rulers and receive emancipation for the Catholics of Ireland. One boat did land at Killala in County Mayo but was easily overcome while Tone himself was on the boat *Hoche* that was engaged in a battle on Lough Swilly in October 1798. Following the *Hoche's*

Theobald Wolfe Tone

surrender, Tone was captured and arrested by the English, and this is where the debate begins.

William Theobald Wolfe Tone

The first evidence we have of Letterkenny as the location for Tone's arrest comes from his own son, William, in his *"Memoirs of Theobald Wolfe Tone"*, first published in 1827, twenty nine years after the capture of his father. In it, he states that:

"The two fleets were dispersed in every direction; nor was it till some days later that the Hoche was brought into Loch Swilly, and the prisoners landed and marched to Letterkenny. Yet rumours of his being on board must have been circulated, for the fact was public at Paris...It was at length a gentleman well known in the county Derry as a leader of the Orange party, and one of the chief magistrates in that neighbourhood, Sir George Hill, who had been his fellow-student in Trinity College and knew his person, who undertook the task of discovering him...The French officers were invited to breakfast with the Earl of Cavan, who commanded in that district.

My father sat undistinguished amongst them, when Sir George Hill entered the room, followed by police officers. Looking narrowly at the company, he singled out the object of his search, and, stepping up to him, said, "Mr. Tone, I am very happy to see you." Instantly rising, with the utmost composure, and disdaining all useless attempts at concealment, my father replied, "Sir George, I am happy to see you; how are Lady Hill and your family?" Beckoned into the next room by the police officers, an unexpected indignity awaited him. It was filled with military, and one General Lavau, who commanded them, ordered him to be ironed, declaring that, as on leaving Ireland to enter the French service he had not renounced his oath of allegiance, he remained a subject of Britain, and should be punished as a traitor. Seized with a momentary burst of indignation at such unworthy treatment and cowardly cruelty to a prisoner of war, he flung off his uniform, and cried, "These fetters shall never degrade the revered insignia of the free nation which I have served."...From Letterkenny he was hurried to Dublin without delay, fettered and on horseback, under an escort of dragoons." [1]

The Legend Grows

Eighteen years later, in September 1845, noted Irish Nationalist John Mitchel wrote a letter to his friend Thomas Davis stating that Tone *"was present at Lord Cavan's quarters at Letterkenny when the French officers were assembled for breakfast at Lord Cavan's along with the French officers."*[1] In 1878, eighty years following his capture, it was stated *"the captive officers were landed and marched to Letterkenny, where the Earl of Cavan invited them to breakfast. It was believed that Tone was among them."*[2]

With these statements, Canon Edward Maguire easily picked up the belief that Wolfe Tone was captured in Letterkenny in 1917 when he stated that:

"A noble and distinguished Irish patriot in 1798 met with very indifferent treatment in Letterkenny from a Donegal landlord, whose son afterwards posed as a benefactor of the people. Wolfe Tone was the victim, Lairds Hotel the scene of the treachery, and Wolfe Tone's son the narrator of the facts" [4]

Chapter Six: Was Wolfe Tone Really Arrested in Letterkenny?

The newspaper, Town and Country News from November 20th 1931, tells us that it was not Laird's Hotel at the Market Square, as stated by Maguire, that was the scene of the event but the hotel located next door to it which was

"*…Hegarty's Hotel at Letterkenny. This historic hotel is extremely popular with holidaymakers. It was here that the famous rebel Theobald Wolfe Tone, was detained after his arrest on Lough Swilly…*" [5]

This would have been quite difficult though as Hegarty's Hotel was only established in 1843, forty-five years after the supposed event. However, by now, the idea that Tone was captured in the town (either at Laird's or Hegarty's Hotels) was now well and truly believed by the local residents of Letterkenny.

Hegarty's Hotel opposite the Market Square, supposed site of the capture of Wolfe Tone. Laird's Hotel was next door. Image courtesy of the National Library of Ireland

Two George Hills

Many Letterkenny people believe that Tone's identifier, Sir George Hill, is buried in Conwal Parish Church graveyard. In quoting the 1827 account, Canon Maguire amends William Tone's "*Sir George Hill*" to "*Sir (afterwards Lord) George Hill*" and this is where a distinction must be made. Sir George Hill and Lord George Hill are two different people entirely.

Lord George Hill was indeed a Donegal landlord who owned land in Gweedore. He died in 1879 and is buried in Conwal Parish Church graveyard. However, if we look carefully at this gravestone, we can see that Lord George Hill was born in 1801 making it quite difficult for him to be at the Market Square to

93

Letterkenny - Where the Winding Swilly Flows

identify the rebel three years previously!

Sir George Fitzgerald Hill, on the other hand, was born on 1 June 1763, and died on 8 March 1839. He studied law at Trinity College Dublin, along with Wolfe Tone and was Colonel of the Londonderry Militia, a Member of Parliament for Derry, became Vice Treasurer for Ireland in 1817, and then Governor of St Vincent and Trinidad in 1806. He is buried on the island of Trinidad.

This confusion between the two men was also evident with local historian Sam Fleming who stated that: *"Sir George Hill was at that particular time living in Ballyare House."* [6] It was in fact Lord George Hill who had bought Ballyare House in 1842 whereas Sir George Hill lived at Brooke Hall in Derry. Despite any belief to the contrary, these men are not related and merely share a name. Interestingly though, Lord George Hill who is buried in Conwal Parish Church was married first to Cassandra Jane Knight (1806- 1842) and then, following her death, to her sister, Louisa Knight (1804-1889). Both of these ladies were nieces of the celebrated author Jane Austen, of "Emma" and "Pride & Prejudice" fame.

The grave of Lord George Hill (1801–1879) in Conwal Parish Church. Hill was married first to Cassandra Jane Knight (1806-1842) and then, following her death, to her sister, Louisa Knight (1804-1889). Both of these ladies were nieces of the celebrated author Jane Austen.

First hand accounts

Following the battle off the coast of Horn Head, Tone's ship, *Le Hoche*, (which incidentally was renamed *The Donegal* and fought in the Battle of Trafalgar) was brought into Lough Swilly Port near to Buncrana where Sir George Hill was brought from his residence in Derry to identify the Irish rebel, now disguised as a French Officer. We know this occurred in Buncrana for Hill wrote a letter from there on the day of the capture:

My Dear Cooke,
Until this moment such has been the stormy weather that for two days no boat has been on shore from Le Hoche. This morning some hundreds of the prisoners are just landed. The first man who stepped out of the boat, habited as an officer, was T. W. Tone. He recognised me and addressed me with as much sang froid as you might expect from his character…
Yours etc. G.F. Hill

Tone is sent off to Derry under strong escort; he called himself Genl Smith
Buncrana, Saturday Nov. 3, twelve o'clock [7]

Chapter Six: Was Wolfe Tone Really Arrested in Letterkenny?

This first hand evidence is further corroborated by an account in the Londonderry Journal from Thursday 13th November 1798, ten days after the capture (as opposed to Tone's son's account written twenty nine years after the event).

"Conscious of being detected, this wretch used no means to conceal himself. Had he done so they must have been fruitless. On landing at Buncrana, he was identified by numbers, and on being brought to the Castle, where Lord Cavan resided, he affected a considerable degree of ease but was obviously agitated in the extreme.

After remaining a short time at Buncrana, he was conducted to the gaol here by Lord Cavan's aide-de-camp, Capt. Chester, who, committing him directed that he should be put in irons." [8]

The mast of the Londonderry Journal of November 13th 1798 in which it states that Tone was captured at Buncrana

Lord Cavan was resident in Buncrana Castle at this time and as stated by the newspaper, Tone was brought there following his identification by Sir George Hill before being taken to the jail in Derry, located on Bishop's Street, near to the Diamond. At this time, there were several businesses located here that were owned by people called Hegarty, which may account for the confusion with Hegarty's Hotel at the Market Square.

Buncrana, not Letterkenny

So we can now see from this convincing first hand evidence from Sir George Hill and also newspaper reports ten days after the event that there really can be no further argument as to the location of Wolfe Tone's capture. His son, William, was only three years old at the time of his father's capture so his version of events may not be as trustworthy as the contemporary evidence from the time. He may have heard when he was much older that Letterkenny was the scene of the identification and as such set in motion a chain of events which led to the popular belief amongst locals that connected the town to an event of national significance.

The main culprit for the growth of this legend appears to be a combination of various confusions that have expanded over time. A confusion over the identities of Lord George Hill and Sir George Hill; a confusion over the Hegarty's businesses located near to Wolfe Tone's prison and Hegarty's Hotel in Letterkenny. And lastly, a confusion over a local legend that grew in belief with each subsequent generation, which of course is a major problem in local history studies everywhere.

Letterkenny - Where the Winding Swilly Flows

However, perhaps the confusion comes from a much simpler source. A local legend tells us that the sword used by Tone was once proudly on display in the bar of Laird's Hotel. When this weapon was brought to the hotel, 'Wolfe Tone's sword' being in Laird's evolved into 'Wolfe Tone's capture' being in the hotel. This belief then could have spread for Tone's son to hear it and set the chain of events in motion.

Despite evidence to the contrary, many locals continue to believe that Theobald Wolfe Tone was captured in Letterkenny at Hegarty's or Laird's Hotel on the Market Square; that he was identified by Lord George Hill who is now buried in Conwal Parish Church; and that, as a result, Letterkenny has an indelible connection to the celebrated rebel, without any convincing evidence to back it up. In the end, people will believe what they want to believe. However, historian Seamus Brady perhaps said it best. In 1948, writing in the Donegal Annual, he stated that:

"Letterkenny need not feel aggrieved at the loss of its connection with the arrest of Tone; it has other and prouder associations with history. The danger of relying too heavily on tradition, which often descends to mere legend, is palpably evident here." [9]

Endnotes

1 Wolfe Tone, William Theobald (Ed), "Memoirs of Theobald Wolfe Tone", Vol. II, London, 1827 pp348-350
2 Moody, T.W. et al (Ed), "The Writings of Theobald Wolfe Tone, 1763-98, Vol. III", Oxford University Press, 2007, p363
3 Webb, Alfred, "A compendium of Irish biography: comprising sketches of distinguished Irishmen, and of eminent persons connected with Ireland by office or by their writings", Dublin, 1878, p533
4 Maguire, Canon "Letterkenny Past and Present", 1917 pp32-33
5 Town and Country News 20/11/1931
6 Fleming, Sam, "Letterkenny Past and Present", 1979, p33
7 Moody, T.W. et al (Ed), "The Writings of Theobald Wolfe Tone, 1763-98, Vol. III", Oxford University Press, 2007, p359
8 Ibid p362
9 Brady, Seamus, "Wolfe Tone and Donegal", Journal of the County Donegal Historical Society, 1948, p131

Chapter Seven: Nineteenth Century Change

The nineteenth century was a period of gradual and sustained growth for the once small market town of the post-Plantation period with many prominent buildings in the town's architecture today having their origins. St. Conal's Hospital, the AIB and Bank of Ireland premises, the Courthouse, the Gospel Hall, Mount Southwell Place, Trinity Hall, the Loreto Convent and the original boys and girls primary schools all date from the nineteenth century, as well as the most notable building of all, the Cathedral of Saints Eunan and Columba. Other buildings dating from this period, such as the Literary Institute and Robertson's Parochial Hall, have only recently been demolished and replaced.

What facilitated this marked growth of the town in the nineteenth century was a combination of various events. Sweeping reforms in local government at a national level coincided with the sustained development in the markets and shops of the town's mercantile classes, which in turn led to a gradual and continuous growth in confidence by the residents as being viewed as the principal town of the county. Each event had a knock on effect towards continual growth. For example, the ever-increasing development of the market town led to the subsequent need for the construction of a railway that would connect with Derry and Strabane in the east and Burtonport and Gweedore in the west. This in turn led to the opening of many more businesses in the town to cater for the growing trade. As such, Letterkenny began to grow steadily as a 'gateway' town, whereby traders from the east in the Laggan and the west in the Gaeltacht areas could converge and do business; the Hiring Fair being the most notable example of this.

The top of the Main street around the late nineteenth century.

Letterkenny - Where the Winding Swilly Flows

The change in the town's fortunes from the preceding century is best illustrated through the comparison of two first hand descriptions given over 100 years apart. On a visit through Donegal in 1752, Dr. Richard Pococke did not describe the town very favourably:

"Letterkenny is more beautiful in prospect than when one enters it, consisting of one street meanly built with gardens behind the houses; and there are remains of an old square castle. The chief trade of the town consists of shops to furnish the country to the north, and a market for oats and barley, wheat, some yarn and flax."[1]

Whereas, by 1865, after considerable change through various reforms and a growth in the town's prosperity, Dr. MacDevitt described the town as:

"...a pleasant little town, occupying the side of a hill, and overlooking a large expanse of country; the quarter sessions are held here; and it has a very good weekly market. Its clean street, its range of gas lamps, and other pleasant tokens of an improving spirit, bear honourable testimony to the efficiency of the town commissioners and their excellent chairman Joseph Gallagher, Esq."[2]

Indeed by 1917, and the publication of his history of the town, Canon Edward Maguire, a witness to some of the town's most noticeable changes at this time, pointed out that:

"Few, if any, towns of its size in Ireland, have undergone so sweeping changes in their administration of public affairs, the relative social status of families, and leading business firms as have marked the steady progress of Letterkenny, if not towards prosperity and affluence, at all events on the path of democracy and of the distribution of wealth."[3]

Local Government

The first major factor attributable to the town's economic growth was a nationwide series of reforms in local government that facilitated vast improvements in the layout and structure of the town. Prior to the nineteenth century, two main institutions undertook local government - the Grand Jury for the County and the various civil parishes of the Established Church (i.e. Church of Ireland). The Grand Jury was a panel of local nobility and landlords with responsibility for civil government, the maintenance of roads and bridges and the provision of county hospitals. It did this by raising a local tax called the county cess, the calculation of which varied from county to county. For Donegal, the Grand Jury tended to consist of the local Ascendancy families such as the Boyds and the Chambers. The civil parishes of the Established Church, on the other hand, were responsible for poor relief, graveyards, education, sanitation and the enforcement of law and order, paid for through the collection of the tithe.

Since 1639, the town of Letterkenny was within the district of Manor Sempill (i.e. the area covered by the original 1,000 acres Ulster Plantation land grant of 1611 that included the surrounding areas of Ballyraine, Sallaghgraine,

Chapter Seven: Nineteenth Century Change

Gortlee, Glencar, Carnamuggagh and Killylastin). The care of various parts of the town was to be carried out by prominent townspeople assigned by the local jury. One such set of assignments from 8th December 1821 were given by the Seneschal for Manor Sempill, **Ralph Young**:

"We appoint the following persons as conservators of the streets of Letterkenny: **George Leech** *and* **James Foy** *from the Market House to the lower end of the street.* **George Russell**, **John Hunter** *and* **William Fisher** *from the Market House to the upper end of the town.* **John O'Donnell** *and* **Alexander McCollum** *for Castle Street etc. We appoint* **James Gallagher** *as town constable and allow twenty five pounds sterling as his salary, to be collected from the Manor.*
Jury of: **William Fisher, John Rankin, George Russell, Gabriel King, Robert Philson, Roger McMenamin, William O'Donnell, John Bonner, William Ewing, John Robinson, Alexander McCollum, Cornelius Curran, Neil McGinley, John Gallagher, John Harkin, William O'Donnell, James Foy, George Leech, Robert Gallagher, Henry Coyle, Philip Divitt, James Kelly** *and* **A. Sweeney**" [4]

However, this system of local government was flawed on many levels. Small cliques, who were unrepresentative of the local townspeople, mostly ran these juries and as such, throughout the country they tended to be rife with corruption. A series of acts were introduced that brought about a change to this system beginning with the Lighting of Towns Act of 1828 which provided a framework under which an urban area could elect a body of commissioners. However, only those with property worth £20 or more could serve as Town Commissioners and only those with property worth £5 or more could vote. This act was further enhanced with The Towns Improvement (Ireland) Act of 1854 that reduced the property valuation for voting to £4 and the elected commissioners' property valuation to £12. Through the implementation of both of these acts, Letterkenny, like so many other towns, received its first elected Town Commissioners in the mid nineteenth century who were responsible for street paving, cleaning and lighting and the control over the fairs and markets.

This new administration of Town Commissioners wasted no time in implementing improvements to the appearance of the town, erecting gas lighting for the Main Street in 1856 and establishing a new fair for the town. The Londonderry Sentinel reported on 18th December 1857:

"It is gratifying to see the spirit and energy with which the inhabitants of Letterkenny carry on the improvements of that important town. Last year the lighting of the town was accomplished in a very handsome manner, the gas being of superior quality. In the next place, every effort is being made to promote the cleanliness of the town. A new fair has been established on the last Friday of each month, in addition to the old fairs. John R Boyd Esq. is gradually extending market accommodation – a want that has long been felt; and he is further about erecting a handsome town clock in the market square, which place has of late been vastly improved. We congratulate the people of Letterkenny on their general improvement, and we trust

Letterkenny - Where the Winding Swilly Flows

the day is not far distant when the railroad shall connect their town with this city, affording those facilities of transport which are so essential for developing the resources of the great county of Donegal, of which Letterkenny is the central and principal town." [5]

Letterkenny Town Clock, erected by John Robert Boyd in the late 1850s.
Image courtesy of the National Library of Ireland

In 1863, the Town Commissioners welcomed the visit to Letterkenny of the Lord Lieutenant General and General Governor of Ireland, George William Frederick Howard, Earl of Carlisle. Chairman of the Town Commissioners, John R. Boyd, addressed the Lord Lieutenant General in Hegarty's Hotel at the Market Square on behalf of Letterkenny. Town Commissioners present were **Edward Murray**, **Joseph Gallagher**, **William Elliot**, **Robert McMullan**, **William Hegarty**, **John Gallagher**, **Matthew Wilson**, and **Robert Henderson**.[6] Another recorded Town Commissioner at this time was **Henley Thorpe** while the Town Clerk was **John Storey** (a former Baptist pastor in the town and one of the founding members of the Christian Brethren, who built the Gospel hall on the Church Lane in 1895.)[7]

These Town Commissioners served the needs of Letterkenny for almost half a century but they were still being drawn from the landlord and propertied classes of the town. The Local Government (Ireland) Act of 1898 significantly removed the property qualifications for councilors to be elected, which gradually facilitated the emergence of the 'working-class councilor', more representative of the people that could now elect them. The key result of this 1898 Act was the final

Chapter Seven: Nineteenth Century Change

overthrow of Protestant Ascendancy dominance in local government in Ireland. New Urban and Rural District boundaries were drawn up with the Letterkenny Rural District following the same boundary as the Poor Law Union boundary of 1838 while the Urban District followed the same territorial boundary of the former balliboe of *Leitir Ceanainn*.

The election for this new Urban Council aroused much interest in the locality:

The grave of John Storey (1817-1916) in Conwal Parish Church

"On Monday, the polling for the elections of nine Councillors for the urban township of Letterkenny took place. There were sixteen candidates seeking the suffrages of the electors for the vacancies, nine of whom were Nationalists and six Unionists and an Independent, and the elections gave rise to considerable interest. The Nationalists of the town, though the vast majority of the inhabitants, have hitherto been deprived of that representation which their numbers and interest in the town entitled them to. They have never had a controlling voice in the government of Letterkenny, the Town Commissioners being with a couple or three exceptions, Unionist and Protestant."[8]

Prior to the election, the Unionists candidates of Letterkenny were offered three out of the nine seats on the new Council, a number that was felt was representative of their population in the town but this offer was rejected and all of the candidates went to the polls against each other on Monday January 16th 1899. The returning officer was **John G. Larkin** with voting booths set up in the Literary Institute and in the 'Old Seminary' next door. The results of this election were as follows:

Edward McFadden	228
Connell Bradley	225
Thomas Mulhern	225
Patrick Doherty	207
Bernard Langan	204
Philip Carroll	202
John Sweeney	186
James Gallagher	174
Francis Ward	174
Wm. G. McKinney	125
W.H. Boyd	124
David McAuley	96
Major Doyne	82
Thomas Patterson	82
Robert McClure	76
James Corry	70

Letterkenny - Where the Winding Swilly Flows

The first nine of these candidates were duly elected as the first Urban District Councilors for Letterkenny while John G. Larkin was selected as the first Town Clerk. Although **Robert McClure** and **William G. McKinney** missed out on being elected in 1899 they would later become members of the council in 1909 and 1920 respectively. Other elected councilors in the first decade of the twentieth century include **Patrick McAteer, Henry Gallagher, John Gallagher, Daniel McDevitt, James Gibbons, Thomas Sweeney, Patrick Doherty jnr.** and **John Ward**.[9]

The boundary of the new Urban Council of Letterkenny created in 1898

Through these various reforms in local government the appearance of the town of Letterkenny was vastly improved in the nineteenth century by the work firstly of the Town Commissioners created in 1854, and then by the Urban District Councilors created in 1898. The knock on effect of this improvement in the town's appearance led to increased commerce by visiting traders, which in turn greatly facilitated further economic growth, leading to more improvements in the town's appearance. Canon Maguire compared the town of 1870 with the improved appearance of 1917:

"Blocks of unsanitary dwellings have been cleared away and their former occupants transferred to commodious cottages, possessing the most modern equipments and very moderately rented; the gas works are the property of the Town Commissioners and are most economically and satisfactorily managed; and the water supply is pure and copious. Recently telephonic communication with all public departments and important business firms throughout the kingdom, has been most successfully introduced both for the general public and for the private convenience of shopkeepers, bankers, etc."[10]

Chapter Seven: Nineteenth Century Change

Were it not for these changes in the appearance and governance of the town, the next factor in the town's nineteenth century growth might not have occurred, that of the growth of the shops and markets of the town.

Growth of the Market Town

Letterkenny as a market town had existed since the town's inception in the early seventeenth century. A Royal Patent was granted for a:

'Tuesday market and two fairs on 29th June and 28th October. Patent granted to Sir George Marbury, Kt., December 9th 1616. Re-granted to Sir William Sempill, Kt., June 22nd 1639'[11]

while another market for nearby Oldtown was granted over a hundred years later for a:

"Wednesday market and four fairs, on the 20th October, 23rd April, 28th May and 20th July. Patent granted to Nicholas, Bishop of Raphoe, December 26, 1725" [12]

These fairs were modest at first but slowly grew in popularity and increased their trade over time so that by the middle of the nineteenth century, the town's shops and markets had felt the effects. For a full list of the merchants and traders of Letterkenny in 1824, see Appendix D. We also have several descriptions of the town's retail layout in the mid nineteenth century that give us a picture of the trade and commerce in the growing town and also of the honesty and integrity of the wholesalers at that time. In 1834, we are informed that:

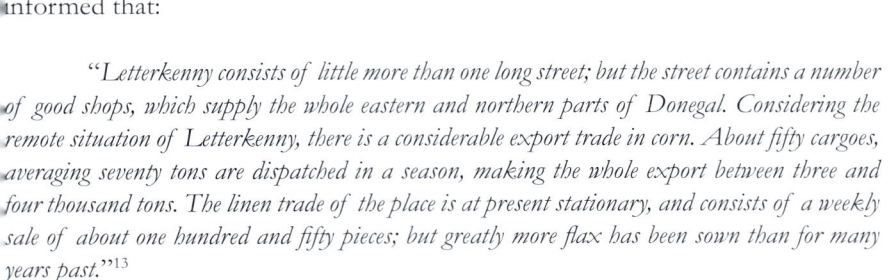

"Letterkenny consists of little more than one long street; but the street contains a number of good shops, which supply the whole eastern and northern parts of Donegal. Considering the remote situation of Letterkenny, there is a considerable export trade in corn. About fifty cargoes, averaging seventy tons are dispatched in a season, making the whole export between three and four thousand tons. The linen trade of the place is at present stationary, and consists of a weekly sale of about one hundred and fifty pieces; but greatly more flax has been sown than for many years past."[13]

John G. Larkin, first Town Clerk of the new Urban Council. Courtesy of Donegal County Library

Letterkenny - Where the Winding Swilly Flows

A town resident by the name of **Walter Hunter** wrote to the Londonderry Sentinel newspaper in November 1851 informing us that:

"In Letterkenny there are some good shops, well supplied with goods, and as fair and honest traders as in the north. In Messrs. H. Peoples, Gallaghers, McMullan's, Ramsays and Mitchells, as good value will be given in woolens, silks, cottons and haberdashery as in any part of Ireland. In the general grocery, wine and spirit trade, the same; and some are extensive dealers; and one lady in particular for assiduity, integrity and honest dealing, can only be excelled by her amiable disposition and gentle manners. And for bakeries, Elliots is famous, and the bread baked in Letterkenny is superior to most parts of Ireland."[14]

A final extract informs us that Letterkenny at the time was *"beyond question an industrious and meritoriously ambitious little metropolis, where there is much hard-headed honesty, and where good fortunes have been realised by trade."* [15]

Letterkenny Main Street at the beginning of the twentieth century. Image courtesy of the National Library of Ireland

This growth in the markets and the increased arrival of traders led to the rise in popularity of arguably the most famous type of fair, one that over time did not endear the town to many people throughout the county. Poverty stricken families, predominantly from West Donegal, would take their children to Letterkenny to strike bargains with the richer Presbyterian farmers of the Laggan for six month terms of work - a process held twice a year and known by many as the 'Hiring Fair'.

Chapter Seven: Nineteenth Century Change

Endnotes
1. Pococke, Richard, "A Tour in Ireland in 1752", London, 1891, p52
2. Maguire, Canon "Letterkenny Past and Present", 1917 p33
3. Ibid p68
4. Documents of Local Interest: Manor Semple, Donegal County Library papers
5. The Londonderry Sentinel 18/12/1857
6. The Londonderry Sentinel 19/6/1863
7. Maguire, Canon "Letterkenny Past and Present", 1917 p68
8. Derry Journal 18/01/1899
9. Donegal County Council Archives
10. Maguire, Canon "Letterkenny Past and Present", 1917 p69
11. McGill, P.J., "Some Old Fairs of Co. Donegal", Donegal Annual, 1960 p228
12. Ibid p230
13. Inglis, Henry D., "A Journey Throughout Ireland, During the Spring, Summer and Autumn of 1834", Vol. II, London, 1834 p190
14. The Londonderry Sentinel 14/11/1851
15. 'A Ride to the Head of Glenswilly', Dublin University Magazine 1853.

Chapter Eight: Hiring Fairs & the Workhouse

A key component of the evolution of the market town of Letterkenny was the growth in popularity of the Hiring Fair, or Rabble Days as they were also known. Having been a part of the English and Scottish way of life since the fourteenth century, many of the large farmers who had been brought to Ulster in the Plantation made use of the Hiring Fairs to secure cheap labour for their farms. The fairs tended to be held in towns that lay between areas of poor land (where the labourers came from) and areas of good farming land (where labour was required). For this reason, Letterkenny was an ideal location, situated as it is between the mountainous land of west Donegal and the rich fertile land located in the Laggan area to the east. Letterkenny acted as the gateway through which the labourers could pass to find work. Strabane and Derry were also chosen for this reason in the northwest with smaller fairs held in Limavady, Cookstown, Ballybofey and Omagh.

The Hiring Fairs took place twice a year, on May 12th (the beginning of the harvest season) and November 12th (the preparation of the ground and planting) with more workers usually taken on for the May to November term because of the heavier summer workload.

The Fair Day was a busy affair as people crowded the streets looking to do business. The actual hiring of labourers was done early in the morning, giving everyone involved the chance to either tend to business or enjoy the lighter side of the fair. After the hiring of the labourers, the farmers would adjourn to the local alehouses before heading back to the farms in the evenings. The labourers were then free to attend the many stalls and amusements throughout the Main Street. The excitement and thrill of the Hiring Fair day in Letterkenny in 1853 was recorded at the time:

"It was market day… and the peasantry were thronging in from the country; and the shops and stalls swarmed like beehives with buyers and sellers. Here were sturdy Presbyterian farmers, blue coated and well-fed; many of them riding their own nags, or driving their jaunting cars and giving every evidence that they were well to do in this world. And here were wild Irish kerne, from the hills beyond Glen Swilly, with frieze great coats, and worsted hose ungartered, and corduroy smalls unbuttoned, and disreputable-looking rakish caubeens cocked on the side of their heads, and large sticks in their hands"[1]

The labourers were mostly children, typically from the Glenties and Gweedore areas who would either be sent by their parents or accompanied to the fair to look for work. Usually coming from large families, sending children to the fairs ensured one less mouth to feed as well as generating income from their six-month terms of work. Upon arriving at the fair, the children would stand around with a parcel of belongings under their arms to show that they were available for hiring.

Today at the Market Square in Letterkenny, a monument commemorates

Chapter Eight: Hiring Fairs & the Workhouse

the Hiring Fair Days showing children awaiting employment. While it is true that some hiring took place at the Market Square, typically the main hiring took place at the top of the Main Street at the corner of Speer's Lane, then an area known as 'The Diamond' (owing to the convergence of four streets – Main Street, Ramelton Road, Asylum Road and Speer's Lane). **Michael McGowan** who was 9 years old was hired at Letterkenny in 1874 and gives us an account of the process of hiring:

> *"Two big men came over to my mother and started to bargain with her. One of them had plenty of Irish and I think the other man had brought him along to translate. They offered a wage of a pound. My Mother wasn't satisfied to let me go with them for that, but the end of the story is that the bargain was made for thirty shillings from May until November."*[2]

Of course, when viewed from today's perspective, the Hiring Fair seems a barbaric example of cruel exploitation of children. However, in the nineteenth and early twentieth century, hiring was simply a rite of passage for many poor children and their families. It was a stepping-stone along the way towards the inevitable process of emigration.

By the 1930s, Irish farming underwent major social and economic changes that gradually ended the use of the Hiring Fair. The mechanization of farms resulted in less need for labourers while from the labourer's point of view, unemployment benefits from the state began in the 1930s, which broke down the centuries old tradition of the six-month hiring term, as people now wanted to be employed on a weekly basis so they could claim unemployment benefits for periods of days and weeks when there was no farm work to be done. At government level, the School Attendance Act 1926 in the new Irish Free State meant that younger workers could not travel to fairs anymore, depriving the fair of its chief assets. Even though hiring continued into the 1940s, the fairs gradually ceased as by now, new jobs in the urban areas attracted farm workers into the expanding towns, gradually reducing the need for skilled workers on farms. The Letterkenny Official Guide in 1952 tells us that *"nowadays the hiring fair is more a holiday when labourers, freed from winter or harvest work, don their best clothes and make merry in the town."*[3]

The Fair Day in Letterkenny would have been a great spectacle with people arriving from all over the county, not just for the hiring but also for the 'craic' in the pubs, stalls and amusements. It was a busy day for the merchants and

Artist's impression of a child with his parent awaiting hiring in Letterkenny

County Donegal Railways

LETTERKENNY
Hiring Fair
14th November, 1924.

For the convenience of Passengers attending this Fair a SPECIAL TRAIN will run from Letterkenny, as under:—

LETTERKENNY	Dep.	3.50 p.m.
GLENMAQUIN	,,	x
CORNIGILLAGH	,,	x
CONVOY	,,	4.20 ,,
RAPHOE	,,	4.30 ,,
COOLAGHEY	,,	x
BALLINDRAIT	,,	4.42 ,,
LIFFORD	,,	4.48 ,,
STRABANE	arr.	4.50 ,,

x Will stop to set down Passengers as required.

The above Special will connect with the Great Northern train leaving Strabane at 5.1 p.m. and arriving at Derry at 5.35 p.m.

Market Tickets will be issued from Derry and above Stations at reduced fares.

HENRY FORBES,

A railway poster of 1924 concerning departure times from the Hiring fair of Letterkenny.
Courtesy of Christmas Annual

Chapter Eight: Hiring Fairs & the Workhouse

traders of the town who benefited greatly from the added business. In the end, the Rabble Days were consigned to history and became just a memory but there is no doubting the impact they had on the growth of the town's fortunes in the nineteenth century.

By the 1930s and 1940s the Hiring Fair was beginning to die out in the town but it was still a busy place. Image courtesy of the National Library of Ireland

Hiring mostly took place at the corner of Speer's Lane but a monument to the children of the Hiring Fair was erected at the Market Square in 1996

Letterkenny - Where the Winding Swilly Flows

Poor Relief & Workhouse

Even though the Rabble Days brought great trade to the town, we must not forget the plight of many of those that were hired. It was hard, backbreaking work, often in terrible conditions and must have been very difficult for those that were hired. The principal reason for the availability of this cheap labour was the economic state of the country at that time. Poverty was rife amongst the rural and predominantly Catholic population of the country in the years before the Famine and the ruling British Government, who had experienced similar conditions and had passed a New Poor Law in 1834, had to act to overcome these conditions. In 1838 the British passed a Poor Law for Ireland that set up 130 unions nationwide. They were called unions as the new system united a number of parishes and townlands into one area with each principal market town in that area becoming the centre of a union. There were eight such unions in Donegal – Glenties, Dunfanaghy, Milford, Carndonagh, Stranorlar, Donegal Town, Ballyshannon and Letterkenny Union, coming into operation on 31st July 1841. The boundaries of these unions would later act as the Rural District Council boundaries established in 1898 and abolished in 1925.

A board of Guardians, elected annually, controlled each of these unions. The first Chairman of Letterkenny Union was **Daniel Chambers** while **George Langan** was elected Clerk and Workhouse Master and his wife **Anna Lane** was appointed Matron. **Jane Thompson** was the schoolmistress. One of the first acts of the Letterkenny Union was to make plans for the building of a Workhouse that would cater for the able bodied poor of the local area. A site was purchased from Captain Chambers for £480 and **Alex Deane** of Cork was given the contract for the construction of the workhouse. The cost of building was £5,792.

An aerial photography from the 1950s showing the site of the former Workhouse being used by Lymacs bottling

Work began on the construction in 1842 and was completed in 1845. **George Wilkinson** designed the workhouses of Ireland and all had a similar layout, differing from each other only in size. When the doors of the new workhouse in Letterkenny opened in March 1845, forty-six paupers were admitted. It was built to cater for 900 paupers but with the onslaught of the Great Famine, it far exceeded that. In 1847, for example, 1,309 people were admitted. The ethos behind the workhouse system was to make the place as uncomfortable as possible for the inmates, they were designed only for those who had no other

Chapter Eight: Hiring Fairs & the Workhouse

choice but to go there. The authorities believed that this current poverty was merely the result of laziness and an unwillingness to work and so to remedy that, the male inmates broke large stones and females knitted and spun wool for workhouse uniforms while their meagre portions of food consisted of oatmeal, potatoes and buttermilk, rations designed to just about sustain life.

Upon admittance to the reception area, families were separated as fathers, mothers, sons and daughters were divided into their respective groups and assigned specific areas in the building. They were forbidden to meet at all while living there, except for mass on a Sunday. The Master of the Workhouse ran a strict code of behaviour and anyone who stepped out of line would be flogged with a cane. Not surprisingly, many people died in Letterkenny Workhouse and were taken and buried in unmarked plots in a small adjoining piece of land. In the early 1970s, when road improvements were being carried out on New Line Road, a large mound grave was uncovered and their remains were reverently gathered and reinterred in Leck Cemetery with the full burial rites of both the Roman Catholic and Protestant churches. A stone memorial now stands in the area of this Peace Garden.

By 1923, the Dáil of the Irish Free State passed an act that abolished all workhouses, removing this terrible blight of British rule from the Irish landscape. Letterkenny Workhouse still had forty remaining inmates at this time, so they were sent to the new County Home in Stranorlar in February 1922.

The Porter's Lodge continued to be used as the headquarters of Letterkenny Rural District Council until it was abolished in 1925 and was made into a Fever Hospital in 1928. The fever hospital was later used as St. Anne's Maternity Hospital from 1954 until the new County Hospital was opened opposite St. Conal's Hospital in 1960. When the Maternity Hospital closed, the Letterkenny Urban District Council had their offices in the building until 1979 when they moved to Murrac A Boo, and in 1987, it became the County Museum, after serving a short time as the County Library. The middle building continued to be used as a Dispensary until 1927 and it was later refurbished to be a Nurses Home in 1930. In 1928, Watts of Derry leased the main building of the Workhouse where they manufactured mineral waters and had a bottling store until 1938, when Lyttle and McAuley (Lymacs) took over and continued this business until 1968.

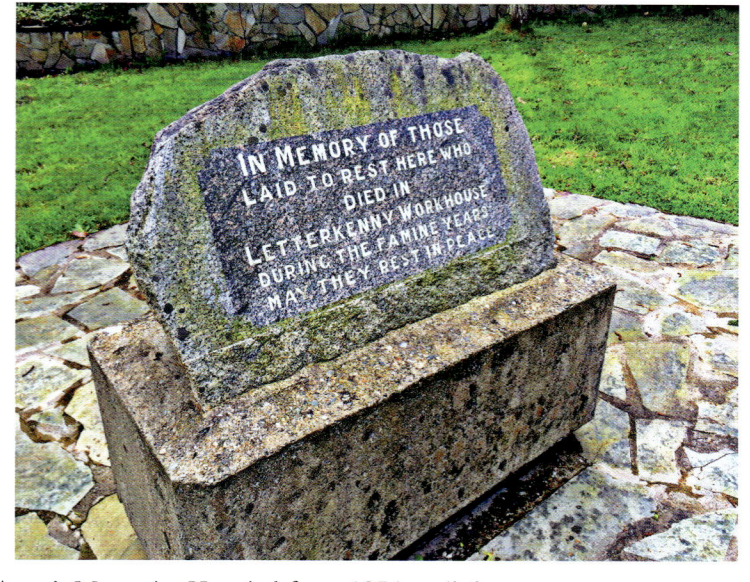

A stone plaque commemorating those that died in Letterkenny Workhouse during the Famine years

Letterkenny - Where the Winding Swilly Flows

Above: By the 1980s, the Workhouse building was in a terrible state of decline. From Christmas Annual 1992

Below: The front of the former Workhouse, home to the County Museum today

Following the closure of Lymacs, throughout the 1970s and 1980s, the cold, grey remains of the old Letterkenny Workhouse were deemed an eyesore on the architectural landscape of the town. It served as a constant reminder of a harsh past and it slowly collapsed around itself and fell into disrepair. The site was cleared to construct the new Garda Station for the town in 1988, eradicating the memory of the brutal workhouse, except for the Porter's Lodge front entrance which today, aptly, still houses the Donegal County Museum.

All that remains of this once harsh domineering structure is the front portion of the former Reception Area that still serves as a timely reminder of the extreme poverty that existed in this area in the not too distant past. Today, if you stand on the steps at the front and look at the original wooden door, you can get a sense of what it must have felt like for the poor unfortunate paupers standing there in the rain as they waited for it to slowly open for them to enter the miserable existence of the Workhouse.

Buildings

Many other notable buildings were built in Letterkenny in the nineteenth century, some of which are thankfully still standing as a reminder of our heritage whilst others unfortunately fell victim to the ravages of time or indeed the bulldozers of the Celtic Tiger.

Chapter Eight: Hiring Fairs & the Workhouse

The **Courthouse**, originally built in 1831, was designed by **John Hargrave** and cost £963 to build. Prison cells had already been built next door to the Police Barracks at the top of the Main Street in 1828 and it was only an afterthought to have the Courthouse built on top of them. In 1836, the Petty Sessions (also called the Parish Courts) were held there every Wednesday while the Quarter Sessions for the County were held in Letterkenny Courthouse in April and October.

Another notable building still in existence from this period is **St. Conal's Hospital**. George Wilkinson, who had designed the Workhouse, drew up plans for the building of a new hospital in the early 1860s for the Lunacy Board and **Matthew McClelland**, a Letterkenny man, was chosen as the contractor. Construction began on the Donegal District Lunatic Asylum in 1862, and was completed by 1866 at a cost of £37,887.5.3. A letter to the Londonderry Sentinel in 1865 gave a description of the new building:

"The Asylum is situated about a quarter of a mile on the road leading from Letterkenny to Dunfanaghy. The site is on a gentle eminence, and the building runs from east to west, commanding fine views of the surrounding scenery, which is here both bold and picturesque. The first sight of the structure impresses the spectator with a feeling somewhat akin to wonder – the front presenting a noble façade three storeys in height…the people of Letterkenny feel a little pride that Mr. M'Clelland, the contractor, is a townsman of their own, and that his name is associated with a building of which the entire County feels proud."[4]

The hospital was originally designed to accommodate 300 patients and was under the control of a Board of Governors that included **Sir James Stewart**, **AJR Stewart** of Ards and **John Vandeleur Stewart** of Rockhill and whose Chairman was **Lord George Hill**. **Dr. Eames** was the resident physician, **Dr. Thorpe** was a visiting physician while **Mrs. Malseed** was the Matron. By 1883, the number of inmates had risen to 354, exceeding its capacity and two expansions of the building took place - first in 1880 and again in 1895. By 1900 though, the numbers had increased to 596 and so accommodation for an extra 250 patients was completed by 1904. The building continued to serve as a hospital for people with a mental illness for a further 100 years but the process of phasing out the numbers admitted began in 2006 with the last patient leaving the hospital on 18th June 2010. Today, the large building houses various offices of the Health Service Executive (HSE) West.

On the Port Road, **Robertson Parochial Hall** was built in 1878 on the site of an older Sabbath School which itself had been built in 1833. Originally used as a day and Sunday school for the local Church of Ireland community, it also served as the Masonic Lodge of Letterkenny from 1886 until the current Lodge was erected in the 1920s. The Parochial Hall was a school until 1976 when a new National School was erected in Ballyraine. Over time, the hall was used less and less and with new traffic arrangements in the town that changed the Main Street to one-way traffic, it was deemed too distant from the Parish Church to serve any useful purpose. The Church of Ireland sold the hall in October 1997 and built a new parish hall beside the church in 1998. Sadly, the Parochial Hall is now gone but the nearby Presbyterian church (and later school) of **Barkhall**, built in 1820, still stands opposite An Grianán Theatre.

The houses of **Government Terrace** located behind Gallagher Hotel, were built in 1889 and were put up for auction in 1905. The first occupants were all Government Officials, hence the name. **Mount Southwell Place** at the top of the Market Square was built in 1837 while the **Royal Garrison Artillery** under the command of **Col. Saunders Knox-Gore** built a barracks at Sprackburn in 1880, which still stands today as a residential building, having been used as a hosiery factory between the 1920s and 1960s. The first bank to open in County Donegal, the **Belfast Banking Company** had its Letterkenny branch built on the Main Street in 1835 and stands today as the Allied Irish Bank while the **Hibernian Bank** also opened opposite the Market Square in 1873 and houses the Bank of Ireland today. While both of these buildings have undergone extensive refurbishments, they still retain the original facades.

The original Christian Brethren in Letterkenny consisting of **John Davis**, **Robert Dobson**, **William C. McKinney**, **John Stewart**, **William McKay** and John Storey erected the **Gospel Hall** off the Church Lane in June 1895. John Storey, a former Town Clerk, had been a Baptist pastor in the town and joined the assembly of the Brethren who met in the yard of John Davis, whose merchant business was on the Main Street. When they erected a hall in the yard, they cleared away a building to gain access to the Church Lane, hence the fact that the entrance to the hall today is further back than the other buildings on the street.[5]

Letterkenny **Methodist Preaching House** was built in 1823 although a Methodist Society had been in Letterkenny since 1784 under **Mary and James Elliott**. Since 1816 there were two branches of Irish Methodism - Wesleyan and Primitive Wesleyan – the latter remaining loyal to the Established Church and both branches were active in the town with the Primitive Wesleyans building a church at the Market Square in 1823 and John Noble officiating at meetings. Following the reunification of the two branches in 1878 to become the Methodist Church in Ireland, the building was sold and in later years was used as a Market Hall, a cinema and a printing works. Today it is home to an architects business.[6]

Endnotes
1 'A Ride to the Head of Glenswilly', Dublin University Magazine 1853.
2 O'Hanlon, Michael, "Hiring Fairs and Farm Workers in North West Ireland", Guildhall Press, 1992, p10
3 Letterkenny Official Guide 1952, p5
4 Londonderry Sentinel 14/2/1865
5 Information courtesy of William Harris, Letterkenny Gospel Hall
6 Information courtesy of David Dobbie, Archivist, Methodist Historical Society of Ireland

Chapter Eight: Hiring Fairs & the Workhouse

Some of the buildings in Letterkenny dating from the nineteenth century, most of which are still here

115

Chapter Nine: The Derryveagh Evictions 1861 and Tenant Rights

Approximately 20 km to the west of Letterkenny, in August 1857, a land speculator from Queen's County, **John George Adair** made his first purchase of land on the Derryveagh Estate, having fallen in love with the scenery on a previous visit. Over the next couple of years, he acquired more and more land in the area, and, about a year after purchasing this first portion of the land, while hunting for wild fowl, twelve local tenants beat the bushes and spoiled his day's hunting. As he marched indignantly away he promised them that one day they would pay dearly for this outrage. In 1859, having finally acquired the title to all of the estate of Derryveagh, Adair was now in a position to make good on his threat.

However, he could not just throw his tenants off the land without just cause. His 'justifiable reason' duly arrived with the murder of his Scottish land steward in November 1860. Adair had imported Scottish sheep to his estate and hired Scottish shepherds **James Murray, Dugald Rankin** and **Adam Grierson**, to look after them. In November 1860, Murray's body was found on the mountains with his skull fractured by a large stone and the coroner returned a verdict of murder.

As the police could identify no single person as the murderer, on St. Patrick's Day 1861 Adair obtained a Writ of "*Habere Facias Possessionem*", an obscure Norman law that gave him the right to hold the entire community guilty when one culprit could not be identified and he duly took possession of the land and houses in Derryveagh. In correspondence between Adair and Thomas Larcom, assistant to the Lord Lieutenant of Ireland, he outlined his reasons for the proposed evictions, conveying the fear of injury that might befall him on his estate:

The notorious John George Adair (1823-1885)

"*I beg you to convey to His Excellency that it is with the deepest pain and regret I have most reluctantly come to the resolution to evict the people of Derryveagh...a previous proprietor of my estate, Mr. Marshall, was a few years ago murdered; that I myself was attacked by an armed party on the very spot where my manager was murdered; that upwards of 600 of my sheep have been destroyed; and that in not one single instance have the perpetrators been brought to justice...Law establishes the principle, in cases of malicious injury to property, that the district be made responsible.*"[1]

Chapter Nine: The Derryveagh Evictions 1861 and Tenant Rights

Adair gathered together a 'Crowbar Brigade' from County Tyrone to carry out the deed and a large police force from Roscommon and Leitrim were drafted in to protect them under the command of sub-inspectors William Henry from Ballyshannon, **John Corr** from Letterkenny and Robert Griffin from Carndonagh. This large force of over 200 men stayed in Letterkenny the day before the evictions. On the morning of Monday 8th April 1861, they left Letterkenny and proceeded towards Loughbarragh, at the extreme boundary of Derryveagh. Upon reaching the house of the 60 year old widow Mrs. McAward, who lived with her six daughters and one son, the sheriff entered the house, removed the tenants and instructed the 'Crowbar Brigade' of six men to level the house to the ground.

"The scene then became indescribable. The bereaved widow and her daughters were frantic with despair. Throwing themselves on the ground, they became almost insensible, and bursting out in the old Irish wail - then heard by many for the first time - their terrifying cries resounded along the mountains for many miles. They had been deprived of their only shelter - the little spot made dear to them by association of the past - and with bleak poverty before them and with only the blue sky to shelter them, naturally they lost all hope and those who witnessed their agony will never forget the sight"[2]

Over the next two days, the evictions continued unabated. The report of another evictee informs us that:

"one old man, near the "four score years and ten," on leaving his home for the last time, reverently kissed the door posts, with all the impassioned tenderness of an emigrant leaving his native land. His wife and children followed his example, ere those familiar old walls gave way before the crowbars, and in agonised silence, the afflicted family stood by and watched the destruction of their dwelling."[3]

A typical eviction scene in Ireland in the nineteenth century

By two o'clock on Wednesday afternoon, Adair's work had been completed and a deathly silence had descended over the whole district. The official Derryveagh Eviction Report tells us that there were 47 families from 46 houses evicted. Of the 244 people evicted, 159 were children while 28 homes were unroofed or leveled and 11,602 acres of land was seized. On the following

Letterkenny - Where the Winding Swilly Flows

Friday, 43 heads of the evicted families applied for admission to the Workhouse in Letterkenny.

Funds were collected to assist the homeless in starting a new life in Australia with the Donegal Relief Committee paying their passage and purchasing small farms for them. In January of 1862, many took advantage of this offer and departed for Australia, travelling first by train to Dublin accompanied by **Father James McFadden**, the parish priest in Falcarragh who gave a moving farewell address at a dinner arranged for them in a Dublin Hotel. 143 persons from Derryveagh, now joined by 130 Gweedore residents, boarded the ship to Australia, never to return to Ireland again.

The tragedy of the Derryveagh evictions lies in the simple fact that most likely the tenants on the estate were not hiding the culprit; they were entirely innocent of the crime. It was thought by many at the time that Dugald Rankin, another Scots shepherd on the estate, was having an affair with Murray's wife and killed her husband on the mountains of Derryveagh. In the House of Commons on 24 June 1861, J. F. Maguire, the MP for Dungarvan, claimed that *"there was one man in Donegal who was openly suspected of the crime. Whether he was guilty or not was a matter between God and himself, but it was a curious fact that this man wore the dead man's clothes at his funeral, that he was extremely intimate with the dead man's wife."*[4]

In April 1863 Adam Grierson, Adair's land steward was shot and mortally wounded when returning home late one evening. He identified **Francis Bradley**, the son of one of the evictees of 1861, as his murderer in a dying declaration. Bradley was put on trial for the murder but three juries disagreed between 1863 and 1865 and he was discharged and cleared of the murder. Following his acquittal, Bradley's return to Letterkenny *"was awaited by thousands; old people grasped his hand and burst into tears of joy; young people cheered until they were hoarse."*[5]

A Derryveagh eviction cottage

Tenant Rights

The mass eviction of 244 people from Derryveagh in 1861 was an example of the lack of rights that tenants had on their lands in Ireland at the time and highlighted the ease with which they could be evicted. The feelings of revulsion at the impotency of the law was expressed in an editorial of the Derry Journal:

Chapter Nine: The Derryveagh Evictions 1861 and Tenant Rights

"But what we would complain of is the law which permits or enables any mortal man to do what Mr. Adair has done. This has been our view throughout, and to effect a change in the law is the only certain mode of preventing the recurrence of similar clearances. The tale of Derryveagh and the sufferings of its evicted inhabitants have excited the pity of the whole community, and, while Parliament and public opinion are condemning Mr. Adair, the highest legal functionary in the land officially declare that the gentleman has not overstepped his legal authority. Is the law as it should be when this is so?"[6]

This was the question that many Tenant Rights campaigners now sought to address. Tenant farmers had no rights to be given a written lease, and when a rental agreement ended they could be swiftly evicted. Tenants also could not claim compensation for any improvements that they made on their farm, although this was not always the case in Ulster, due to the 'Ulster Custom'. However, as this custom was decided on the whim of the landlord, a change was needed.

On February 3rd 1870, over ten thousand people were packed into the Market Square in Letterkenny for one of the largest Tenants Rights meetings ever recorded in Ulster. This was over five times the population of the town at this time, composed of people of various classes and religions from the surrounding districts. No doubt some survivors of the Derryveagh evictions would have been present also. A large platform about fourteen feet high had been erected near the recently built clock tower but when the first speaker began his remarks, it collapsed under the weight of the people on it. Nobody was seriously hurt and

Artist's impression of the ten thousand people present at the Market Square attending the Tenant Rights meeting of 1870

so a second platform was erected on the higher ground of Mount Southwell Terrace and the speeches in which to air their grievances began. The landlord John Robert Boyd of Ballymacool rode past on his grey horse several times and he was repeatedly booed at until he left.

Since 1850, the leading Tenant Right campaigners of the Letterkenny area were **Edward Gallagher, Ned McFadden, Father McGroarty, Robert Ramsay** and his son **Robert Ramsay**[7] but there is no doubting the most prominent of all the local supporters of Tenant Rights was **Rev. John Kinnear**.

Kinnear was born in 1823 near Dungannon, County Tyrone and was ordained to the charge of First Letterkenny Presbyterian Church on 27th December 1848 where he served as minister for fifty years until his retirement in 1889. He had three children from his marriage to Margaret Fanny Alexander but they all died of consumption. Margaret herself died in 1863, thirteen years after they were married.

Since his arrival in the town of Letterkenny, Dr. Kinnear had supported Tenant Rights on public platforms and through the press and was no doubt angered by the eviction of so many families at Derryveagh by John George Adair. His oratorical skills and public persona were greatly admired by all:

"At all times extremely popular, he was welcomed with enthusiastic acclaim whenever he appeared on a public platform; for though he was by no means revolutionary, he was a born demagogue, and his refined oratory was attuned to the ear of the multitude."[8]

Kinnear spoke at this large meeting in 1870 in which the grievances of tenants against their landlords were debated. Amongst his remarks on that day were:

"I rejoice to see all denominations harmoniously mingling in this great constitutional assemblage. I am glad to see Episcopalians and Roman Catholics, and Presbyterians, assemble constitutionally and peacefully to proclaim their grievances, and claim that protection of tenant capital and expenditure which justice and equity demand..."

The demands at this meeting were simple:
"We claim our inalienable right to the fruits of our industry and our toil and we demand that the landlord's irresponsible power over our peasantry shall be swept away as a barbarism iniquitous and unjust...

We want capricious evictions to cease, capricious and arbitrary rent raising to be abolished, irresponsible power swept away from the landocracy of this country, and we want the free and unfettered liberty to exercise the franchise, unmolested by the mandate of the bailiff, or the nod of the agent, or the tyrannical power of the landlord (loud cheers)"[9]

On the 27th March 1880, Dr. Kinnear decided to stand as a last minute Liberal candidate for Co. Donegal in the United Kingdom Parliament elections. In his mandate to his voters he proclaimed:

Chapter Nine: The Derryveagh Evictions 1861 and Tenant Rights

"Having been urgently requested by a most influential deputation of Electors to offer myself as a Candidate for the representation of your County, I have resolved to place myself at your disposal.

During all my public life I have lived amongst you, and my political principles are well known, being those I have so often advocated during the past thirty years through the Press and on public platforms over your county...

Should you return me to Parliament, I shall esteem it to be the proudest era of my life, and my loyalty to the land and to liberty, and my fealty to the memories of the men associated with me thirty years ago in our first Tenant-right campaign will stimulate my efforts to close down, as they and I resolved, another chapter in the history of oppression, and register on the statutes of the realm a new act of Emancipation for the enslaved peasantry of the land."[10]

Kinnear was running with another Liberal candidate, **Thomas Lea** against the Tory **Marquis of Hamilton**. As two candidates were to be returned, the two Liberals united in their campaign with both men appearing at a large rally in the Market Square on Friday April 2nd 1880 just days before the voting began.[11]

The election took place on Wednesday April 7th and Dr. Kinnear was triumphantly elected with 2,015 votes, defeating the Marquis of Hamilton who had received 1,954 votes, a mere sixty-one votes difference. Thomas Lea topped the poll with 2,274 votes. Dr. Kinnear now had the honour of being the first clergyman in charge of a congregation to sit in the House of Commons.

Great rejoicing took place throughout the county at the election of Dr. Kinnear. The Derry Journal reported that large crowds were cheering in Letterkenny and tar barrels burning when the results were read out. The day after the elections, Kinnear returned to his home town amidst great celebrations:

Rev. John Kinnear (1824-1909) MP for Donegal 1880-1886, From Christmas Annual 1999

"On last Thursday...when the joyful tidings of the Donegal election resulted in the defeat of the Tory candidate, reached Letterkenny, the town was the scene of unbounded joy. Words fail to express the feelings of the Liberals, when they were informed that their townsman, Dr. Kinnear, was returned M.P...

At eight o'clock, the town presented a gay appearance. The houses were illuminated, and the Tyrconnell Flute Band, headed by tar-barrels, and followed by about three thousand people, paraded the street. In the midst of the excitement, Dr. Kinnear and party arrived from Lifford and proceeded to Hegarty's Hotel, receiving such a reception as may be better imagined than expressed."[12]

Letterkenny - Where the Winding Swilly Flows

A large banner reading "*Long live Lea and Kinnear*" was carried by torchlight before the wagonette that contained Kinnear and his closest supporters which was drawn by several young men of the town. The procession paraded from the Port Bridge to the Market Square amidst great cheering and excitement. When they arrived at the Square, Dr. Kinnear took to the stand and informed his fellow townspeople:

"In my humble person I care little for the elevation, but I rejoice that in me there is now the triumph of those principles I believe to be founded on justice and righteousness...

We have now done what, thirty years ago, a small band of men in Letterkenny resolved to do, to close down another chapter in the history of oppression..

I shall enter the Senate House of the Empire determined to continue my advocacy of these principles I have espoused during all my public life and I hope soon to see them immovably registered on the statutes."[13]

Michael Davitt (1846-1906) who spoke out against Rev. Kinnear at the Market Square in 1881. Image courtesy of National Library of Ireland

However, Rev. Kinnear was soon to discover the fickle nature of politics. Nine months following his election, on January 19th 1881, amidst heavy snow and biting cold winds, a monster meeting for the Irish National Land League was held at the Market Square at which ten thousand people were present when **Michael Davitt** openly attacked Kinnear's position in government. Rev. Kinnear had voted against Charles Stewart Parnell at Westminster and for doing so, was verbally attacked by several speakers at this meeting with groans being reported from the crowd whenever his name was mentioned. Davitt told the crowd:

"I am sorry to find your representative, elected by the tenant farmers at the last election, has gone against the people of Ireland in the present emergency, and has given his vote in favour of coercion and of the Whigs, who are trying to rule Ireland by police and dragoons and flying columns. I am very reluctant to talk about this, as your representative is a minister of religion, and I shall never stand on any platform in which a single offensive word is said against a minister of any religion, Catholic or Protestant. (Cheers.) But as he is one of your representatives, elected by you, and fails to carry out your views, I hold you are perfectly justified in claiming an account of his conduct, and that he place in your hands the trust you gave him at the last election."[14]

Chapter Nine: The Derryveagh Evictions 1861 and Tenant Rights

It is no surprise then that Dr. Kinnear did not seek re-election in 1885. Disillusioned at the increasingly Nationalist aspect within Irish politics, he concentrated instead on the religious needs of his parishioners.[15]

By 1888, a new strategy for land reform was under way in County Donegal with Fr. James McFadden of Gweedore and Fr. Daniel Stephens of Cloughaneely to the forefront of the Plan of Campaign. The idea of the plan with its 'No Rent Manifesto' was to cause so much cost to a landlord in evicting a tenant that it would be better for the landlord to reduce the rent for the tenant instead. Both priests were arrested by the authorities for their involvement in the plan on the Ards estate and sentenced to three months imprisonment at Dunfanaghy in January 1888. In April of that same year, their appeal was heard at Letterkenny Courthouse where a large reception of townspeople was awaiting them. Heavy police and military force patrolled the streets to keep order amongst the thousands of people from the district that had arrived in the town from early morning. At the hearing, John Dillon M.P. sat with his old schoolfriend and newly appointed Bishop of Raphoe, Dr. Patrick O'Donnell, to hear their sentence of six months imprisonment in Derry jail.

John Dillon (1851-1927) friend of Bishop O'Donnell who attended the trial of Father Stephens and Father McFadden in Letterkenny in 1888. Image courtesy of National Library of Ireland

On their return to the town in October, both priests were hailed enthusiastically by almost three thousand people who met them at the train station and, unhooking their horse from their wagonette, many townspeople carried them triumphantly to the Market Square through the flags, banners and arches that decorated their route. Fr. McFadden, now dubbed *'The Patriot Priest of Gweedore'*, addressed the large meeting at the Square:

> *"I have had on many occasions abundant proof of the patriotism of the good people of Letterkenny and the surrounding parishes, and their eternal hatred of the wicked class laws that misgovern the country. But I may safely say that no demonstration in the past has approached either in numbers or in enthusiasm the vast multitude gathered in from every point of the compass, which I see before me here today. (Cheers)"*[16]

The land question in Donegal and Ireland was eventually defused by a series of Land Acts, which culminated in the 1903 Wyndham Land Purchase Act. Thankfully, Dr. Kinnear lived long enough to see these changes in land ownership at the turn of the century. He died on 8th July 1909 and was buried in

Fr. James McFadden, the 'Patriot Priest of Gweedore'. From Christmas Annual 2001

the graveyard of Conwal Parish Church, not far from the grave of the founders of Letterkenny, the Marburys. Canon Maguire, who witnessed these significant events first hand, wrote of the importance of these monster meetings that took place in Letterkenny in these turbulent years:

> "...*outside the Letterkenny district, the county appeared to be asleep during that campaign, but Letterkenny, to its eternal honour, carried the Tenant Right banner to victory.*"[17]

The grave of Rev. John Kinnear in Conwal Parish Church

Endnotes

1. Derry Journal 24/4/1861
2. Derry Journal, 17/4/1861
3. Derry Journal 17/4/1861
4. Vaughan, W.E. "*Sin, Sheep and Scotsmen, John George Adair and the Derryveagh Evictions, 1861*", Appletree Press, 1983, p43
5. Maguire, Canon "Letterkenny Past and Present", 1917 p57
6. Derry Journal 1/5/1861
7. Maguire, Canon "Letterkenny Past and Present", 1917 p59
8. Ibid p59
9. Derry Journal 1870
10. Derry Journal 29/3/1880
11. Derry Journal 2/4/1880
12. Derry Journal 12/4/1880
13. Derry Journal 12/4/1880
14. Derry Journal 21/1/1881
15. Weir, A.J. "Letterkenny Congregations, Ministers, & People 1615-1960", 1960
16. Derry Journal 22/10/1888
17. Maguire, Canon "Letterkenny Past and Present", 1917 p64

Chapter Ten: The Growth of Catholic Confidence

One of the most significant changes to the town of Letterkenny in the nineteenth century was in the rise in status of the Roman Catholic community in the hitherto Protestant dominated market town. Almost fifty years after the formation of the town at the beginning of the seventeenth century, the 1659 Census informs us that the population of Letterkenny consisted of 73 people, 49 listed as "English/Scottish" and 24 listed as "Irish". Taking the general assumption that the English and Scottish were most likely Protestant (i.e. Established Church or Presbyterian) and the Irish were Catholic, this gives us a percentage of 67% for the former and 33% for the latter. By the census of 1901 however, these figures had been reversed; 69% of the population were Catholic and 31% were Protestant (by 2011, this gap further widened to 84% and 12% respectively).[1]

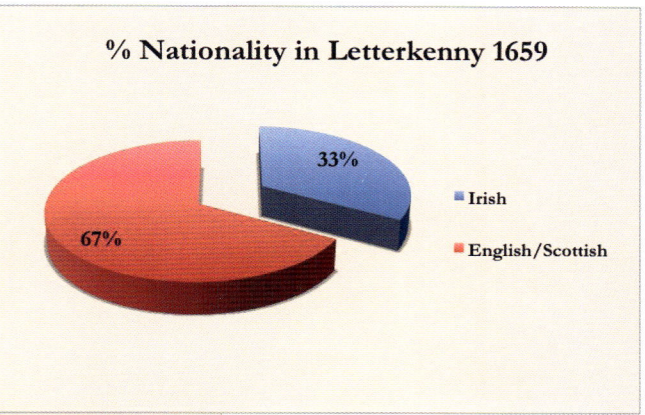

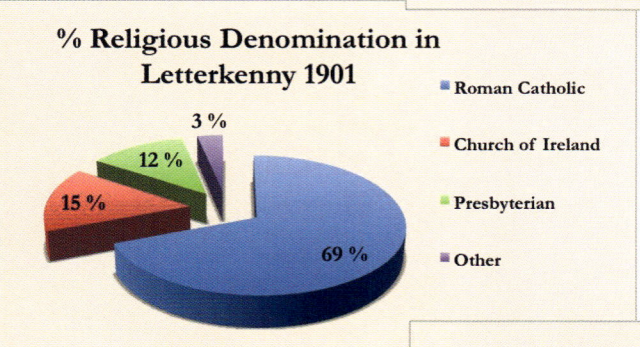

Pie Charts showing the growth of Roman Catholicism in the town of Letterkenny between 1659 and 2011

This of course did not happen over night, it did so gradually throughout the century, primarily as a result of national events such as the relaxing of the Penal Laws at the end of the eighteenth century and the granting of Catholic Emancipation in 1829 that had enhanced the status of Catholics throughout the country.

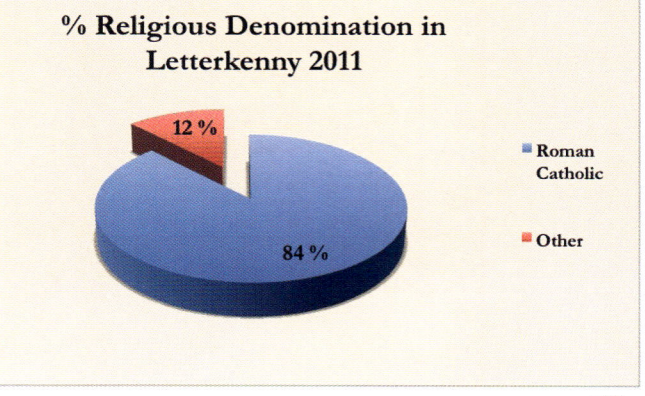

Letterkenny - Where the Winding Swilly Flows

The Mass Rock

The Penal Laws of the early eighteenth century had prohibited the public practice of Catholic worship in Ireland, which led to private masses taking place in secluded wooded areas throughout the country. Isolated locations were sought to hold these religious ceremonies, as observing the Catholic mass was a matter of severe danger for those in attendance, but especially for the priest. 'Priest hunters' were employed to seek out those who contravened these laws so their parishioners often hid them for protection.

A Mass Rock (*Carraig an Aifrinn*) was a large slab of rock used as an altar in these secluded areas for the Catholics to attend service. There were several of these in the Letterkenny area - Sam Fleming listed one in the Windyhall area while the 1836 OS Memoirs notes a "*Craignasiguart*" (The Priest's Rock) in the townland of Dooballagh, near Listillion - but the one that is best known locally is located near Roger's Burn, a small stream that divides the townlands of Sallaghgraine and Ballymacool.

Generally, the stone used for an altar would be taken from a church ruin nearby and relocated to this secluded area. The stone for the Mass Rock altar at Roger's Burn would most likely have been taken from the old abandoned 12th Century church at Conwal. According to a report entitled "*An Abstract of the State of Popery in the Diocese of Raphoe*" carried out on November 4th 1731 there were two '*Popish priests*' in the parish of Conwal '*who officiate in the open fields*' and one in the parish of Leck who '*officiates in the open field or in some poor Cabbin*' (most likely this refers to Craignasiguart).[2]

Six years after this, we know from a petition from the Diocese of Raphoe from 1737 that **Canon Francis Mac Devitt** was the Parish Priest of Conwal so he was most likely one priest who would have said mass '*in the open fields*' at Roger's Burn. **Dominick O'Donnell** is listed as Vicar of Leck so he would have been the priest who officiated at Craignasagairt. In 1704, '*An Act for Registering the Popish Clergy*' required all priests to register their names and pay £50 to be of '*peacable behaviour*' and from this we know that the parish priest for Conwal was a **Rev. James Dougherty**, aged 60, who lived in Pollans near Templedouglas[3] while the parish priest for Conwal in 1777 was listed as **Rev. James Harkin**.[4] As these years predate the building of the first Catholic Church in the town, it is most likely that these were also priests who would have officiated mass at Roger's Burn.

Lookouts, or 'sentries', were usually posted on good vantage points near to the mass rocks, and would then send a series of signals to warn the mass-goers of approaching British troops

The restored Mass Rock near Roger's Burn

Chapter Ten: The Growth of Catholic Confidence

(referred to as 'Redcoats' due to the colour of their uniform). Local sentries for Roger's Burn were positioned on a hilltop that overlooks the Main Street and Market Square areas where the Redcoats were stationed, and thus, the locals informally christened the area 'Sentry Hill'. A lookout would stand at various points around this area and on seeing the movement of the Redcoats, he would send a signal to other lookouts who would pass on the warning until the message was relayed successfully to the mass-goers and priest at Roger's Burn. In 2013, a commemorative stone sculpture, designed by Redmond Herrity, was unveiled at Sentry Hill to mark this site by the Letterkenny Community Heritage Group. A poem was written about the Mass Rock at Roger's Burn, which appeared in a 1980 leaflet that accompanied a special mass:

Carraig an Aifrinn	Mass Rock
Ag Carraig an Aifrinn ag Sruth Ruairí,	*At the Mass Rock at Roger's Burn*
Bhí dochas an phobail go lag 'e bhrí,	*The hope of the community was weak*
A gcinn crom ag urnai faoi bhrón fadó,	*Their heads bent in prayer for the sorrows of the past*
Ag iarraidh a gcreideamh a choinneail beo.	*Trying to keep their faith alive*
An sagart ag seachaint on namhaid dhur,	*The priest avoiding the enemy*
A dhaoine ag gealluint do Rí na nDuí,	*The people promising to the King of the Duí*
O thaobh Leitir Ceanainn go lar Ghleann Cheo,	*From Letterkenny to the centre of Glenceo*
Bheith dílis do Aifreann Chríost go deo.	*Being faithful to God's mass forever*
Ag Carraig an Aifrinn ag Sruth Ruarí,	*At the Mass Rock at Roger's Burn*
Tá dochas an phobail go fóill gan chloí,	*The hope of the community was without restrictions*
Na cinn crom ag urnaí mar bhí fadó,	*Their heads bent in prayer as was long ago*
Go dílis do Carraig an Aifrinn fós.	*Still faithful to the Mass Rock*
A Thiarna go mairimid faoi do threoir	*Lord we live under your guidance*
'Sna laethe 's na blianta cruaidhe romhainn	*In the days and years to come*
Ar nduchas ar díoladh a luach go daor	*Our heritage sold for a high price*
Gur buan é do Charraig an Aifrinn fíor	*It's true that the Mass Rock will last*

Letterkenny - Where the Winding Swilly Flows

Monument sculpted by local artist Redmond Herrity and erected by the Letterkenny Community Heritage Group in 2013 to commemorate the location of Sentry Hill

The use of Mass Rocks ceased with the relaxation of the Penal Laws at the end of the eighteenth century. The first known Catholic Church in Letterkenny was built during the episcopacy of **Bishop Anthony Coyle** (1782 – 1801) around 1784 on a site opposite Sentry Hill where St. Eunan's College now stands. This replaced the Mass Rock at Roger's Burn as the principal place of worship for the Catholic population of Letterkenny until a new church was erected nearer the town in 1820 on the site of the present Cathedral. 'The Liberator' Daniel O'Connell had achieved Catholic Emancipation in 1829 and throughout the nineteenth century, the sites of these Mass Rocks throughout the country came to be overgrown and forgotten about.

This first church for the worship of Catholics in Letterkenny was a small barn-like structure and stood until 1820 when it was decided that it was too far from the Main Street for the parishioners to travel. A new site was chosen for the building of a church on the site now occupied by the Cathedral. The man behind the building of this new church was **Fr. James Gallagher**, who had been promoted to the united parishes of Conwal, Leck and Aughaninshin in 1808.

Father Gallagher was also involved in an incident on 12th July 1822 known as the **Battle of Sprackburn**. An altercation between a marching group of Orangemen from Milford and the Catholics of Letterkenny threatened to spill into terrible bloodshed only for the intervention of Fr. Gallagher. Even though

Chapter Ten: The Growth of Catholic Confidence

was referred to as the Battle of Sprackburn, it appears to have taken place in a field just below it nearer to Gortlee.

"The majority of the invaders, who threatened to sweep the streets of Letterkenny with the bodies of the "Papishes", came from the Milford district, but they received re-inforcements from Raphoe and elsewhere. Gortlee was the trysting ground; the battle was short and decisive." [5]

Despite this though, thankfully there have been very few reports of sectarianism in Letterkenny throughout its history. In general, the Catholic, Church of Ireland and Presbyterian communities have lived together in relative harmony in the town with marriage between faiths very common. In 1891, for example, the Derry Journal reported that constabulary from Letterkenny were sent to Derry for the July 12th demonstrations and that:

"It speaks favourably for this harmony existing amongst all our local religious denominations that our town and adjacent stations are almost depleted of police who are drafted to less similarly favoured districts." [6]

The rising status of Catholicism in Letterkenny at this time was represented by the arrival of the residency of the Bishop of Raphoe in the late eighteenth century. Bishop Anthony Coyle had studied in the Irish College Paris but had been expelled in 1755 and completed his training in Nantes. While returning to Paris in 1779, he is believed to have rescued Frederick Augustus Hervey, Earl of Bristol and Anglican Bishop of Derry from an angry mob during a riot. Showing his gratitude, Bishop Hervey used his influence with the Boyd family to secure a residence for Bishop Coyle on the Ballymacool estate.

As well as overseeing the development of the first place of public worship in the town, Bishop Coyle set up a small secondary school for Catholics and often taught in it himself but it ceased to function following his death in 1801. **Bishop Patrick McGettigan** (1820 – 1861) also set up schools in the town on Castle Street between 1825 and 1833 and on the Port Road between 1841 and 1846. Bishop McGettigan was responsible for inviting the Loreto nuns to open schools for girls' education in the town in 1854, using his residence to accommodate their needs.

Further progress in the growth of Catholicism in the town was made by Bishops **Dr. Daniel MacGettigan** (1861 – 1870), **Dr. James MacDevitt** (1871 – 1879) and **Dr. Michael Logue** (1879 – 1888) but perhaps the greatest

Dr. James McDevitt, Bishop of Raphoe 1871-1879. Image courtesy of Diocese of Raphoe

Letterkenny - Where the Winding Swilly Flows

symbol of this new found rise in the confidence and status of Catholics in Letterkenny in the nineteenth century came under the episcopacy of **Bishop Patrick O'Donnell** (1888 – 1925). In 1891 under his watchful eye, the foundation stone was laid for a building that would rise up brick by brick over the following ten years to eventually dominate the skyline of the market town - St. Eunan's Cathedral.

Dr. Michael Logue,
Bishop of Raphoe
1879-1888

Endnotes
1 Census statistics available at www.cso.ie
2 Archivium Hibernicum or Irish Historical Records Volume I, St. Patrick's College Maynooth, 1912, p20
3 Silke, Re. John J & Hughes Mrs. Moira, "Raphoe Miscellany 1", 2012, p67
4 Maguire, Canon, "A History of the Diocese of Raphoe," Vol 1, Brown & Nolan Ltd., 1920, p339
5 Ibid p340/1
6 Derry Journal 13/7/1891

Chapter Eleven: The Cathedral of Saints Eunan and Columba

When entering Letterkenny from any direction, the towering spires of the Cathedral of Saints Eunan and Columba dominate the skyline. In fact, it would be pretty difficult to imagine the town without them. The building stands as a permanent reminder of the determination and zeal of **Bishop Patrick O'Donnell** who supervised the construction of the Cathedral from the laying of the foundation stone in 1891 through to its completion in 1901. At the dawn of the new century, it embodied the new confidence of Catholicism, symbolically towering over the nearby Protestant churches.

The Cathedral of Saints Eunan and Columba. Courtesy of Redmond Herrity

Early Churches

Towards the end of the eighteenth century, the first Catholic Church in the Letterkenny area had been erected on a site inside the northern gates of the present site of St. Eunan's College while we have seen that Fr. James Gallagher erected a church around 1820 where the Cathedral presently stands. By 1830, **Bishop Patrick McGettigan** built a larger church on the same site and was making significant improvements by 1851 in the hope of building a pro-cathedral. The Derry Journal from January 15th 1851 tells us that the "*highly gifted and popular preacher, Dr. O'Connell of Waterford*" would be giving a Charity Sermon in the church with a collection:

"*to enable the Right Rev. Doctor McGettigan to carry out some important improvements in his Church, among which are contemplated the erection of a Tower and Belfry, the purchase of an organ etc….the venerable prelate has already collected in that poor locality, and extended in the erection of the new church, in the construction of three spacious galleries, in the purchase of a very beautiful marble altar and in other internal decorations of the building, a sum of nearly £3,000.*"[1]

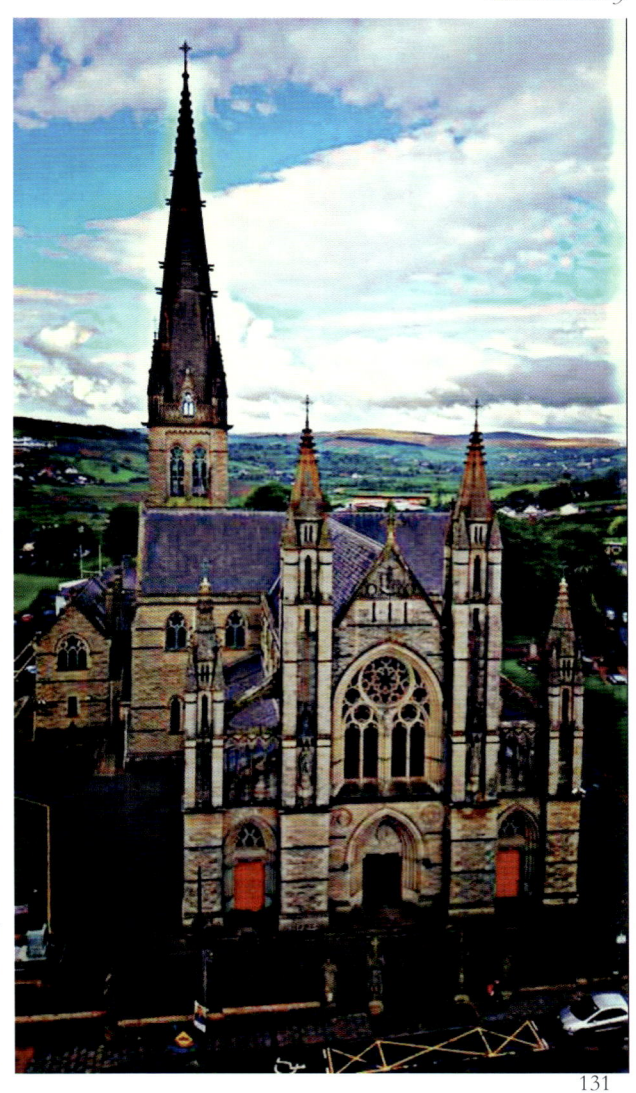

The Charity Sermon by Dr. O'Connell raised £180, a significant sum for the time. These sums raised by Bishop McGettigan were used to build **St. Patrick's Catholic Cathedral** (or the pro-cathedral as it was later known) on the site occupied by the current Cathedral, consecrated on Thursday 3rd August 1854 with Archbishop Dixon of Armagh and Archbishop Cullen of Dublin in attendance.[2]

St. Patrick's Pro-Cathedral, consecrated in 1854. Image courtesy of the National Library of Ireland

By 1865 though it was decided that a much larger Cathedral was needed for the ever-growing town. Following Bishop McGettigan's death in 1861 (incidentally this occurred in the same week as the Derryveagh Evictions), it was his successor **Bishop Daniel McGettigan**, who started the process by raising £500 but the scheme had to be abandoned due to the depressed economic conditions prevalent in the county at the time.

No real progress occurred during Bishop MacDevitt's occupancy of the bishopric (1871-1879) but under **Bishop Michael Logue** (1879-1888) the project was resurrected with large sums of money bequeathed to the building of a Cathedral by **Neil Gillen** (£11,000) and **J.D. McGarvey** (£10,000) but again the project fizzled out due to economic hardship. When Bishop Logue became Cardinal in Armagh, the seat of the Bishopric of Raphoe became vacant and the 32-year-old Fr. Patrick O'Donnell became the youngest Catholic bishop in the world at the time. The task of building a Cathedral for the town was now in his hands.

Chapter Eleven: The Cathedral of Saints Eunan and Columba

Patrick O'Donnell

Patrick O'Donnell was born on 28th November 1856 in Kilraine near Glenties, the son of Dan O'Donnell and Mary Breslin. At the time of his birth, it must be remembered that Catholic Emancipation had only been granted twenty-seven years previously and the Great Famine had been only the decade before. Times were tough in the Gaeltacht area of Glenties and these conditions made quite an impression on the young Patrick.

Following national schooling in Kilraine, Patrick attended the High School in Letterkenny in the Old Seminary on the Main Street before attending the Catholic University in Dublin and the seminary in Maynooth. It was here that he was ordained a priest in July 1880. It is quite a testament to his ability and determination that he became Bishop of Raphoe only eight years after his ordination as a priest.

He was consecrated as Bishop of Raphoe on 3 April 1888 and following the ceremony, a banquet was held in the Literary Institute. His predecessor, Dr. Logue stated of O'Donnell that:

"Not only was their young bishop deeply interested in the religious welfare of the people, but there was no legitimate National aspiration of the people that he would not do his best to further and promote."[3]

A keen Nationalist, O'Donnell was not only involved in the day to day running of his diocese but he was also involved in the **Plan of Campaign** and **Congested Districts Board** to aid his parishioners and his fellow countrymen in their struggles against landlordism.

Fundraising

However, Bishop O'Donnell's primary focus was on the building of a Cathedral, which he knew would cost a large amount of money in very tough times. In 1890, the Cathedral Building Committee was formed and despite the bleak economic conditions prevalent at the time in Donegal, Bishop O'Donnell called on generous people, especially of Irish descent, all over the world to help with the fund as the building of the cathedral would generate employment to people who needed it most. What Bishop O'Donnell wanted most of all was: *"a building to gladden the hearts and ennoble the ideas of our downtrodden race, and remain for ages, not only a memorial, but a resurrection of the fallen shrines of Donegal"*[4]

Dr. Patrick O'Donnell (1856-1927), Bishop of Raphoe 1888-1922, Co-adjutator Bishop of Armagh 1922-1924, Cardinal 1925-1927

The cost of building the cathedral would be immense, and although his

Letterkenny - Where the Winding Swilly Flows

previous prelates in the diocese had raised money for the task, a substantial amount was still needed. To that end, **Fr. Daniel Stephens** and **Fr. James Walker** set sail for Canada and America in 1893 to raise necessary funds for the building. Upon their return to the town a year later, the Glenswilly flute band and torch bearers met them and paraded through the town to the Market Square where a crowd of 8,000 people assembled.[5]

The 'Patriot Priest of Gweedore', **Fr. James McFadden**, went to America in 1897 for fundraising also, while other priests who undertook this arduous task included **Fr. Hugh MacDwyer**, **Fr. Daniel Sweeney**, **Fr. John Dorrian** and **Fr. J.C. Cannon**.

The Aonach Tir Chonaill

Funds were also being raised annually for the project through diocesan collections but more money was still needed. Bishop O'Donnell saw a great opportunity with the centenary anniversary of the 1798 Rebellion approaching. The 1300th celebrations of Colmcille at Gartan in 1897 had been a great success for the revival of interests in all things Gaelic and so he decided to hold an Aonach (or Festival) that was modeled on the ancient Féis Teamhrach at Tara, where St Eunan had attended in 697. The primary aim of the Aonach would be to raise the funds for the Cathedral but it would also celebrate and highlight the best in Irish language, music, culture and games as a part of the overall Gaelic Revival, a national focus that Dr. O'Donnell was a keen supporter of.

Artist's impression of the great Aonach Tirchonaill which took place in 'Halla Eithne', the unfinished Cathedral in 1898

Chapter Eleven: The Cathedral of Saints Eunan and Columba

By this time, the building had risen to wall height and was chosen as the venue for the Aonach. It was renamed 'Halla Eithne' after the mother of Colmcille, and stalls for each parish were set up in the aisle and transepts. Raffles, concerts, art exhibitions and drama performances were performed by each stall to raise various funds while a large marquee was used as a tea pavilion for the crowds that would be attending.

On November 22nd 1898, the former Bishop of Raphoe and now Cardinal, Michael Logue officially opened the Aonach Tir Chonaill while the Féis Adamnan, running concurrently on the grounds of the Loreto Convent, had been opened the previous night. The Literary Institute held the Gaelic Congress for the week where Cardinal Logue presided and **Dr. Douglas Hyde**, later to be the first President of Ireland, gave an address on behalf of the Gaelic League. Performances of a Gaelic play '*The Passing of Conal*' took place by the members of the Letterkenny branch of the Gaelic League as well as a raffle in which the first 100 prizes were front row seats for the opening of the Cathedral. The Aonach lasted for the whole week and was a phenomenal success both culturally and financially, so much so that it eventually became an annual Féis Tirchonaill, which lasted for many decades in the county. A similar Aonach an Dún festival was used eight years later for the opening of St. Eunan's College.

The Building

William Hague was appointed architect for the Cathedral in 1890 and **James McClay** of Strabane was the builder. McClay built a small (100ft x 40ft) wooden temporary church for the duration of the project, the altar from which is still held in the sacristy of the cathedral. Archbishop Logue had laid the foundation stone in 1891 while rubble from the previous Pro-Cathedral was used for the foundations. Boats transported the Mountcharles quarried stone to the Thorn where local farmers volunteered on Sundays to cart them the several miles to the building site. When they got to the bottom of the Church

Dr. Douglas Hyde (1860-1949), later to become first President of Ireland, spoke in the Literary Institute as part of the Aonach Tírchonaill. Image courtesy of National Library of Ireland

Below: The temporary church erected in the grounds of the Convent in 1891 and used while the Cathedral was being built

Letterkenny - Where the Winding Swilly Flows

Lane, 1/3 of the cargo was unloaded, to be taken up on a second trip. The stone for the spire were then raised by sets of horses pulling ropes to the desired height. James McClay went out of business in 1895 and so Fr. Stephens was recalled from America to supervise the completion of the building while in 1899 the architect William Hague died and was succeeded by his colleague **Thomas Francis McNamara**. Hague's work was later commemorated by having a stained glass window of St. William placed in the cathedral in his honour located on the left hand side of the aisle.

The construction site of St. Eunan's Cathedral as it was nearly completed. Courtesy of Raphoe Dioceasan Archives.

The Opening of the Cathedral

By June of 1901 the new Cathedral was ready for opening. People came from all parts of Ireland, England, Scotland, America, Australia and New Zealand to witness this wonderful occasion for the town of Letterkenny and the overall Diocese of Raphoe. The consecration took place on Friday June 14th by Cardinal Logue while the first mass took place at 1 o'clock on Sunday June 16th 1901. Various festivities throughout the town followed this with the bells ringing throughout the day and music performances into the early evening. At 10pm, fireworks were set ablaze for over two hours. The visiting dignitaries of priests, bishops, archbishops and Cardinal Logue visited Gartan and Glenveagh over the weekend where Cornelia Adair entertained them to dinner. The Derry Journal describes vividly the vibrant atmosphere in the town that weekend:

"Yesterday an historic scene – a great celebration – was witnessed in Letterkenny that stirred the feelings, influenced the minds eye and touched the hearts of all beholders…In the early morning the town was alive with preparation, gay with hope and outward cheer.. Hearty words of greeting streamed from every side and

Chapter Eleven: The Cathedral of Saints Eunan and Columba

the whole effect and display exhibited the feelings and warmth of a populace who greeted in enthusiastic welcome those numerous visitors who crowded the town."[6]

Large triumphal floral arches greeted the visitors throughout the town, with flags fluttering from houses and trees. Outside the railway station, a large floral semi-circular span had the greetings *"Céad Mile Fáilte"* and *"Welcome to the Cardinal and Hierarchy of Ireland"* while on the Main Street, an arch outside McCarry's Hotel, had *"Eire go brath"*, *"Tir agus credimh"* and *"Stay long, return soon"*. The houses and footpaths of the town were one continuous line of flags, bunting, banners and decorations.

Bishop O'Donnell's Later Life

Bishop O'Donnell continued to be involved with national politics long after the Cathedral was completed. He had been friends with John Dillon MP since his university days and was a key supporter of the Home Rule movement and the Irish Parliamentary Party. He even helped to unify the party following the split after the scandal of Charles Stewart Parnell's affair with Kitty O'Shea in 1891. When the prospect of partition loomed in 1912, he was an advisor to John Redmond on the best political stance to take and he was chosen as key speaker at the Irish Convention of 1917-18 which was set up to decide on the best solution to the 'Irish Question'. At the Convention he showed a deep understanding of the Unionist position in any possible outcome. Having been a member of the Congested Districts Board since 1892, he was its longest serving member until its dissolution in 1923.

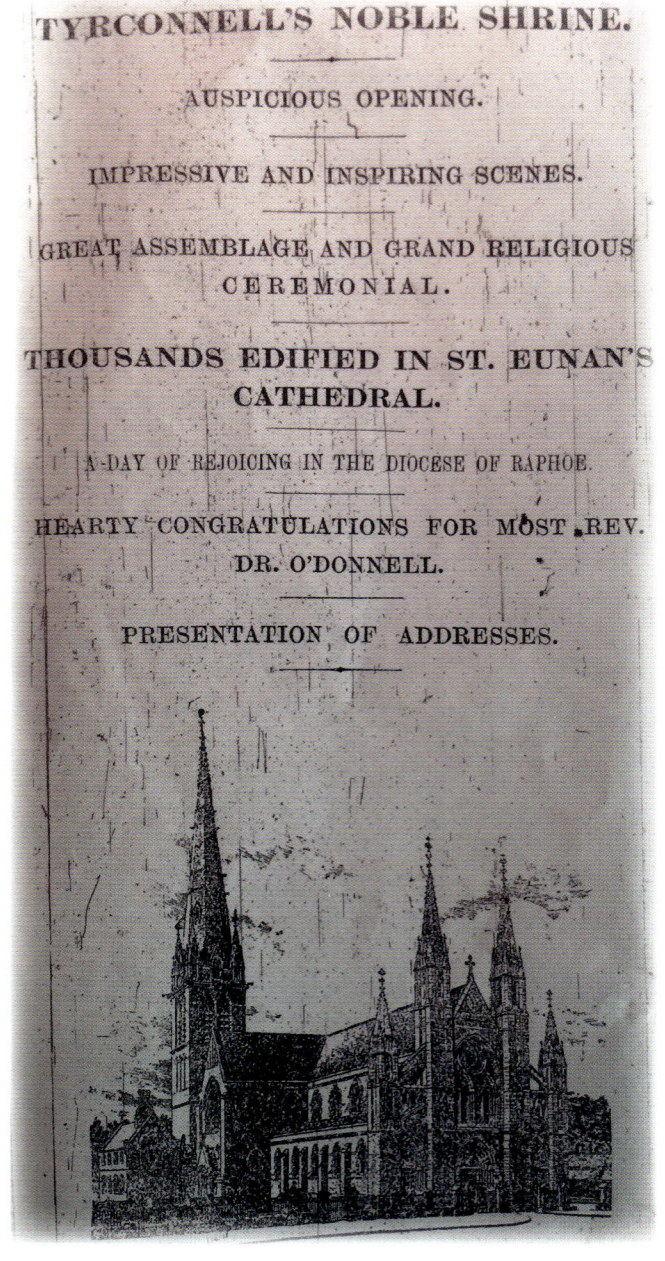

He became co-adjutator Archbishop of Armagh in 1922 and Archbishop in 1924, with **Fr. William MacNeely**, from Donegal Town and veteran of World

Newspaper headline from the Derry Journal in 1901 concerning the opening of the Cathedral

TYRCONNELL'S NOBLE SHRINE.

AUSPICIOUS OPENING.

IMPRESSIVE AND INSPIRING SCENES.

GREAT ASSEMBLAGE AND GRAND RELIGIOUS CEREMONIAL.

THOUSANDS EDIFIED IN ST. EUNAN'S CATHEDRAL.

A DAY OF REJOICING IN THE DIOCESE OF RAPHOE.

HEARTY CONGRATULATIONS FOR MOST REV. DR. O'DONNELL.

PRESENTATION OF ADDRESSES.

Letterkenny - Where the Winding Swilly Flows

The floral arches that decorated the street at the opening of the Cathedral in 1901. Images courtesy of the National Library of Ireland

Chapter Eleven: The Cathedral of Saints Eunan and Columba

Did you know?

- Over the ten years it took to complete the construction, the final cost of the Cathedral was over £300,000 - approximately €20.5 million today.
- It measures 200ft x 100ft with the spire rising to 240ft.
- The twelve bells in the belfry are all named after Donegal saints: Columba, Eunan, Fiacre, Conall and Dallan, Baithen and Barron, Ernan and Assicus, Naul and Mura, Finan and Davog, Carthage and Cairneac, Catherine and Taodhóg, Croine, and Rian.
- The beautiful Columban arch in the middle of the aisle celebrates the life of Columba on the right and of Eunan on the left. Engraved also in the arch is St. Patrick blessing Conall Gulban's shield, the laying of the foundation stone of the Cathedral in 1891, the writing of the Annals of the Four Masters and the Flight of the Earls giving the viewer a pictorial history of the Diocese of Raphoe.
- The ambulatory (sides and rear of the altar) are guarded by the stone sculptures of Red Hugh O'Donnell and Hugh O'Neill.
- The Pulpit of the Four Masters was paid for by the teachers of the diocese and designed and made by the Pearse family of Dublin. This was the family of the 1916 revolutionaries **Patrick and Willie Pearse** and as both men were working in their father's business at that time, it is most likely that they would have worked on it.
- There are several graves on the grounds of the Cathedral that predate the building itself. The Gallagher family of **James** (1834), **Catherine** (1840), **Rosanna** (1830), **Joseph** (1863), **Patrick** (1864), **Henry** (1881), **William** (1881), **Joseph** (1881), **Edward** (1887) and **Sarah** (1890) have a gravestone there. Joseph Gallagher was a former chairman of the Town Commissioners. **Elizabeth Dougherty** (1878), her son **Charles** (1893) and **Michael Doherty** (1895) have a plot while **Nicholas Francis Ball** (1884) is also buried there.

Archbishop O'Donnell attending the ordination of Dr. William McNeely as Bishop of Raphoe in 1923

Letterkenny - Where the Winding Swilly Flows

War 1, succeeding him as Bishop of Raphoe. In 1925, he was appointed Cardinal but he died on 22nd October 1927 at the age of 71. While on holiday in Carlingford, Co Louth, he had been out swimming and injured his knee, which led him to develop double pneumonia and pleurisy. His death was mourned not just in his adopted hometown of Letterkenny but throughout the country. He is buried in Armagh Bishop Mc Neely supervised the building of a bronze statue in his honour that was unveiled in 1929 and stands proudly beside the magnificent building that he worked so tirelessly to complete.

Newspaper heading on the death of Cardinal O'Donnell in 1927

It is sometimes easy to forget the impact that Patrick O'Donnell had on national politics as a whole and the esteem in which he was held in but also the sizeable impact he had on our local history. His role in the development of education in Letterkenny at the dawn of the twentieth century will be examined in the next chapter while his love of the preservation of the Gaelic language is evidenced by his promotion of the Aonach Tir Chonaill which continued in various venues throughout the county until the 1950s as well as the publication of An Crann, the journal of the Crann Eithne movement. His greatest legacy, however, is without doubt the beautiful structure that dominates the hillside town and captures the attention of all who visit here, the Cathedral of Saints Eunan and Columba.

Bishop McNeely unveiling a statue to Cardinal O'Donnell in 1929. Image courtesy of the National Library of Ireland

At the time of its opening in 1901, a book entitled "An Illustrated Guide to Saint Eunan's Cathedral" was published which tells us much about the pride with which the people of Letterkenny had for their grand new building:

"*The Cathedral cost much money, much thought, much anxiety, much sacrifice, but no life, thank God. It was meant as a "resurrection of the fallen shrines of Donegal". It is that, and more, Letterkenny is not a large town, but the scattered children of Tirconnail are a numerous race, with the same virtues, ideals and inclinations that were theirs in the past. Henceforth the Cathedral is a rallying point, a source of inspiration, a common*

140

Chapter Eleven: The Cathedral of Saints Eunan and Columba

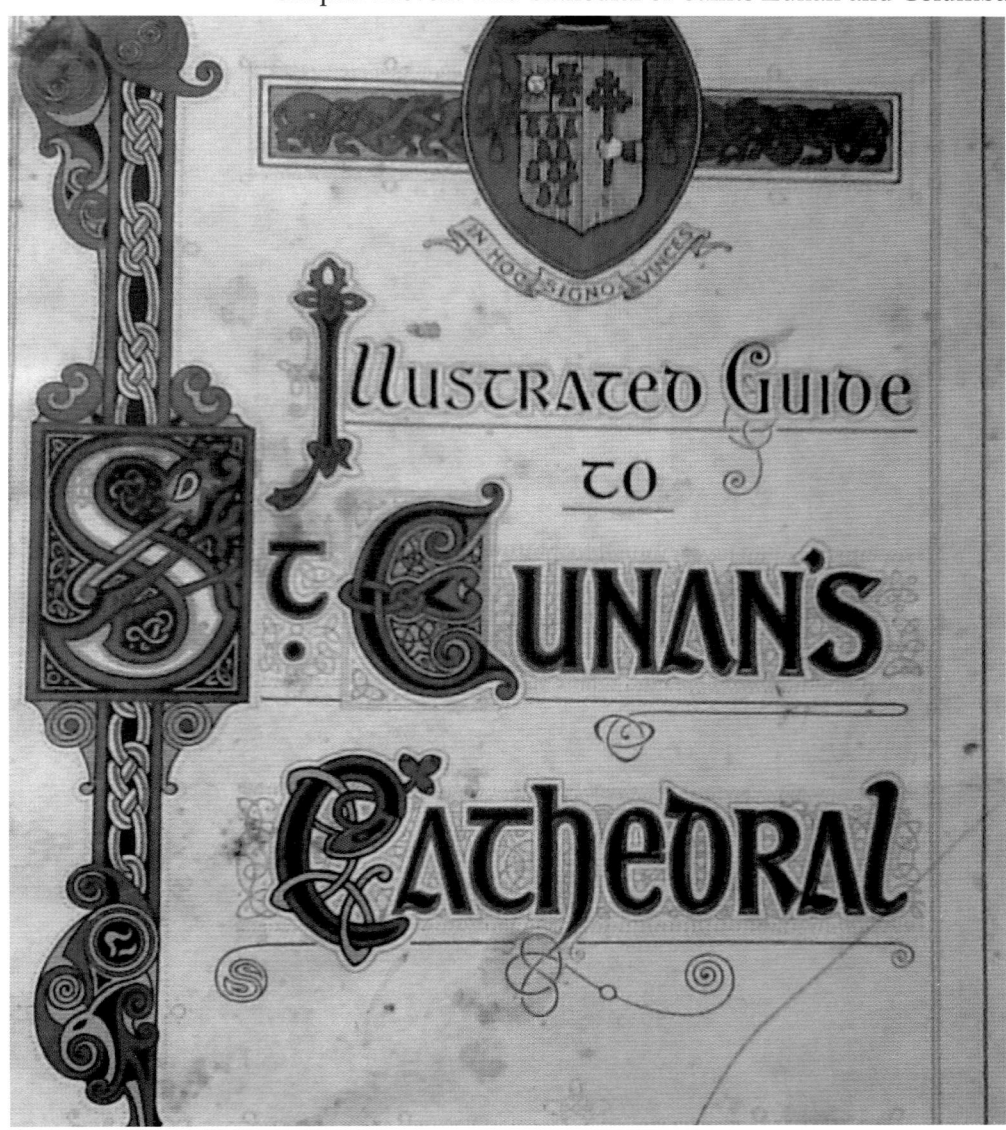

The cover of the Illustrated Guide to St. Eunan's Cathedral which accompanied the opening

"...joy and a common inheritance for them all. And not for them only. But for every visitor who loves the beauty of the Lord's House and the place where His glory dwelleth."[7]

Endnotes
1 "Fragmenta Rapotensiana", Donegal Annual 1956, p 130
2 Ibid p 131
3 Derry Journal 4/4/1888
4 "Cathedral of S.S. Eunan and Columba", Conwal and Leck Parish, June 20001, p8
5 Derry Journal July 1894
6 Derry Journal 17/6/1901
7 "An Illustrated Guide to St. Eunan's Cathedral", 1901, p43

Letterkenny - Where the Winding Swilly Flows

St. Eunan's Cathedral with the stone Celtic Cross sculpted by local artist Redmond Herrity

Chapter Twelve: Educational Establishments in Letterkenny

Naturally, the many personalities we are meeting on our journey were adults when they shaped and defined the history of Letterkenny. However, as the old saying goes, mighty oaks from little acorns grow! Just as the River Swilly has rather humble origins as a trickle of water, so too did these personalities – as children. The lessons that they learned whilst attending school helped forge and determine the characters that they would later become and, as such, the schools that they attended and the teachers that they met along the way played pivotal roles in their development.

Today there are ten primary schools and five secondary schools in Letterkenny catering for the education of almost 6,000 children from the town and surrounding regions, but the growth and development of these schools took a long time. With the gradual repeal of the Penal Laws in the early nineteenth century, Catholics were allowed to receive education and in the predominantly Catholic town of Letterkenny various attempts to open schools were sporadic and chaotic at first, owing mostly to the availability of teaching personnel. For that reason, several schools opened and closed within short periods of time. It wasn't until the Loreto Sisters arrived in 1854 and the Presentation Brothers in 1894 that stability emerged for the education of the Catholic girls and boys of the town. Prior to this, those that could afford to attend school did so at multi-denominational schools, at Oldtown for example. Presbyterian children generally attended Barkhall School on the Port Road from 1860 while Church of Ireland

Graph showing the numbers of pupils attending each of the primary and secondary schools of Letterkenny as of June 2014

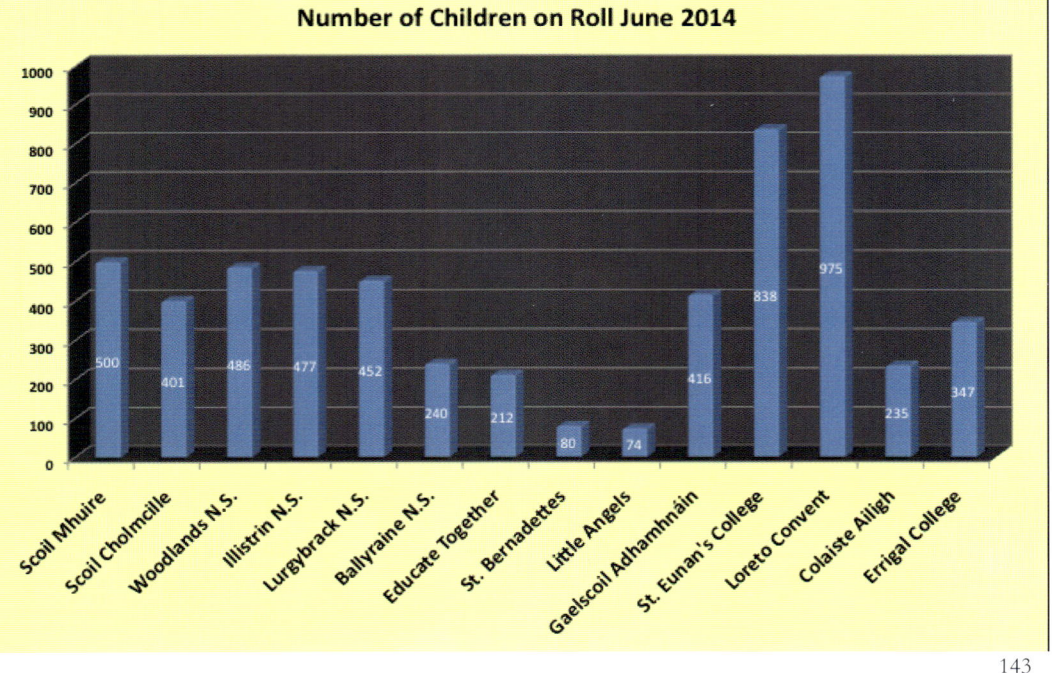

Number of Children on Roll June 2014

Scoil Mhuire	500
Scoil Cholmcille	401
Woodlands N.S.	486
Illistrin N.S.	477
Lurgybrack N.S.	452
Ballyraine N.S.	240
Educate Together	212
St. Bernadettes	80
Little Angels	74
Gaelscoil Adhamhnáin	416
St. Eunan's College	838
Loreto Convent	975
Colaiste Ailigh	235
Errigal College	347

children attended the Robertson School, also on the Port Road, from 1878. Other schools, such as at Woodlands, Lurgybrack and Illistrin - once on the outskirts but now considered to be a part of the town – have seen dramatic growth in recent years, owing mostly to the rising population but also the gradual de-centralisation of families moving to housing estates on the periphery of the town.

Early Schools

For over a century following the Plantation, the commercial nature of the growing market towns resulted in the recognition by the Gaelic Irish of the necessity for the education of their children. Receiving the correct education would open doors to employment in the many businesses that were springing up. However, the Penal Laws of the eighteenth century forbade Catholics to attend schools and consequently, 'hedge-schools' became the dominant form of education for many years in the diocese of Raphoe. These usually consisted of a local man instructing his classes in the hedgerows or barns throughout the countryside. We know that one such school existed in the Parish of Conwal in 1731 with '*one Popish school in the mountain*' being recorded.[1]

Following the relaxation of the Penal Laws, the first Catholic school that we know of for Letterkenny was established during **Dr. Anthony Coyle**'s episcopacy of Raphoe (1782-1801). However, following his death in 1801, this 'classical academy' was abandoned as his successor, Dr. Peter MacLaughlin (1802-1819), preferred to live in Ballyshannon and focus his attentions there.[2]

His successor, **Bishop Patrick McGettigan**, arrived in Letterkenny in 1820, and the need for a formal educational establishment in the town once more came to the fore. Between 1825 and 1833, Bishop McGettigan supervised the running of a school at Castle Street, at the top of the Market Square, and appointed **Rev. John Feely** to conduct classes in Greek, Latin and Mathematics. **Fr. McGarrigle** took over from Fr. Feely in the teaching of the school but later transferred to the parish of Killybegs where he died in 1833. When his successor, **Fr. Drummond**, was transferred to Killybegs, due to the dearth in the number of priests in the diocese at the time, this school was abandoned.[3]

With the closure of the school on Castle Street, a **Mr. MacGoldrick** from Castlecaldwell in County Fermanagh opened a school with his family in the 1830s on the road that is now called College Row near to the present St. Eunan's College. Three of Mr. McGoldrick's sons later became priests while one of them, James McGoldrick, became Bishop of Duluth in Minnesotta. For unknown reasons, Mr. McGoldrick left Letterkenny after 5 or 6 years and this school closed up.[4]

Unperturbed by the departure of Mr. McGoldrick, Bishop McGettigan oversaw the opening of a new school on the Port Road in 1841, appointing **Fr. Hugh O'Donnell** as teacher there. It was initially a great success with students coming from all areas of the diocese and also from Derry. A report from 1842 tells us that:

"*The new college at Letterkenny is in a flourishing condition. Although 20 years ago, there were only 23 priests in the diocese, there are now 50 on active duty and work for 10 more.*"[5]

Chapter Twelve: Educational Establishments in Letterkenny

However, this promising school did not last long either, as after five years, Father O'Donnell was transferred to the parish of Kilcar and the school closed.

From 1790, the will of Colonel Robertson, the son of a clergyman from Donegal Town, bequeathed a large sum of money, from which the interest of £15 per year was to be paid to each of the parishes in the diocese of Raphoe for the support of a schoolmaster to instruct children of all religious denominations. This fund was later increased to £40 for the erection of schoolhouses also. One such school existed at Oldtown, as evidenced by the letters of Lieutenant Wilkinson as part of the Ordnance Survey of 1836. At this Oldtown School, the teacher was **Mr. Hamilton Doggan**, a Protestant, and they had 43 children on their registry (Males – 8 Protestants, 8 Presbyterians, 11 Catholics; females – 7 Protestants, 4 Presbyterians and 5 Catholics).[6]

From these letters we also learn of schools at nearby Drumminny (one for boys, one for girls but under the same roof) that were maintained by the Kildare Place Society and were also multi-denominational (Male – 18 Protestants, 3 Presbyterians, 30 Catholics; Females – 4 Protestants, 20 Presbyterians and 1 Catholics) and their teachers were **John Wilson** and **Ellen Russell**. **John McShane**, a Catholic, taught at Listillion School where he had 24 children enrolled (Males – Presbyterians 4, Catholic 10; Females – Presbyterian 4, Catholic 6)[7] while another national school opened in Glencar in 1841, which remained open until the early 1950s.

Barkhall and Robertson National Schools

On the Port Road, following the death of Dr. Spratt in 1858 and the dissolution of Second Letterkenny Presbyterian Church, the building was converted to a schoolhouse and in 1860 Barkhall National School was officially opened for the education of Presbyterian children. **Mr. Robert Quigg**, from Derry, was one of the earliest principals of the school and "*as an educationalist, he stood in the front rank of National teachers, and was noted as well for his charm of manner, which gained him the love of his pupils, as for his success as a teacher.*"[8]

Mr. Quigg obtained the Carlisle and Blake premium award for excellence on several occasions and, following his retirement in 1897, he was succeeded by his son, **Mr. James Quigg** as Principal of Barkhall National School.

From 1833, a Sabbath School existed slightly further up the Port Road but was replaced in 1878 by the Robertson School (named after Colonel Robertson). Following disestablishment, the hall became a day school in 1881 for the education of the Church of Ireland children of Letterkenny, becoming a national school two years later. It was also used as a Sunday school and as a hall for private functions.

By the 1960s, due to the need for repairs in both schools, a decision was made that, rather than update these old buildings, a new school premises would be built to cater for the children of both Protestant communities. A site was purchased in Ballyraine from the Baird family for £250 in 1965 and both Barkhall and Robertson schools closed in 1976 following the erection of this new Ballyraine National School – the nearby schools of Ednaharnon and Glendooen also amalgamated with them at this time. **Mrs. Delia Harris**, the former principal of

Robertson School, became the new principal of Ballyraine with **Ms. Ine Orr**, the former Princip of Barkhall becomin deputy Principal. Dr. Robe Eames, Bishop of Derry an Raphoe, and **Archdeaco Crooks** officially opene the school in 1977 with enrollment of 164 childre **Anne McKinley** took ov as Principal in 1987 un 2000 when **Mr. Dav Oliver** became Principal an today the school has ov 240 children on the roll.[9]

Ballyraine National School opened in 1977

1855 Schools Inspection

We know that two National Schools existed in the town in the mid 185(for Catholic children, one for the boys and one for the girls (the latter run by th recently arrived Loreto Sisters). The National Schools Inspector, Patrick Josep Keenan, arrived to inspect the "Letterkenny Male" school in 1855 reporting th it had an:

"Excellent house, in good repair. Furniture good…two large maps; a fair supply reading and arithmetical tablets…order and cleanliness very good; discipline fair…(Teache not trained, class 2, sixty years of age, a national teacher since 1834, was trained in t establishment of the Kildare-Place Society, in 1814, and served for twenty years under th body, method of teaching sensible and rather intelligent, but full of old fancies; examines wi tolerable judiciuosness…he is a deserving and respectable man. Considering the short time t pupils attended school and the age of many of them at coming, there is a fair amount intelligence and knowledge exhibited by them when examined. This school is a little beyond t average class…The female school here happens to be a remarkably superious one."[10]

This 1855 report also informs us that there were 75 pupils on the roll this time. Sometime around 1870, **Mr. J. Sweeney** was headmaster of this schoo and under his successor, **Mr. Hugh O'Donnell** of Kilcar, the male school too first place in the county for attendance and proficiency.[11] This school remained the foremost educational establishment for young Catholic boys within the tow until the arrival of the Presentation Brothers in the 1890s.

The Loreto Sisters Girls' School

Coinciding with the growth of Catholic confidence in the middle o the nineteenth century, one of the main catalysts for the stable developmer

Chapter Twelve: Educational Establishments in Letterkenny

education in the town was without doubt the arrival of the Loreto Sisters. In October 1851, Bishop Patrick McGettigan visited the Loreto Order in Rathfarnham as his niece, Ellen Gallagher, attended the convent there. Unable to afford the money for her continued studies in the impressive establishment, Dr. McGettigan wrote a letter to the Superior, Mother Teresa Ball, and offered his residence on nine acres of land to open a convent in Letterkenny for the education of the girls of the diocese:

You are aware I presume that for some time past my pecuniary means have been limited and that I have no money to give her at present. The only remuneration I can give is to make you a present of my house, a beautiful place which cost me two thousand pounds and which I shall hand over to you whenever you think proper to found an establishment here, a thing much required and would be productive of very great benefit to the females of this locality."[12]

Taking up this invitation, on August 28th 1854, **Mother Conception Lopez** arrived in the town with six Loreto nuns and was greeted by over 2,000 people:

On their arrival at Letterkenny, a scene took place which will not be hastily forgotten in that beautiful locality. The Chapel-yard was lined on both sides, to the entrance of the grand door, by the confraternities and the school children, under the direction of the teachers and truly Apostolic Father McGettigan. No sooner had the nuns descended from the carriages than a simultaneous burst from some hundreds of voices filled the air with the strains of the "litany of the Blessed Virgin"[13]

On September 5th 1854, the Loreto sisters opened two schools, one for younger girls known as the 'Free School' and a boarding and Day School for older girls (the Convent). The 'Free School' was located where the Adoration Chapel is today near the Cathedral, noted by the location of a date stone for *'Letterkenny National School 1854'* at the gable. Fifty pupils originally attended this Free School while only five were enrolled for the senior Day School. As the numbers increased in the Free School (or Seanscoil as it would eventually become known as), classes were held in the Literary Institute but by the 1890s, it was decided that larger premises were needed.

By 1898, under the

The 'Seanscoil' opened by the Loreto Order in 1854 now houses the Adoration Chapel. The original datestone can still be seen in the gable

Letterkenny - Where the Winding Swilly Flows

guidance of Father William Sheridan, the Loreto sisters built a new school ne[xt] to the as yet unfinished Cathedral and Parochial House, calling it St. Columba[′s] Convent National School. This building catered for the national school educatio[n] for the Catholic girls of Letterkenny (and boys up until first class) for half [a] century until enrollment numbers had increased to such an extent that yet aga[in] another new building was required. Scoil Mhuire gan Smál was completed acro[ss] the road at Sentry Hill by 1956 with **Sr. Angelica Mulcahy** serving as the fir[st] Principal of this new school.

The Presentation Brothers' Boys' School

Just as Bishop McGettig[an] had invited the Loreto Siste[rs] to the town for the setting u[p] of a school for girls in 185[4,] Bishop Patrick O'Donne[ll] invited the Presentatio[n] Brothers to Letterkenny t[o] formally set up a prima[ry] school for Catholic boys fif[ty] years later. In August 189[6,] **Brother Aloysius Rahil[ly]** and **Brother Domini[c]**

St. Columba's Convent National School which was opened in 1898

Murphy arrived in the town from Cork to set up this new school, the forme[r] becoming the first Principal. Originally housed in the Seanscoil (as the girls we[re] by now in the Literary Institute on the Main Street), on 30th November 1896, th[e] new St. Eunan's Monastery School for boys was formally opened on the rock[y] ground directly opposite the construction site of the Cathedral and above Trini[ty] Hall (today it houses the Pastoral Centre). In this school, there was a large roo[m] in the middle with a fireplace at each end with two smaller end rooms. There we[re] originally 70 pupils on the registry but, as the numbers began to increase, **Broth[er] Columba Bateman** and **Brother Gilbert Leahy** arrived to assist. Interesting[ly,] according to the 1901 Census, the address for the school was given as 26 Churc[h] Street, indicating that the Church Lane was once much longer, stretching up t[o] the current location of the Pastoral Centre.

A Monastery was opened next to the school in June 1911 and for a tim[e] Trinity Hall was used for the overspill of pupil numbers and Wolfe Tone Ha[ll] (a small hall behind Hegarty's Hotel at the Market Square) was also used but b[y] the early 1950s, a decision was made that as the girls were moving into the new[ly] erected Scoil Mhuire gan Smál building, their former premises next door to th[e] Parochial House would be used to cater for the boys.

The building underwent major renovations and an extension was added t[o] the Sentry Hill end to accommodate the arrival of the 250 boys now enrolled. [It] was renamed Scoil Cholmcille and was opened in February 1959 with the origin[al] school building later becoming the headquarters of a boys' club. It was also use[d]

Chapter Twelve: Educational Establishments in Letterkenny

to cater for the overspill of students from the Technical School. By 1973, there were 373 boys on the roll with five Brothers and nine lay teachers on the staff. In 1974, work began on a new building on the Convent Road and the school took in all the infant boys who had previously attended the Loreto School up until first class. Four classes were accommodated in the old school, eight in the new school and one in the Cathedral conference room. In May 1976, extension work began on the new building and by September 1977, it was finally possible to house all sixteen classes under one roof. By 1981 the number on the school roll was almost 700 boys.

The presentation Brothers School and Monastery. Courtesy of Brother Donatus Brazil

However, by the early 1980s, there was a significant reduction in vocations for the Presentation Brothers and Brother Eunan Page, Provincial Superior, visited the town in February 1983 to discuss this crisis with **Bishop Seamus Hegarty**. In April 1983, it was left to Principal **Brother Raphael O'Halloran** to inform the 22 members of staff of the decision of the Presentation Brothers to leave Letterkenny and **Mr. Tom Redden** became the first lay principal of the school. The 'Old School' continued to be used by both Scoil Cholmcille and Scoil Mhuire gan Smál to cater for the overspill of classes but by 2012, due to a gradual drop in numbers and an extension to the girls' school, the building ceased to be used.[14] The current principals of both Scoil Mhuire gan Smál and Scoil Cholmcille are **Ms. Irene Simmons** and **Mr. Padraig Cannon** respectively.

Woodlands, Lurgybrack and Illistrin National Schools

One of the oldest surviving schools in the Letterkenny area is Woodlands National School. The first schoolhouse was built in 1861 on a site that was leased from William Wray of Oak Park. It consisted of one large room with 18 pupils (12 boys, 6 girls) attending. **Mr. Edward Lynch** was principal with **Mr. Bernard Callaghan** succeeding him in 1878. The school moved to new premises in Rough Park in October 1952 but they retained the name of Woodlands School and in 1994, due to increased numbers, a new building was erected near to the former school.[15] **Mrs. Gabrielle Fitzsimmons** succeeded **Mr. Kevin Caulfield** as principal in 2014.

In 1880, two small schoolhouses were recorded for the Illistrin area, 'No. 1 School' catered for the Protestant community and 'No. 2 School' catered for Catholic children. No. 1 school was built on the site of a former schoolhouse that can be seen on Ordnance Survey maps of 1841 while No. 2 school was located on the main road to Letterkenny next to a forge, approximately where the

Letterkenny - Where the Winding Swilly Flows

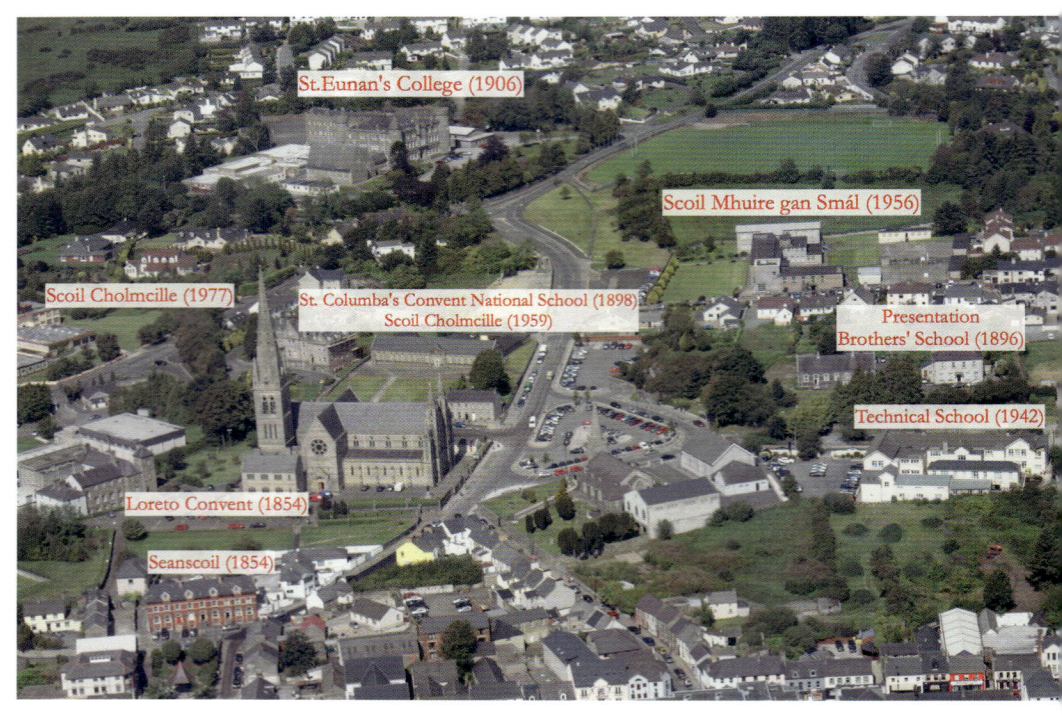

The location of the various schools in close vicinity to each other

petrol station is today. After much needed renovations in both buildings, No. school was re-opened in January 1929 and No. 2 school was re-opened two yea later. Following the closure of No. 1 School in 1952, a new school was built th catered for all of the children of the Illistrin area until 1988 when, under Princip **Charlie McGinley**, a new building was erected next to the former site. A furthe extension was completed in 2002 under the principalship of **Mr. Tom Feene** and the school currently has 477 children attending with **Mr. Luke Kilcoyne** principal from 2014.

Lurgybrack School was built in 1927 amalgamating the surroundin schools of Corravaddy, Drumlodge and Knockbrack and was officially opene on the 21st April 1928 with 85 children on the roll. Due to increasing number an extension was built in 1982 when **Maurice Sweeney** was principal. With th continual development of Letterkenny and the erection of houses on the outskir of the town, numbers attending the school continued to grow throughout th 1980s and 1990s with many prefabs being used to cater for the growth. A extension commenced in January 2012 and the school currently has 24 teache including the principal, **Anne Foxe**, with 452 children enrolled.

Modern Primary Schools

St. Bernadette's Special School was originally established as two classe within Scoil Mhuire gan Smál in 1969 before formally gaining recognition as separate school in 1978. Initially accommodated in the former boy's school of th Presentation Brothers, under principal **Norah Flynn** a new building was erecte

Chapter Twelve: Educational Establishments in Letterkenny

n the Glencar Road in 1981 and continues to educate boys and girls up to 18 years of age with mild general learning disabilities under the present principal **Mrs. Elaine Bonner**.

Little Angels School opened in a three bedroomed semi-detached house in the Ballyraine Estate in 1980 with two teachers and catered for up to 40 pupils. In 1989, Minister for Education Mary O'Rourke opened the current building in Knocknamona and today, under principal **Angela Keane**, the school caters for pupils with moderate, severe and profound learning difficulties and pupils with Autism ranging in age from 3-18 years with 74 children with special needs currently on the roll.

The most recent addition to primary education in Letterkenny is Educate Together, opened in Ballyraine in 2006 with a multi denominational ethos in the education of its pupils and **Máire Lynam** as principal, who was succeeded by **Line Fabisiak** in 2014.

The Loreto Convent, opened in 1854 in the former home of Bishop McGettigan. Image courtesy of the National Library of Ireland

Secondary Schools – the Loreto Convent

In secondary education, we have already seen that the Loreto Sisters opened a Convent School for girls in the middle of the nineteenth century. After the poor enrollment in the first week, numbers soon began to climb steadily. In fact, by 1861 a new building at a cost of £3,000 was built next to Bishop McGettigan's former residence. **Sister Josephine Gallagher**, daughter of local merchant John Gallagher 'of the Store', succeeded Mother Conception Lopez as Mother Superior of the Convent while **Mother Xaveria Kelly**, a sister of Charles Kelly, merchant of Ramelton and later Letterkenny, became Mother Superior in 1874. Further extensions to the school took place in 1922, 1938, 1971, 1980, 1986 and 2004 and by 2014, there were just under 1000 students on the roll with **Mrs. Susan Kenny** as Principal.

Dr. Crerand's High School 1849

Typically, for many years a boy's education would end at primary level, as they would then go out and find local employment or learn a trade. However, for those that had the means to attend secondary school, a new High School opened in 1849 with the permission of Bishop McGettigan, located on the site of the current County Library. **Dr. Crerand**, originally from Illistrin, had practiced as a physician for twenty years in Paris as well as being a tutor to the son of King Louis Philippe in France. Due to the increase of revolutionary activity in the city in 1848 however, he decided to return to his hometown and opened this new school.

151

Letterkenny - Where the Winding Swilly Flows

George Sigerson (1836-1925) who attended Dr. Crerand's School on the Main Street. Image courtesy of National Library of Ireland.

One of his most illustrious students was **George Sigerson** from Straban in County Tyrone who attended the High School for one year in 1850. Sigerson later became a renowned poet, scientist, writer and politician, noted as a leading member in the Irish Literary Revival in the late 19th Century. He is perhaps best remembered as the donor of the GAA Sigerson Cup contested annually by Third Level colleges in Ireland. Sigerson donated his salary from his post at UCD in 1911 for the purchase of the trophy.

Due to alleged sectarian trouble in the area, his parents decided to remove him from the Letterkenny High School in 1851 and send him to Paris to continue his education. Dr Crerand often spoke to his pupils about the beauty and wonders of the French capital and his profound influence remained with Sigerson for many years as he often spoke fondly of his old teacher and his time in Letterkenny. When his brothers John and James fell ill, George even wrote to his father stating: *"I hope Dr. Crerand has been to see them for he is a better doctor than those in Strabane"*.[16]

The former Literary Institute on the Main Street opened in 1876. The County Library presently stands on its site. From Christmas Annual 1993

Following the death of Dr. Crerand sometime around 1855, the school and several small plots of land were bequeathed to the Bishop of Raphoe and the school continued for two years with **Mr. Francis Martin** of Bomany as teacher.

Having had great success with a school in Stranorlar, **Mr. Hugh Heron** from Glenfin was brought to Letterkenny as headmaster to achieve similar results. As the school by now was being run by the Diocese it began preparing many young men for their further studies in Maynooth to become priests and so came to be known as the Diocesan Seminary.

Following Mr Heron's death in 1860 **Dr. McFadden** from Kilmacrennan continued as headmaster but left soon after. **Francis Gallagher** from Glencolmcille was

152

appointed headmaster in 1871 who was *"hard-working, sympathetic and unostentatious, he was an excellent teacher, whose reputation rests on solid and conspicuous results."*[17]

The Literary Institute 1876

With the blessing of Bishop James McDevitt, **Fr. F.B. Gallagher** from Portnoo opened the Literary Institute adjoining the Seminary in 1876. It comprised of

"a grand hall in the second storey, with a stage or dais, and chairs for 250 persons. A spacious school room and a well-furnished reading room occupied the first storey, and on the ground storey were a caretaker's apartments, and a recreation hall."[18]

The Lord Chancellor of Ireland, Thomas O'Hagan gave an address at the opening of the Literary Institute in 1876 and it was to be his introduction of the Intermediate Education Bill to the House of Lords in 1878 that led to a radical redefinition of Secondary schooling in Ireland. The resultant Intermediate Act (Ireland) 1878 allowed the payment of public money to schools that was dependent on their success in examinations with an Intermediate Education Board established to conduct the examinations and disburse the funds.

With the passing of this Act and the death of Francis Gallagher, the Diocesan Seminary became an Intermediate School under **Fr. Edward Maguire** in 1879. In his book, "Letterkenny: Past and Present", Maguire himself informs us of the conditions in this new school:

"The premises were very unsuitable both structurally and on the score of light and ventilation, not to speak of the total absence of equipment or even grounds for recreational purposes."[19]

At this time there were 47 boys in attendance with only one teacher and so **Rev. James Scanlon** was appointed to assist, being succeeded by **Mr. Mark Molloy** from Galway. In 1888, fees for the school were £5 a year while a subsidy from the Intermediate Act was £110 10s each year. The school day was long with students attending morning classes from 9.45am until 3.00pm and returning for evening classes from 5.30pm until 9.00pm while students were only allowed to board in houses specifically approved by the Bishop. The students learned English, Latin, Greek, French, Irish, Mathematics and a Science and Art course.

Following Dr. Maguire's appointment as Professor of Rhetoric in Maynooth in 1883, Rev. Patrick McCafferty became President of the school.

Rev. Edward Maguire, first President of St. Eunan's College and local historian of Letterkenny and the Diocese of Raphoe. Image courtesy of National Library of Ireland.

Father P.J. Brennan succeeded him in 1888, followed by **Rev. J.J. O'Doherty** and then **Rev. Hugh A Gallagher**, the last President of the 'Old Seminary'.

St. Eunan's College

By the end of the nineteenth century, this building was in much need of repair. One former pupil of the 'Old Seminary', Bishop O'Donnell, turned his attention towards this need following the completion of the Cathedral in 1901 with the aim to complete:

"the erection of an institution, at once reminiscent in its architecture of the most famous Irish ecclesiastical edifices of bygone days, and inferior to no existing college, either in interior equipment, or in the outdoor appurtenances of an up-to-date teaching establishment"[20]

Purchasing a site from **Mr. Andrew McDaid**, the foundation stone for the new school was laid on 23rd September 1904, symbolically marking the Feast of St. Eunan. Thomas Francis McNamara, the architect who had taken over the building of the Cathedral from William Hague in 1899, designed the new school. The cost for its construction was £22,000 and it was built with great speed and efficiency, being opened a mere fourteen months after the laying of the foundation stone.

The Derry Journal described the school at the time:

"The new College itself, with its courses in religion and Gaelic, its classical and scientific departments, will supply a want that has long been felt in this diocese. Whether our young men aspire to the clerical order or to lay pursuits St. Eunan's should be to them a safe and happy home in the opening years of life."[21]

St. Eunan's College was formally opened on July 6th 1906 as part of the Aonach an Dún, a fund-raising fair similar to the Aonach Tír Chonaill that had raised money for the Cathedral eight years previously. Stone from the immediate area surrounding the college had been excavated for use in the construction and not all of it had been cleared by the time of its opening.[22] 72 students were enrolled for the September 1st opening of the school.

The former principal of the Old Seminary, **Fr. Edward Maguire**, returned to the town to become the College's first President while staff at the time included **Fr. Patrick O'Doherty, Fr. Michael Ward, Fr. Patrick D. McCaul, Mr. John Magner, Mr. James P. Craig** and **Mr. Denis Murray**. In 1910 Dr. Maguire left Letterkenny to become Parish Priest to Fanad and Fr. Michael Ward succeeded him as President. The first lay principal of the school, **Mr. Chris Darby**, was appointed in 2010 following the retirement of **Fr. Michael Carney**.

Technical School

The passing of the 1891 Land Act helped set up the Congested Districts Board, a body which aimed to improve conditions through education and training to help small communities survive. Bishop O'Donnell was the longest serving

Chapter Twelve: Educational Establishments in Letterkenny

member of the Congested Districts Board in his aim to help ease the plight of rural communities. To escape the problems of poverty in rural life at the time, proper training and education would be needed. In 1899, the Agricultural and Technical Instruction (Ireland) Act was passed which came into operation on 1 April 1900. This new department set about organising schemes in manual instruction, rural industries and domestic science in rural areas through the use of Technical Committees. The first meeting of the Donegal Committee took place on 27th November 1900 and Bishop O'Donnell was appointed Permanent Chairman, being reappointed every year until 1923.

In 1905, this County Donegal Agricultural and Technical Committee was split in two, with an Agricultural Committee focusing on the agricultural needs of the community and the Joint Technical Instruction Committee provided for education. For the latter, trained teachers travelled around the county to various rural areas providing classes and instructing on various technical subjects. By October 1914, though, permanent facilities were provided for these itinerant instructors as the first Technical Schools in the county opened in Ballyshannon and Letterkenny. The first principal who shared his responsibilities between the two schools was **Mr. James O'Neill** and suitable premises for the new school in Letterkenny were located on the Main Street, near to the Literary Institute:

"The Secretary also reported that he had visited Letterkenny with Mr. O'Neill and inspected the only two houses which were in any way suitable for school purposes viz. a vacant house in Southwell Terrace and a vacant house in the Main St. known as Henderson's premises. This latter was much the more suitable and could be had at a rent of 20 per annum"[23]

This school was located in a building opposite where the Voodoo Nightclub is today. When it opened, 174 students enrolled in the new school and instruction was provided in subjects such as domestic science, Irish, metal workshop, technical instructions and engineering. Day classes began at 4.30pm while Night classes began at 7.30pm.

In 1930, through the implementation of the Vocational Education Act, the Joint Technical Instruction Committee became the Vocational Education Committee (VEC) and the school in Ballyshannon was used as its headquarters. By the end of that decade, an inspection of the Letterkenny Technical School by the County Medical Officer of Health left the committee in no doubt that they urgently needed a new school. The current premises were:

The former Technical School on the Main Street. Courtesy of Donegal County Archives

Letterkenny - Where the Winding Swilly Flows

"very unsuited to a large town like Letterkenny. The building appears to be pretty old, and the classrooms are not adequate for the number of scholars in attendance. In addition, there is no ground available at the rear. As a result, there is no yard or play-ground accommodation where students could congregate at lunch-hour and other free periods. I am of opinion that a new Technical School is required, owing to the unsuitability of the present premises, which were evidently not built for the purpose they now serve." [24]

The former Technical School at Ard O'Donnell built in 1942

To cater for the building of this new school, the Urban Council donated a site of just over 1 acre adjacent to Trinity Hall in August 1940. This site was known locally as Ewing's Field and work commenced immediately on the building of the new school, completed within two years. **Mr. Joseph McVeigh**, principal since 1937, oversaw the transfer of the Technical School into their new premises in 1942. It was originally a four roomed building that taught General Subjects, Science, Woodwork and Home Economics and later, Engineering, Shorthand and Typewriting. The VEC moved into the building in 1949 from their previous county headquarters in Ballyshannon.

Mr. McVeigh remained principal until 1955 when **Mr. Patrick McGeehan** succeeded him. In 1963 an extension was added with nine more classrooms available and the curriculum was extended to include Arts & Crafts, History and Geography. A new gymnasium was built in 1974 but with continued increases in enrollment, the old building was deemed insufficient and so a new site was purchased at Windy Hall for £35,000 and the school moved premises in 1987. The VEC remained in the building, which still acts as their headquarters in the county, while the Letterkenny Vocational School was renamed Errigal College in 2007.

Gaelscoils

In his inspection of schools in Donegal in 1855, Mr. Keenan reported on the impact that the new National School system was having on the knowledge of the Irish language in schools throughout the county in the years following the Great Famine:

"23.3 per cent of the population spoke Irish in the year 1851. The National System is every year diminishing this number…the language of the National Schools, the books, the teaching, etc. are entirely English…In this way the Irish language will gradually fall into disuse,

Chapter Twelve: Educational Establishments in Letterkenny

and be, perhaps, entirely forgotten...During my inspection last year, I was frequently engaged in the examination of classes of children who exhibited neither intelligence nor smartness, nor even ordinary animation whilst being questioned in English; but when the questions were given or the answers required in Irish, at once their eyes flashed with energy, their voices became loud and musical, and their intellectual faculties appeared to ripen up and to delight in being exercised."[25]

As children were being taught in the primary school system through the medium of English, gradually the decline of the Irish language in the non-Gaeltacht areas of the county, such as Letterkenny, became more pronounced. English was the language of commerce, especially in the growing market town and gradually the native language was dying out. However, the Gaelic Revival of the late nineteenth and early twentieth centuries sought to address this decline with bodies such as the Gaelic League and Gaelic Athletic Association (GAA) being set up. Again, Bishop O'Donnell was to the fore of this revival locally, promoting the Aonach and Féis Tir Chonaill, annual events that continued in various venues throughout the county until the 1950s as well as through the publication of An Crann, the journal of the Crann Eithne movement. In the Loreto Convent also, all subjects in the school had been taught through Irish up until 1976.

By the 1990s, a new school was established on the grounds of the VEC at Ard O'Donnell, which would teach all of its subjects (except English) through the Irish language. In September 1991, Gaelscoil Adhamhnáin was opened to 26 pupils with **Bernadette Ní Aingléis** as the principal. With increased numbers each year, more teachers were required and the classes moved to various premises, such as the former Monastery School of the Presentation Brothers, the VEC building and Trinity Hall, until a new school was opened at Glencar in September 2000. Today the school has 416 pupils with a staff of 19 teachers and **Máire Nic Ghairbhe** as Principal since 1994.

In 2000, a post-primary Gaeilge school was also opened in the town to primarily cater for those children who were graduating from Gaelscoil Adhamhnáin, while also receiving students from other primary schools who wished to be educated through the Irish language. Coláiste Ailigh was opened

The new building of Coláiste Ailigh opened in 2013

157

in the former residential premises of Pat and Sally Dunnion on the High Road with an enrollment of 25 pupils and **Micheál Ó Giobúin** as Principal. Again though, due to increased numbers enrolling each year, overcrowding of students became an issue and a site for the building of a new school was purchased in Knocknamona, receiving students in November 2013.

Education and Letterkenny

Were it not for the education received when they were children, many of the personalities that we associate with the development of Letterkenny today perhaps would not have come to the fore. The influence that various teachers and principals had on their formative years would leave a lasting effect and played a major role on their intellectual and moral growth. For example, Lieut. Col. James McMonagle who was the O/C of the Letterkenny Company of the IRA in the early 1920s stated:

"I was born in Letterkenny, Co. Donegal on the 16th May, 1898. I attended school at the local monastery staffed by the Presentation Order of teachers…Practically every day one or other of them would point to the map of the world, across the face of which was printed in large letters, "British possessions coloured red", and drew our attention to the fact that Ireland was included in that colour and pointed out to us our duty to have this rectified when the opportunity arose." [26]

Were it not for the influence of his teachers at the Presentation Brothers School, would Mr. McMonagle have later played such an active part during the War of Independence? We shall never know, but there is no doubt that the impression left by teachers – either by the cane, or by a smile – on shaping the minds of the future men and women that these children would grow up to be, had a natural knock on effect for the town. Without this education in these schools of Letterkenny, perhaps these children would not have grown up to eventually open their own successful businesses and the town today would quite conceivably be a different place. To all of these primary and secondary teachers then, in all of the schools of the local area throughout the years, this town owes a sincere debt of gratitude.

Chapter Twelve: Educational Establishments in Letterkenny

Endnotes
1. Archivium Hibernicum or Irish Historical Records Volume I, St. Patrick's College Maynooth, 1912, p20
2. Maguire, Canon Edward, "Letterkenny Past and Present", 1917, p11/12
3. Maguire, Canon, "A History of the Diocese of Raphoe", Vol. I, p346
4. Ibid p347
5. Ibid p348
6. Day, Angelique and McWilliams, Patrick, "Ordnance Survey Memoirs Of Ireland, Vol 39: County Donegal I, 1835-36" Institute of Irish Studies, 1997 p119
7. Ibid p119
8. Derry Journal 18/06/09
9. Sterritt, Marina, "Changed Times: Ballyraine National School, The Background and its History 1976-2007)", 2007
10. McGill, P.J., "Donegal Schools a Century Ago", Donegal Annual 1956, p102
11. Maguire, Canon "Letterkenny Past and Present", 1917 p71
12. Carroll, Anne (ed),"Loreto Letterkenny 150: Loreto Convent Letterkenny 1854-2004", 2004, p6
13. Derry Journal 13/9/1854
14. O'Connor, John J., "The Presentation Brothers in Letterkenny", Presentation Studies 11, June 2001
15. Gallagher, Adrian, "A Short Walk, A Long Journey – Woodland National School 1860-1994", Donegal Printing & Stationery, 1994
16. McGilloway, Ken, "George Sigerson Poet, Patriot, Scientist and Scholar", Stair Uladh, 2011, p9
17. Maguire, Canon, "A History of the Diocese of Raphoe", Vol. I, p350
18. Maguire, Canon "Letterkenny Past and Present", 1917 p72
19. Ibid p23
20. Ibid p86
21. Derry Journal 6/7/1906
22. Derry Journal 6/7/1906
23. Buchanan, Sandra (ed), "County Donegal Vocational Educational Committee 1905, 2005", County Donegal Vocational Educational Committee, 2005, p34
24. Ibid p59
25. McGill, P.J., "Donegal Schools a Century Ago", Donegal Annual 1956, p108/9
26. McMonagle, Col. James, "National activities, Letterkenny, Co. Donegal, 1917-1921", Statement by Witness, courtesy Bureau of Military History, Document Number 1385

Chapter Thirteen:
World War 1 & Letterkenny

I wish that I were back again in the glens of Donegal,
They'd call me a coward if I return but a hero if I fall! [1]

These are the words of Donegal poet and writer, Patrick McGill when he was serving with the London Irish Rifles during World War 1. McGill was born in Glenties and he was one of the 8,000 Donegal men who fought in this terrible conflict. Many men from Letterkenny answered the call to arms also, including those that were living overseas when the war broke out. However, for many years there has been a confusion over the reasons for Irishmen enlisting in the British Army for this war. The most common answer was that they were simply serving for the 'British shilling' as they needed the money, but the reasons were of course much more complex than that.

Against the backdrop of the war in Europe, this period was also a defining moment in the history of the modern Irish State. When those who had enlisted in 1914 returned to their homes and families in 1918, they found that the perception of Irish nationality had been 'changed utterly' by the events of Easter 1916. The rising republicanism in the country and the actions of the British army in Ireland during the War of Independence created an antipathy towards the combatants in the years following their return home. As a result, they were, by and large shunned and castigated by their fellow Irishmen for daring to serve in the army of 'the enemy'. Sadly, this treatment occurred in Letterkenny also, just as it did in towns and cities throughout the country.

200,000 men from Ireland fought in World War 1 (plus 300,000 Irish immigrants or people with Irish parents). Of these numbers who enlisted somewhere between 35,000 and 50,000 Irishmen never returned home, including 1,200 from Donegal and approximately 91 from the Letterkenny area.

From Letterkenny, the youngest man to die was aged just 17 (**Albert Mills Knipe** from the Main Street) while the oldest was 40 (**Jeramiah McDaid** from Crieve). Eight men from the town died in the Battle of the Somme between July and November 1916, four of them on the very first day of the battle. From what we know, fifty Letterkenny men are buried in France, twenty-one in Belgium and eight in Turkey. Many from the same family enlisted and lost their lives also such as **David** and

The Doherty brothers from Sentry Hill with their mother, Elizabeth. Courtesy of Johnny Keys

Chapter Thirteen: World War 1 & Letterkenny

bert Dobson from Ballymacool, Charles and Paddy Doherty from Asylum
ad, Hugh and John McKelvey, Charles and John Stewart of Rockhill House
d Daniel, James and John Doherty from Sentry Hill.[2]

Three of the four Doherty brothers of Sentry Hill died during the war;
illiam Doherty was the only son to survive. A newspaper report informs us
these four sons of Elizabeth Doherty and how she received a letter from the
ng as a result of their enlistment:

*His Majesty the King has heard with much interest of the loyalty of Mrs. Maurice Doherty
poor widow residing at Sentry Hill, Letterkenny, who has given four sons to the army. Her
ungest son who is under the age limit for enlisting is being trained in the Letterkenny company
the U.V.F and hopes to serve his King and country as a soldier. Mrs. Doherty's two
ughters are married to soldiers, one of whom is now at the front. The King's congratulations
re expressed in the following letter:*

*Madam I have the honour to inform you that the King has heard with much interest
at you have at the present moment four sons in the army. I am commanded to express to
u the King's congratulations and assure you that his Majesty much appreciates the spirit of
triotism which prompted this example in one family of loyalty and patriotism to their sovereign
d empire"*[3]

easons for enlisting

However, the question remains for many
ationalists in the town today, why would these
en from Letterkenny and its hinterland serve
a British army? Firstly, a significant fact often
rgotten is that service in the British Army had
en an element of Irish life for centuries prior
World War 1. For example, Irish troops had
ught for opposing English kings at the Battle
the Boyne while Irish rebels fought Irish
giments in the 1798 Rising. Approximately 30%
Wellington's army against Napoleon were Irish
hile by 1860, this number had risen to 60%.[4]

Serving in the army gave a lot of
nemployed men an opportunity to work and of
urse earn a wage and have job security. Poverty
as rife in rural areas at the dawn of the twentieth
ntury and the need to feed a hungry family far
tweighed any sense of moral duty of nationality. For others, they were enticed
the prospect of living in an exotic land and were inspired by the propaganda and
les of adventure and excitement that came with serving in the army. For some,
ere was the family tradition of being a soldier, their fathers and grandfathers
ving served with distinction in previous conflicts and who were held with great
spect within the family since. Others saw enlisting as an opportunity to escape
e clutches of the law by 'hiding out' in the army. For example, a dentist by the

James Doherty of Sentry Hill. Courtesy of Johnny Keys

161

Letterkenny - Where the Winding Swilly Flows

name of **William H. Boland** who had a practice in the town shot and killed love rival on the Port Road and rather than face five year's penal servitude, volunteered for service in the army.[5] Of course, some simply believed that t conflict would 'not last beyond Christmas' and a few months adventure would interesting.

The plight of Catholic Belgium was arguably the major reason for ma Catholic Irishmen to heed the words of their public representatives and sign for war. John Redmond, leader of the Irish Party said in 1916:

Below and next page: Propaganda posters such as these were used to entice Irishmen to enlist in the army. Images courtesy of the National Library of Ireland

"*What has Ireland suffered in the past which Poland, Alsace, Belgium and Ser have not suffered at the hands of Germany?...What has been the record of Germany but suppression of nationality, of freedom, and of language – in short, the suppression of all things for which for centuries Ireland has struggled, the victory of which Ireland has achiev Take the case of Belgium. Has there not been there the same ruthless shedding of the blood priests and people that is part of Ireland's own history?*"[6]

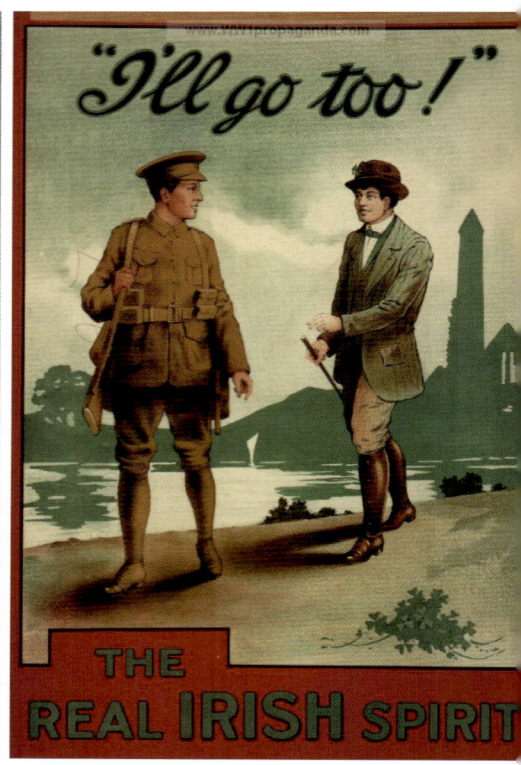

This attitude of a moral duty to assist the plight of a fellow Cathol dominated country was shared by many priests and bishops, including Cardin Logue, former Bishop of Raphoe. At a public meeting of the Nationalists of Letterkenny district in the Market Square on Sunday September 27th 1914, **Fath John McCafferty**, Administrator in the Cathedral and noted Nationalist, told t large assembled crowd:

162

Chapter Thirteen: World War 1 & Letterkenny

"Not many days ago they (Irish Nationalists) were called upon to give practical proof their sympathy with the suffering victims of the present war in one small nation of Europe, d well they responded to the call...German armies of destruction are let loose on Belgium. er churches and her homes, her libraries and Universities are destroyed, and Belgian soil is enched with the blood of her people. If justice is to prevail, the wrongs of Belgium must be hted, and the sympathies of right-thinking men will be with her, as I am glad to think your mpathies are with her in her hour of trial and distress. (Cheers.)..."

In his speech at the same meeting, **Rev. James C. Cannon** stated:

"This war is as much Ireland's war as it is England's war. It is a war for human erty, for the rights of small nations against the domination of larger and more powerful ones. Cheers.) It is a battle for right against might. It is more, it is a struggle for our very existence a nation, a struggle to keep from our shores the brutal and unscrupulous Prussian vandals, ho in defiance of treaty rights, robbed and ruined and plundered gallant little Belgium, the ost prosperous nation in the world. In the present terrible war crisis, Ireland will do her part, guided by her leaders, and be faithful to a tradition of bravery that has never yet been sullied. Cheers.)"

163

Letterkenny - Where the Winding Swilly Flows

Mr. Edward Joseph Kelly, M.P. for East Donegal spoke next at the meeting:

"We in Donegal have already sent men to fight on the plains of France and to beat invader on his ground when the time comes. We are proud of those men who are gone and wish them a hearty God-speed and a safe return... The result of carrying out this policy will that by the end of the war there will be here in Ireland a seasoned, disciplined force, whose a and whose devotion will guarantee the smooth working of the new Irish Government (Cheers.)

Home Rule

This last point by the Nationalist politician Kelly leads us into anoth crucial reason why Letterkenny men signed up so readily. These speeches the Market Square were made several days after Home Rule had received Roy Assent in the British Parliament (which was suspended for the duration of t war) and they give a remarkable insight into the mindset of the Irish people this time. For over 100 years, from Daniel O'Connell to Charles Stewart Parne generations of Nationalists in Ireland had fought constitutionally to remove t Union between Britain and Ireland, and now in 1914 under John Redmond, th had at long last achieved it. The scenes of jubilation in Letterkenny at this histor occasion were described in the Derry Journal:

"Every Nationalist house in the town was illuminated, most of them with gre artistic taste. The green flag flew from many windows while vari-coloured bunting was gener On the Sentry hill, Market Square, and at street junctures large bonfires blazed, and around the town the hilltops and hillsides were lit up. At eight o'clock the Nationalist ba headed a procession of extraordinary proportions. There were 60 torchlight bearers, follow by 200 National Volunteers, under County Commander Carrigan, and with at least 2,0(Nationalists of town and district traversed the streets. At the Palace grounds loud cheers we given for Most Rev. Dr. O'Donnell, who delivered an address of burning eloquence. Returni to the Market Square the patriotic and popular administrator (Father McCafferty), in a f speech, congratulated all on the achievement of National Freedom. On the conclusion of Fat McCafferty's speech loud cheers were given again and again for the reverend gentleman, t Bishop, Messrs. Redmond, Dillon, Devlin, and the Irish Party."[8]

Now, after having finally received Home Rule, there was the perceptic that Ireland had to prove that it was worthy of it, especially in the face of t rising resistance from Carson and the Ulster Volunteer Force. The UVF had bee formed by Unionists to oppose, by force of arms, the introduction of Home Ru in 1913 and in response, the Nationalists of Ireland formed the Irish Nation Volunteers to protect the smooth implementation of Home Rule. By servir in Irish Regiments within the British Army, these Volunteers could receive t necessary training to become a disciplined force to protect the rights of t people in the 'new' Ireland. In other words, they saw themselves not as fightir FOR Britain but rather ALONGSIDE Britain as a new and independent natior

Chapter Thirteen: World War 1 & Letterkenny

Pre-1916 Attitudes

Several days after the outbreak of the war, the Derry Journal from Friday August 7th 1914, gives us an interesting pre-1916 perspective of the Irish Nationalists in Dublin, Castlebar and Ballinasloe as they bade farewell to their loved ones:

"Probably never in the history of Dublin were such scenes presented as those at the North Wall, when several hundred reservists left for Holyhead. Fully 50,000 people, drawn from all classes, thronged the quays. The vast majority were working class people whose husbands, fathers or brothers were leaving for the front…During the waiting hours the crowd sang national songs, and a band played "A Nation Once Again." As the steamer moved down the Liffey, the cheers were deafening. Hats and handkerchiefs were waved and many women, and even men wept…In Castlebar the departures of close on 100 men was made the occasion of a remarkable display. They were escorted to the railway station by close on 2,000 people headed by the local Volunteers' band. The Ballinasloe reservists were escorted to the station by the local corps of the National Volunteers, headed by a fife and drum band. As the train steamed out they were loudly cheered." [9]

This image of over 50,000 Dubliners thronging the quays and cheering the departure of troops for the front contrasts sharply with our post independence image of the attitudes of the people of Ireland at this time. In the eyes of the people in 1914, these men were not going off to fight for Britain at all. These men were considered Irish, and the crowds singing '*A Nation Once Again*' at their departure viewed these men as a distinct Irish Regiment within the British army, a view no doubt shared by the Nationalist soldiers on the departing boat.

However, despite John Redmond's plea for Irish enlistment, out of a membership of over 150,000 Irish National Volunteers, only approximately 4,000 enlisted with 80% remaining to protect Ireland's interests at home. Worse for Redmond though was that a small number (approximately 10,000) of the National Volunteers did not agree with his policy of serving in a British army and split to form their own military force, the Irish Volunteers. This group of men would eventually form the nucleus of the participants in the Easter Rising and would in time bring down Redmond and his Irish Party in the elections of 1918.

Outbreak of War

The assassination of Archduke Franz Ferdinand of Austria in Serbia on the 28th June 1914 is cited as the spark that lit the fuse of World War 1, although it is generally accepted that the rapid growth in arms of both German and British Empires in the years building up to it made a conflict inevitable at some stage. As a result of the assassination, Austria declared war on Serbia on the 28th July and due to a complex set of pre-war alliance pacts, on the 1st August, Germany (Austria's ally) declared war on Russia (Serbia's ally) and two days later, the Germans implemented the long-mooted Schlieffen Plan to invade Paris by marching through Belgium and Luxembourg. Due to a pact from 1839 that

Letterkenny - Where the Winding Swilly Flows

guaranteed Britain would protect Belgium in the event of any invasion, Brita[in] declared war on Germany on 4th August 1914 and the 'war to end all wars' w[as] now in progress.

To the surprise of the advancing Germans, there was much Belgi[an] resistance to the attack on their country, both by the army and by civilians. [At] Aarschot, a single brigade of Belgian infantry held up the German advance f[or] several hours, but after suffering heavy losses and being attacked from three sid[es] they withdrew. In retribution for this defence of their country, a large number [of] wounded Belgian soldiers were marched to the banks of the River Demer, whe[re] they were shot, while those that attempted to escape were thrown in the river [to] drown. The Germans then turned on the citizens of the town with 400 hous[es] being plundered and set on fire while 150 innocent people were executed. This fu[ry] of the Germans on the Belgia[ns] continued unabated as over t[he] next few days the towns of Die[st], Schaffen, and Tremelo were al[l] razed while between 25th a[nd] 28th August, to the horror of t[he] rest of Europe, the historic o[ld] town of Louvain was set aflam[e]. Thousands of Belgians were le[ft] homeless by this destruction a[nd] their plight did not go unnotic[ed] by other countries in Europ[e]. Attitudes towards Germa[ny] internationally at these atrociti[es] were at an all-time low.

Memorial in Conwal Parish Church to the Stewart brothers of Rockhill who died within six weeks of each other

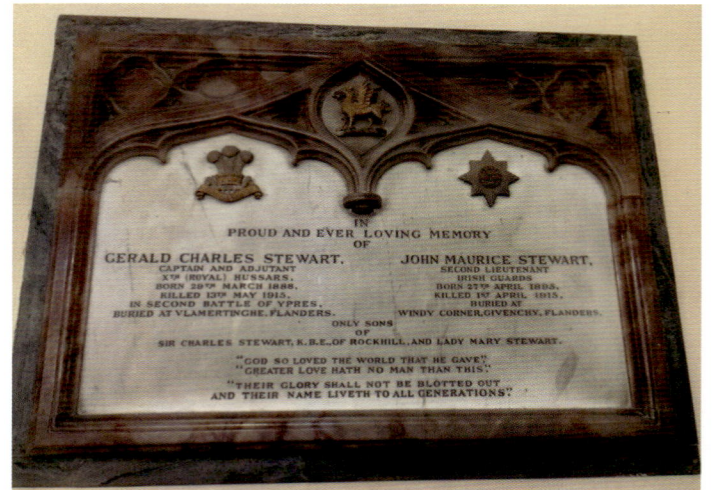

Belgian Refugees

In Letterkenny, a Belgian Refugee Committee was set up to assist t[he] refugees of this conflict with **Thomas McFadden** as chairman. On Tuesd[ay] 12th January 1915, ten Belgian families of 48 people arrived in the town a[nd] were received by Bishop O'Donnell, **Rev. Dr. Molloy, Fr. John O'Doherty** a[nd] members of the Relief Committee at the train station. Crowds of Letterken[ny] people met them also and the families were then taken to the Technical School [on] the Main Street where the committee had prepared a dinner for them. **Profess[or] Cooney** from St. Eunan's College acted as interpreter for the Belgians, who we[re] reported as deeply gratified by the reception. Following dinner, the families we[re] then taken to their accommodation in the new council houses that had bee[n] built at Ballymacool Terrace. The families that arrived in Letterkenny include[d] a government clerk, a railway official, a motor mechanic, a draper, a baker, a[nd] a chauffeur. The day after they arrived, groups of the refugees walked abo[ut] Letterkenny and were pleasantly greeted by the townspeople.[10]

166

Chapter Thirteen: World War 1 & Letterkenny

Various fundraising efforts to assist the refugees in the town took place such as a large Fancy Dress Ball in the Literary Institute in February 1915. The Derry Journal tells us:

*"In aid of the funds of the local Belgian Refugee Committee a highly successful fancy dress ball was held in the Literary Institute, Letterkenny…From the town and district the number present was very large. Scarcely a town or village in Donegal was unrepresented, and there were also visitors from Derry City and Strabane. Fully two hundred and fifty were in fancy dress, and great variety and originality were shown in the costumes. All wore masks until midnight, and attempts at recognition led to many humourous incidents…This was to a great extent due to careful preparations made by the committee, and in this respect a special meed of praise is due to the hon. Treasurer, **Mr. E.J. Butler** and the hon. Sec. **M.J. Clancy**, Messrs. Kyle Henderson (piano) and **James Kearns** (violin), musical artistes known all over the North West, gave entire satisfaction to the dancers, and **Mr. James Daly** acted capably and courteously as master of ceremonies…It may be mentioned that interested and pleased spectators of the night's entertainment and participators therein were a number of Belgian refugees resident in the town, who were present on the invitations of the committee."*[11]

Cornelia Adair of Glenveagh Castle had also allowed her residence to be used as a hostel for wounded Belgian soldiers since the end of 1914. The soldiers had the use of a nurse and masseuse while two Belgian priests catered for their religious needs.[12] The Belgian Gardens in the grounds of the castle today were developed in memory of their presence there. **Charlotte Agnes Boyd** of Ballymacool House also requested the use of a Belgian nun to teach the children of the refugee families so that they would not fall behind in their education.[13]

Hugh Bonar from Letterkenny with his ambulance in Belgium. Courtesy of Niall McGinley

Letterkenny Survivors of the War

Although 91 people died, following the war, many others from the Letterkenny district were able to return safely home following their harrowing experiences in the trenches, such as James Duffy, Charlie Collins, Eddie Greene, Peter Duffy and James Roarty while others came to live in the town following the war such as Tom McClintock and Fr. William MacNeely. These men and many

167

others did not wish to talk about their experiences and for many years afterward remained silent about what they had witnessed.

James Duffy from Letterkenny is one of only thirty-seven Irishmen who received the Victoria Cross (VC), the highest military decoration awarded for valour in the face of the enemy, during his service in World War 1. Duffy was born on 17th November 1889, the son of Peter Duffy from Bonagee and Kate Doogan of Gweedore. Like so many Irishmen at the time, he was working in a Glasgow shipyard when he joined the Iniskilling Fusiliers upon the outbreak of the war. On the 27th December 1917 at Kereina Peak in Palestine, despite heavy gunfire and bombing, Private Duffy ran out to the area under attack with another stretcher-bearer to rescue an injured comrade. When his partner was wounded by the gunfire, Private Duffy, under very heavy fire from the enemy, succeeded in getting both of the wounded men to safety and attended to their injuries. His bravery in the face of such an onslaught earned him the award of the Victoria Cross.

On his return to Letterkenny after the war, his gallant bravery on the battlefield largely went unnoticed by his fellow townspeople, a casualty of a change in attitudes following the events of 1916. He was treated with suspicion in the town and rarely mentioned his Victoria Cross when he was working at Ballyraine Port unloading coal boats. In 1964, he sold the medal to the Royal Iniskilling Museum for £ per week until his death but a replica can still be seen in the County Museum. James Duffy died on 7th April 1969 at the age of seventy-nine and he is buried in Conwal cemetery.[14]

Private James Duffy (1889-1969) Victoria Cross medal winner for bravery

Another Letterkenny man who survived the war was **Charlie Collins** from College Row. Affectionately known as 'Bovril', (due to a game of football against a team from Derry who had a goalkeeper with the nickname of 'Oxo', the Letterkenny captain replied, you may have an 'Oxo' but we have a 'Bovril'!) Charlie was born in 1893 and like James Duffy was working in Scotland when the war broke out. He enlisted in the 6th Battalion of the Inniskilling Fusiliers on September 8th and he was trained in Omagh and then Dublin. In July 1915, he was sent to the Dardanelles and later Suvla Bay before serving in the trenches of Lille and Amiens.

Following the war, he returned to Letterkenny and joined the Volunteers, being part of the new Irish army that took over the Letterkenny R.I.C. barracks in 1922. In 1941, like many Irishmen he joined up with the British army again to combat the threat of Adolf Hitler but this time was stationed in England, Scotland and Wales only.[15]

Chapter Thirteen: World War 1 & Letterkenny

Eddie Greene, born in Pluck in 1892, joined up at the Market Square on March 15th 1915 and served in the 16th Division of the Irish Brigade. He was trained at Omagh, Tipperary and Finner and then sent to the trenches of Flanders before being wounded at Massines. He returned to Letterkenny after the war and died on 11th December 1979.[16]

Peter Duffy from the Cullion Road was born in 1888 and joined the Irish Guards in Letterkenny in April 1915. After training in Kettering, he served on the Western Front at Belgium and France before returning home in 1919 when, like Charlie Collins, he joined the Volunteers.[17]

James Roarty was born in Letterkenny in 1896 and enlisted in the Royal Scots in January 1915. He was wounded in combat on 6th November 1917. He returned home after the war and died on 7th November 1973, being buried in Conwal graveyard.[18]

Tom McClintock was born in Derry but following the war, set up business in Letterkenny for many years. He served in the 1st Battalion Royal Irish Regiment and also the 173rd Brigade of the Royal Field Artillery becoming a Major in the process. In 1919, he moved to Letterkenny and set up his veterinary business in the town until his death in 1974.[19]

William MacNeely was born in 1888 in Donegal Town and educated at the High School in Letterkenny before continuing his studies in Rome from 1906. He was ordained to the priesthood in 1912 and was appointed to the teaching staff of St. Eunan's College shortly afterwards. Following a request from Cardinal Logue for Donegal priests to enlist as chaplains, Fr. McNeely volunteered in 1917, and saw action on the Western Front where he was injured in a gas attack. Following the war, he was curate in the Cathedral from 1918 until 1922 when he was sent to Finner camp to serve as chaplain to the newly formed Irish Army. Archbishop O'Donnell, now transferred to Armagh, ordained him as his successor as Bishop of Raphoe on 27th July 1923 where he served for

James Duffy's funeral passing solemnly down the Main Street in 1969. Courtesy of the Duffy family

Charlie 'Bovril' Collins (1893 - 1989). Courtesy of the Collins family

Major Tom McClintock. Courtesy of Niall McGinley

Dr. William McNeely (1888-1963) Bishop of Raphoe 1923-1963

forty years. He died on 11th December 1963 and is buried in the grounds of the Cathedral.

In Conwal Parish Church, there is a war memorial with the names of several parishioners who lost their lives engraved on a stained glass window with a poppy wreath before it. To the right of this is a special brass plate inscribed with the names of those Letterkenny men of the parishes of Conwal, Leck and Aughaninshin who gallantly served in battle and were fortunate enough to return home alive. Those names are:

- William Anderson
- William Birney
- William Bonar
- Thomas Bovaird
- Charles K. Boyd
- George Boyd
- John D. Boyd
- James A. Buchanan
- John D. Buchanan
- Matthew Carre
- Robert Clarke
- Thomas Clarke
- David Delap
- William Doherty
- John Elliot
- Robert Elliot
- Thomas Elliot
- George Field

- John R. Fleming
- Percy Fleming
- Samuel H. Fleming
- George Garstin
- John Garstin
- Richard Garstin
- J. F. Gerald Hanlon
- Robert Harper
- Samuel Harper
- Robert Harris
- Joseph Harron
- Robert Horraner
- Alfred I. Horobin
- Christopher Ingram
- James A. Johnston
- William Kennedy
- Hugh Laird
- George Lucas

Chapter Thirteen: World War 1 & Letterkenny

- Edward McAuley
- James McAuley
- Thomas McAuley
- Wm. John McIntyre
- Henry McKelvey
- Alexander Mitchell
- James Moore
- William Park
- John Patterson
- Matthew Patterson
- Charles Schoales
- John Schoales
- Henry Spratt
- Richard Spratt
- John White
- William J. White
- James Wilson
- William Wilson

Other Letterkenny men not listed on this plaque who served in the war and returned home include **Neilly Carberry**, **Charlie, Cornie and Barney Sweeney**, **John Hegarty**, **Robert McLoughlin**, **Arthur Kerr**, **Jimmy Drein**, **Joe Gallagher**, **Charlie "Bump" Coyle**, **John Hayes**, **Hugh Bonar**, **James Kerins**, **Charles Drein** and **Danny Murray**.[20]

Memorials

World War 1 ended on 11th November 1918 with the signing of the Armistice by Germany in an unconditional surrender and a victory for the Allies. But at what cost was this victory? Somewhere between 35,000 and 50,000 Irishmen lost their lives in the trenches of France, Belgium or Turkey, their memories now preserved in memorials at Flanders, the Somme, Tyne Cot and Ypres amongst others.

Towards the end of the twentieth century, a new attitude of reconciliation and acceptance permeated the Irish consciousness. At Messines in Belgium, a memorial site was dedicated to all of the soldiers of Ireland, regardless of political or religious beliefs, who died, were wounded or went missing in the war. Known as the Island of Ireland Peace Park, a Celtic Round Tower was built as a symbol of reconciliation by An All-Ireland Journey of Reconciliation Trust and was constructed using stones from a demolished workhouse in Mullingar, County Westmeath. As part of the design the sun lights up the inside of the tower each year on the 11th hour of the 11th day

The brass plaque in Conwal Parish Church which lists the men from the parish who returned home alive from the war

171

Letterkenny - Where the Winding Swilly Flows

The stained glass window memorial in Conwal Parish Church to those that died in the war

Chapter Thirteen: World War 1 & Letterkenny

of the 11th month, the time at which the Armistice was declared and the guns fell silent after four years of fighting. The Island of Ireland Peace Park was officially opened at 11am on 11th November 1998 by the then President of Ireland Mary McAleese in the presence of Queen Elizabeth II and King Albert II of Belgium and each year a commemorative Remembrance Day service is held at the Tower.

In Islandbridge in Dublin, the Irish National War Memorial Gardens was constructed in the 1920s to remember the Irishmen that died during World War I. Over time, it fell into disrepair and neglect and it wasn't until 1988 that the restored gardens were re-opened to the public. As a symbol of Ireland's new attitude to reconciliation, Mary McAleese and Queen Elizabeth II visited the gardens in 2011 on the Queen's historic visit to the country, laying a wreath in recognition of the brave men and women who lost their lives.

Post-1916 Attitudes

However, despite these renewed efforts at recognizing the thousands of Irishmen who served in the war of 1914-1918 (most notably in Donegal through the efforts of Niall McGinley, Paddy Harte and the County Donegal Book of Honour Committee), the attitudes of many Irish people towards those that served remains. In their eyes, these men served in the British Army, the army of the 'enemy', simple as that. Many Irish people share Sir Roger Casement's attitude that they were *not Irishmen but English soldiers*, their views and attitudes being molded and shaped by years of misunderstanding as to the motives of those that fought. From our post-1916 viewpoint, it is difficult to imagine the emotions that prevailed in the country in 1914. At long last Ireland had received Home Rule, an occasion that their fathers and grandfathers did not witness. It was a 'new Ireland'. Those that served would receive the necessary training and discipline that would be implemented in a new Irish army after a war that would no doubt 'be over by Christmas'. If Home Rule was to be successfully implemented following the war, the State would need an efficient army to combat the threat of Carson and the UVF and avoid a partition of the country. Serving in the war would also show that Ireland was an ally of Britain, not an enemy, and that we could be trusted in our new found situation.

Private Patrick Boyce from Main Street, killed 1st July 1918. From Christmas Annual 1999

173

Letterkenny - Where the Winding Swilly Flows

As John Redmond stated in 1916:

> "*Leave the question of principle out and consider the question only of the mere interest of Ireland herself. What did the situation demand? Neutrality? That was impossible. Hostility to the just cause of the Allies? Is there a sane man in Ireland who does not see this meant the drowning of the newly won liberties of Ireland in Irish blood. Be these views right or wrong this was the opinion of the overwhelming majority of the Irish people. It was the opinion which thousands of Irish soldiers have sealed with their blood by dying in the cause of the liberty of Ireland and of the world.*" [21]

Tellingly, those words of Redmond's were printed in the Derry Journal on May 3rd 1916, the very same day that Patrick Pearse was shot in Dublin. Over the days that followed, with each bullet that was fired in retribution by the British against the insurgents of the Easter Rising, the attitudes of the people of Ireland including Letterkenny, slowly changed - attitudes it must be said, that were shared by many of the Irishmen in the trenches. Many of those that returned to Ireland after the war wasted no time in joining the Volunteers, whose name was changed to the Irish Republican Army, and fought against the British army in the War of Independence. Many others did not join up, having seen enough bloodshed and battle on the war fields of Europe. Those who had served in the British Army were commonly branded traitors and 'not Irish' in the new zeal of nationalism and republicanism that came following the General Elections of 1918. However while the harrowing experiences that they went through on the battlefields of Europe might be difficult for us to comprehend, their names should never be forgotten.

Letterkenny men in the Royal Inniskilling Fusiliers, 1915. VC James Duffy from Bonagee is pictured sitting bottom left. Also in this picture are Denis Gallagher killed 2 Apr 1916, John Gallagher who survived the war and George Gibbons killed 6 Apr 1916. Courtesy of Jimmy Sweeney

Chapter Thirteen: World War 1 & Letterkenny

Letterkenny Men Who Died in World War 1

From the County Donegal Roll Book of Honour

NAME	BORN/LIVED	RANK	DIED	AGE
Anderson, Samuel	Newmills	Private	29 Mar 1918	22
Beattie, Robert James	Letterkenny	Gunner	16 July 1916	
Blistine, John	Conwall	Private	4 Aug 1915	
Bonar, James	Ballyboe	Private	5 Sept 1917	21
Boyce, Patrick	Letterkenny	Private	1 July 1918	
Boyle, Hugh	Letterkenny	Private	10 July 1917	
Boyle, John	Rareagh	Private	21 Mar 1918	29
Boyle, Robert (Bertie)	Letterkenny	Private	Sept 1916	23
Callan, George	Letterkenny	Private	24 May 1916	31
Cleary, Thomas	Cullion	Private	29 Sept 1918	33
Colhoun, John	Port Bridge	Bombardier	10 July 1917	
Collins, John	Letterkenny	Private	27 Nov 1917	
Curran, John	Newmills	Private	30 April 1915	
Deery, John	Bomany	Rifleman	9 May 1915	
Diver, Redmond Joseph	Asylum Rd, Letterkenny	Private	14 July 1916	19
Dobson, David	Ballymacool	Trooper	30 March 1918	25
Dobson, Robert James	Ballymacool	Private	8 May 1916	18
Dobson, Robert Thomas	Ballyconnelly	Private	9 May 1916	24
Doherty, Charles	Asylum Rd/ Oldtown	Private	19 May 1917	36
Doherty, Patrick	Asylum Rd/ Oldtown	Private	27 April 1916	38
Doherty, Daniel	Sentry Hill	Lance Corporal	1 July 1916	
Dougherty (Doherty), James	Sentry Hill	Corporal	16 Aug 1917	20
Doherty, John	Sentry Hill	Coy. Quartermaster Sergeant	22 Mar 1918	
Doherty, Michael	Church Street	Private	29 Apr 1916	34
Doohan, Edward	Letterkenny	Private	1 July 1916	
Drain, John	Ballymacool Tce	Private	21 Mar 1918	18
Elliot, Robert	Ballyboe	Private	27 Jan 1917	
Finn, J.	Port Road	Lance Sergeant	17 May 1918	38
Friel, William	Ballymacool Tce	Private	8 Oct 1918	

Letterkenny - Where the Winding Swilly Flows

NAME	BORN/LIVED	RANK	DIED	AGE
Gallagher, Denis	Cullion	Private	2 Apr 1916	32
Gallagher, Frank	Letterkenny	Private	27 Nov 1917	31
Gallagher, J.	Port Road	Corporal	29 Aug 1917	
Gibbons, George	Hollyhill Cullion	Private	6 Apr 1916	20
Gibbons, Neil	Letterkenny	Private	13 Oct 1916	24
Gregg, Richard	Killydesert	Gunner	12 Oct 1918	21
Hannigan, John	Main Street	Sapper	18 Dec 1915	
Harkin, Joseph	Letterkenny	Private	7 Aug 1915	
Hawkins, David	Letterkenny	Private	25 Apr 1915	29
Hegarty, John	Ballybocunagh	Private	3 Oct 1918	37
Hegarty, John	Drumany	Corporal	28 Feb 1917	
Hunter, William Mortimer	Barnhill	2nd Lieutenant	29 June 1917	26
Ingram, Charles Alper	Ballyraine	Private	26 Oct 1914	
Keenan, John Arthur	Letterkenny	Private	29 Oct 1914	34
Kelly. Patrick	Oldtown	Private	21 Aug 1916	28
Kennedy, Thomas	Letterkenny	Private	10 July 1916	
Knipe, Albert Mills	Main Street	Rifleman	20 Oct 1918	17
Lucas, Alexander	Conwall	Private	21 Oct 1918	19
Martin, Patrick	Asylum Rd	Private	15 Aug 1915	
Millar, James Lytton	Hillmount	2nd Lieutenant	28 July 1916	19
Moore, John	Letterleague	Private	19 Mar 1918	
Moore, Morgan Edward Jellett	Letterkenny	Lieutenant	24 Mar 1918	24
Moore, Samuel	Conwall	Private	3 Oct 1917	
Murray, John	Glenswilly	Sergeant	5/6 Jan 1916	36
Murray, Joseph	Coolboy	Private	16 Aug 1915	32
Mc Afee, Richard	Curraghalea	Private	31 Oct 1917	29
Mc Bride, John	Letterkenny	Sergeant	19 Sept 1915	37
Mc Bride, Thomas	Letterkenny	Private	31 July 1917	
Mc Cafferty, John	Letterkenny	Sergeant	29 Apr 1916	
Mc Cauley, James Edward	Rareagh	Rifleman	16 Oct 1918	40
Mc Clure, David	Letterkenny	Private	1 Oct 1918	26
Mc Clure, John	Letterkenny	2nd Lieutenant	29 June 1917	33
Mc Daid, Jeramiah	Creave	Private	7 June 1917	46

Chapter Thirteen: World War 1 & Letterkenny

NAME	BORN/LIVED	RANK	DIED	AGE
Mc Devitt, Patrick	Kilmacrennan Rd	Private	25 Sept 1916	23
Mc Gaughey, Patrick James	Letterkenny	Private	11 Apr 1917	26
Mc Grenra, James	Church St	Private	17 Nov 1918	32
Mc Kelvey, Hugh Alexander	Letterkenny	Sergeant	29 Sept 1918	22
Mc Kelvey, John	Letterkenny	Private	15 Oct 1918	19
Mc Laughlin, R.	Crieve	Private	3 Oct 1918	
Mc Laughlin, Samuel	Dromore	Private	12 Dec 1915	20
Mac Lennan, Allan Alexander	Leck View	Air Mechanic 2nd Class	30 Apr 1918	19
Mc Monagle, Francis	Letterleague	Private	1 Sept 1914	25
Moore, J.	Newmills	Private	13 Oct 1917	31
O'Donnell, Robert	Letterkenny	Private	5 Aug 1917	31
Porter, Robert	Letterkenny	Private	5 July 1916	22
Ramsey, James	Loughnagin	Private	22 May 1915	21
Robinson, James	Letterkenny	Private	20 Jan 1916	
Robinson, James Andrew	Letterkenny	Private	29 Mar 1918	23
Schoales, James	Letterkenny	Private	3 Nov 1918	34
Scott, James Tees	Killylastin	Private	1 July 1916	20
Scully, Patrick	Port Road	Private	13 Oct 1915/ 1 Aug 1916	
Speer, Albert Victor	Letterkenny	Sergeant	1 July 1916	19
Starritt, James	Killyclug	Private	6 Dec 1917	22
Starritt, Joseph	Letterkenny	Private		
Stephens, D. Bertie	Killyclug	Lance Corporal	6 Dec 1917/ 21 Aug 1918	25
Stewart, Gerald Charles	Rockhill	Captain & Adjutant	13 May 1915	28
Stewart, John Maurice	Rockhill	2nd Lieutenant	1 April 1915	19
Sweeney, A.	Letterkenny	Lance Sergeant	11 Sept 1917	23
Watkinson, Margaret Lita	Letterkenny	Motor Transport	31 Dec 1919	24
White, John	Letterkenny	Private	9 Aug 1916	23
Wray, John	Letterkenny	Private	7 June 1917	34
Wright, Alexander	Letterkenny	Private	21 Aug 1915	

Letterkenny - Where the Winding Swilly Flows

A sculpture by Redmond Herrity to commemorate those from the Letterkenny area who lost their lives in World War 1. It was unveiled by the Letterkenny Community Heritage Group in August 2014.

Endnotes
1 From "A Lament from the Trenches" by Patrick McGill
2 The County Donegal Book of Honour, pp108-119
3 Newspaper extract courtesy of Johnny Keys, great grandson of Mrs. Doherty
4 Richardson, Neil, "A Coward If I Return, a Hero If I Fall – Stories of Irishmen in World War 1", O'Brien Press, 2010 p23
5 MacFhionnghaile, Niall, "Donegal, Ireland and the First World War", An Crann, 1987, p35
6 Derry Journal 3/5/1916
7 Derry Journal 30/9/14
8 Derry Journal 23/9/14
9 Derry Journal 7/8/14
10 Derry Journal 15/1/15
11 Derry Journal 12/2/15
12 Derry Journal 22/3/15
13 MacFhionnghaile, Niall, "Donegal, Ireland and the First World War", An Crann, 1987, p13
14 The County Donegal Book of Honour, p7
15 MacFhionnghaile, Niall, "Dr. McGinley, His Life and Times", An Crann, 1985, pp212-213
16 Ibid p213
17 Ibid p214
18 MacFhionnghaile, Niall, "Donegal, Ireland and the First World War", An Crann, 1987, p119
19 Ibid p113
20 nGiallach, Naoi, "Not So Long Ago – World War One", Letterkenny Christmas Annual 1987 p38
21 Derry Journal 3/5/16

Chapter Fourteen:
The Growth of Nationalism

As the town of Letterkenny has its origins in the Plantation of Ulster, it is not surprising to see that from its initial growth in the early seventeenth century the descendants of the original Scottish settlers largely dominated the growth of the market town and its politics. As a result, Letterkenny in the nineteenth century, like other towns throughout Ireland, was considered to be a 'British' town, or at least a town loyal to the Crown in the upper echelons of its society. We have already seen that certain aristocratic Ascendancy families had their residences on the outskirts of Letterkenny and the Town Commissioners who governed the town were by and large made up from these families or from successful businessmen and traders who tended to be from Protestant backgrounds. This all started to change though as the nineteenth century progressed. The rise in confidence of Catholicism following the repeal of the Penal Laws and Catholic Emancipation resulted in a large and rejuvenated Catholic population in the town and the successes of the various Land Acts resulted in an ever-rising Catholic landholding class while the local government reforms at the end of the nineteenth century resulted in the rise of the Catholic politician, at least at local level. At the dawn of the twentieth century therefore, a new Catholic and Nationalist landowning majority existed in Letterkenny that was to be affected by the national events of Easter 1916, the War of Independence and the Civil War.

The 'Britishness' of Letterkenny

Evidence of the 'Britishness' of nineteenth century Letterkenny can be found in various historical sources. Following the failure of the 1798 Rebellion of the United Irishmen and the capture of Theobald Wolfe Tone at Buncrana, on behalf of the clergy of the Diocese of Raphoe, on 3rd December 1799 **Bishop Anthony Coyle** wrote a letter to King George III in which he professed loyalty to the King and even supported the idea of a union between both countries, a union that would occur three years later:

"Being called upon to give our assent, if necessary, to a Union between Great Britain and Ireland, We, not only consent to that measure, but also wish for it, and hope it will answer the great and important ends wisfully expected from it"[1]

Further evidence of a town loyal to the Crown comes from the Londonderry Guardian newspaper on 17th March 1863, which gives a report of celebrations in Letterkenny on the marriage of the Prince of Wales:

"Tuesday last was celebrated in a becoming manner by the inhabitants of this prosperous town, who had made every preparation to testify loyalty to their Sovereign and her illustrious family. The streets and principal buildings were illuminated, and every demonstration of joy was manifested by people of all ranks and creeds. Fire-works, torch lights, and tar barrels blazed in all directions, and in front of Mr. Hegarty's Hotel, the Band of the Donegal Militia Artillery performed a number of loyal and appropriate airs. A Royal salute was discharged from the barrack square, and the police force paraded the streets, and fired a feu de joie in honour of the

Letterkenny - Where the Winding Swilly Flows

A reminder of former British rule. This Post Box in Letterkenny was painted green after independence but the Crown with the initials VR (Victoria Regina) are still visible

The sash of the Ancient Order of Hibernians

event. *The proceedings passed off with the utmost decorum and regularity."*[2]

The Londonderry Sentinel from 19th June 1863 gives us a report of t visit to Letterkenny of the Lord Lieutenant General and General Governor Ireland, George William Frederick Howard, Earl of Carlisle. Chairman of t Town Commissioners, John R. Boyd, addressed the Lord Lieutenant General in t hotel on behalf of the inhabitants of Letterkenny and the Town Commissione *"May it please your Excellency, We, the Town Commissioners of the Town of Letterken would appear to be deficient in the loyalty and attachment feel for our beloved Queen, if we did not avail ourselves the present opportunity of welcoming your Excellency to County of Donegal, and to this its chief Town. We ass your Excellency that the County of Donegal, and this To especially, have always shown their loyalty to their Soverea not only in words, but, whenever opportunity has offered, substantial deeds. Also, to your Excellency in your indivia capacity, we beg to offer our humble thanks for your visit to a remote District."*[3]

Following the large Tenant Right Meeti at the Market Square in 1870 at which Rev. Kinn spoke, the Derry Journal reported that ten thousa people from all around the district gave cheers for " *Queen and her Majesty's Government."* [4]

Today, evidence of the former British r in the town can still be seen on the Post Office b opposite Ard Eunan Parochial House. Like many p boxes across the country, after independence v gained in 1922, to save money on replacing the red post boxes, most of them were simply paint green with the old British insignias still emblazor on them. On this post box in the town, the initials 'VR' (Victoria Regina) and the crown are still visibl

The Rise in Nationalism

By the dawn of the twentieth century, howev the rise of Irish nationalism in the by now Catho dominated town of Letterkenny was clearly evident. 1891, for example the number of Parliamentary vot for Letterkenny was reported as 792 Nationalists a 467 Unionists.[5]

The United Irish League and the Ancio Order of Hibernians (AOH) had become popu throughout the country in raising national support and branches soon appeared in the to of Letterkenny. Joseph Devlin, MP from Belfa had organized the AOH from 1905 and its memb

Chapter Fourteen: The Growth of Nationalism

largely came from supporters of the Irish Parliamentary Party. To be a supporter of one usually meant to be a supporter of the other. The AOH would later build a hall in 1939 at the bottom of the Main Street and name it after Devlin, which was used for social functions, dances and dramatic performances. The Devlin Hall most recently housed the Society of the St. Vincent de Paul and their second hand clothes shop, Déjà vu.

In response to the introduction of the Third Home Rule Bill at Westminster in 1912, Unionists signed the Ulster Covenant and formed the Ulster Volunteer Force (UVF) to resist any implementation of what they saw as 'Rome Rule'. September 28th 1912 was celebrated as 'Ulster Day' when special gatherings for signing the covenant took place. Meetings at Letterkenny took place in both Presbyterian churches, on the Main Street and Trinity Hall, where 671 signatures were collected.[6] One year later, 82 men from Letterkenny were listed as members of the UVF[7] under the command of **Captain A.J. Horabin**[8] showing that despite the rise of Nationalism, there was still a significant element of Unionism in the town. The Ulster Volunteer Force also used a drill hall locally for a number of years on the Boyd estate at Ballymacool.[9]

In response, in November 1913, Nationalists in Dublin formed the National Volunteers to safeguard the introduction of Home Rule. A National Volunteer force was soon set up in Letterkenny and they began parading and drilling, albeit largely with wooden sticks and hurleys due to a lack of guns. The Derry Journal from Wednesday July 15th 1914 tells us of a large National Volunteer meeting that took place in Letterkenny:

A parade of Irish National Volunteers at the Cock Pit on Sentry Hill in 1913. Courtesy of Niall McGinley

181

Letterkenny - Where the Winding Swilly Flows

"The "Twelfth" was celebrated in Letterkenny on Sunday by the holding of a rev[iew] of National Volunteers. At 2.30 pm 400 men of the regiment fell in on parade at Sentry H[ill] and were put through the usual drill exercises. At three p.m. 80 men of the Rosemount (Der[ry]) Volunteers who had come to Letterkenny with a large excursion from Derry, mustered at bu[gle] call on the Market Square, from whence headed by the Rosemount Sarsfield Band they marc[hed] to Letterkenny drill ground. Shortly afterwards 180 men of the Drumbollogue and Drumk[een] companies arrived, accompanied by the Drumkeen Band. The joint companies were subsequen[tly] marched to the Isle Meadows. After inspection by Rev. John McCafferty, Adm., chaplain [of] Letterkenny Regiment the forces marched in column and quarter column past the sainting b[ox] at which was erected a flag pole flying the National flag and advanced in review order...Th[ere] were 640 Volunteers on review, and fully 1,500 of the general public attended at the rev[iew] ground. A collection, realising a very considerable sum, was taken up from the spectators in [aid] of the Equipment Fund."[10]

So we see that now by 1914, Letterkenny held a dominant National[ist] majority in the population who were mostly members or supporters of the Unit[ed] Irish League, the Ancient Order of Hibernians, the Irish Parliamentary Pa[rty] and/or the National Volunteers, all with the vested interest of the success[ful] introduction of Home Rule into Ireland. When this Bill received the Royal Asse[nt] in 1914 (although delayed for the duration the war), there was much celebrati[on] and rejoicing in the town, just as in many other towns and cities througho[ut] the country. Many National Volunteers, under the advice of John Redmond a[nd] other politicians and priests, enlisted to fight the Germans and protect the liber[ty] of Belgium upon the outbreak of war. Most hoped to be home for Christmas a[nd] live in this 'new Ireland' of Home Rule and finally to be governed by 'themselv[es] alone'. However, the ideals of Nationalism in Ireland, and by consequence in t[he] town of Letterkenny, were to take a drastic change following the events of East[er] 1916.

Easter 1916

Following Redmond's encouragement to National Volunteers to enlist [in] the army and fight in the war, there was a split, with almost 10,000 membe[rs] forming their own distinct "Irish Volunteers" - mostly made up of the mo[re] radical thinking members of the Irish Republican Brotherhood (IRB) such [as] Padraig Pearse. These Irish Volunteers were seen as a minority in the National[ist] community of Ireland and when they took over the General Post Office on East[er] Monday 1916, both the Irish Parliamentary Party and the media condemned th[eir] actions. Local newspaper, the Derry Journal for example, on Wednesday May [3] 1916 reflected the general opinion when it stated that *"the dangerous, disruption[al] and demoralising movement stands utterly condemned."*[11]

John Redmond, appalled at the actions of these men to derail all t[he] political efforts to attain Home Rule believed that *"it is a German invasion of Irela[nd] as brutal, as selfish, as cynical as Germany's invasion of Belgium…I do not believe that t[his] wicked and insane movement will achieve its ends. The German plot has failed… Home R[ule] has not been destroyed, it remains indestructible."*[12]

Chapter Fourteen: The Growth of Nationalism

The initial revulsion felt by many Nationalists at these actions of a minority on the streets of Dublin soon began to change though as between the and 12th May, the British army executed 15 men (including the 7 signatories of e Proclamation) in Dublin Castle. With each bullet and execution, the British ly encouraged support and sympathy for the separatists. Evidence of the anging mood can be seen from the Derry Journal from Monday May 8th 1916. ill condemning the actions of the rebels as a crime committed against the Irish ople, it reflected the growing sympathy of its readership when it stated *"There ould, in short, be no more shootings in any barrack yard of the Irish metropolis. The walls of ublin are already too much blood spattered."*[3]

> **Did you know?**
>
> Even though the political party was not formed until 1905, the first time the phrase 'Sinn Féin' was used in a political speech took place in Letterkenny, when **Timothy Healy**, an anti-Parnellite politician in the Irish Parliamentary Party, spoke in the town in June 1892:
> *"Now they (Parnellites) say against us that we put our hopes in the Liberal Party and that we are bound hand and foot to the Liberal Party. Now, I give you the good old watchword of Old Ireland – Sinn Fain – Ourselves Alone"*

he Rise of Sinn Féin

Following this failed rebellion, the crackdown on Nationalist behaviour the British forces in Ireland resulted in arms searches throughout the country, hich only agitated the Nationalists even more, forcing them into more militant es of thought. One such arms raid took place in the Literary Institute in etterkenny, a suspected arms dump, on Wednesday 16th August 1917 and the next y, at a large assembly in Letterkenny, **Father John McCafferty**, the chaplain of e National Volunteers and Administrator in the Cathedral requested the 150 olunteers in attendance to form up and march through the town to give: *"public anifestation of their purpose of protecting the liberty and property of the people."*[14]

Actions such as these by the British combined with a general dissatisfaction nongst Nationalists following the increased delay in the implementation of ome Rule. Also, the apparently never-ending war (not to mention the sympathy wards the executed rebels of 1916) resulted in the steady rise in support of e new republican party Sinn Féin throughout the country and in Letterkenny. ormed by Arthur Griffith in 1905, the party had only small support at first but e events of Easter week 1916 and the growth in militancy amongst disaffected ationalists led to an ever-growing swell in their numbers. On the 16th eptember 1917, **James Gibbons** presided over the enrollment of 130 members om the Letterkenny town and district in the new "Jim Connolly" cumann of nn Féin. This took place in the backyard of Willie Boyle's premises, where e Voodoo nightclub stands today.[15] At the meeting, Mr. Gibbons introduced seph O'Doherty, of Derry, who dealt with the aims and objectives of Sinn

Letterkenny - Where the Winding Swilly Flows

Féin while a resolution was proposed by **John McMonagle**, seconded by **Joh Curran**, pledging to support the Sinn Féin policy to realize the nation's aim independence. Prior to and after the meeting, the Derry Pipers' band marche through the town playing national airs.[16] **Dr. J.P. McGinley** became president this local Sinn Féin body.

The Letterkenny cumann received a considerable coup with the arriv of Padraig Pearse's mother, sister and niece as guests of honour on St. Stepher Night 1917.

"On St. Stephen's Night Mrs. Pearse (mother), Miss Pearse (sister), and Mrs. McGart (niece), of the Republican leader P.H. and William Pearse, were the guests of the Jim Conno Sinn Féin Club, Letterkenny, at a ceilidh held in the Club Hall. Dr. J.P. McGinley, preside of the Club, introduced the lady visitors, who were accorded an enthusiastic welcome. Duri an interval in the programme, Mrs. Pearse delivered a touching address on the boyhood a manhood of her illustrious sons. The night's programme, which was in all detail of a high ord of merit, consisted of an exhibition of pictures on the cinema, which was operated by **M James Kearns**. *Songs were contributed of Irish patriotic character by* **Mrs. McGarve Miss C. Gillen**, *Derry*, **Messrs. John and Connell Bradley, C.A. Flattery, V McMenamin, James Langan, M. Dawson, Eaman Coyle, James O'Donne** *Presentation Brothers' Boy Choir*, **James Friel**, *recitation by* **Master C. Bradley**, *and mandoline solo by* **Mr. J. O'Donnell**. *The accompaniments were effectively played by* **Mr Clancey** *and* **Miss D. Gallagher**. *An enjoyable dance commenced at the termination of t concert and continued until 5.30,* **Mr. John Curran** *acting with courteous ability as mas. of ceremonies. Light refreshments were supplied during the night, the stewards being* **Messr Jim Dawson** *and* **Jim Murphy**. *The following orchestral party gave entire satisfaction the supplying of the dance musical programme –* **Miss S. Gallagher** *(piano)*, **Messr William McManus, sen., William MacManus jun., Wm. McMenamin, Kearns,** *and* **James O'Donnell** *(violins)"* [17]

Eamonn DeValera pictured in the Sinn Féin Hall in Letterkenny on his visit to the town in February 1918. Also included in the picture are Dr. J.P. McGinley, Nellie Grey, Willie McManus, Sam O'Flaherty and Jimmy O'Donnell. Courtesy of Liam O'Duibhir

Chapter Fourteen: The Growth of Nationalism

Eamonn DeValera, the new President of Sinn Féin, arrived in Letterkenny five weeks after this, on February 7th 1918 with Seaghan McEntee and Sam O'Flaherty on his tour of the North West to whip up support for the party. DeValera and his entourage were met by a torch light procession from the Port Bridge and escorted to McCarry's Hotel, at the top of the Main Street, accompanied by many local supporters.

A public meeting was held in the Market Square the next afternoon when a large body of supporters, including a contingent from Raphoe, were led by the Derry Pipers' Band, and marched through the town to the hotel where they escorted the leaders to the square. When DeValera spoke to the hundreds of supporters that were gathered there, he whipped the crowd up by reflecting on the growing tide of dissatisfaction with the old Irish Parliamentary Party and their antiquated politics. He stated that:

'If there were any men who ought to be Sinn Féiners more than another it was Ulstermen...Sinn Féin represented the great majority of the Irish people... The Irish Party were pro-Britishers, and had given themselves heart and soul to the British Empire. Sinn Féiners thought of Ireland first'[18]

The Conscription Crisis

Despite this impressive growth in Sinn Féin locally, there was still an Irish Party and Ancient Order of Hibernians (AOH) supporting majority in the town of Letterkenny in 1918. The Irish Party was now, since the death of John Redmond, under the leadership of John Dillon, a former schoolmate and close friend to Bishop O'Donnell. What united the Irish Party and Sinn Féin supporters though were the attempts by the British to force conscription on the people of Ireland for the war in Europe. A large Anti-Conscription rally was held at Sentry Hill on Sunday April 21st 1918 with over 2,500 people in attendance and 500 supporters of Sinn Féin and 80 students from St. Eunan's College marching in military formation being led by a joint AOH and Sinn Féin band. Fr. McCafferty presided over the gathering where he read out a letter from Bishop O'Donnell:

"The enactment of conscription against the will of Ireland would always constitute unwarrantable aggression on the highest rights of our people and nation...Forcible conscription is a reckless attack on our nationhood as well as a great wrong on our people. We cannot encourage it under either aspect by tamely submitting to it."[19]

Large cheers followed the reading of this letter. Edward McFadden, William Kelly, E. Mahony, (United Irish League), Dr. J.P. McGinley, (President

Eamonn DeValera (1882-1975) Image courtesy of National Library of Ireland

of the Sinn Féin Club) and Charles A. Flattery. (Sinn Féin) also addressed the large crowd assembled. After an Anti-Conscription pledge was administered to the crowd, a Committee was formed, consisting of three representatives from the United Irish League (**Edward McFadden, William Kelly,** and **E. Mahony**) three from the Ancient Order of Hibernians (**Charles Ward, Edward Lynch** and **H.J. Allison**), three from Sinn Féin (**Dr. J.P. McGinley, Charles A. Flattery** and **John Curran**), and two from the Labour Association (**James Semple** and **A. McMonagle**), with a third member to be decided at a later date. Father McCafferty was elected as Chairman of the Committee.[20]

A Conscription law for Ireland was passed by the English government but was never put into practice – not one man from Ireland was forcibly conscripted into the British army. By now though, the tide of the war had changed. America had entered the conflict in late 1917 and by summer 1918, a resolution was finally in sight. The armistice on 11th November 1918 signaled the end of the war in Europe and those Letterkenny soldiers lucky to have survived the trenches returned home to the 'new' Ireland. By now however, events in the country had swung Nationalist opinion away from the Irish Party and towards Sinn Féin and the measure of their support was about to be witnessed in the General Election of December 1918.

1918 Elections - East Donegal Campaign

On November 10th, the day before the Armistice, a large meeting was held at the Literary Institute, presided over by **Fr. John O'Doherty**, successor as Administrator in the Cathedral to Fr. McCafferty who had moved to Stranorlar. Fr. O'Doherty stated that he hoped that the differences that kept the Nationalist Party and Sinn Féin apart would be settled before the General Election, so that a united Nationalist Ireland would address the Peace Conference that would take place now that the war was over.

Fr. McCafferty, still as keen an activist as ever, addressed a Nationalist crowd in support of **Mr. Edward Joseph Kelly** from Ballyshannon, Irish party M.P. for East Donegal since the 1910 General Election:

"The election now in swing is of more grave importance and of more far-reaching effect than any which has taken place in Ireland in our time or at any time…The question is whether…the people will send Irish representatives to Parliament to fight the battle of Ireland in the stronghold of the enemy, and use the most effective platform we possess today, from which the clear articulate voice of Ireland can be heard throughout the world; or whether by a senseless policy of abstention they will leave every Irish Catholic and National interest at the mercy of the British members and the Orangemen of Ulster".[21]

Concerned that a division in Nationalist opinion would split the votes in the election and thus lead to Unionist victories in several constituencies in Ulster, Cardinal Logue called for both parties to work together and work towards a compromise. If the Unionists were to gain victory in these constituencies their call for a partition of the country could gain legitimacy and this had to be avoided. He divided the eight key constituencies in Ulster between both parties, allocating 4 to each – the Irish Party to be supported in East Donegal (Letterkenny's constituency), South Down, North East Tyrone and South Armagh and Sinn Féin to be supported in Derry City, East Down, North West Tyrone and South Fermanagh.

"The object of this friendly understanding is to enable Nationalist voters of both parties specified

Chapter Fourteen: The Growth of Nationalism

to unite and give their whole hearted support to the candidate of the Party to whom the seat has been allocated, and in consequence, secure that seat for Ireland, and overthrow the Unionist aim to have the constituency branded as being in favour of being cut off from the native soil and made an English shire. The plain duty cast upon nationalist voters, therefore, in honest fulfilment of the agreement is: Irish party and Sinn Féin electors of the constituency actively to support and vote for Kelly."[22]

Bishop O'Donnell gave his full support to this plan by Cardinal Logue and encouraged his diocese to follow it to avoid the danger of partition: *'The 'new departure' for Ulster leaves nationalists in the eight constituencies no option but to stand together as one man in the election...the Nationalists of Ulster can paint the political map of the election in such a way as to dispose of the six-county project'.*[23]

And so, on December 9th 1918, following this announcement by Cardinal Logue, Fr. John O'Doherty addressed a meeting in Letterkenny calling for the unified Nationalist and Republican support of Edward Joseph Kelly, the Nationalist candidate. At the meeting, Charles Flaherty, the Sinn Féin Director of Elections pledged active support for Kelly. As a result of this agreement, Kelly swept to victory in East Donegal receiving 7,596 votes to the Unionist candidate's 4,797. Despite this victory by the Irish Party in East Donegal however, they were emphatically and overwhelmingly defeated throughout the country by the electorate in favour of the now dominant Sinn Féin party. The party won a paltry 6 seats, down 61 since the previous election and they slowly diminished as a political force. Edward Joseph Kelly chose not to be a member of the abstentionist First Dáil in Dublin but he remained active in the UK House of Commons representing East Donegal until his retirement in October 1922 on the establishment of the Irish Free State. He was made a Senior Counsel in the Irish Free State in 1930. With such overwhelming success in these elections, Sinn Féin now believed they had the complete backing of the people to remove the British Government from Ireland once and for all in a guerilla style War of Independence.

Endnotes
1	Silke, Rev. John J., and Hughes, Mrs. Moira, "Raphoe Miscellany 1", 2012, p53
2	Londonderry Guardian 17/3/1863
3	Londonderry Sentinel 19/6/1863
4	Derry Journal 5/2/1870
5	Derry Journal 19/10/1891
6	O'Connell, Aidan, "The Ulster Covenant in Donegal 1912", Donegal Annual 2011, pp45-54
7	O'Duibhir, Liam, "The Donegal Awakening: Donegal & the War of Independence", Mercier Press, 2009, p24
8	MacFhionnghaile, Niall, "Dr. McGinley, His Life and Times", An Crann, 1985, p8
9	McMonagle, Col. James, "National activities, Letterkenny, Co. Donegal, 1917-1921", Statement by Witness, courtesy Bureau of Military History, Document Number 1385
10	Derry Journal 15/7/1914
11	Derry Journal 3/5/1916
12	Derry Journal 3/5/1916
13	Derry Journal 8/5/1916
14	Derry Journal 20/8/1917
15	MacFhionnghaile, Niall, "Dr. McGinley, His Life and Times", An Crann, 1985, p23/24
16	Derry Journal 21/9/1917
17	Derry Journal 28/12/1917
18	Derry Journal 11/2/1918
19	Derry Journal 22/4/1918
20	Derry Journal 22/4/1918
21	Derry Journal 2/12/1918
22	Derry Journal 11/12/1918
23	Derry Journal 11/12/1918

Chapter Fifteen: Independence and Civil War

The first shots of the War of Independence against the British were fired in January 1919 at Soloheadbeag in County Tipperary. The Irish Volunteers, renamed the Irish Republican Army (IRA), targeted Royal Irish Constabulary (RIC) and British Army barracks and ambushed their patrols, capturing arms and forcing the closure of barracks in isolated areas. The British Government responded by importing recruits from Britain—the Black and Tans and Auxiliaries—who became notorious for their ill discipline and reprisal attacks on civilians in Ireland.

Ernie O'Malley, training officer to the IRA rural units, visited the Letterkenny area in early 1919 to organize the local Volunteers. Up until now the Irish Volunteers had been generally employed at drill parades, route marches and occasional raids for arms on the homes of Ulster Volunteers, mostly in the predominantly Unionist Laggan area to the east of the town, but from 1919 the organization had a military structure, divided into:

- Divisions
- Brigades
- Battalions
- Companies

Donegal was now the 1st Northern Division, within which there were four brigades - East Brigade was under the command of Samuel Flaherty from Castlefinn with **James Dawson** of Castle Street, Letterkenny Vice O/C.

Within this Brigade was Letterkenny Battalion (known as 4th Battalion) under the command of Dawson, with four companies, Letterkenny Company (**James McMonagle** O/C), Manorcunningham Company (William Holmes O/C), Churchill Company (Hugh McHugh O/C) and Fanad Company (Niall Blaney O/C).[1] It was the responsibility of **Anthony Dawson**, James' brother, to care for the safe custody of the arms of the unit, which were hidden in a 'dump' under the heating chambers of St. Eunan's Cathedral.[2]

In August 1920, under instructions from the Brigade at Castlefinn, ten men from the Letterkenny Company - **Dr. J.P. McGinley, James Dawson, Eddie Gallagher, Hugh McGranaghan, Hugh Sweeney, Hugh McGrath, William McLoughlin,** and brothers **Patrick** and **James McMonagle** – were among a party that carried out a daylight raid on Drumquinn R.I.C. barracks in County Tyrone where a constable was killed and a sergeant was badly injured in the attack. At this time, a District Inspector of the R.I.C. named **Patrick Walsh** had been recently stationed in Letterkenny. After this raid at Drumquinn, D.I. Walsh called to the surgery of Dr. McGinley and produced a slip of paper, telling the doctor that he had a description of three men from the raid that he knew were in Letterkenny: "*You answer the description of one, James Dawson fits in with the description given of the second man and James McMonagle is the third.*" After a short

Chapter Fifteen: Independence and Civil War

panic by Dr. McGinley, Walsh informed him that he was working with Michael Collins and was therefore going to destroy the document so that nobody else would see it, warning the doctor to be more careful in the future.[3] Over his years in Letterkenny, D.I. Walsh would help the local Volunteers evade capture on many other occasions, later becoming Assistant Commissioner of the Garda Síochana force following their formation in the new Irish Free State.

In May 1921, Peadar O'Donnell was commanding a flying column in West Donegal and large detachments of British forces from Derry were sent to that area in an attempt to capture them. O'Donnell issued an order to Anthony Dawson, now O/C in the absence of his brother, to carry out an attack on the British forces in Letterkenny in an effort to relieve the pressure on those men in West Donegal. Dawson organised an attack on the Main Street of Letterkenny on Wednesday 18th May against a patrol of three RIC Constables and one Sergeant. Dawson and his company lay in wait in McGlynn's Walsteads near the Literary Institute (approximately where the Library is today) and opened fire on the patrol shortly after 11pm while at the same time, another group of men fired at the No. 2 Barracks at the bottom of the town. **Constable Albert Carter** was shot dead by a revolver bullet to the throat while **Sergeant Charles Maguire** received two wounds in the hip and the calf of the leg. All the available police, reinforced by military located at Sprackburn, paraded the streets, which were by now practically deserted by civilians.[4]

The last of the British troops leaving Letterkenny from the top of the Port Road in 1922. Courtesy of Niall McGinley

Letterkenny - Where the Winding Swilly Flows

Artist's impression of the shootings by the Black and Tans at the top of the Main Street in which Anthony Coyle and Simon Doherty were injured

Chapter Fifteen: Independence and Civil War

However, the Black and Tans, located in No. 1 Barracks beside the Courthouse, heard the shots and were quick to retaliate on the streets of Letterkenny. Two local civilians, **Anthony Coyle** and **Simon Doherty**, were injured in the reprisals while McCarry's Hotel, location of the Sinn Féin Courts, was shot up and a grenade thrown through the window:

"There were heavy and continuous fusillades, which continued for several hours, and two civilians were wounded by rifle bullets, Anthony Coyle in the wrist and leg, and Simon Doherty in the foot. McCarry's hotel was injured, the smoke room windows being completely demolished, pictures and mirrors shattered. A large hole was torn in the floor, apparently by a grenade or bomb. There are several bullet marks on the ceiling and walls. Terror prevailed during the night, few people retiring to bed." [5]

The attack had the desired effect of drawing off the forces from West Donegal who then concentrated on the Letterkenny district in the belief that the Column had moved in that direction. Dawson and his Company made plans on two more occasions in June of 1921 for a daylight attack on the British forces in Letterkenny but on each occasion the British troops did not turn up.[6] By July of that year, a truce had been agreed between the British and the Irish and Michael Collins and his team of delegates signed the Anglo-Irish Treaty in December creating the Irish Free State and ending British rule in Ireland, at least in 26 counties.

On Tuesday 28th March 1922, both Letterkenny Barracks were vacated by the R.I.C. and handed over to **Col. Commandant Glennon**, 1st Northern Division I.R.A. at 7a.m. The old coat of arms was taken down from over the main entrance, and a large tri-colour flag was hoisted through the window. About 30 R.I.C. then left for the railway station and members of the I.R.A., supplied by Letterkenny Company, occupied the barracks.[7]

However, the handover of the barracks was not without its tragedy. On the previous weekend, the police had dumped a lot of their explosives over the bridge at the Port into the Swilly. When the tide went out, the explosives were stuck in the silt and were found by a group of young boys, one of whom was **James Moore** of Rosemount and his friend **P. Curran**. While toying with one device, Moore was killed while Curran was badly wounded. The Derry Journal reported the tragedy as follows:

"It appears that on evacuating the police barracks the R.I.C. "dumped" bombs, rockets and verey lights over the wharf at the port during high tide, but when the tide ebbed a number of boys discovered some of the explosives, including bombs and were actually found using the latter as footballs along the road.

Young Moore and Curran brought a bomb to the latter's house, where it exploded while they were toying with it, causing frightful havoc. Portion of Moore's head was blown off, and he died shortly afterwards. One of Curran's hands was blown off. He also received a nasty wound in the neck, and as result of injury to one of his feet had to get a toe amputated. The windows of the house were blown out, and the interior of the building greatly damaged." [8]

Letterkenny - Where the Winding Swilly Flows

The former barracks of the RIC in Letterkenny. No.1 Barracks is now a solicitor's office while No. 2 barracks at the bottom of the Main Street later housed the Garda Station

From Christmas Annual 1994

Chapter Fifteen: Independence and Civil War

The Irish Civil War in Letterkenny

Not everyone agreed with the signing of the Anglo-Irish Treaty and it split the Sinn Féin party resulting in an outbreak of Civil War in Ireland in 1922. The Treaty debates split Nationalist opinion, even within families, with the result that Pro-Treaty supporters faced off against Anti-Treaty supporters in towns and villages throughout the country.

In the early hours of Wednesday morning 27th April, one month after the handing over of the barracks in the town, No. 1 barracks was attacked by rifle fire from the Anti-Treaty IRA with a bomb blowing out the glass windows. Shots were also fired at No. 2 Barracks and a dance in progress in the Literary Institute was entered and searched but nothing was found. The Free State patrol remained on the streets until 6 a.m.[9]

Rockhill House and Ballymacool House were both occupied by the Anti-Treaty forces in June of 1922. Rockhill was empty at this time making the takeover relatively straightforward but Col. John Boyd and his wife were forcibly removed from Ballymacool. On 22 June 1922, an attack was launched on both houses by Pro-Treaty forces under the command of Lt. James McMonagle. The Anti-treaty forces in both houses were caught by surprise in the dawn attack and **Lt. Daniel Larkin** was fatally injured on the front lawn of Rockhill.

In July 1922, almost 100 Anti-Treaty Volunteers took possession of the schoolhouse, the old R.I.C. Barracks and a number of houses at Knockbrack, near Letterkenny but then moved away in the direction of Glenveagh Castle which was to become GHQ for the Anti-Treaty forces in Donegal.[10]

Also that month, an Anti-Treaty garrison had taken control of Skeog House, near to the border with Derry. After five and a half hours resistance, 41 Anti-Treaty prisoners were captured by Free State forces and brought to Letterkenny Courthouse. Shortly after their arrival, in the early hours of the morning the prisoners started to wreck the interior, smashing the front windows and throwing out portions of the gallery, judges' bench, solicitors' table, and books and papers containing the record of the court for the previous 50 years. By noon smoke was seen at the front of the building, and shortly afterwards flames engulfed the building as prisoners stood at the windows and waved the tricolour and called for cheers for an 'Irish Republic', singing the 'Soldier's Song'. Eventually they came out to the street, and were surrounded by the

Letterkenny Courthouse after being burned out by the Skeog prisoners in 1922. Courtesy of Niall McGinley

Letterkenny - Where the Winding Swilly Flows

Artist's impression of the takeover of Ballymacool House by Anti Treaty IRA forces in 1922

Chapter Fifteen: Independence and Civil War

ee State troops, who lined them up on the footpath. The Fire Brigade arrived d the fire was brought under control but not before considerable damage was ne.[11]

By August 1922, many Anti-Treaty forces were captured in the areas rrounding Letterkenny. On Wednesday 2nd August, Free State troops under eutenant **Martin** encountered Anti-Treaty forces on Cark Mountain, three les from Letterkenny towards Drumkeen. Shots were exchanged and a nning fight ensued for over two hours. The Anti-treaty force then made signs surrender but as they advanced towards the troops they opened fire before reating towards Drumkeen where they were rounded up, thirteen of whom re taken prisoner. Two days later, **John Mulla**n from Glendowan, a member the Letterkenny Rural District Council, **Mr. O'Hare**, a clerk in Belfast Bank Letterkenny, **Hugh Murray** of Termon and **Seamus O Griana** (who would er write the Irish novel *Caisleáin Óir*) were all arrested in Letterkenny for Anti-eaty activities.[12]

On Saturday, more prisoners were captured by the Letterkenny troops in Glenfin district. While on patrol in the area, the troops accidently came upon lying column of 17 men, who were concealed behind turf banks. Fire was ened on them, and there was a quick fight, lasting about 20 minutes.[13]

On the 19th August, six prisoners who had been caught in this round up aped from No. 1 Barracks by using a piece of steel which they fashioned into aw. The prisoners cut through the iron bars of the cell and made an opening ge enough to pass through. Once outside they covered the barbed wire with ir blankets and gained access to the adjoining premises and made their escape.[14]

At 1.45am on 16th January 1923, a Free State military patrol was passing garty's Hotel at the Market Square, when they believed shots were fired on m from the elevated area on the height of Mount Southwell Terrace. The trol returned the fire for about een minutes. The family Patrick Dawson at Mount uthwell had a narrow escape as bullets struck inches from the ndows and also near the front or. No one was injured but one the telephone wires across Main Street at the Square s cut in two by a rifle bullet. ter the gunfire had ceased the litary were called out of the rracks and made a thorough rch of the neighbourhood t no evidence of activity could found. People going to the ly mass in the Cathedral were stopped and questioned but again any would-be ooters could not be identified.[15]

The new Garda troops arrive in the town. Courtesy of Niall McGinley

Letterkenny - Where the Winding Swilly Flows

By now, though, the Civil War was starting to peter out. More and mo[re] victories for the Free State forces throughout the country eventually brought t[he] Anti-Treaty forces to their knees and a ceasefire was called at the end of Ap[ril] 1923. But it was not without its consequences. It resulted in an irrevocable split [in] Sinn Féin with the Pro-Treaty element becoming first the Cumann na nGaedh[eal] party and later Fine Gael while the Anti-Treaty supporters would eventua[lly] form the core of the Fianna Fáil party under DeValera in 1926. Former Si[nn] Féin comrades in the War of Independence were now split in this new politi[cal] atmosphere. For example, Dr. J.P. McGinley, former President of the Letterken[ny] Sinn Féin Cumann and who welcomed DeValera to the town in February 19[ ] voted in favour of the Treaty while S[am] O'Flaherty former Brigade commander [of] the Letterkenny district voted against it.

Due to the civil war amongst t[he] Nationalists of Ireland, the new state [of] Northern Ireland was also allowed [to] consolidate its existence and the partition [of] the country was confirmed as a necessity [for] many Unionists. The town of Letterken[ny] with its close proximity to the border of t[he] new state was of course affected by vario[us] events that took place over the followi[ng] years, both politically and economica[lly]. For example, following the rioting of t[he] Battle of the Bogside in Derry in Augu[st] 1969, a field hospital was set up at Rockh[ill] to aid the refugees while, as debates rag[ed] in the Dáil about whether Irish troo[ps] should be sent in to assist or not, a sm[all] garrison of troops were stationed on t[he] outskirts of the town awaiting orders. T[he] 'Camp Arrow' was situated at Lisnenn[a] and although no orders arrived, it led [to] the permanent residency of Army troo[ps]

J.P. McGinley, Johnny Seáin Mac Lochlainn and President W.T. Cosgrave on Letterkenny Main Street 1923. Courtesy of Niall McGinley

in the town at Rockhill Barracks for over forty years.[16] Another example was [in] January 1972, when several people who were injured in the horrific events [of] Bloody Sunday were treated in Letterkenny General Hospital.[17]

By the third decade of the twentieth century then, the town [of] Letterkenny had finally shed its long held British identity. What was once [a] Protestant Ascendancy market town was now very much a predominan[tly] Catholic and Nationalist controlled urban area in the new Irish Free State. T[he] new ruling system of a more working class dominated local government, alli[ed] with a determination amongst the various businesses of the town, ensured a rap[id] growth in Letterkenny's development as the new century progressed.

Chapter Fifteen: Independence and Civil War

Endnotes
McMonagle, Col. James, "National activities, Letterkenny, Co. Donegal, 1917-1921", Statement by Witness, courtesy Bureau of Military History, Document Number 1385
Dawson, Anthony "Activities of Letterkenny Company, Letterkenny Battalion, Irish Volunteers, Co. Donegal, 1917-1921" Statement by Witness, courtesy Bureau of Military History, Document Number 1546
McMonagle, Col. James, "National activities, Letterkenny, Co. Donegal, 1917-1921", Statement by Witness, courtesy Bureau of Military History, Document Number 1385
Derry Journal 20/5/1921
Derry Journal 20/5/1921
Dawson, Anthony "Activities of Letterkenny Company, Letterkenny Battalion, Irish Volunteers, Co. Donegal, 1917-1921" Statement by Witness, courtesy Bureau of Military History, Document Number 1546
Derry Journal 29/3/1922
Derry Journal 27/3/1922
Derry Journal 29/4/1922
Derry Journal 5/7/1922
Derry Journal 10/7/1922
Derry Journal 4/8/1922
Derry Journal 7/8/1922
Derry Journal 21/8/1922
Derry Journal 17/1/1923
Longwill, Edward, "Donegal and the Outbreak of the Northern Conflict 1968-69", Donegal Annual 2010, pp70-81
Derry Journal 31/1/1972

Chapter Sixteen: The Port and Railway

One of the major factors in the early development of economic grow in Letterkenny in the nineteenth and early twentieth centuries was undoubted the role of the Port at Ballyraine. Set up in the late eighteenth century to facilit the arrival of goods into the nearby small market town, on January 10th 1775, **Monck Mason** reported on its poor condition:

"The port of Ballyrain is yet in its infancy, but is worthy of your attention from the circumstan of its situation within a quarter of a mile of Letterkenny, a very considerable town in the m of a populous country, and in one of the finest harbors in the world; for such I may venture pronounce Lough Swilly. There never was a port however in a more deplorable condition, th it is at present: without a quay, Custom House, or boat; without a road passable for carria from thence to the town, & provided with scarcely a single officer, who both knows his busin and is able to execute it.
The Grand Jury of the County of Donegal have granted a presentment for making a road fr Ballyrain to Letterkenny, which will probably be completed early in the spring."

People who worked at the Port at this time were **John McCauslan Henry Cooper**, **John Witherall**, **William McMullan** and **William Birch** wh the boatmen were **John Hunter** and **George Swiney** but *"as there has never bee boat provided for them, these officers have hitherto had nothing to do."*[1] **William Boyd** Ballymacool and later of Gortlee was the Collector for the Port at this time. 1824, conditions at the Port appeared to have improved:

A plaque in Lower Main Street indicating the location of the Corn Market from 1852

"Within half a mile is Port Balliraine, whither vessels of one hundred tons bring ir salt, colonial produce, and whence they export hides, butter etc. This is the market for a v considerable tract of county: the principal commodities sold here are linen, yarn, cattle, a provisions."[2]

While visiting Letterken in 1854, Henry D. Ing remarked that:

"...there is a considera export trade in corn. About f cargoes, averaging seventy tons dispatched in a season, making whole export between three a four thousand tons."[3]

This thriving co market was located on t Main Street from 1852, evidenced by the sign still existence today.

In 1900, one of Letterkenny's most successful businessmen at the tim **William George McKinney**, bought the Port with the surrounding coal yard

Chapter Sixteen: The Port and Railway

...eds and warehouses from the Ramsay family. Another successful businessman, ...arles Kelly from Ramelton, was a tenant of the Ramsays in one of the ...rehouses and was negotiating to buy the property himself when McKinney ...tbid him and became his new landlord. The Kelly family would eventually get ...nership of the Port forty years later though.

W.G. McKinney (not to be confused with the McKinneys on the Port ...ad who later owned Oatfields) ran a very successful business on the Main ...eet selling ladies and gents shoes while also working a funeral business and ...arm at the bottom of Rosemount and serving on the Urban Council. His ...rchase of the Port effectively gave him control of the River Swilly in this area ...d for many years he held the large contract for supplying St. Conal's Hospital ...h 12,000 tons of steam coal while he sold and delivered up to 5,000 tons ...coal per year throughout the local area. McKinney died in 1931 in what was ...scribed as a largely attended and solemn funeral. Ten years later **A.D. Kelly**, ...son of Charles Kelly, successfully purchased the port from Cecil McKinney ...d from then until the 1960s the firm of Charles Kelly Ltd. imported coal, salt,

A boat arriving at Port Ballyraine at the turn of the twentieth century. Image courtesy of the National Library of Ireland

...ber, and fertiliser through the port. Sawn timber was imported from Finland, ...eden and Norway for their Mill at Ballymacool while coal came from North ...st England, Scotland and South Wales and later from Poland and Holland.

In 1937, **Paddy Tinney**, then working with another successful local ...sinessman **Sam Roulston** at the bottom of the Main Street, began importing ...al through the port and opened a business with his sons Charlie and Eddie ...the Port Road. The Electrification of Rural Ireland programme began in

Letterkenny - Where the Winding Swilly Flows

1945 and again the Port was instrumental as large vessels brought thousands wooden poles from Europe after being treated with creosote in Dublin, Cork a Limerick. These large poles were then taken to all parts of the county and erecte connecting the various outlying areas with electricity.

By the 1960s, the days of large and small ships arriving at the Port Ballyraine appeared numbered as a new pier had been built downriver at Thorn. This could accommodate much larger coasters meaning that Ballyrai was gradually used less and less. In 1980, due to repairs being done at the Tho a Scottish ship, the *Polarlight*, arrived with a cargo of salt for Kelly's and sai off into history as the last boat to use the Port at Ballyraine. In July 2001, the warehouses that were so synonymous with the area were demolished to facilit the construction of a new roundabout while the importance of the Port in t early growth of the market town was recognised with the erection of the Poles monument in the centre of this new roundabout. Designed by Locky Morris was erected in 2003 and as the 'Pole Star' was the navigational tool for sailors guide them home, it is a fitting memorial to all those who worked there in t busy days of the Port.

The Polestar monument designed by Locky Morris erected at the Port Bridge. The 'Polestar' was used by navigators to direct their boats home

Railway Development

Another key factor in the initial growth of Letterkenny in the ea twentieth century was the construction of a railway system that connected t town to Derry in the east and later Burtonport to the west and also to the tow in the south of Donegal. There were two railway companies that ran the lir

Chapter Sixteen: The Port and Railway

n Donegal, the **County Donegal Railway** (CDR) and the **Londonderry and Lough Swilly Railway** (L&LSR). The CDR controlled the lines in the south of he county while the L&LSR exclusively ran the lines in the north and northwest. situated between both regions, Letterkenny then was the only town in the county hat housed both rival networks.

Since the mid 1850's, several projects had been mooted to bring the town nto the existing railway network coming from Derry. This led to the incorporation of the **Letterkenny Railway Company** in 1860 and after nearly twenty years of

The Railway network in Donegal. Letterkenny was the only town to house both rival networks the L&LSR and the CDR

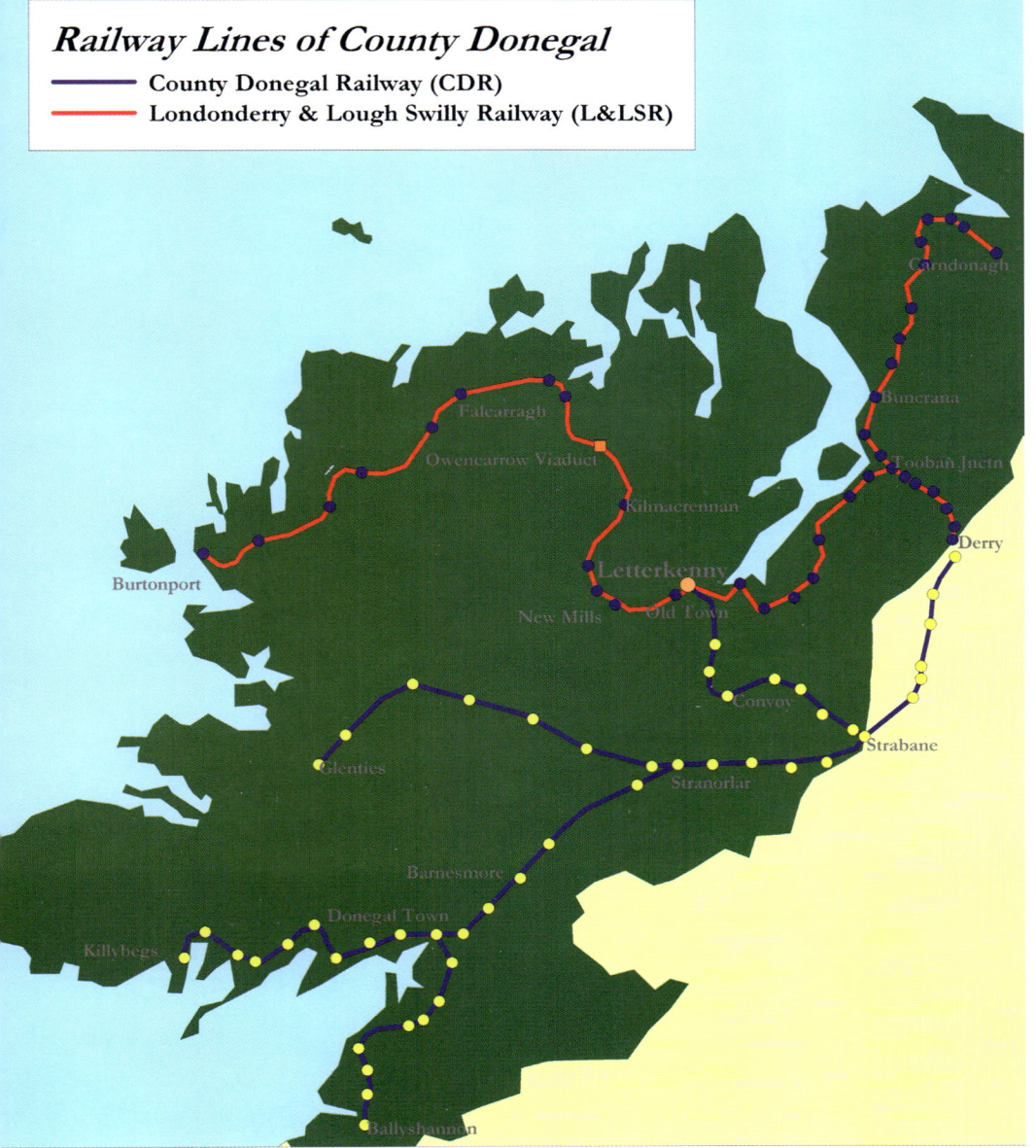

Railway Lines of County Donegal
— County Donegal Railway (CDR)
— Londonderry & Lough Swilly Railway (L&LSR)

201

Letterkenny - Where the Winding Swilly Flows

discussion and delays, in 1883 the Letterkenny Railway Company's narrow-gauge line from Tooban Junction was finally opened as an extension of the Londonderry and Buncrana Railway. This line was the property of the L&LSR and they had their station at the entrance to the town at the junction of the Port Road and the Ramelton Road. By 1903, a further extension was built that connected the town to Burtonport through Kilmacrennan, Dunfanaghy and Gweedore and a new Station House and stop was built at Oldtown with the track running alongside the Isles. By 1903, through their connection via the railway, the markets of Derry and Letterkenny had access to the fisheries of Burtonport by an efficient rail service that was much quicker than the traditionally used method of horse and cart. Large viaducts and bridges were built for this Burtonport extension through a mountainous and boggy terrain, most notably over the Owencarrow River, and fish, potatoes, livestock, turf and mail could now be delivered quickly to and from Letterkenny from these surrounding stations. Connections to these small rural towns and villages also facilitated the arrival of more and more people for the Hiring Fairs, a legacy over time that did not endear the rapidly growing town to many rural Donegal families. Seen as the place where they would be separated from their families, the town grew less popular with those that arrived to be hired.

In 1892 the Finn Valley and West Donegal Railways were amalgamated and became known as the Donegal Railway, changing its name to County Donegal Railway in 1906. An extension of the line from Strabane to Letterkenny through Raphoe and Convoy was opened in January 1909, most likely to gain access to the thriving fish industry that was passing through the town from Burtonport. From Strabane, you could then travel to Glenties in the west of Donegal or switch at Stranorlar and head south to Donegal Town, Killybegs and Ballyshannon. The CDR had their Station House immediately next door and at a right angle to the L&LSR Station House at the Port Road/Ramelton Road junction and both of these rival companies ran side by side in the town for almost 50 years.

With the construction of the railways, Letterkenny had fast and efficient

The CDR and L&LSR stations were situated right next to each other in the town. From Christmas Annual

Chapter Sixteen: The Port and Railway
Courtesy of Niall McGinley

Courtesy of Niall McGinley

Letterkenny - Where the Winding Swilly Flows

Courtesy of Gabriel Flood

access to the cities of Derry, Belfast and Dublin as well as the fishing ports of Burtonport and Killybegs. Being the only town that housed both companies, acted as a gateway through which both rail networks had to pass. As a result, the markets and shops of the town thrived while the trains could also load up with cargoes from the Port at Ballyraine and vice versa. This economic growth of the town by mutual assistance of the ship and railway systems continued right up until the 1940s.

Train Crashes

The train system was however not without its tragedies. On Saturday February 22nd 1908, the morning passenger train from Burtonport reached the Owencarrow Viaduct on the way to Letterkenny. A strong gale that blew through the valley managed to derail two carriages but amazingly, nobody was killed. A more serious accident occurred at this same spot seventeen years later. On stormy night of 28th January 1925, the L&LSR train had left Derry at 5.15pm and after unloading goods at Letterkenny, continued on its destination toward Burtonport. By Kilmacrennan, the driver, **Bob McGuinness**, knew that the winds had picked up considerably. The train approached the viaduct, which was approximately 380 yards in length and 40 feet high, at a speed of about 10 miles per hour. There were now 14 passengers on board, having left Kilmacrennan Station at 7:52pm, running only 5 minutes late.

When the train was on the viaduct, there was a great gust of wind that lifted the carriage next to the engine off the rails. **John Hannigan**, who was working on the train that night, recalled the experience fifty years later:

Chapter Sixteen: The Port and Railway

Bob slowed down to a snailpace and as we crossed the bridge we did not think that the storm was all that bad. We were almost at the end of the viaduct when it all happened and quite suddenly. The carriage behind the two front wagons was raised up on the line; it was like a hump in its back. It then fell against the parapet and the roof was smashed."[4]

The severe gust of wind had lifted two of the big coaches from the rail and flung them onto the parapet, their roofs being smashed and passengers hurled from the carriages into the valley below. The masonry of the parapet also gave way and masses of it thundered down upon the injured passengers. The victims flung down the precipice amongst the huge boulders and rocks were horribly mutilated, and agonising scenes were witnessed by the band of workers, who under circumstances of great peril, and in the teeth of a raging gale, devoted themselves during the dark hours of the night to the work of rescue."[5]

The Owencarrow Viaduct disaster 1925

Of the 14 passengers on board, 4 people were killed - **Philip Boyle** (53) and his wife **Sarah** (45) from Arranmore, **Mrs. Una Mulligan** (48) from Falcarragh and **Neil Duggan** (67) of Meenabone. Only one passenger escaped unhurt; a **Miss Campbell**, who was flung from an upturned carriage and miraculously landed on soft, boggy soil, sinking knee-deep into it.

Another minor crash occurred in the summer of 1938, this time on the CDR line connected to Strabane. A railbus that had left Letterkenny for Strabane built up its speed as it neared the crossing at the Port Bridge but due to the failure of a worker to correctly change the line of the track from the turntable to the main thoroughfare, the railbus headed straight for the turntable and crashed into a clay bank at the Ramelton Road. People were thrown from their seats across the railbus but thankfully, nobody was seriously injured in the crash.[6]

205

Letterkenny - Where the Winding Swilly Flows

The End of An Era

After the Second World War, traffic on both railway networks began to fall off, a consequence of the competition from road transport. Cars and lorries had become much more popular and people could now access the outlying towns and villages much easier and quicker than using the railway system.

The Derry-Letterkenny line of the L&LSR closed on 1st July 1953, running only a goods service since 1940. It was followed seven years later by the closure of the Burtonport extension. Various lines and stations of the CDR throughout the county were by now in need of immediate repair and as the parent companies could not provide the necessary capital for replacement, a formal application for complete closure of the CDR system was made in May 1959 and all services ceased on 31st December 1959. The railways in Donegal never lived to see the coming of the 1960s. As the last trains left the Letterkenny stations, mini explosives detonated the railway lines and they were lifted shortly thereafter. The last Station Masters in Letterkenny were **Rory Delap** (L&LSR and grandfather to the Premiership footballer of the same name) and **Matt Patterson** (CDR and father of the successful singing group The Pattersons). The CDR survived as a separate transport company until it was eventually absorbed by Coras Iompair Éireann (CIÉ) in 1971, while the Lough Swilly Bus Company took over the duties of the L&LSR, sadly closing its business in 2014.

The legacy of the train system can still be seen around Letterkenny. The former CDR station is now the Bus Éireann depot (successor to CIÉ) while reconstruction of the Dry Arch bridge at Bonagee with its tin men building the

Below and following page: Memories of the railway network in Donegal at Owencarrow, Oldtown and a replica of the Dry Arch bridge.

Chapter Sixteen: The Port and Railway

Letterkenny - Where the Winding Swilly Flows

lines can be seen as you enter the town from Derry/Dublin. Remnants of the actual bridges can be seen at Owencarrow, Oldtown and Newmills while the Oldtown Station House was demolished and rebuilt as a large hotel, fittingly called the Station House Hotel. The section of the line that connected Letterkenny and Oldtown stations along the area known as the Isles became a road for the cars, buses and lorry systems that replaced the trains and although it may be officially called Pearse Road, to many Letterkenny residents, it will always be known as the 'Railway Road'.

Endnotes
1 Dickson, David "A Donegal Revenue Inspection of 1775" Donegal Annual 1972, pp172 – 181
2 "Letterkenny down the years: Letterkenny in 1824", Letterkenny Christmas Annual 2009, p92
3 Inglis, Henry D., "A Journey Throughout Ireland, During the Spring, Summer and Autumn of 1834", Vol II, London, 1834 p190
4 "Footplate man recalls Viaduct Disaster 59 Years ago", Letterkenny Christmas Annual 1984
5 Derry Journal 2/2/1925
6 Watson, Billy, "On the Day of the Crash", Letterkenny Christmas Annual 1992, p81

Chapter Seventeen: Twentieth Century Development

At the end of the nineteenth century, Slater's Directory described the town of Letterkenny as consisting of *"one principal street and a spacious Market square   has been much improved by supply of gas to the shops, and which the streets are also ted. A clock tower has also been erected in the market square. Trade in the town supplies a siderable tract of country and is an extensive one for flax during the season."*[1]

The 'one principal street' was of course the Main Street, with two roads ding off at the top, one leading to Ramelton and one to Kilmacrennan, forming junction. This junction is still visible in the modern layout with the Ramelton d (referred to as the Port Road today) and the Kilmacrennan Road, (later wn as the Asylum Road but now known as the High Road). For almost three dred years, this had been the traditional layout of the town and anything side of this was simply considered to be the countryside. As the twentieth tury was beginning however, all that was about to change.

Letterkenny at the beginning of the twentieth century. The town was quite compact then with residential areas close to the Main Street. to Image Courtesy of National Library of Ireland

By this time, Letterkenny had become the principal market town of negal. At the Market Square a weekly market for farm produce was held each day with a flax market on every alternate Friday. The 8th of every month was r Day' when farmers from the surrounding countryside areas would bring their ep or cattle to sell at the 'Fair Green' at Sentry Hill. The Oldtown Fair was a cial occasion held on the 8th of June each year. Hundreds of cows, horses and ep would line the bottom of the Main Street and out into Oldtown where the mers would strike deals for the various livestock. Children were entertained also h travelling shows and ice cream vendors creating a great carnival atmosphere oughout the area. The 'Scotch Fair' catered for those returning home from ir labours in Glasgow and Clydebank during the weeks of July while as we e seen, the Hiring Fairs were also held in the town on the first Fridays after 12th

Letterkenny - Where the Winding Swilly Flows

May and 12th November when deals were struck for children, women and you[ng] men to work on the farms in Derry, Tyrone and East Donegal. As a result [of] these continuous influxes of people from the surrounding countryside to do th[is] trade, it wasn't long before more and more drapers and grocers set up busines[s] in the town creating a thriving town for shopping and commerce. In 1824, th[ere] were 15 pubs in the town[2] but by 1889, a Public House Register showed t[hat] there were a total of 31 pubs in Letterkenny to cater for these great influ[x] of traders.[3] To put that into perspective, the thriving Letterkenny of today h[as] approximately the same number of bars and hotels but with a vastly increa[sed] number in population.

The Oldtown Fair was an annual spectacle when deals were struck from Oldtown all the way up the Main Street. Image courtesy of the National Library of Ireland

In 1836, the population of Letterkenny was recorded as 2,160. O[ne] hundred years later, in 1946, the population was 2,848, showing that the tow[n] population had only increased by about 700 people in this time. By and lar[ge] despite the economic growth of the town, the town's population had stay[ed] relatively the same for almost one hundred years. By 1996 however, the tow[n] population (urban and rural) had grown to 11,996 people. In just fifty years, t[he] population of the town had exploded by 400%.

Many factors contributed to this explosion in numbers, such as the drawing of the urban boundary in 1953, the point at which the town's populati[on] overtook the county's other major towns to become the largest urban populati[on]

Chapter Seventeen: Twentieth Century Development

he county (see county population graph on page 13). The opening of the new gional Technical College in 1971, the first Third-Level institution in the county, ant that students from all over the country were coming to Letterkenny to receive ir training and highly skilled students were available for industrial development. other significant factor was the arrival in town of the large UK textile business urtalds with their new plant at Kiltoy. The impact that the opening of this large iness had on the town of Letterkenny cannot be over-stated. Supermarkets ne to the town in the 1970s leading the town away from the traditional small cers and drapers and into the new age of the large supermarket with shoppers ning from all over county to avail of new phenomenon. th further industrial elopment in the 1970s 1980s, Letterkenny dually moved away m its traditionally epted market town us and fully embraced new position as a large mmercial and industrial a in the North West so by the late 1990s and arrival of the new millennium, the town was almost unrecognizable from at it had been only 50 years before.

The premises of John Gallagher on the Main Street of Letterkenny. From Christmas Annual 1997

own for Employment

Several large industries existed in the town in the first half of the ntieth century that provided much needed employment to the residents, as l as enticing others to move to the town from the surrounding countryside. ef amongst these was the business of **Charles Kelly Ltd**. The Kelly family l a successful grain, butter, bacon and egg business in Ramelton since around 0 and expanded their business ventures into Letterkenny at the turn of the century. They purchased the Oatmeal Mill in Ballymacool from the Boyds 1900 followed by the Corn Market at Lower Main Street in 1910 where they ned their hardware store. The family acquired the Port at Ballyraine in 1940 they followed this up with the purchase of the Thorn Quay in 1950, therefore ctively controlling the importing and exporting of goods on the River Swilly t up until the 1960s. They opened the Model Bakery in Oldtown in 1955 so by the mid 1950s they were employing many people in the town through er their Hardware shop on the Main Street, importing goods at the Port, their ber and grain mill at Ballymacool or their bakery in Oldtown. In 1938, they played their new status as the most influential family in the area by purchasing Boyd mansion at Ballymacool with its gatehouses and large gardens. They also ned Kiltoy Lodge, which they had bought in 1910 and later sold to the IDA in '5 for the development of the site for the Courtalds Factory.

Letterkenny - Where the Winding Swilly Flows

The firm of Charles Kelly Ltd. Was a large employer in the town for many years. From Christmas Annual 1996

Another significant employer in the town was **Oatfield** Sw Factory. **William McKinney** had started a small grocery business on the Ramelt /Port Road in 1900 and with the help of his two sons, **Ira** and **Haddon**, he beg a wholesale business in 1920, covering all of Donegal from 1923 with his V Wholesale Run. It was in 1927 at the back of their premises with a copper p a hand roller, a small slab and a coke fired home made kiln, that they made th first batch of pineapple drops. They proved so popular locally that they decid to expand their business and in February 1930 they purchased a site in the nea area of Oatlands opposite Gortlee House for the erection of a large factory. T was undoubtedly a brave decision just one year after the Wall Street Crash a the worldwide economic depression. Sadly though, William died just before factory went into production in August 1930.

Their original trading name was "Mayfield Confectionary" but another firm in Manchester were using the same name, they decided to merg with the name of the area in which the factory was built and thus became "Oatfi Sweets". The first manager in 1930 was **Joe Harrison**, who worked there for years while many other local people found long term employment in the la factory. The sweets were originally cooked on stoves but from 1934, cook was done by steam and on average they were producing 3 tons of sweets a we Sugar and glucose were imported from Holland through the Port at Ballyraine a their most successful products were the Emeralds, Eclairs, Orange Chocola and boiled sweets. By 1964, they began exporting to Northern Ireland, Malta a Canada and by the 1990s, they were exporting 65 tons of sweets and chocolat

Chapter Seventeen: Twentieth Century Development

...eek to 103 countries throughout the world. William's son, Ira McKinney, died in ...y 2000, a year after Donegal Creameries PLC had purchased a 76% share in the ...mpany. This was the beginning of the end for the long standing business as in ...ril 2007 Zed Candy of Dublin purchased the entire company, deciding to close ...wn the factory with the loss of the final 15 jobs in May 2012 and the demolition ... the building in April 2014. It was a sad day for people in Letterkenny, as the ...ctory had become an institution in the town. For many, there was always an ...ment of local pride in seeing bags of Emeralds or Colleen sweets around the ...rld and knowing that the only factory ...s located in Letterkenny.

Lymac's Bottling Store on ... High Road was yet another major ...ployer in Letterkenny. In 1928, Watts ... Derry had leased the main building ... the former Workhouse where they ...nufactured mineral waters and had ... bottling store. Ten years later, two ...ployees of the factory, **Mr. Lyttle** and ... **McAuley** took over and continued ... business. They amalgamated their ...mes to form the name of the new ...mpany, "Lymacs", and operated their ...ge factory here, employing over 100 ...ople until they closed down in 1968.

Across the road from this factory, ...**Hosiery Factory** was opened in the ...rly 1920s on the site of the former Army ...rracks at Sprackburn. The factory ...ployed 135 people by the 1930s, the ...jority of whom were women, making ...rdigans, jumpers, socks, stockings and ...derwear that were exported to many ...untries around the world but mostly to ...itain. The factory closed down in 1961 ...th the loss of around 60 jobs.

Two major iron works foundries ...isted in the town at this time also, ...own's and Wallace's. William Holmes ...ablished **Brown's Foundry** at the bottom of the town next to the Gas Works ...here Dunnes Stores is today) in 1934 and the work involved moulding various ...etal parts for plough parts, fire-bars, window weights, man-hole covers and pot ...ens. A similar business owned by the **Wallaces** was also in operation on the ...ain Street on the site of the former Hogg's Shirt Factory. Joe Bonner eventually ...ok over the business of Brown's and opened his own metal craft company that ...still in operation today, located on the Neil T. Blaney Road.

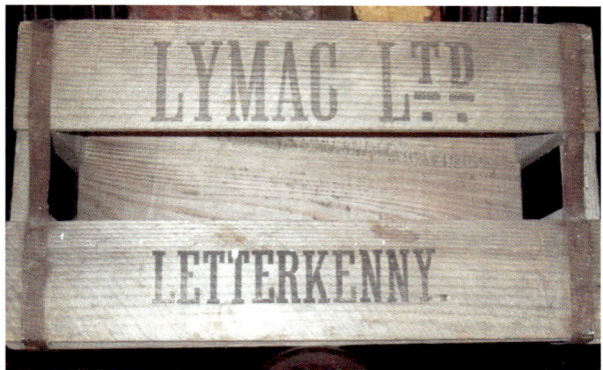

An old ad for Watts Distillers who were located in the former Workhouse building

A crate from the former Lymac's bottling factory

213

Letterkenny - Where the Winding Swilly Flows

William McKinney outside his shop on the Port Road where he first produced his sweets before building a new factory at Oatlands. From Christmas Annual 1991

Below: The former sweet factory of Oatfields prior being demolished in 201

Chapter Seventeen: Twentieth Century Development

Letterkenny - Where the Winding Swilly Flows

The Donegal Bacon Factory was opened by O'Meara's of Limerick 1939 on the Railway Road and provided much employment as well as business the local pig farmers while **George McFeely** and **Joseph Crumlish** opened **Letterkenny Steam Laundry** in 1935 in Oldtown. These businesses employ many local people until they closed down in 1987 and 1991 respectively.

Industrial growth in Ireland by the late 1940s called for the inception of the **Industrial Development Authority** (IDA) in 1950 and a branch the association was set up in Letterkenny. The Association gave assistance a information to corporations or individuals who were interested in establishi industries and gave detailed information concerning sites, power, labour, r materials, water, transport facilities, housing and educational facilities etc. It v composed of the leading businessmen, professionals and workers of the tov and held conferences with prominent industrialists and various Governm Departments. The programme for the 'An Tostal' festival in 1954 tells us:

In 1953, the Urban Council extended their boundary to take in Oldtown for the first time

"That business is booming so strongly in Letterkenny to-day reflects an enterprising commur drive which finds expression in the constant vigilance and readiness for action of the Indust Development Association, set up some years ago. This body, which counts in its membersr the majority of the town's most progressive business men, is always on the alert to sponsor setting up of a new industry and to provide facilities for those prepared to invest capital in s projects." [4]

Chapter Seventeen: Twentieth Century Development

The Letterkenny Town Guide of 1952 also tells us of the local support for the IDA:

"The community is solidly behind its efforts, as demonstrated by the financial support accorded to it. No wonder then that here business thrives and over the town there is an air of quiet prosperity and confidence in the future."[5]

With the assistance and promotion from the IDA, Nestles Ltd. founded the **Donegal Milk Products** factory at Crieve in 1952 and a year later, the **Letterkenny Co-Operative Dairy Society** was set up and ran a creamery in connection with the Nestle factory, both of which again provided employment in the town. These companies formed the backbone of the future business of Donegal Creameries, which would be formed in 1970. Just as the local pig farmers benefited from the opening of the Bacon Factory, so the local dairy farmers

A town about to change: Letterkenny Main Street in the late 1950s/ early 1960s. From Christmas Annual 2010

prospered with the opening of these businesses and after much hard initial work by local farmer **Sam Fleming**, Donegal's first livestock mart was opened on the Fair Green on Sentry Hill on 8th March 1958.

Local agriculture was key to the success of many businesses in the town. Butchers and grocers received their supplies of milk, meat and eggs from these local farmers as well as trading their goods at the weekly markets. After the

217

Letterkenny - Where the Winding Swilly Flows

formation of the Irish Free State in 1922, the **Irish Agricultural Wholesale Society (IAWS)** was set up to supply many local co-operatives with everything that the farmers needed to develop their farms and produce. The Conwal Co-Op had owned a building on the Main Street but due to accruing debts with the

> ### Did you know?
>
> The oldest shop still in existence in the town is Speer's Drapery. If you were to walk through the doors of this business on the Main Street, it is like taking a step back in time as the original décor of wooden floors and counters remain the same as they did when the business opened in 1880. A **Mr. Magee** had operated a large drapery, haberdashery and millenary business here for thirty years; the name Magee Bros. still appears on the tiles as you enter the shop. In 1910, **James Benson** bought the store from Mr. Magee and for forty-five years the business was known as Bensons. In 1955, an employee of Mr. Benson, **Ernest Speer**, bought the premises and took over the running of the business from his employer and the Speer family continues to run a successful drapery business in the town.

IAWS, the building was taken over by the IAWS in 1924 with **Michael Mellet** from Mayo becoming the new manager. As well as continuing to assist farmers, the business also dealt with hardware and grocery goods until 1967 when it closed its retail outlet. By 1976, the Council were looking to build a new road to ease traffic congestion on the Main Street so the company sold its premises to the Council for the construction of this new Oliver Plunkett Road and moved its wholesale business to the Pearse Road where it remained until 1985.

Dillon Bros. Supermarket, Main Street Letterkenny. Courtesy of Brian McDaid

Shopping Town

Many local shops and grocers operated like the IAWS at this time in that the customers would ask the shopkeeper for what they wanted, like a loaf of bread or a pound of sugar, and the shopkeeper or his assistant would

Chapter Seventeen: Twentieth Century Development

etch the goods, weigh them out and bag them up for the customer at the counter. This was standard practice until the opening of the first supermarket in Donegal at the end of the 1960s. **Bernard** and **Jimmy Dillon** had already opened their small grocery business on the Main Street in 1957 but ten years later, they decided to expand and bought up much of the adjacent land and buildings to construct their new supermarket, **Dillon Bros. Supermarket**. Now customers could take the various goods off the shelves themselves, place them in their basket or trolley and pay for them at the counter. This new system of shopping was quite revolutionary for its time, changing the way that local people shopped for their groceries and brought many people to the town from around the county to do their shopping and witness this exciting new way to buy their groceries.

It was with the opening of Dillon's Supermarket that the town of Letterkenny really started to move towards its status as a shopping town for tourists, a status still enjoyed today. A documentary about Letterkenny broadcast on RTÉ in 1975 entitled "Portrait of an Irish Town" highlighted a key factor in the sustained growth of the town at this time as a centre for shopping for many people throughout Donegal and its adjoining counties:

An aerial view of the site for the new Shopping Centre in the early 1980s. Courtesy of Brian McCracken

Letterkenny - Where the Winding Swilly Flows

"While the neighbouring urban communities across the border, Derry and Strabane, ha suffered some of the worst scars in the Northern conflict, Letterkenny's shopkeepers have some extent benefited. Many of the County Donegal people who regularly crossed the border shop in the North before the Troubles now consider it more prudent as the bombs go off to she in the south and Letterkenny has benefited in consequence."[6]

As more and more people came to shop, even more businesses decided t capitalize on this new status. **Best's Supermarket** was next to follow when the opened their large supermarket on the site of the Old Gas Works in 1972. Seve years later, the large national supermarket of **Dunnes Stores** decided to open business in the town and after an initial decision to purchase the site of the o Fiesta Dance Hall, decided to purchase the premises of Best's Supermarket at th bottom of the Main Street where they remain today. More national chain store soon followed and in 1985, Quinnsworth and Penneys opened their stores in th newly constructed **Letterkenny Shopping Centre** complex, built on the site c the old railway lines behind the bus station. The **Courtyard Shopping Centr** opened on the Main Street in 1993 and brought with it Super Valu, Iceland an British Home Stores.

It is fair to say that Letterkenny as the shopping town we know toda really began with the opening of Dillon Bros. Supermarket in 1967. Sadly, th original supermarket of the county closed down in 1997 and the building wa demolished making way for a new hotel, the Letterkenny Court Hotel but the fittingly called their bar Dillons, in recognition of the previous owners of the si and what they did for the town of Letterkenny.

Housing

By the 1950s, Letterkenny was beginning to shed its long held Marke town status and was embracing its new position as an industrial town of economi growth providing much needed employment to many people in the local are This rise in employment and population led to the construction of new housin estates at Ros Suilghe (1940), Ard O'Donnell (1949) and Ard Colmcille (195 and in 1954, the guide for the An Tostal Festival proudly declared:

"Within recent years, Letterkenny has so expanded and modernised itself as to virtually unidentifiable with the backward, poorly housed, thinly populated town that the o people still with us, recall, with reluctance, when recalling the hard days of their youth.

For long, bad and insanitary housing disfigured the town and coupled with enforce overcrowding, was a menace to the health of those who found it impossible to get decent livin accommodation. To-day, complaint on that score is but rarely heard, thanks to the unremittin and enlightened crusade of the Urban Council, in recent times, to promote large scale housin schemes to meet a persistent and ever increasing demand."[7]

However, by 1968, the Buchanan Report, when identifying the tow as an area for future industrial growth, highlighted the need for new housin schemes as important to the town's future that would cater for this expansior

Chapter Seventeen: Twentieth Century Development

in the early years of the 1970s, new housing schemes were constructed in the surrounding fields that lay in the town's immediate hinterland and slowly and gradually, the town of Letterkenny expanded outwards from its previously dominant residential area of the Main Street. McNeely Villas (named after Bishop McNeely) was constructed in 1970 at Oldtown while in 1973, the Beechwood Estate was constructed, followed a year later by Gartan Avenue and Ballyraine Park. In 1975, Derryveagh Ave, Muckish Avenue, Cnocnar Avenue, Binnion Ave and Croagh Patrick Avenue (estates all named after mountains), were constructed near to the new County Hospital, which had been built in 1960. The estates of Hawthorn Heights, behind St. Eunan's College, and Ashlawn, near Gortlee were also built at this time while many privately built homes in the Glencar and Ballyraine areas were also erected. Before long, the once centralized residential layout of the town had expanded outwards, gradually claiming land from the surrounding hillsides, and Letterkenny was now ready for significant industrial expansion.

Industry

Having grown significantly as a result of the commercial boom of the first sixty years of the Twentieth Century, the arrival of large industries further enhanced the town's growth as a large urban centre. In the early 1970s, the government were opening several new regional colleges throughout the country. Local T.D., **Neil T. Blaney** was instrumental in pushing through the need for a Third Level institution in the North West and in September 1971, the **Donagh O'Malley Regional Technical College** (renamed Letterkenny Institute of Technology, LYIT, in 1997) opened on the Port Road. With the opening of the new college came the training of many young locals for advancement in the industrial sector. Certificates in Business Studies, Science Technology and Construction Studies were available for these new students and many would go on to get jobs in the industrial and business sectors of many large companies. With the training of many new students for the industrial sector, Letterkenny moved even further away from its traditional agricultural background and new industries were enticed to the town by the IDA, the biggest of which was the major UK firm of Courtalds.

Letterkenny Regional Technical College (now the LYIT) admitted students for the first time in 1971

221

Letterkenny - Where the Winding Swilly Flows

The availability of a trained workforce was no doubt a factor in attracting many new industries to the town, including this large UK business.

The arrival of **Courtalds** was a watershed moment for the town of Letterkenny. It was a defining moment that changed the image and status of the town forever, as it heralded the arrival of 'large-scale industry'. The IDA worked tirelessly to entice the company to set up its factory in the town and great rejoicing took place by many when Letterkenny was chosen as its new location. It was the first major industry to open in the county offering large-scale employment in the late 1970s and many more were soon to follow. Although industries had existed in the town previously and gave employment to many local people, none of these were on the same scale as this new factory, which offered its employees the new concept of 'shift work' where they would be working throughout the night producing polyester yarn.

In the 1975 RTÉ documentary about Letterkenny, Ken Worrall the Director and General Manager of Courtalds expressed his slight concern that the town would not be able to cope with this new development. However, he was also confident that with the proper training the employees would learn to cope with these new demands. This documentary did not portray the town too favourably with many interviewees expressing their concern at the lack of amenities in the town such as a swimming pool, a community centre or

The construction of the Courtald's factory at Kiltoy was a watershed moment for the town as it heralded the arrival of large scale industry

adequate housing to cater for this new industrial growth. By 1975, Letterkenny was at a crossroads and if it were to expand industrially, then it would also need to expand in its housing and social outlets to cater for the thousands of new people who were now arriving in the town for employment.

By 1982, the Urban District Council had acted on the fears and concerns of the lack of amenities highlighted in the documentary and the town proved to be an enticing prospect for many more industries to come and set up businesses. Local businessman **Sean Curran** noted that there had been 517 people in industrial employment in Letterkenny in 1973 but by 1982, this number had almost tripled to 1,304.[8] As well as the large businesses already established such as Charles Kelly Ltd., the Donegal Bacon Factory and of course Courtalds, new industries had been established in the town such as IMED, Gaeltext, Sigro, James Doherty Meat Processing and Donegal Co-Op Creameries that provided massive

Chapter Seventeen: Twentieth Century Development

The former UNIFI plant at Kiltoy. From Christmas Annual 1984

nployment for many people in the area. In March 1984, the large U.S. firm **UNIFI Textured Yarns Ltd.** acquired the Courtalds factory and opened eir first off shore production base outside of America manufacturing textured olyester yarns for use in the textile industry. By 1986, the company was employing ver 400 people at its plant in Kiltoy.

Spurred on by how the town was perceived in the RTÉ documentary, e Urban Council set about meeting this demand for social opportunities and a ew Community Centre and athletic track was opened at the Isles in 1983 soon ollowed by a swimming pool off the High Road. The Letterkenny Tidy Towns ommittee, formed originally in the 1960s, was rejuvenated in the 1980s and set out cleaning the town up and ridding it of the unsightly litter and overgrown edges and trees. With increased community involvement each year, the efforts of e Committee were apparent as the town gradually became much more visually ppealing to visitors and the Tidy Towns judges. Letterkenny would win many old Stars for its community efforts in the 1990s and eventually in 2007, to the elight of the chairman **Jim McCormick** and his hard working committee, they aimed the coveted Large Urban Area trophy for the town.

The Main Street was converted to one-way traffic in 1983 to cater for e increased number of cars now arriving on the street while new schools were ected at Ballyraine (1976) and Convent Road (1977) as more and more children ere being enrolled. As the town kept on growing, the Garda Barracks at the ottom of the town was not able to cope with the increased demands in such small confined building. A new station was built on the site of the former orkhouse in 1987, much more befitting of a town of Letterkenny's size.

Despite the growth though, Letterkenny was not immune to the recession at hit Ireland in the early 1980s, with many young men and women from the area cing no other option but to emigrate to England and the USA for employment.

Letterkenny - Where the Winding Swilly Flows

By the late 1990s, Letterkenny had been transformed from the town that many people grew up in throughout the 1950s and 1960s. It began the century with a population of almost 4,000 people and had *"one principal street and a spacious Market square"* and ended it as the largest commercial and industrial town in the county with a population of just fewer than 12,000 people. The economic growth was initially facilitated by the boat and railway systems that developed the weekly and monthly markets and led to a gradual growth in the town's businesses and population. By the 1970s though, the arrival of the supermarkets in the town changed the way that people shopped and annually, more and more of the smaller grocers began to close down, unable to compete with the thriving new supermarkets. While the supermarkets brought many people to the town for their shopping they also had the detrimental effect on the local bakeries and farmers. Bread, meat and other products now came from all over the country, and even internationally, rather than from the local agricultural hinterland.

Since the 1950s, the town openly embraced its industrial expansion and following the arrival of Courtalds in the 1970s, the town really expanded as an industrial hub of employment. More and more industries arrived soon after expanding the town's size throughout the 1980s and 1990s. New industrial parks were built to accommodate these new businesses while an AnCo (later FÁS) training centre assisted the RTC in providing a trained workforce for the local industries. The Church of the Irish Martyrs, a new Catholic church for the parish of Aughanunshin, opened in 1994 to cater for these ever-growing numbers in the town's hinterlands while the schools of Lurgybrack, Woodlands and Illistrin increased steadily in size as more and more people relocated to new housing estates built in the surrounding districts.

The traditional market town of Letterkenny, with its centrally located residential areas, was no more and at the dawn of a new millennium and the boom of the Celtic Tiger, it was about to evolve once again. This time into a thriving, multicultural urban centre whose population would almost double in ten years, and gain with it all the associated dangers that comes with a rapid and uncontrollable expansion.

Endnotes
1 Farrell, Noel, "Exploring Family Origins in Letterkenny", 1996
2 "Documents of Local Interest", Donegal County Library papers, see Appendix D
3 Farrell, Noel, "Exploring Family Origins in Letterkenny", 1996
4 An Tostal Guide 1954 p5
5 Letterkenny Official Guide 1952, p2
6 Portrait of an Irish Town, RTÉ, 1975 available to watch in full on YouTube
7 An Tostal Guide 1954, p3
8 Curran, Sean, "A Growing Letterkenny With A Bright Future", Letterkenny Christmas Annual, 1982

Chapter Eighteen: Sports Clubs in Letterkenny

As the town of Letterkenny was growing throughout the twentieth century, the community naturally required a means of social interaction with each other. Aside from frequenting the local 'watering hole', one of the best ways for this to happen is through participation in sport or attendance at a sporting event. Today, the town has many sports clubs and noted athletes. Residents can choose from a variety of sports, such as football, GAA, athletics, golf, boxing, tennis or basketball as a means of social interaction. In the early years of the twentieth century, as the town started to develop economically and people arrived looking for work, these sports took root in the town, although it wasn't until the 1970s when the town's population rose significantly that the majority of the present clubs in the town have their origins.

With the building of the Royal Garrison Artillery Barracks in 1880 at Blackburn, Letterkenny officially became a Garrison Town, although the Donegal Artillery were present in the town for many years prior to this.[1] The arrival of British troops brought the playing of predominantly English games such as football, rugby and cricket to the town. The large tracts of land between the railway track and the Swilly were known locally as 'the Isles' consisting of fields that were rented out by their owners for the playing of various sports. One such field was known for many years as the 'Cricket Meadow' (approximately where the car garages on the Canal Road are today) where cricket, and later football, was played. In the 1870s and 1880s, there were four cricket teams based in the town – Swilly, Letterkenny, the County Donegal Cricket Club and the Military Barracks team while by 1895, a Letterkenny team were competing in the County Donegal Cricket League against Convoy, Raphoe, Manorcunningham, Lifford and Monleigh (notably all areas within East Donegal with strong Plantation roots).[2] Even though it had been introduced by the arrival of garrison troops, the playing of cricket did not cease with their removal from the town, as it continued to be played into the late 1920s with games occurring on the grounds of the Asylum Hospital.[3] Golf is also reported to have been played in 1894 although for a long time, like cricket, this was considered an elitist sport for the more 'well to do' of Letterkenny society.

Football Clubs

A sport more suited to the working class members of society was of course football or soccer. On 30th January 1882, two years after the arrival of the garrison troops in the town, the first record of a football match in Letterkenny took place when the two lady proprietors of Hegarty's Hotel granted "Letterkenny Athletic Club" the use of their field at the Isles for "*a well contested match of football… under association rules*". The 9-a side match was played between the "Friendly Club" and the "Town Club" and the referee was Mr. Hugh Gallagher. The Friendly Club team was made up of **S. Russell, Henderson, McCrossan, Allison, Lyons, Cooke, Starritt, Lafferty** and **Ferry** while the Town Club team was composed

225

of **John Diver**, **M. O'Brien**, **P. McAteer**, **John Doherty**, **Richard Barry** **Mulheron**, **J. Bolster**, **James O'Donnell** and **Hugh Kelly**.

"The play was of the most spirited kind. Both teams struggled pluckily for victory. A fine of athletic fellows it would be hard to find. After an excellent contest, fortune favoured teams and gave each a goal, which left the game to be decided on another day...The utmost humour and satisfaction were felt by all and hearty cheers for both teams closed the proceeding

Later that same year, Hugh Gallagher was again the referee for games football as part of the St. Patrick's Temperance Guild Athletic Sports tournam Various athletic sports were competed for that day again taking place at Hega Isle and both games of football once again ended in a draw.[5]

The seasonal migration to Scotland and England for work gre influenced the development of football in Donegal as labourers returned ho with the new association rules. However, it appears that the rules took a w to be understood amongst many people more used to playing other sports. example, in September 1891 a team called Milford Swifts defeated Letterkenny 1-9 to 1-4. Not that alarming a result at first until you read that this was actual game of soccer![6]

By the early 1890s, the first official competitive team in the to "Letterkenny F.C.", was competing in the North West Football Association aga teams from Donegal and Derry. The team held their meetings in the rooms **Michael Doherty**'s Hotel (now the Central Bar) on the Main Street receiv subscriptions from **W.H. Boyd** and **Major Doyne** while Town Commissio **Mr. P. Doherty**, let them use his field at the Isles to play in.[7] This team composed of **Charles McCafferty**, **Joseph Cullin**, **James Sweeney**, **P. Peop W. McLaughlin**, **John Sweeney**, **James Gallagher**, **W. Roarty**, **Joe Di Barney Crampsey** and **James Peoples**.[8] On Christmas Day 1891, they pla against Young Ireland of Derry with the visiting team winning by 6 goals to

"After the match was over Young Ireland and friends were entertained to a sumptuous dinn Mr. Michael Doherty's Hotel, which was heartily partaken of; songs etc. being kept up till in the evening, when they again started home. Never in the history of Young Ireland did meet a more hospitable team than Letterkenny F.C. and it is certain that their visit will ne easily forgotten."[9]

By 1894, a new team, "St. Adaman's Swifts" had joined Letterkenny in competing in the North West Football Association competition, but the i that Donegal teams could compete in their own league without teams from De was now put forward by Daniel Deeney from the Carradoan Club of Rathmu One week later, **Joseph Devenney**, the secretary of St. Adaman's Swifts Letterkenny, backed Deeney's proposal for a Donegal only league, stating tha

"the majority of Letterkenny footballers are in favour of raising a Cup for Donegal clubs a I think it would be the best and most achievable method of spreading the game in our county

Chapter Eighteen: Sports Clubs in Letterkenny

On the 24th March 1894, these men got their wish as the County Donegal otball Association was founded in Boyle's Hotel, Ramelton. The following nth, at the Sunburst Football Club ground in Ramelton, the Whites (players m Letterkenny and Ramelton) defeated the Pinks (players from Milford, nford, Cratlagh, Carradoan and Kerrykeel) 2-1. At a meeting following the ne, both Letterkenny F.C. and a new team from the town, "Letterkenny Celtic", representatives - Mr. J. Peoples for the former and Mr. J. Gallagher for the er.[11]

There appears to have been no love lost between these two rival teams m the town. In December 1894, a representative from Letterkenny Celtic te a long letter to the Derry Journal complaining about Letterkenny F.C. He ed that the team should not be called "Letterkenny" at all as: *"...it is not strictly posed of players belonging to that town, and in addition its style of play is not of the highest s."*[12]

By the middle of the 1890s, Letterkenny F.C. had garnered an unpopular utation. Ramelton Athletic Football Club removed themselves from the negal Association in March 1895 owing to the actions of the Letterkenny b. According to a lengthy statement in the Derry Journal, the two teams were to play each other in the cup semi final but at the last possible minute, the terkenny club pulled out saying that they couldn't travel. As the referee had ady travelled, he awarded the game to Ramelton. However, after Letterkenny ealed to the Committee, the match was played on 16th February, ending in raw, 3 goals each. For the replay, again Letterkenny refused to travel but they lly met on 9th March, Ramelton winning 4 - 3. Letterkenny F.C. once again tested the result and to the surprise of Ramelton, the Committee upheld protest, awarding the tie to Letterkenny. Dr. Patterson, the President of the ociation, resigned at this outrageous decision and advised the Ramelton club o the same. In their resignation letter, the Ramelton club also highlighted the that Letterkenny F.C. had been playing three ineligible Strabane players (King, te and Kearney) against them all season. In a final barbed attack they stated:

"Since the game started in this county, about three seasons ago, out of ten matches een Ramelton and Letterkenny, Ramelton have seven wons, two draws, and one loss as record. Letterkenny have established an unique record in the annals of football, as they appear in the final of the Donegal Challenge Cup without having won a single match in the petition."[13]

As a result of this ruling, Letterkenny F.C. competed in the County negal FA Challenge Cup Final against Derrybeg Celtic in Kerrykeel on 20 ril 1895 but unsurprisingly for this problematic club it was not without its controversy. After twenty minutes of the second half, and trailing 1-0, when ball was accidentally burst, Letterkenny left the field and refused to play the ainder of the game with the new ball. This led to a concession of the game Derrybeg were awarded the cup.[14] Letterkenny F.C. dropped out of the league following year and were replaced by Letterkenny Celtic who competed against lly Rangers, Cresslough, Cranford and Milford Swifts in the County Donegal ior League.[15] On 29 Feb 1896, Letterkenny Celtic made it to the cup final to

Letterkenny - Where the Winding Swilly Flows

face Derrybeg Celtic but were defeated 5-1.[16]

By the end of the 1890s, the County Donegal Football Associat[ion] gradually faded away with less teams competing in the competition. In Feb 190[?] ban was placed on Irish men participating in playing the so-called 'English' sp[orts] of rugby, soccer, hockey and cricket supported by the clergy of the country. [On] 9 Oct 1905 Bishop O'Donnell stated in a thinly veiled attack against these sp[orts] that: *"Irish games in Irish terms are the games for Irish people…no sports are so good for [?] people as those of native growth."*[17]

Bonagee F.C. 1911/1912. From Christmas Annual 2002

In the first three decades of the new century, several small cl[ubs] participated in occasional friendly matches. "Bonagee F.C.", "Letterkenny Hea[rts]" and "Letterkenny United" are three such local teams said to have been in existe[nce] immediately prior to World War I, while the 1920s saw the "Lily Whites" and [?] St. Conal's Hospital Staff teams compete regularly in Summer Cup competitio[ns]. Following the demise of the Letterkenny Rovers Gaelic Football team in Aug[ust] 1927, a "Letterkenny Rovers Association Football Club" played several gam[es] at Ballymacool w[ith] 'Hanlon', 'Roarty' [and] 'Loughrey' noted as [?] players.[19]

St. Conal's Hospital football team 1920s. Courtesy of Liam Blake

In January 19[??] "Letterkenny Crusade[rs]" were formed, play[ing] their home matches [at] the ground of Pat[?] Doherty at the Cri[cket] Meadow, even erect[ing] a pavilion there [for] spectators, and compet[ing] in the Connau[ght] Football Associati[on]

Chapter Eighteen: Sports Clubs in Letterkenny

ich was the controlling body for football in Donegal at this time.[20] Players the Crusaders included **Denis McGlynn**, **N. McGroarty**, **T. Whyte**, **M. Monagle**, **T. Gavigan**, **W. Whyte**, **J. Friel**, **G. McCaul**, **D. Crampsie**, **J. vine**, **J. McLaughlin**, **A. McNelis**, **D. MAteer**, **A. McKinley**, **M. Logue**, Quigley, **P. McLaughlin**, **T. McRoarty** and **T. Loughrey**.[21] This club was stly successful in Summer Cup competitions with a victory dance being held he Devlin Hall in September 1939 with over 300 people in attendance.[22] With outbreak of World War II though, this team was no more.

For many years, the Main Street of Letterkenny was divided into 'East' l 'West' (as opposed to Upper and Lower as it is today). Evidence of this can seen, for example, in 1927 when the Derry People reported incidents in the 'est End of Letterkenny" while as we shall see, a "West End Tennis Club" yed near the Garda Barracks.[23] In November 1947, following a meeting in Devlin Hall, a new team based at the bottom of the town took the name of est End United" with Mr. Joseph Blake as Chairman.[24] They played in a field ind Larkin's Bakery initially before moving to play their games at McCaul's Isle Ballymacool. **Danny Blanchflower**, the Northern Ireland and Tottenham F.C. tain, is believed to have guest played for West End United in a Summer Cup npetition.[25]

November 51, "Letterkenny saders" were ormed with **lphonsus llagher** as airman and **draig Henry** as cretary. In 1953, y finished runners to Swilly Rovers in Donegal League by 1955 they l their first cup cess, winning the terkenny Summer Cup and finishing runners up in the Donegal League to anmore Hibs. The following year, they won the Lifford Cup defeating their n neighbours West End United 3-2 and once again finished runners up in Donegal League. The 1957 season saw them victorious in the Letterkenny, phoe and Buncrana Cup competitions but by now it was noted that the expense l difficulties of bringing in outside players from Derry and Sligo was getting much.[26]

The club name of "Letterkenny Rovers" was revived in May 1957 with intention of confining membership only to players residing in the town l district, making their debut in the Convoy Summer Cup of 1957 against

Letterkenny FC from 1936. From Christmas Annual 1982

Letterkenny - Where the Winding Swilly Flows

Letterkenny Crusaders from the mid 1950s. From Christmas Annual 2002

Eunan Blake (right) in action for Derry City at the Brandywell. From Christmas Annual 1996

Drumoghill Hibernian The Crusaders c officially amalgama with this new Letterker Rovers club with forn Crusaders players such brothers, **Eunan** and **Li Blake**, **Charlie 'Bov Collins** and Alphon Gallagher helping Rov win the Letterker Summer Cup in 195 In 1960, the club w competing in the Done Association Footl League against Kildr Tigers, Swilly Rovers, Dunmore Utd., Raphoe, Lifford Celtic and Drumog Hibs.[29] The club purchased land in the Isles from the Crumlish family in early 1960s, and officially opened their new ground, "Leckview Park", in 19 Six years later, the team joined the new Donegal League, founded by Letterker man **Dick Duffy**, and won the league for the first time in 1979/80 and agair 1980/81.

By this time, anot Letterkenny team h been set up also. "Arca Athletic" were forn in 1970 by **Brian Dre Paddy McFadden**, **Pe McGlynn** and others a played their games in Bonagee area of the to with **Frankie Dohe** serving as their f manager. In 1971, the te purchased two and a h acres of land behind Dry Arch Inn from a lo farmer, George Bates a in 1973, they changed th name first to "Bonag Celtic" and finally in 1975 to "Bonagee United". Other teams from the Letterker area to have competed in the Donegal League since its inception in 1971 were "Dodgers" (playing their games at St. Conal's Hospital), "Rockhill United", "CYMS", "Downtown United", "Orchard United", "Glencar Celtic" and "G Rovers" (playing their games at Rashedoge). Since its formation in 1986, b

Chapter Eighteen: Sports Clubs in Letterkenny

tterkenny Rovers and Bonagee United have en competing in the Ulster Senior League h Letterkenny Rovers winning the league 2005 and again in 2009.

A Clubs

As part of an overall late nineteenth tury national Gaelic revival, the Gaelic letic Association was formed in Thurles 1884, which set about codifying games that re played with different rules in various ts of the country. Although attempts were de to form clubs, it was a slow start for the v organization to penetrate into Donegal. wasn't until 23rd October 1905 that the negal GAA County Board was officially med at a meeting in Mountcharles hough the first GAA club in the county, t Hibernians had been in existence ce the 1890s and won the Aonach an Dún Festival at St. Eunan's College in 06). **Canon Edward Maguire**, the former President of the Old Seminary in tterkenny, became the inaugural President of the County Board.

One month prior to the formation of the Board, on the 18th September 05, a Gaelic club was established in Letterkenny for the first time following eeting in the Literary Institute. Bishop O'Donnell was chosen as patron of "Lámh Dearg" club while **Patrick Sweeney** was made captain and **James**

Ryan McLaughlin of Letterkenny Rovers and Sam Murphy of Bonagee United in the Ulster Senior League 2014. Courtesy of Stephen Doherty

Did you know?

Rory Delap, grandson of the former Station Master of the L&LSR, was born in England but has strong Letterkenny connections from his father. He made his professional debut with Carlisle United, before joining Premiership teams Derby County, Southampton, Sunderland and Stoke City. Famed for his long-throw technique, Rory won 11 caps for the Republic of Ireland before retiring in 2013 after short spells at Barnsley and Burton Albion. Brazilian World Cup winning manager Luis Felipe Scolari, when manager of Chelsea said *"I have never seen anything like this in my life; 10 metres outside midfield, this boy puts the ball inside the area. Maybe it's not beautiful football but it's effective."* Another player with Letterkenny connections is Everton's **Shane Duffy**, whose father Brian comes from Ard O'Donnell while **Anthony Gorman** from Glencar had spells with Portadown and Coleraine before joining Linfield in 1996 winning every honour in Irish League football.

Letterkenny - Where the Winding Swilly Flows

> **Did you know?**
>
> Celtic manager Jock Stein's final signing for the club took place in Letterkenny, at the Ballyraine Hotel, when he signed goalkeeper **Packie Bonner** in May 1978. Incidentally, when Glasgow Celtic was formed in 1888, one of the founder members was a man of Donegal descent by the name of Dominic McCreadie who welcomed the boatloads of Donegal workers off the Derry boat into his pub in Glasgow. Perhaps his son, who worked in the bar at the time and greeted many seasonal immigrants from Letterkenny, may even have had something to do with the writing of a famous local song, for his name was indeed Pat McCreadie!

McMonagle vice-captain.[1] On 26th December 1905, the club competed in a ga of camán (hurling) in the East Donegal division against St. Mura's of Fahan. T match was played in Letterkenny on the grounds of the Asylum Hospital draw a sizable crowd with Bishop O'Donnell in attendance. St. Mura's won the ga 2-3 to 3 points. The match report stated:

> *"Lamh Dearg did very well considering that they are practically a new team, and practice should show much improvement. When it is considered that their opponents were su superior lot it cannot be denied that they have made great progress indeed in hurling circles."*

The Lámh Dearg team on that momentous occasion of the first recor Gaelic match in the town was: **Patrick Sweeney, Edward Sweeney, Edw Coyle, Bernard Crampsey, James McMonagle, Lawrence Robbins, Jan Rodden, John Blake, Joseph Cullen, John Campbell, Joseph Harkin, McLaughlin, A. McClean, John McGinley, David Gallagher, James Gil** and **James Peoples**. From this we can see that the games of hurling and foot were played as 13-a-side, and would remain so until the 1930s.

On 22nd April 1906 the Lámh Dearg football team (comprised mostly the same players from the hurling team) were defeated by the Gweedore C in the Gaelic Football Championship with over 2,000 spectators present. I strange game in Gweedore dictated by the weather conditions, the home te failed to score a single score in the first half and Lámh Dearg failed to score the second. The final score was 1-08 to 1-06.[3]

The GAA movement slipped into decline throughout Donegal after 19 This was due to several factors such as the popularity of soccer, arranging transp to games and also organizational difficulties within the County Board. Howev teams still were in evidence in Letterkenny playing in occasional tournaments. 1911, two new hurling clubs had replaced Lámh Dearg in the town, "Tircona and "Faugh A Ballagh". In June 1911 the Tirconaill hurling club were defeated the final of the Assaroe Cup played in Letterkenny.[4] This club was primarily m up of most of the former members of the Lámh Dearg club in the town.

Chapter Eighteen: Sports Clubs in Letterkenny

One month later, Ardaghy defeated the same team in a hurling match in Donegal Town at the Féis Tír Chonaill:

At the end of a contest in which both teams exhibited a knowledge of the game, and an appreciation of its merits which augurs well for the future of hurling in Donegal, the Ardaghy boys were declared the victors...I never witnessed a contest of the kind in which such earnestness and determination to win were accompanied by such good temper. The Letterkenny club has come into existence only recently...Both teams if they continue to practice may be trusted to give a good account of themselves in the near future."[5]

On 4th August 1911 the Faugh A Ballagh team of Letterkenny defeated Éire Óg in the Junior Championship at the grounds of the Tirconaill Club at the Isles.[6] (The name Faugh A Ballagh comes from an old battle cry from 1798 meaning "Clear the Way" - Fag an Bealach).

By 1919, a new attempt at revitalizing the GAA took place, with a new County Board put in place following a meeting in Letterkenny with local man Sean Curran appointed as Secretary-Treasurer. A county championship was set up, to be played on a league basis with the county divided up into East and West divisions. "Letterkenny" competed against Castlefin, Killygordon, Clady and Labstown in the East Donegal section of the County Championship in 1919.

With the formation of the Irish Free State in 1922, the new forces of An Garda Síochana arrived in various towns throughout the country. Needing a social outlet in their new locations and also with the need to keep fit, many new clubs were formed throughout the country as a result, catering for these enthusiastic young men in their new surroundings.

In 1924, following the arrival of An Garda Síochana in the town, two new clubs were established in Letterkenny, the "Geraldines" and "Letterkenny Rovers", although a team from the 'Mental Hospital' also played occasionally in friendly matches.[7] As well as competing in the championship, both of these teams competed in the Dr. McGinley Cup, or East Donegal Hospital League against teams from Raphoe, Stranorlar, Ballybofey, Clonleigh and Carrigans. The rivalry between both town clubs was quite fierce with many matches between them developing into hard-hitting and raucous affairs. In a Dr. McGinley Cup match in January 1926, for example, which ended in a draw, it was reported that:

Fr. John McMonagle, Johnny McClean and Michael McGovern, Faugh a Ballagh players from 1917. From Christmas Annual 1982

Letterkenny - Where the Winding Swilly Flows

"Fouls seemed to be the order of the day, and play was of an uninteresting nature, due to the necessity of the whistle... More football and less grumbling would be preferable on the next occasion when the Letterkenny rivals meet."[8]

Both of these clubs shared a pitch at Ballymacool, known locally as the Burn Field, but sometimes reported in the press as either 'Geraldine Park' or just simply 'Ballymacool Grounds'.[9] The 1925/26 season saw mixed fortunes for the Letterkenny clubs. The Geraldines won the Dr. McGinley Cup (League) without defeat while Rovers were defeated in the County Championship Final by Ardara 5 points to 2.[10] The Rovers team did not have long to wait for success though - the following season saw them win the County Championship. Run on a league format, victory in Newtowncunningham against Carrigans on 4th March 1927 assured them of the title with a scoreline

A GAA football team from the 1920s, most likely the Geraldines. From Christmas Annual 1991

The Letterkenny Rovers team who won the Senior GAA Football Championship in 1927 shortly before the team broke up. From Christmas Annual 1987

of 1-5 to 0-3. A 6-1 to 1-2 home victory against Ballybofey the following week was a mere formality for this strong Rovers team consisting of **Patrick Doherty** (capt.), **Michael Peoples**, **John Harvey**, **William O'Donnell**, **John McManus**, **Anthony Gallagher**, **Frank Larkin**, **Jack Doherty**, **William Strain**, **William Roarty**, **Hugh McGlynn**, **Patsy Sweeney**, **Phil Doherty** and **John Larkin**.[11]

There was again a lull in GAA activity in the county in the mid 1920s with

Chapter Eighteen: Sports Clubs in Letterkenny

many fixtures not being fulfilled. Emigration due to harsh economic conditions was playing a key part in the decline. After winning the County Championship, following a celebration dance by Letterkenny Rovers in the Central Hotel, it was noted that several players were leaving for America.[12] Interest in the game was waning as a result of long intervals between matches and only four months after securing the county championship, the Letterkenny Rovers GAA team broke up:

"A disquieting feature of the decadence which seems to be taking hold of the GAA in Donegal is the approaching disbandment of the Letterkenny Rovers G.F.C. Although not many years in existence, this plucky little combination made its presence felt in GAA circles, and its passing will be regarded with regret by Gaels all over the country."[13]

The remaining Rovers team decided to amalgamate with the Geraldines to form a new club called "St. Eunan's GAA Football Club" in 1927. The name St. Eunan's for a GAA team in the town was not new. The ladies of "St. Eunan's Camogie Club" had supplied the catering for the Geraldines' McGinley Cup victory dance in 1926 in the Literary Institute[14] while a "St. Eunan's" team competed in the juvenile Wednesday evening league in the town against "Young Bloods" (Barkhall School), "Lamh Deargs" (Presentation Brothers School), "Hearts of Steel", "Swilly Harps", "O'Toole's", "Red Hearts", "Eire Oge" and "Holy Terrors".[15]

This newly formed St. Eunan's club played their games at John Crumlish's field in Ballymacool making their debut against Killygordon on 17th August 1927. Dying their old jerseys blue, the combined players of Geraldines and Rovers forming the new St. Eunan's team consisted of **John Doherty, Michael Peoples, Anthony Gallagher, Frank Larkin, John Larkin, Hugh McGlynn, John Harvey, Patrick Murphy, P. McBride, William Curran, Frank Crain, John Curran, Tommy**

The cover of the original minutes of St. Eunan's GAA club from 1928. Courtesy of Connie Maguire

The Donegal Junior team of 1933 who won the Ulster Junior title against Derry in Gaelic Park, Glencar.

Campbell, Hugh Doherty, Hugh McGrath, Charles McGrath, Domini[c] Kearns, H. Hegarty and Patrick Dawson.[16] This club was in existence for on[ly] a short time though, playing 15 matches, mostly friendlies against Killygordo[n] and Dungloe, and accruing a sizeable debt of £22 in unpaid liabilities before [it] ceased to be in June 1928.[17]

Two years later, on the 19th February 1930, a meeting was held in th[e] Catholic Club Rooms consisting of *'representatives of An Garda, Tirconaill Ment[al] Hospital and former members of the GAA in the town'* with the view to reform th[e] old St. Eunan's club and take on all liabilities and assets of the former club. M[r.] D.F. Ryan was elected chairman of the new club and Anthony Gallagher fro[m] Sallaghgraine was chosen as the club captain.[18] The committee chose as the[ir] colours *'black jerseys with amber hoops and black stockings'* and they approached th[e] Asylum Hospital Committee for the use of their field for matches.[19] The fir[st] match for the new St. Eunan's Club took place on 2nd March 1930 on the groun[d] of the Asylum Hospital, losing to Killygordon 1-4 to 3 points. A year later, th[e] club secured the hiring of a playing field in Glencar from Mrs. Margaret Kel[ly] of Bomany where they played their matches until 1937. After renovations to th[e] grounds, this field became known as 'Gaelic Park, Glencar' and even hosted th[e] Ulster Junior Football Final in 1933 between Donegal and Derry, the home tea[m] winning on a scoreline of 3-7 to 1-3.[20] Donegal went onto to compete in the A[ll] Ireland Junior Final that year, making its first appearance at Croke Park but lost t[o] Mayo on a scoreline of 2-15 to 2-2.

The opening of O'Donnell Park in 1937. Image courtesy of the National Library of Ireland

Chapter Eighteen: Sports Clubs in Letterkenny

In 1931, St. Eunan's first success came. The hurling team won the Derry People Cup that year while a new club in the town also made its bow. "St. Pat's" were formed in April 1931, with former Letterkenny Rovers player Frank Larkin their star player. The first match between the town rivals took place on 24th May 1931 in Gaelic Park, Glencar, a venue that was shared between the clubs. St. Eunan's achieved moderate success in their early years, winning the Minor Championship in Rashedoge in 1932 and their hurling team winning the Championship of the Northern Area in October 1933.

The club soon wanted a permanent residence rather than hiring a pitch and under the chairmanship of **John Crumlish** and through the tireless work of club secretary **John Hourihane**, they bought a 7-acre field that was formerly part of the Boyd estate in Sallaghgraine for £300 from the Urban District Council and called it "O'Donnell Park", after the former Bishop of the Diocese, Patrick O'Donnell. At the official opening of 'the county's premier Gaelic stadium' on 2nd May 1937, Antrim hurlers defeated Donegal by 5-5 to 2-2 and Armagh defeated the Donegal footballers 2-5 to 1-7. [21]

The short lived St. Columba's team who won the Dr. McGinley Cup in 1938. From Christmas Annual 2001

In this same year, another new club was formed in the town. St. Pat's had broken up in 1932 and, after a short lived attempt to form a new 'Letterkenny Rovers' a year later[22], a meeting was held in O'Donnell's Hotel on 16th September 1937 attended by 53 people with the object of establishing a new team in the town to:

"...*promote better support for the native games and to bring the people back to their GAA allegiance from which they seem to have greatly departed....a determined effort was being made by the Masonic club in Letterkenny and indeed throughout the rest of Ireland as well to try to ensnare the Irish youth in 'soccer' to make Imperialists out of them*"[23]

John Flynn was elected as Chairman of this new club of "St Columba's", with other prominent members including **Michael Moriarty**, **Edward McCaul**, **Peter McMonagle**, **Frank Larkin**, **Hugh McGrath**, **Connell Carbery**, **Lawrence Gildea**, **P.J. Mulchay** and **Hugh McGovern**. The team shared O'Donnell Park with St. Eunan's for their home matches and they did not have long to wait for success. In March 1938, they secured the Dr. McGinley Cup with an unbeaten record against St. Eunan's, Porthall and Ballybofey, taking the cup back to the town for the first time since the Geraldine's success in 1926.

GAA Football in the town was now going through a purple patch with a sensational result at the time occurring in O'Donnell Park in May 1938. In

Letterkenny - Where the Winding Swilly Flows

The Senior Championship winning St. Eunan's team of 1956. From Christmas Annual 1991

front of a crowd of 1,10[] people, a Letterkenny sele[] team comprised of playe[] from both town clubs heavi[] defeated a fancied Doneg[] county team 4-8 to 1-[] Up until this point, ve[] few Letterkenny men ha[] represented the county, b[] opinions were changed aft[] this memorable encounter:

"The sweeping success achiev[] by the joint Letterkenny teams has finished all future thought of excluding Letterkenny fro[] the county selection. Certainly, to judge from Sunday's result, the county team would have do[] well on a few recent occasions to have had players from the Cathedral Town in their side. Letterkenny men will feature more prominently in future county engagements than they have be[] doing for some considerable time past"[24]

Despite the initial early success of St. Columba's, the club broke up [] the early 1940s. The sole remaining GAA club in the town, St. Eunan's, lost thr[] Championship county finals [] 1944, 1946 and 1947 again[] an all-conquering Gweedo[] side before finally securin[] the Dr. Maguire Cup (name[] after Canon Maguire followin[] his death in 1926) for the fir[] time in 1948 with a 1-7 to 2-[] victory over Gweedore. B[] now the club were playing in [] changed strip of red and gree[] horizontal stripes due to fabr[] shortages during the war an[] although they made it to thr[] further county finals, the clu[] had to wait until 1956 to secu[] their second championshi[] Fittingly this was the sam[] year that they returned to the[] original colours of black an[]

Rory Kavanagh of St. Eunan's after winning the Sam Maguire for Donegal in September 2012. Courtesy of Donna McBride

amber. Since then, the club has won at least one senior county championship p[] decade and, since the late 1990s in particular, has become a dominant force i[] county club football.

Two St. Eunan's players, **Peadar McGeehin** and **James 'Gouldi[] McGettigan** played in the All Ireland Junior Final against Kerry in 1954 while i[] 1982, when Donegal won their first U21 All Ireland title, three players from th[]

Chapter Eighteen: Sports Clubs in Letterkenny

ub, **Eunan McIntyre**, **Charlie Mulgrew** and **Paul Carr**, were on the team. 1984, two St. Eunan's players, **Seamus Hoare** and Peadar McGeehin, were elected on the Donegal County Board Team of the Century. Charlie Mulgrew, aul Carr and **Mark Crossan** were on the Senior All Ireland winning squad when e coveted Sam Maguire Cup was won for the very first time in 1992. However, e honour of being the first St. Eunan's player to play in a Senior All Ireland inal goes to midfielder **Rory Kavanagh** in 2012, while his club mate **Kevin afferty** was also a part of the All Ireland winning squad.

Since the disbandment of the St. Columba's team in the 1930s, the adition of having rival clubs in the town had waned for approximately fifty years. 1996 though, a new club, "Letterkenny Gaels", were formed to cater for the sing population in the rapidly expanding town. The eagerly anticipated first clash etween the two clubs came in a league game of Junior Football on 20th April 997 in which St. Eunan's won on a scoreline of 4-9 to 1-6. Initially, Letterkenny aels with **Jim Frain** as their first chairman, played their games at various venues, Heaton's Field at the Port Road, the grounds of Letterkenny Rugby Club at e Silver Tassie and at Errigal College), before finding a permanent home. In 999, along with Letterkenny Rugby Club, the club acquired land at the Glebe for e development of a GAA pitch and opened their new playing field "Páirc na Gael" in March 2008. The club have been most successful in underage football particular and this still relatively young club are continuing to make great strides their development.

ugby

Like cricket and football, rugby was deemed an 'English sport' for many ears but unlike those sports, very little evidence exists of it taking place in onegal in the early years of the twentieth century. By the 1930s though, these titudes were changing. The first recorded rugby match concerning a Letterkenny am took place in April 1932 when the team lost to Milford 1 try (3 points) to l. This team played their ome games at the Asylum ospital grounds, and espite protests from arious GAA officials at the romotion of the sport, the oard of the hospital ruled at: *"these matches brought a ttle variety into the very drab ves of the patients, and there as nothing more exhilarating an a rugby match."*[25]

Five players from t. Eunan's GAA club, e **Callaghan**, **George Corabin**, **William Dillon**,

Aerial view of Dave Gallaher Park, home to Letterkenny R.F.C. and Letterkenny Gaels

239

Robert Russell and **Patrick McLaughlin**, were suspended from playing for th[e] team in March 1932 for attending a rugby game at the Asylum Hospital Ground[,] McLaughlin having also played in the game.[26] Much to the outrage of Gael[ic] clubs throughout the county, rugby was also being promoted amongst the you[th] in St. Eunan's College under the eye of **Fr. J. McMenamin**, with three Doneg[al] Town players being suspended from their club as a result of participating.[27] [In] 1933, at an Asylum Hospital committee meeting, at which once again the use o[f] the ground for rugby matches was being debated, **Mr. J. P. McIvor** stated tha[t] *"he did not believe it was possible to make the people more loyal or Irish by these coercive acts. People had a perfect right to play any games they liked."* [28]

As time went on, attitudes against rugby became more relaxed. Occasion[al] games took place but no official club existed until the 1970s. Up until then, tho[se] players interested in the game usually travelled to nearby Derry or Limavady [to] get a game and so they decided to form their own club in the town. In 197[4] "Letterkenny Rugby Club" was officially formed with games played at Robinso[n] Field at the Port Road while training took place at O'Donnell Park. This u[se] of the St. Eunan's training ground for rugby shows the more relaxed attitu[de] between the GAA and the so-called 'foreign' sport by now. Given the similariti[es] of physicality of players and the use of the hands, it was no surprise to see sever[al] successful Gaelic football players playing for the new rugby club, including J[o] **'Dodo' Winston** (St. Eunan's) and **Declan O'Carroll** (St. Joseph's).

In 1974 the club purchased four acres of land at Drumnahoagh near th[e] Dry Arch and constructed a small clubhouse, while in 1985 they moved to a fie[ld] near the Silver Tassie Hotel known as the Halfway Line. In the late eighties an[d] early nineties, for various reasons, rugby began to decline but the club was ke[pt] alive through the enthusiasm and dedication of several members. By 1999, [in] conjunction with Letterkenny Gaels GAA club, land was purchased at the Gle[be] for the development of their pitch and since then the club have played the[ir] games at "Dave Gallaher Park", named after the former New Zealand All Bla[ck] Rugby Captain, originally from nearby Ramelton who died in World War I.[29]

Golf

The first mention we have of the game of golf being played in Letterken[ny] comes from a letter from **Robert R. Robinson** to **Major Gen. A.C.H. Stewar**[t,] the landlord at Rockhill from 19 April 1894:

"I beg to say Mr. Chambers, Manager of the Ulster Bank, Dr. Carre a[nd] *a few others have been playing golf in the lawn starting at McDaid's old lodge and going acro*[ss] *into the fort field. They say it is splendid golfing ground and are envious to get what they call s*[and] *pots made in it."*[30]

There are various reports of golf being played at Carnamuggagh, Ballybo[fey] and Windyhall in the early years of the twentieth century[31] but it wasn't un[til] 1913 that a 20-acre course was formally laid out at Crievesmith, on land owne[d] by the Stewart family of Rockhill. **Sir Charles John Stewart** was made the fir[st] honorary President of the new Letterkenny Golf Club, even though he didn't pla[y] the game himself. In January 1920, the club purchased the land from the Stewa[rt]

Chapter Eighteen: Sports Clubs in Letterkenny

ily for £725 with improvements being made to the layout. A clubhouse was pleted in 1925 and by now the membership had risen to 54 men, mostly from wealthy tradesmen and clergy of the town. In 1926 Bishop McNeely became President and remained so until 1963.

Letterkenny Golf Club remained at Crievesmith until June 1967 when the purchased land from the Hunter family at Barnhill for £6,600 for the building new 18-hole course, although golf continued to be played for a number of s at the course at Crievesmith under the new owners, the McKendricks.

By 1974, membership at the club had risen to 350 people and, as a result, clubhouse at Barnhill needed to be extended. Membership continued to rise the gradual expansion of Letterkenny in the seventies and eighties so that and new clubhouse was needed, opened in June 1998. A year later, the club ed the Donegal Irish Ladies Open with great success while in 2007, a newly eloped €1.75 million 18-hole course was opened to the public. Success in the er Cup followed in 2010, the first time it was won by the club since 1987 and n in 2012. The club also won the Pierce Purcell Shield National title in 2009. erkenny Golf Club celebrated its centenary in 2013 and to mark the occasion, lan O'Carroll wrote a book detailing the entire history of the club where e details on the history of golf in the town can be obtained.

Danny McDaid competing in the Marathon in Greece 1970. From Christmas Annual 2004

letics

As we have seen, as part of the Patrick's Temperance Guild under the onage of Bishop Logue, an Athletics rts contest was held in August 1882 on the nds of Mrs. Hegarty at the Isles. As well as ball matches, contests included a 300 yards s' race, won by **A. Peoples**, a blindfolded ow race, won by **John McGlynn**, men's -yard race won by **Henry McGrath** and en's 600-yard race won by **Charles Frise**. prizes were presented by '*our popular sman Dr. Dunlop and Mr. Lyndon, manager er Bank.*'[32] This was the general pattern athletics in Letterkenny for many years – tests and tournaments at fairs and local erings. In the 1920s, the Garda Sports letics Tournament was held annually in the nds of the Asylum Hospital with **General n O'Duffy** attending in 1926. Contests ded the 100-yard sprint, the long jump the tug of war. Although events such as e were common at these Fair Days, no anized athletic club existed in the town in e years.

241

Letterkenny - Where the Winding Swilly Flows

As there was no athletics club available in Letterkenny, **Danny McD** from nearby Glenswilly joined the Cranford Athletic Club in 1965 winn several Ulster Championships in that season. Moving to Dublin for worl 1967, he first represented Ireland in the World Cross Country Champions in 1969. Taking up marathon running soon after, in 1970 he won the Nati Marathon Championship in Leitrim and came eleventh in the European Marat Championship in Helsinki in 1971. Due to this fine form, Danny was selecte compete in the marathon event for Ireland in the Olympic Games of Munic 1972 where he finished 23rd and was the first Irish man home.

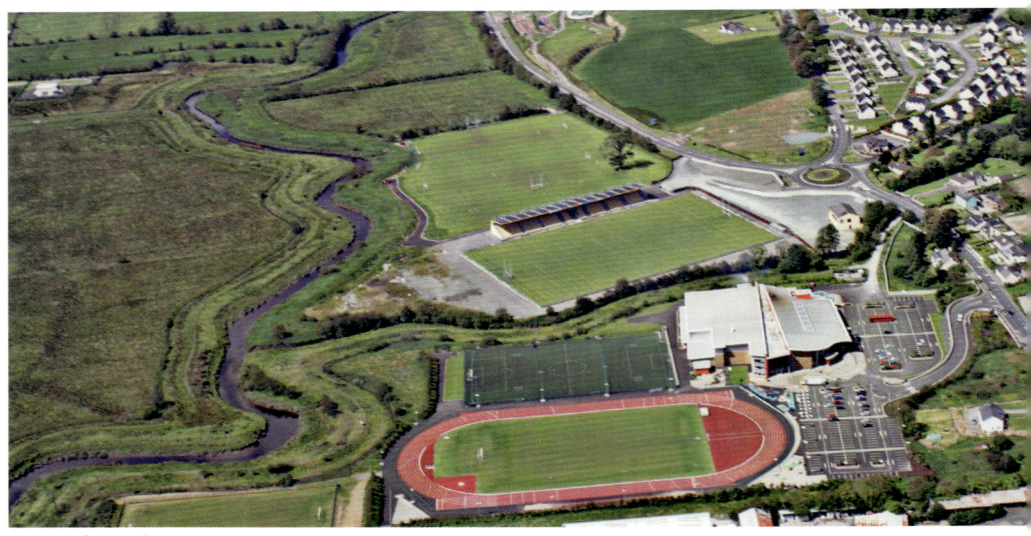

Aerial view of O'Donnell Park and the Aura Leisure Centre with the Danny McDaid running track, as the Swilly meanders gently past them

Due to the national success of Danny, a keen interest was revived lo in athletics and in 1972, "Letterkenny Athletic Club" was officially formed **Eddie Gibson**, **Liam O'Donnell**, **Brother Austin Lyons** and **Patsy Durn** Returning to work in the town in 1974, Danny continued to compete in marath all over Europe and in 1976 he was again selected to compete in the Olyr games, this time in Montreal. Three months after this, Danny competed in New York marathon finishing in 6th place.

In 1979, Danny was captain of the Irish team that won the Silver m at the World Cross-Country Championships in Limerick along with John Tr and Eamon Coughlan, when he was the second Irishman home, finishing in place.[34] His teammate on that occasion, **Eamonn Coughlan**, officially ope the new all weather 400m running track of Letterkenny Athletic Club in 1 and five years later, a new clubhouse was built beside it.

Between 1967 and 1987, Danny McDaid won 13 Ulster Senior cr country titles, competed in two Olympic marathons and represented Letterke with pride on each occasion. In recognition of these achievements, a mo was passed in 2008 by the Letterkenny Town Council to name the new ta running track built at the Aura Sports Complex at Sallaghgraine after Da and the Letterkenny Athletic Club have made it their home ever since. The

Chapter Eighteen: Sports Clubs in Letterkenny

Poster for an open air Boxing tournament held at O'Donnell Park in 1939. From Christmas Annual 2000

Letterkenny - Where the Winding Swilly Flows

Letterkenny Boxing Club 1950. From Christmas Annual 1987

Letterkenny Boxing Club 1956 with trainer John McLaughlin pictured at the rear. From Christmas Annual 1982

currently has a membership of c 100 people and competes in cro country, road running and track field competitions throughout country.

Boxing

Open air boxing tournaments recorded as taking place in the to at the Asylum Hospital Grounds August 1933[35] and O'Donnell I in July 1939[36]. These tourname mostly featured fighters from De Ramelton or Glasgow but sev fighters from the "O'Donnell Bo Club" of Letterke also fought such **Reggie McCauley Billy Gibbons. J McLaughlin** came the town in 1938 f Carndonagh and met I Gibbons and the boxing fanatics set ab forming an official clul However, it took sev years to accomplish due to the outbreak of World War II and it was not until 1946 that the two r resurrected their plans and the "Letterkenny Amateur Boxing Club" was offic founded in the Devlin Hall. The club moved to various premises in the e years, first to **Manus Regan's** rooms in 1948 and then **Tommy Nee's** Hal Main Street around 1949. Shortly after that, the club moved their training facil to rooms in the Old Workhouse.

The first major success for the club came in 1957 when **Malachy P** won both the Ulster and National titles. Many more titles followed for the including bouts won by John's sons, **George, Jack** and **Niall McLaughlin**. W John retired he had trained 11 National champions, 7 of the titles won by his s In 1970, the Urban District Council gave the club a site for the building of a gym between the Port Road and the High Road and Letterkenny Boxing C continues to train promising young pugilists to this day.[37] To mark the role pl by John McLaughlin in developing boxing in the town, in 2013, Letterkenny T Council approved the naming of the laneway from the High Road to the Bo Club gym as "John McLaughlin's Way".

Chapter Eighteen: Sports Clubs in Letterkenny

Tennis

Racquet sports such as Badminton held tournaments at the Recreational Hall on the Port Road in 1927[38] but the first evidence of tennis in the town is the "Letterkenny Tennis Club" who ran a cup competition in 1926.[39] In 1927, the "West End Tennis Club" of Letterkenny issued a challenge to the Manorcunningham club to a doubles tournament.[40] This club played their games on a lawn court behind the Garda Barracks at the bottom of the town and their existence was criticised in the weekly column of a GAA reporter bemoaning the demise of GAA sports locally:

"Under the shade of the Garda Barracks, the young men who thought hurling too vigorous and the young ladies who think camogie not 'class' enough, meet in a miniature Wimbledon and discuss developments in the tennis world with an accent more characteristic of the West End of London than of Letterkenny."[41]

Letterkenny Tennis Club Centre

The "O'Donnell Tennis Club" was formed following the construction of a tennis court at the new O'Donnell Park in 1937 and played tennis there up until the end of the 1940s.[42] Over the years, other tennis courts were available to play on such as at the rear of Barkhall School, and next to the Boxing gym, but it wasn't until 1978 that the "Hospital Tennis Club" was formed playing their games in the grounds of Letterkenny General Hospital and developing into one of the leading tennis clubs in the northwest. Later changing their name to "Letterkenny Tennis Club", due to increased membership in the late eighties and early nineties, the Letterkenny Tennis Centre was opened in August 1997 on land next to Murraghatoo and behind the Swimming Pool with four new courts and a new clubhouse being erected and is now the largest tennis club in County Donegal.

Other Notable Sports

While football, GAA, rugby, golf, boxing, tennis and athletics are noted above as the dominant sports in Letterkenny's history, there are many other sports that are catered for in the town and several athletes who deserve special mention. Since 1975, for example, Letterkenny has been the centre for the **Donegal International Rally**, whose headquarters are at the Mount Errigal Hotel with **James Cullen** from Letterkenny a two-time winner of the event and **Rory Kennedy** and **Seamus McGettigan** also successful over many years. Since 1985, the **Swilly Seals Swimming Club** have trained young swimmers and have

245

competed annually in events at the Community Games in Mosney. The game snooker had been played in the **CYMS** since it was first opened and form entered competitions from 1964. In rowing, Letterkenny girl **Sinead Jenni** competed in the World Championships in Munich, Vienna, Lucerne, Zag Seville, Milan, Poznan and Linz winning several gold and silver medals.[43] later switched to cycling and only narrowly missed out on qualifying for the 2 London Olympics with the Irish team. Her sister **Catriona Jennings** did man to compete for Ireland in the London Olympics Marathon, while in cycl **Philip Deignan** from Magherennan represented Ireland at the Beijing Olymp of 2008 and has been competing in cycling championships throughout Eur since 2005. In August 2014, 21 year old **Mark English** claimed a bronze me for Ireland in the European Track and Field Championships in Zurich in 800m event and holds a bright future ahead of him in athletics. In 1999, **Patr Quinlivan** won seventeen medals at the Special Olympics in North Carol while **Shaun Bradley** took silver in the 200 metres Kayaking competition the Special Olympics in Athens in 2011 with **Oliver Boyle** and **Hugh Swee** also receiving silver medals as part of the soccer team in the same tourname When Donegal won the Sam Maguire Cup in 2012, it was **Michael Murphy** fr Bomany, just outside Letterkenny, who had the honour of being only the seco Donegal captain to do so. A former St. Eunan's College pupil, the Glensw clubman also captained Ireland to International Rules victory in 2013. On M 19th 2013, Letterkenny man **Jason Black** tested his endurance to the limit succeeded in being the first Donegal man to scale the summit of Mount Ever a tremendous achievement.

Sport has been crucial to the development of Letterkenny. As more more people arrived in the town for work over the years, a social outlet was nee for them to mix and integrate with their new community. Sport provided s an outlet. Without these sports clubs, many friendships, which have lasted decades in the town, could not have been possible. Due to significant investm in their infrastructure in the late 1990s, most notably through the assistance then Minister for Tourism and Sport, **Dr. James McDaid**, the town can bo today of having several top class facilities that cater for all sports and intere No matter which sport it is, each competitor continues to strive to be the best their club and Letterkenny, and for that, and raising the profile and civic pride the town, they deserve to be richly applauded and acknowledged.

Endnotes

Londonderry Sentinel 27/6/1862
Curran, Conor, "Cricket in Donegal 1865-1914", Donegal Annual 2011 pp64-70
Derry People 9/7/27 and 29/6/29
Derry Journal 30/8/1882
Derry Journal 9/8/1882
Curran, Conor, "Sport in Donegal: A History", The History Press, 2010, p50
Derry Journal 8/1/1892
Derry Journal 7/10/1891
Derry Journal 30/12/1891
Derry Journal 16/3/1894
Derry Journal 25/4/1894
Derry Journal 12/12/1894
Derry Journal 25/5/1895
Derry Journal 24/4/1895
Derry Journal 4/3/1896
Derry Journal 4/3/1896
Derry Journal 9/10/1905
Duffy, Dick, "The Growth of Soccer in Letterkenny", Letterkenny Christmas Annual 1982
Derry People 15/10/1927
Derry People 1/3/1941
Derry People 19/2/1938 and 12/8/1939
Derry People 16/9/1939
Derry People 9/7/1927
Derry People 10/11/1947
Duffy, Dick, "The Growth of Soccer in Letterkenny", Letterkenny Christmas Annual 1982
Derry People 11/5/1957
Derry People 4/5/1957
Derry Journal 22/8/1959
Derry People 9/1/1960
Derry Journal 20/9/1905
Derry Journal 29/12/1905
Derry Journal 27/4/1906
Derry Journal 14/6/1911
Derry Journal 7/7/1911
Derry Journal 4/8/1911
Derry People 9/5/1925
Derry Journal 1/1/1926
Derry Journal 15/1/1926 and 26/3/1926
Derry Journal 14/5/1926
Derry Journal 11/3/1927
Derry Journal 25/3/1927
Derry Journal 11/7/1927
Derry Journal 14/5/1926
Derry Journal 29/7/1927
Derry Journal 26/8/1927
Official St. Eunan's Club minutes
Ibid 3/2/1930
Ibid 6/3/1930
Derry People 19/8/1933
Derry Journal 3/5/1937
Derry People 28/10/1933
Derry People 18/9/1937
Derry People 14/5/1938
Derry People 16/4/1932
Official St. Eunan's Club Minutes 9/3/1932
Derry People 16/4/1932
Derry People 23/12/1933
Downey, Lee, "Letterkenny RFC", Letterkenny Christmas Annual 2006, pp116-117
O'Carroll, Declan, "Letterkenny Golf Club, The Centenary Years 1913-2012", Letterkenny Golf, 2012, p17
Letterkenny Christmas Annual 1992 p118
Derry Journal 9/8/1882
"Twenty Five Years a Growing", Letterkenny Christmas Annual 1997 p105
Delap, "The Glenswilly Flyer", Letterkenny Christmas Annual 2004, pp28-31
Derry People 26/8/1933
Boxing Poster, Letterkenny Christmas Annual 2000, p134

Letterkenny - Where the Winding Swilly Flows

66. "A Life Time of Boxing in Letterkenny", Letterkenny Christmas Annual 2001 and "The History of Letterkenny Amateur Boxing Club", Letterkenny Christmas Annual 1987
67. Derry Journal 21/1/1927
68. Derry People 24/7/1926
69. Derry People 9/7/1927
70. Derry Journal 11/7/1927
71. Derry People 11/9/1948
72. Lynch, Jim, "Row, row, row your boat, gently down the stream", Letterkenny Christmas Annual 2007, pp 37-39

Chapter Nineteen: Theatre and the Arts

Sports clubs in the town were of course hugely important for the social integration of many of Letterkenny's residents throughout the twentieth century, but equally important were the local musical and drama groups. Attending plays, musicals or dances offered the local residents the perfect opportunity to mix with each other, either as participants in the productions or simply as members of the audience. Various venues throughout the town were used for these gatherings, such as the Literary Institute and the Devlin Hall on the Main Street and later the College and Convent Halls, so that generations of residents of Letterkenny were treated to celebrations of music, comedy or drama all performed by their local townspeople. Although economic hardships may have been prevailing in their day-to-day lives, before television and cinema, attending these performances offered the audience a brief respite from the daily hardships. Plays, musicals and pantomimes provided rare glimpses into strange lands and cultures, fired the imagination and inspired the ambitions of many an audience member. In that regard, as much as anything, the arts were hugely important to Letterkenny's development throughout the twentieth century.

The first mention of a theatre group in the town comes from September 1891 when **Joseph Diver**, **John Doherty** and **John McElwaine** met in Doherty's Hotel (now the Central Bar) to hold the first meeting of the "Letterkenny Amateur Dramatic Club", although members of this group are noted to have previously performed in several plays including "The Lady of Lyons", "The Rivals", and "Robert Emmet".[1] Three months later, a concert was held in the Literary Institute by the "Letterkenny Young Men's Catholic Association" with enjoyable performances from **Thomas Mulhern, John Harrity, James Gallagher, James Collins, John McMonagle, Hugh Sweeney, James Sweeney**, and **John Larkin**,[2] while at another concert held a couple of weeks later, M.C. for the evening, James Collins *"complimented the various performers on their musical talent, and said it was highly creditable to find so many and so proficient musical artistes in Letterkenny"*.[3]

The Literary Institute on the Main Street had been opened in 1876 and, as well as serving as a school at various stages of its existence, the second storey contained a stage and a large hall that could seat up to 250 people. This hall served as the main focal point for many concerts and dramatic performances in Letterkenny for over sixty years until the opening of the Devlin Hall in the late 1930s.

As part of the Aonach Tirconaill of 1898, for example, several dramatic and musical performances took place in the Institute (as well as the unfinished Cathedral building, Halla Eithne). **Fr. Hugh Gallagher**, the President of the St. Eunan's Seminary directed "The Passing of Conall" which was performed over several nights, a review of the performance stating: *"for amateurs they exhibited a remarkably accurate knowledge of dramatic requirements. Some of the members, indeed, proved themselves possessors of a high order of histrionic ability."*[4] In the Girl's National School also, visitors to the Aonach were treated to a performance by pupils and past

Letterkenny - Where the Winding Swilly Flows

pupils of the Loreto Convent of the operetta "Finola".

Following the success of the Aonach of 1898 as a fundraiser for th[e] erection of the Cathedral, when it came to completing St. Eunan's College [in] 1906, the Aonach an Dún proved highly successful also, with Gaelic game[s,] arts and literature to the fore. Drama was represented by Seamus MacManu[s'] farce "Dinny O'Dowd" while several other musical performances took place [at] the various stalls.[5] Later that same year, the "Letterkenny Dramatic Club" agai[n] presented Dion Boucicault's drama "The Colleen Bawn" in the Literary Institut[e,] having previously performed it as part of the opening of the Cathedral in 1901[.]

The Silver Screen

However, by now a new invention had caught the imagination of th[e] paying public – that of moving pictures on a screen. In 1909, Mrs. McFadde[n] hosted a free "Cinematograph Performance" in the Presentation Brothers' scho[ol] for the children of Letterkenny and was attended by many prominent townspeop[le] who availed of the opportunity to witness this new wonder.[7]

Between 1926 and 1928, a Cinema was located on the Port Road in th[e] Recreational Hall, a simple wooden and corrugated iron structure, which was use[d] also for dances and music. Originally operated by **Mr. J. Gregg**, Leo McCarro[n] took over the business in April 1927 with his brother **Paddy**, and called [it] McCarron's Cinemas.[8] It showed silent films with musical accompaniments suc[h] as "The Man-Hunter", "The Sleepwalker" (1926), "Galloping Gallagher", "Th[e] Ten Commandments", "Savages of the Sea", and "The Silent Stranger" (1927)[.] This building did not have the opportunity to show the new 'talking picture[s'] phenomenon, instigated by th[e] release of 'The Jazz Singe[r'] in 1927, as it burned to th[e] ground in May of 1928.[10] Th[e] former Methodist church [at] the top of the Market Squar[e] was used by **Jack Doherty** t[o] show the latest talking picture[s] from 1933: *"It is some years n[ow] since Letterkenny boasted a cinem[a] all its own. Mr. Doherty's is t[he] first talkie cinema ever to have be[en] established here. That the townspeop[le] are intending to accord the new proje[ct] deserving support has been indicat[ed] by the numbers who are alrea[dy] attending."*[11]

La Scala Cinema on the Port Road opened in 1935 opposite the former site of the old McCarron Cinema. From Christmas Annual 2001

On 20th April 1935 the new 'La Scala Cinema' opened on the Port Roa[d] near to the former McCarron's Cinema premises, with three pictures showing i[n] its first week - "Tell Me Tonight", "A Southern Maid" and "Lady For A Day"[12] and served as the primary location for silver screen entertainment in Letterkenn[y]

Chapter Nineteen: Theatre and the Arts

...til its relocation in 2001 to its current ten-screen Century Cinemas address at ...eckview Lane.

> ### Did you know?
>
> **Michael Palin**, one sixth of the groundbreaking comedy troupe Monty Python who brought us such comedic gems as The Life of Brian, The Holy Grail, the Meaning of Life and the TV Show, Flying Circus, claims ancestral descent from Letterkenny. His great-grandmother on his father's side, Brita Gallagher, was from the town and left Ireland in 1845 on a "coffin ship" bound for America when both of her parents perished in the Great Famine. Orphaned, with only a label on her dress to identify her, Brita sailed from Kerry to America where she was brought up by a rich spinster called Caroline Watson, who was most likely her aunt. She was then sent back to Europe to receive an education when she was 16. She travelled for several years, before a chance encounter with an English academic called Edward Palin in a hotel in Switzerland. At the time, he was an Oxford Don at St John's College and although there was a 17-year age gap between them, they were attracted to one another and in 1867, once she had reached the age of 21, they were married in Paris. The affair was quite scandalous in this Victorian age and Edward was forced to give up his position in the college but secured a living as the vicar of Linton, Herefordshire. The couple had seven children, one of whom was Michael's grandfather.

Theatre in the 1920s and 1930s

Theatre, of course, was not to be outdone by its moving picture rival. ... 1926 the Loreto Convent's staging of the operetta "Zurika" brought with it *Wonderful stage effects, a riot of gloriously blended colour, picturesque groupings and music ...h in its appeal to our sense of beauty…all combined to impart to us a feeling of pure joy ...d satisfaction such as one rarely experiences in this imperfect world*"[13] while one year later, ...eir operetta "Pearl, the Fishermaiden" brought equal praise from the reviewers: *"t was a world of sunshine and brightness and sweet sounds in which those two hours were ...ent, and it was quite a shock when one found oneself after it on Letterkenny's muddy, ill-lit ...reets."*[14]

The Letterkenny Amateur Dramatic Society continued to perform with ...eir 1927 performance of the comedy "Daddy Long Legs". Performers such as **...rs. E.S. McKinney**, "*who once again delighted a large and enthusiastic audience with her ...amatic power*", **Frances Fleming**, **Jack Speer**, **Ethel Ball**, **Gerald McClintock** ...d **Jack Barr** elicited glowing reviews: "*All the actors acquitted themselves very well ...deed, and the fact that they belong to the locality added to the enjoyment of a production which*

Letterkenny - Where the Winding Swilly Flows

Century Cinemas Letterkenny

An ominous headline from the Derry Journal in 1939

*will be retained in the memory of audience for some time to come." One year later, the Ulster Playe performed **District Judg Louis J. Walsh**'s acclaimed pl "The Auction in Killybuck" the Literary Institute.[16]

The "Letterken Catholic Club Dramatic Societ emerged in 1932 and perform two plays that year; "The Ho in the Harvest" directed **Mr. Moriarty**, a local National Scho Teacher, and also Justice Wals comedy "The Grand Audit Night", both in the Literary Institute. Performe in both plays included **Hugh McKindrick**, **Susie Sweeney**, **Bella Clarke**, **J Doherty**, **Dominic Kearns** and **Harry Mullen**.[17] The society entered two tear into the Féis Tirchonaill that year with the first team restaging "Grand Au Night" and the second team entering with "The Coiner" by Bernard Duffy.[18]

The Féis Tirchonaill continued the work of the Aonach Tirchonaill, wi teams competing annually from all over the county in traditional Irish mus drama and dance competitions. Although held at various venues throughout t county over the years, it later became centralized in Letterkenny and was cruc in keeping alive the spirit of the arts in the town. The music and dance sectio of the Féis were generally held in St. Eunan's College, with language and orato competitions being competed for in the Loreto and Presentation Brothers schoo Drama took place in the Literary Institute and technical exhibits could be view in the Technical School. Each of these venues were importantly within a sho walking distance of each other.[19]

Is Drama Perishing In Letterkenny?

Gloomy Conclusion To Be Drawn From Feis

What is wrong in Letterkenny that there cannot be found people sufficiently interested in drama to stage plays at the annual Feis? the great founders of the movement. Yet, not one drama entry was received from either of these clubs. I don't say it is any part of the work of a G.A.A. club to compete in drama

However, by the end of the 1930s, enthusiasm towards the Féis appeare to be waning locally, at least in the drama sections. Under the ominous headli "Is Drama Perishing in Letterkenny?" in the Derry People newspaper, the writ

Chapter Nineteen: Theatre and the Arts

highlighted the town's poor showing at the 1939 Féis, when, out of a total of seven drama entries, only one was from Letterkenny – "Isogan" directed by **Eunan Coyle**. *"Is drama perishing in Letterkenny? My answer to that question is "No, it is already perished." Presumably there will be many to disagree with me, but not, surely those whose indifference and apathy were responsible for the very poor display which Letterkenny made in the drama competitions this year."*[20]

In an attempt to reignite enthusiasm, it was decided that for the 1940 Féis, the drama section would be held apart from the main competition, with performances in the Literary Institute in March. Two Letterkenny groups entered this festival – the Letterkenny Convent National School performed a play in Irish while Letterkenny C.Y.M.S. Players performed an English play.[21]

Fr. Arthur McLoone, (President of St. Eunan's College 1944-1954), had a great love for the works of Gilbert and Sullivan and directed his pupils in many musicals over the years in the school concert hall since his arrival as a teacher in 1927. In his 1933 production of "The Gondoliers", the reviewer noted that: *"From the leading part to the merest detail of the performance there was a perfectness and beauty of acting that made the combined efforts attractive to a remarkable degree."*[22] In 1939, three notable students arrived at the college who would soon assimilate Fr. McLoone's passion for the arts, especially Gilbert and Sullivan. **Ray McAnally** from Moville, **Danny McGlinchey** from Fintown and **Terry O'Doherty** from Lifford arrived at the school in 1939 and were part of several wonderful performances by the school, not least their own scripted "Madame Screwball" in 1943. Ray McAnally would of course go on to win both national and international acclaim with his performances with the Abbey Theatre and in the movies "The Mission" (1986) and "My Left Foot" (1989). Danny McGlinchey later managed the internationally successful group The Pattersons and was at the fore of the revival of the stage musical in Letterkenny in the 1980s while Terry O'Doherty would be instrumental in forming the Lifford Players in 1952, winning the coveted All Ireland Drama competition in Athlone in 1982, 1985 and 1987.

The 1939 Féis Tirchonaill production of Isogan directed by Eunan Coyle. From Christmas Annual 1999

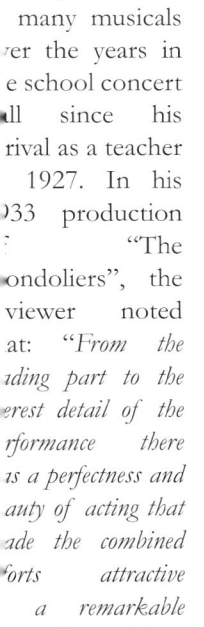

Letterkenny - Where the Winding Swilly Flows

Above: A 1935 St. Eunan's College Gilbert & Sullivan Concert directed by Fr. Arthur McLoone. From Christmas Annual 1991

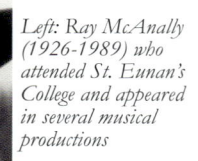

Left: Ray McAnally (1926-1989) who attended St. Eunan's College and appeared in several musical productions

Below: The cast of Madame Screwball, a comic opera written by Ray McAnally and Danny McGlinchey which was performed in the early 1940s. Also included is Terry O'Doherty, founding member of the Lifford Players. From Christmas Annual 2003

The 1940s and the Vocation Players

In 1944, the "Letterkenny Players" presented "Moodie Manitoba" who by now had built themselves up *"to the rank of capable, fairly finished drama group*, with performers including **John Byrne**, **Hugh McKendrick**, **Tommy Nee** and **Desmond Ewing**.[23] Two years later, the Local Defence Force formed the "LDF Players" under direction of Cpl. Eunan Coyle and presented " Damsel from Dublin" with **Vol. V. Conaghan**, **Vol. P. Doherty**, **Adjt. Desmond Ewing**, **Vol. O'Doherty**, **Margaret O'Donnell** and **Patrick T. Cassidy**.[24] The LDF Players were now using a new venue that had emerged to take over from the Literary Institute for dramatic performances in the town. In January 1939, Bishop McNeely officially opened the Joseph Devlin Memorial Hall at Lower Main Street, commemorating the prominent Nationalist and Ancient Order of the Hibernians leader and many dramatic groups would use this hall for drama and music performances. Situated in the so called West End of Letterkenny it was indeed a fitting location for many amateur musical and dramatic productions for almost fifty years.

In late 1946, **Joseph McVeigh**, the principal of the Vocational School at Ard O'Donnell, gathered a group of players together with the view to forming a new drama group in the town. Taking their name from their rehearsal space in the

254

Chapter Nineteen: Theatre and the Arts

[school], the following March, the [L]etterkenny Vocational Players" ([L]VP) staged their first play in [th]e Devlin Hall, B.G. McCarthy's ["T]he Whip Hand", directed by Mr. [M]ichael J. Bradley, which included [p]erformances from **Mary [C]opeland, Patrick McGrath, [A]nnie Campbell, Mary O'Brien, [M]airead O'Donnell** and **[G]eoffrey Prendergast** amongst [ot]hers.²⁵

Later that same year, the [gr]oup returned to the Devlin Hall with George Shiels' "The Rugged Path". *In this three-act play, where pathos and bathos, climax and anti-climax followed one another [in] quick succession, where laughter was often near to tears and where unexpected situations [ab]ounded at every turn, calling for the exercise of all their ingenuity and stagecraft, the Vocational [Pl]ayers gave a well–sustained performance and carried off the honours in a manner which is, [in]deed, a happy augury for the further commendable triumphs which should embellish the fine [re]putation they have now gained."*²⁶

New performers now involved with the group included **Liam O'Doherty, [J].M. Ffrench, Rita McFeely, Pearse Stevenson** and **Patrick Stokes**.²⁷ Building [to] a solid reputation for performances, the group returned in subsequent years [wi]th "Autumn Fire" (1948) and "The Shadow of a Gunman" (1949).

The Golden Era of the 1950s

By the 1950s, the dramatic arts were once again revitalized in the town [wi]th annual performances by the LVP, the Pantomime Society and the short-lived [gr]oup, the St. Colmcille Players. "The Ghost Train" (1950) was produced by **Rev. [P].B. Murphy** for the LVP, which was also brought on tour throughout the county: *[B]y their latest production the Vocational Players have climbed the rugged path and emerged on [to] a vista of great dramatic promise.*"²⁸ In April 1951, the newly formed "St. Colmcille [Pl]ayers" presented "Give Him A House", produced by **Frank Maguire**, in [ha]lls in Letterkenny, Rathmullan, [Ki]lmacrennan, Carrigart and [Ba]llybofey²⁹ while later that same [ye]ar, the first Pantomime was [st]aged in the town. "Cinderella" [w]as directed by Frank Sweeney [an]d starred many recognizable [lo]cal actors including **Harry [P]atterson, Maire Mellett, Mary [M]cAuley**, and of course, the ever [po]pular **Pearse Stevenson**.

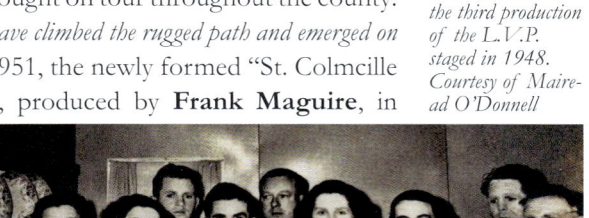

The Devlin Hall Letterkenny, opened in 1939, played host to many plays, dances and performances over the years

"Autumn Fire", the third production of the L.V.P. staged in 1948. Courtesy of Mairead O'Donnell

255

Letterkenny - Where the Winding Swilly Flows

The Pantomime was to witness great success annually throughout the 1950s drawing large crowds to the Devlin Hall to see hilarious productions of "Aladdin" (1952), "Mother Goose" (1953), "Jack The Beanstalk" (1954), "Sinbad the Sailor" (1955), "Dick Whittington" (1956), "Babes in the Wood" (1957), "Little Red Riding Hood" (1958) and "Robinson Crusoe" (1959). Notable names associated behind the scenes with the pantomime in those years include **Leo O'Connor**, **Edward Stevenson** and **Kenneth Corry**. By 1960 though, a combination of diminishing crowds and the problem of enticing new actors resulted in their final production, fittingly a reprisal of their first Pantomime, Cinderella.[30]

Madeline Peoples & Pearse Stevenson from Jack and the Beanstalk 1954. From Christmas Annual 1991

The St. Colmcille Players appear to have dwindled out after only a couple of productions but the LVP continued unabated in the 1950s with stagings of "Arsenic & Old Lace" (1951), "The Money Doesn't Matter" (1952), "Drama at Inish" (1954) and "The Vigil" (1957). By now also the group were performing one-act plays, coming third in the 1952 Ballyshannon Drama Festival with "The Valiant", while also taking it on tour to Milford, Creeslough and Dungloe. In December 1956 the group presented four one-act plays together on one night in the Literary Institute with nineteen members of the group taking part in "The Recco", 'Blunder", "E. and O.E." and "The Valiant".[31]

The Folk and Showband Era of the 1960s

Danny McGlinchey, a former pupil of St. Eunan's College, who was inspired by Fr. McLoone's annual Gilbert & Sullivan productions formed the "St. Eunan's College Past Pupils Musical Society" in 1960 and directed "The Gondoliers" which was performed in the school hall. This group was short-lived as Danny was soon to be preoccupied as manager of the hugely successful Letterkenny folk group The Pattersons.

Chapter Nineteen: Theatre and the Arts

The Pattersons were children of Christine and t Patterson, Station Master he CDR in the town, and e formed officially as a ic group in 1965 with hers **Billy** and **Ronnie,** sisters **Dorothy** and istine taking to the circuit erform their hit songs. By 7, the popular group were orming in the bright lights as Vegas where they met stars as Elvis Presley, my Davis Jnr. and Eartha . Returning to Ireland, they eared on the Late Late Show on many occasions and, although Dorothy left band in 1968, the group continued to have great success where they had their series on the BBC, UTV and RTÉ including memorable appearances over een episodes on the Morecambe & Wise Show and also the Val Doonican w. They appeared several times on the Nana Mouskouri Show, even teaching to sing the words of the famous Irish ballad 'Báidín Fheilimí', which they sang ther on the show. They toured with Val Doonican and Roy Orbison, playing e Royal Albert Hall several times before retiring from the music business in 4.

LVP's 1957 Production of The Vigil. Courtesy of Mairead O'Donnell

Below Left: The Pattersons with Eric Morecambe on the Morecombe & Wise Show. The Letterkenny group appeared over 13 episodes on the hit show. Courtesy of Billy Patterson

Above: The Pattersons album cover

The Showbands and the 'Ballroom of Romance' craze was now sweeping country and it was no different in Letterkenny. In October 1962, the **Keeney** thers opened the "Fiesta Ballroom" on the Port Road with The Capital

257

Letterkenny - Where the Winding Swilly Flows

Showband appearing on opening night while **Senator Bernard McGlinch** brother of Danny, developed a derelict site adjacent to the La Scala Cinema erected a two storey building with a restaurant on the first floor and a small da floor that had music playing while you ate. In 1967 he bought land across the r from this and expanded "The Golden Grill" into a large food, music and da venue for touring bands.

Not to be dismayed by the popular Showband scene, the Vocatio Players continued with their dramatic and comedic productions throughout 1960s with successful stagings of "Today and Yesterday" (1961), "They Got W They Wanted" (1963), "Liberation", "Troubled Bachelors", "The Whitehea Boy" (all 1964), "Winter Wedding" (1965), "Dry Rot" (1966), "See How T Run" (1967), "Ton of Money" (1968) and "My Wife's Family" (1968).[32]

Letterkenny Vocational Players 1964 production of the Troubled Bachelors

The 1970s and the Folk Festiv

On Thursday 28th August 1 **Gay Byrne**, the popular prese of the Late Late Show, opened very first "Letterkenny Internatio Folk Festival" at the Market Squ Throughout the 1970s, the fes committee, with people such **Barney Doherty, Breda Wins Joe Patterson, Patsy Ward** many others, worked hard to en diverse folk groups from Pol Russia, England and all over world to the by now, gradu expanding town. President of Ireland, **Erskine Childers** opened the festiva 1974, while other celebrated guests who 'cut the ribbon' over the years inclu R.T.E. personality **Frank Hall** (1979), artist **Derek Hill** (1972), and singer J **Felix** (1978). Some of the biggest names on the Irish circuit performed at festivals such as **Clannad**, **Ralph McTell**, **Daniel O'Donnell**, **Christy Mo** the **Dublin City Ramblers**, **Dolores Keane**, and **Aslan** and each year it w welcome, celebrated week long event in the town with diverse musical specta dances and singing pubs competitions. Sadly, due to a lack of funding, the an festival came to a close at the end of the 1990s.

By the 1970s, the sole remaining dramatic group in the town, the L continued to keep the flame of drama alive moving from their previous ho of the Devlin Hall and the Literary Institute to performances in the College Convent Halls including "Anyone Can Rob a Bank" (1971), "The Love Ma (1971), "The Haunting of Hill House" (1974), "Troubled Bachelors"(1977), " Evidence I Shall Give" (1977) and in 1979, a reprisal of their very first show, " Whip Hand".[33]

Chapter Nineteen: Theatre and the Arts

On street frolics with the Letterkenny International Folk Festival of 1988. Courtesy of Brian McDaid (Christmas Annual 1988)

1980s and the Pantomime Revival

Now that The Pattersons group were no more, Danny McGlinchey [turned] his attention on reviving the stage musical in the town and in 1980, after [a short] stint with the "Letterkenny Choral Society", he formed the "Letterkenny [Mu]sical Society", along with Billy and Dorothy Patterson amongst many others, [produc]ing "The Mikado" (1981 and 1987), "Pirates of Penzance" (1982), "The [Gon]doliers" (1983), "Iolanthe" (1984), "H.M.S. Pinafore" (1986) and "My Fair [Lad]y" (1988).

After an absence of twenty-two years, the fondly remembered Pantomime [Soci]ety was revived in the town with the availability of a new venue, the newly [buil]t Community Centre on the Pearse Road. "Robinson Crusoe" (1983) was [prod]uced by **Aussie Bryson** and was followed by Cinderella (1984) and Snow [Whi]te & the Seven Dwarves (1985). **Patrick Doherty** took over the reigns as [pro]ducer with Jack and the Beanstalk (1986), Dick Whittington (1987), Mother [Goo]se (1988), Rock Nativity (1989) and Robin Hood and His Merry Men (1990) [stag]ing pantomimes in the Mount Errigal Hotel as well as St. Eunan's College [Hall]. While there have been many stars of the Pantomime over the years, few [wou]ld argue with the status of **Tommy Sweeney** as the 'King of the Panto' since [its r]eintroduction in 1983. Each year, his comic antics regularly bring howls of [laug]hter from the audience and he is highly regarded on the stage in Letterkenny.

Local cabaret competitions had been a key part of Letterkenny life

Letterkenny - Where the Winding Swilly Flows

Morris Dancers were annual visitors to the town during the Festival. Courtesy of Raymond Blake

especially since the first 'Top[s
the Town' competition in 1[
and continued with great succ[
throughout the 1970s and 19[
orchestrated by Convoy r[
Fergus Cleary in particu[
By the 1980s, the Inter-Fi[
Cabaret Competition [
evolved into the 'No-Na[
Club' with local teams (ju[
and senior) competing aga[
each other to large crowd[
venues throughout the t[
such as St. Conal's Hospital,[
College Hall, the Commu[
Centre, the Mount Errigal H[
and the Golden Grill. The No Name Club junior group won the National Tit[
Kilkenny in 1990 with their successful production of "The Year Gone By - 19[

The "Aisteoirí Adhamhnáin" were formed in the town in 1984 as [
of the Glór na nGael initiative. Comprised of female actors only, all of [
plays were performed in Irish in the Convent, winning four national awards[

Assumpta Donaghey, Tina Meehan, Seamus Fennessy, Frances Walsh and Tommy Sweeney from the 1987 panto Mother Goose. Courtesy of Paddy Gallagher (Christmas Annual 1988)

Chapter Nineteen: Theatre and the Arts

...forming at the Peacock and Adelphi Theatres in Dublin, as well as Cork, Kerry ...Galway.

In the 1980s, the LVP continued with "They Got What They Wanted" ...0), "Mick & Mick" (1981), "Many Young Men of Twenty" (1982) and ...celebrate their fortieth anniversary, in 1987, the group staged the hit West ...d Musical, "Blood Brothers" to sell-out shows in the Community Centre. ...wever, despite the success of this show, by now this long-standing group of ...l Letterkenny actors was gradually coming to a close. In 1988 they entered ...r one-act play "End of Term" into the Bundoran and Derry Festivals and the ...owing year, they performed their final one-act plays in the Loreto Convent ...l - "Riders to the Sea", "Scent of Honeysuckle" and "A Galway Girl". Several ...nbers of the group met up in 1990 in Peadar's Bar for script readings of Brian ...l's "Aristocrats" and "Philadelphia, Here I Come" but sadly this fine group ...had kept alive the spirit of drama in Letterkenny for over four decades quietly ...ed stage left, without any noticeable applause.

Jim O'Sullivan, Marion Naughton, Paddy O'Connor and Anne McGowan from the LVP 1981 production of "Mick and Mick". From Christmas Annual 2006

1990s and a ...Theatre

In 1991, ...uincead ...earraigh picked ...the reins of the ...ational Players, ...formed a new ...na group in the ...n, with many ...ner members of ...LVP joining up. ..."Letterkenny ...sic & Drama ...up" announced ...r arrival on the local scene with performances of "The Absent Minded ...legroom" (1991), "Oklahoma" (1992), "Calamity Jane" (1993), "Juno and the ...cock" (1993) "Fiddler on the Roof" (1994) and "The Field" (1995) reaching ...Confined All Ireland finals in 1999 and 2000 with "Wedding Fever" and "All ...King's Horses" respectively, with **Anthony Delap** scooping the All Ireland ...Supporting Actor accolade in 2000. The group generally performed their ...icals in St. Eunan's College Hall and their plays in the Loreto Convent Hall.

Since the 1970s, many local people had been calling for a theatre for the ...-expanding town. The lack of a suitable venue to entice nationally renowned ...ps such as the Abbey and the Druid Theatre, as well as catering for the annual ...ductions of the local groups, resulted in the formation in June 1993 of The ...rth West Theatre Project Committee. This was comprised mostly of members

Letterkenny - Where the Winding Swilly Flows

of the various local groups, old and new, including people such as Billy Patter(Letterkenny Musical Society), **Paddy O'Connor** (Letterkenny Vocational Play and Pluincead O'Fearraigh (Letterkenny Music & Drama Group) to name three, and the hard work and perseverance of the entire committee resulted in opening of the 383-seater "An Grianán Theatre" on the Port Road in 1999 v **Patricia McBride** as Artistic Director. The Department of Arts, Culture and Gaeltacht sanctioned a grant of €1.5 million for the project with the balance €500,000 being met by the Donegal County Council, Letterkenny U.D.C. and Project committee, through various fundraising initiatives.

With this new theatre now available to the local groups, drama musical entertainment once again took on a new life in the town with celebra performances of Séamus Ó Grianna's "Caisleán Óir" (2000 and again in 20 the now rejuvenated Musical Society's "Jesus Christ Superstar" (2000) and Music and Drama Group's production of Patrick McGill's "Children of the D End" (2007). An Grianán Theatre's in-house productions of "Translatio

An Grianán Theatre, Letterkenny, opened in 1999, added a new Town Clock in May 2014

(2000), "Big Maggie", (2001) and "Making History" (2007) also brou magnificent professional productions to the theatre-going public of Letterke while new groups emerged such as the Youth Theatre, the Actor's Workshop Workhouse Theatre. In 2012, the Letterkenny Music and Drama Group brou Ulster and All Ireland Drama success to the town for the very first time with t

Chapter Nineteen: Theatre and the Arts

...rely successful production of the hit West End show, "The 39 Steps". **Elaine ...lespie, John Ruddy** and **Eoghan McGiolla Bhríghde** each won All Ireland ...ng awards while Pluincead O'Fearraigh scooped the Best Director award. The ...owing year, amateur groups from Cork, Clare and all over the country travelled ...etterkenny to take part in the very first ADL affiliated One Act Drama Festival ...he town.

Theatre, music and the arts have always been at the heart of Letterkenny's ...ory, particularly important throughout the twentieth century, offering a social ...et for the many new faces who were arriving for work and providing an enjoyable ...ortunity to meet new people with shared interests. Various musical and dramatic ...ups have come and gone over the years, entertaining their local peers with tales of ...edy, drama and, most importantly in depressed economic conditions, comedy. ...e impressive An Grianán Theatre stands proudly on the shoulders of every ... of those involved in those productions of the past performed in the Literary ...itute, the Devlin Hall and the College and Convent Halls. Their dedication ... determination to proudly stand on the stage and make their audience laugh ... cry, to sometimes ...-filled houses ... ill-informed ...cisms, deserves to ... rightly appreciated ... applauded. Their ...od, sweat and tears ... the foundations ... the theatre and also ... Regional Culture ...tre, built in 2007, ... helped keep the ...it of the arts alive ...e growing town.

In 2012, the Letterkenny Music & Drama Group won the Confined All Ireland Drama Finals and the Ulster Drama Festival with their acclaimed production of The 39 Steps. Courtesy of Noel O'Fearraigh

Letterkenny - Where the Winding Swilly Flows

Endnotes
1 Derry Journal 30/9/1891
2 Derry Journal 9/12/91
3 Derry Journal 24/12/1891
4 Derry Journal 21/11/1898
5 Derry People 13/7/1906
6 Derry People 21/12/1906
7 Derry Journal 6/1/1909
8 Derry People 9/4/1927
9 Derry People and Derry Journal 1926-1928
10 Derry People 12/5/1928
11 Derry People 5/8/1933
12 O'Connor, Leo, "It All Started 66 years ago", Letterkenny Christmas Annual 2001, p16
13 Derry Journal 31/3/1926
14 Derry Journal 30/3/1927
15 Derry Journal 4/5/1927
16 Derry People 25/2/1928
17 Derry People 23/1/1932
18 Derry People 9/4/1932
19 Derry People 2/7/1938
20 Derry People 15/7/1939
21 Derry People 9/3/1940
22 Derry People 30/12/1933
23 Derry People 26/2/1944
24 Derry People 2/2/1946
25 Derry People 22/3/1947
26 Derry People 27/12/1947
27 Derry People 27/12/1947
28 Derry People 28/1/1950
29 Derry People 14/4/1951
30 Derry People 1951-1960
31 Derry People 22/12/1956
32 Derry People 1960-1970
33 Derry People 1970-1980

Chapter Twenty: Boom, Bust and the Future

The Celtic Tiger was a phrase commonly used to describe Ireland's rapid economic growth between the years 1995 and 2008. Low taxation policies by the government and a credit-driven economy led to a boom with many fortune-driven developers instigating huge developments of housing and commercial buildings in almost every town and village throughout the country. Letterkenny, like so many other towns in Ireland, sat happily on the back of this Tiger as it galloped inevitably out of control. The symbol of this boom was without doubt the crane; walking around Letterkenny at the dawn of the new millennium, the skyline was no longer dominated by the imposing silhouette of the Cathedral but by the ominous outline of large cranes constructing more and more new buildings. Long-standing existing structures were torn down along the Main Street to be replaced by new shops and premises and the wrecking ball of development destroyed many links to the town's rich history and heritage that were lost forever.

Many local people looked on with dismay as the town that they had grown up in quickly disappeared. Local poet **John Blake** captured the mood of many local residents when he wrote:

*"O God what are they doing to our
disappearing town,
With everyday that passes another
building's coming down.
The tears are rolling down my cheeks,
there is a sadness in my heart,
As I watch this thing called "progress"
tear our town apart".*[1]

These old buildings that were being torn down were more than just concrete and cement – they were symbols of an 'Old Letterkenny', a link to a time before the industrial development of the 1970s and 1980s and the rapid expansion of the town. Walking down Main Street today, on the left hand side from the Letterkenny Court Hotel to Oliver Plunkett Road, almost every building is a new structure erected within this period (with only the Bank of Ireland retaining its original façade). Many notable buildings were lost during this period such as Robertson's Parochial Hall, Houston's Corner, Gallagher's

The Letterkenny of the mid twentieth century. Courtesy of the National Library

265

Letterkenny - Where the Winding Swilly Flows

The Letterkenny of the early twentieth century. Courtesy of the National Library

Hotel, Dillon's Supermarket, Murr a Boo Rectory, the Literary Institu and many more. Progress in the tow has of course always been welcom but in the early years of the twent first century, it seemed out of contro Little to no thought was given b planners and government officials a to the future well-being of the tow and its inhabitants. Housing estates an apartments were thrown up so quick in certain parts of the town with pair being applied before the plaster wa even allowed to dry that inevitably, i a short space of time, cracks began t appear in the structures, emblemat of the fragile economy as a whole. A damp and decay began to erode at mar of these new residential buildings in th town, several were vacated and left t become run-down within a very sho space of time. Despite the efforts o various local town councilors over th years, Letterkenny now had its 'slum again, a return to the *"blocks of unsanita dwellings"* described by Canon Maguir one hundred years previously.

The vast tracts of land betwee the Pearse Road and the Swilly, know as the Isles, were regularly floode over the years making them marsh boggy and unfit for developmen However, improvements were made t the drainage and surface of the larg area surrounding the existing Can Road and a new road layout to the Po Bridge was constructed (after initi difficulties with sinkage) in the first years of the new millennium. Before lon big-name companies opened up businesses in the new adjoining retail parks wit many British owned companies availing of the secure Peace Process of Norther Ireland to expand their commercial interests into the Republic of Ireland. Mark and Spencers, Homebase, TK Maxx, Boots, Next, River Island and Argos soo opened outlets in this area as well as a new Dunnes Stores premises, McDonald a new 10 Theatre Cinema Complex and a Radisson Hotel. With the developmer of the Retail Parks, thousands of more shoppers began to come to Letterkenr

266

Chapter Twenty: Boom, Bust and the Future

...ch week, enticing more people away from the traditional commercial centre of ...e Main Street.

The Urban District Council, by now renamed Letterkenny Town Council, ...located to this area also, leaving their premises in the former rectory of ...urrac a Boo and moving into a ...w, artistically designed Public ...rvices Centre in 2002. Designed ... McGabhann Architects, the ...ped roof is covered with ...ass in an attempt to blend in ...th the grassland visuals of the ...rrounding hillsides. The same ...chitects also designed a new ...egional Cultural Centre on the ...e of the now fire damaged and ...molished Murrac a Boo.

Aura Leisure Complex ...as opened in McGovern's fields ... Sallaghgraine in 2005. This new ...ate of the art complex has a ...imming pool, fitness suite, sauna, Jacuzzi and steam room, a large indoor hall ...r basketball and fitness classes, an athletic track and several football pitches. The ...d swimming pool, which the Council had worked so hard for many years to build, ...as deemed surplus to requirements and sold in 2006, being demolished in 2010. ...earby, St. Eunan's GAA club ...so expanded, purchasing new ...jacent fields for development, ... well as substantially updating ...eir main playing field and ...nstructing a large stand largely ...rough fund raising such as raffles ...d grants from the then Minister ...r Tourism and Sport, **Dr. James ...cDaid**, a former club player ...d President. Dr. McDaid was ...le to assist many sports clubs ...roughout the county in his term ... T.D. and locally, Letterkenny ...aels GAA club, Letterkenny ...gby Club, Letterkenny Rovers ...otball Club, Letterkenny Tennis Club and many others benefited at this time as ...ey developed their sports grounds and facilities.

Two new Town parks were opened also. The first was built in the fields ...mediately in front of St. Conal's Hospital, the one-time location for the ...gricultural Shows that took place in the early decades of the twentieth century,

The Public Services Centre built on the Neil T. Blaney Road and home to the Town Council from 2002 until 2014

The Regional Cultural Centre built behind An Grianán Theatre on the former site of Murrac a Boo

267

Letterkenny - Where the Winding Swilly Flows

The Bernard McGlinchey Town Park opened in front of St. Conal's Hospital on the former site of the popular annual Show Day. Courtesy of Anne McGowan

and was named after highly respected local councilor Bernard McGlinchey. second park was developed at Ballymacool immediately in front of the form residence of the Boyds. Both of these parks offered people a place to relax ar unwind as well as catering to the younger children with playgrounds and sm football pitches.

The population of Letterkenny continued to rise in the new millenniur By 2002, the combined urban and rural areas were numbered at 15,231; in 20(this had grown to 17,586 while in 2011 the numbers stood at 19,588.[2] Accordir to the most recent census, ov 15,000 people now live in t urban area alone, although this also due to the expansion of t urban boundary that took pla once again in 2005. Since 19! and the beginning of the Cel Tiger, the town's populatic had risen by over 7,500 peop a phenomenal rise in such short space of time. The arriv of many new people to t town from various parts (Ireland to avail of employme and housing coincided al with the arrival of many peop from Poland, Nigeria, Ghar Brazil, China, the Philippin Romania and many oth countries to become part (the ever growing multi-cultu Letterkenny communi Between 2004 and 20(when the boom was arguab at its highest, over 300,0(immigrants moved to Irelan In less than a decade Irelanc non-indigenous population ro from 1% to 12% and almc one in five people living Ireland were now born outsi of the country. In Donegal, th number stood at 8.1%, with t majority of these people livir

Ballymacool Town Park opened in front of the former Boyd house of Ballymacool

in the large urban areas of Letterkenny, Donegal Town, Ballybofey and Buncran Within the space of a decade Letterkenny, like so many other towns and citie had become a significantly more diverse town.

With every boom though comes the inevitable bust. The developme of any economy can only take so much pressure and the predictions of mar economists were proven accurate by 2008. The housing market and bankir systems collapsed, inflation rose and many people lost their jobs in the wor

Chapter Twenty: Boom, Bust and the Future

obal financial crisis to occur since the Wall Street Crash of 1929. Many people ere unable to keep up with their vast mortgages that were so freely given in seemingly unregulated banking system and lost their homes as a result. The rtune-driven developers were declared bankrupt and the sight of many nfinished ghost estates blighted the landscape. Large business and commercial emises lay unoccupied as the Celtic Tiger went into hibernation. The word of sterity entered the dictionaries of many people as a new government tightened e reins by enforcing strict and harsh budgets.

In Letterkenny, several large established businesses shut down as a result cluding Oatfields and Unifi. Many local businesses on the Main Street, unable cope with the high rents and the competition from the Retail Parks with their ger chain stores, were also forced to close and the sight of empty retail units came a common image for many people. Unoccupied houses and buildings on e Port Road and Main Street had wooden boards placed in their windows and e crumbling plaster of dilapidated premises was all too evident. To combat the reat of the decentralization of businesses and custom from the Main Street, in 011 under **Mayor Tadhg Culbert** the Council instigated a renewed development the appearance of the area with new archways and trees lining both sides of resurfaced footpath and roadway. New systems of free half hour parking on e Main Street enticed customers to return and slowly, several new businesses ve recently opened once again. There is more work to do, no doubt, but the re- ergising of the traditional shopping district of the Main Street seems to be on e road to recovery.

In 1991 the **Old Letterkenny Reunion** was established to help foster mmunity spirit and welcome home many people who, for various reasons, had leave the town over the years. The festival, which has been held every three years ice, has grown in numbers and importance throughout the boom years and had en more of a role to play when the bust occurred. The hard working committee ntinues to ensure an opportunity is there for many 'townies' to remember what akes Letterkenny so special and the Reunion continues to foster a civic pride nongst the residents in their homeplace. Similarly, the **Letterkenny Community eritage Group** was formed in 2012 in an attempt to highlight areas of the town's story and remind people of the buildings and heritage that may have been lost nidst the rubble of development. Since 1982, the **Letterkenny and District hristmas Annual** has been produced by the Community Centre and contains any personal recollections of growing up in the town throughout the twentieth ntury as Letterkenny gradually became the town we know today. There is no ubt that the town has changed its physical appearance in recent years, but the eart and soul of the community is still preserved through organizations such as ese.

dnotes
Blake, John, "The Towney's Lament", Letterkenny Christmas Annual 2006 p27
Census statistics available from www.cso.ie

Conclusion

A lot of history has occurred along the banks of the River Swilly. Ancient tribes hunted and fished along it; great battles took place at its crossings; and a burgeoning market town was established on the gentle northern slopes during the Plantation of Ulster, a town that would grow ever gradually into the large urban centre we know today. The railways that crossed over the river came and went, as did the boats that sailed upon it, docking at either the Ballyraine or Thorn port. However, despite all the changes that took place along its banks, the river kept on flowing.

Throughout this book we have seen the growth of the market town through the hard work, perseverance and determination of many far-sighted people, eager for their businesses and the town itself to succeed. Unfortunately not every person important in the development of the town could be mentioned in the pages of this book. Most of the people who contributed to the town through the years simply went about their business in their daily lives, unaware of the impact that they were having on the people and the town around them. People like **Nurse Peg Harkin** who, as a midwife, travelled around the various houses in the local area on her well-worn bicycle, assisting in the birth of over 2,000 Letterkenny children throughout the 1930s and 1940s. Or others such **Mickey 'Fish' Cullen**, **Joe 'Bid' Gallagher** or **Mick Duffy** and his cart of turf – ordinary Letterkenny people who simply through going about their everyday business greatly added to the character and personality of the town they called their own.

An Aerial photograph of Letterkenny in 2013

Conclusion

The Letterkenny of 2014 is a changed town without a doubt. What began as a small and humble market town grew in prominence in the nineteenth century and, through the development of the Port and the onset of the Railways, rose in stature to become the chief town of County Donegal. Small-scale industrial growth in the early twentieth century led to increased development in the 1970s with the IDA enticing many new large industries to the town beginning with Courtalds and later IMED and UNIFI amongst many others. Continued growth in the 1980s and 1990s led to a rapid expansion in the town's commercial, industrial and residential spheres, so much so that many locals stated at the time that it was '*the fastest growing town in Europe*!' However, with the subsequent bust of the late 2000s came a much-needed re-evaluation. Throughout the boom years, in the continued strive for success, many people appeared to forget exactly what it was that made the town of Letterkenny so special - its people. Many feared that the 'heart' of the town had been ripped out with the destruction of many of its traditional buildings occurring amidst constant development. In fact, it has been commented by more than one local person recently that, due to such rapid change in the architecture of Letterkenny, the town no longer has a 'soul'. I disagree.

To find one's 'soul' you must look for it first within yourself. A soul is not visible to the naked eye and can only be perceived by looking 'beyond the physical', and in the case of Letterkenny, the 'physical' is the architecture. What makes the town so special to so many people is not the concrete slabs of either the Cathedral, Conwal Parish Church or Trinity Presbyterian Church. Neither is it the building blocks of St. Eunan's College, the Loreto Convent or Oatfield Sweet Factory. Although it might appear so from a distance, the town of Letterkenny is not just bricks and mortar. It is so much more than all of that. Look beyond the physical and you find something more. The people of Letterkenny are the soul of Letterkenny as it is the people of Letterkenny who make the town what it is, not its buildings. Changes will always occur in the town – they occurred in the past and you can be sure that they will occur again in the future. New buildings and roads will continue to come; old buildings will continue to fall. But Letterkenny will continue to survive through whatever future 'booms and busts' that will come our way, due primarily to the determination and pride of the people who work and live here.

In 2011, Letterkenny officially commemorated the 400th *anniversary of the granting of the land to Captain Crawford in the Plantation of Ulster*

Letterkenny - Where the Winding Swilly Flows

Just like one's soul, the town of Letterkenny is within every single one of us. It was certainly within Captain Patrick Crawford, George and Johanna Marbury, John Boyd, Rev. John Kinnear, and Cardinal Patrick O'Donnell. It was within every man, woman and child that has ever lived in this great town and worked hard to develop and foster its growth. It was within the 91 local people that lost their lives on the battlefields of France, Belgium and Turkey between 1914 and 1918. It was within those that returned home alive from that terrible conflict only to be shunned by a population with a changed political outlook. It was within the successful market traders who made their businesses and homes in the town and within the workers on the railways. It was within those who unloaded the coal, timber and salt at the Port. It was within every one of those people who found employment in the large industries and within those that boarded the boats and planes with heavy hearts to find employment elsewhere. It was within all the players of various sports as they represented the town with pride over the years and within those that treaded the boards in dramatic entertainment. It is now within those that have recently arrived in the town from all parts of the world and within those that strive to hold onto and cherish the memories of the town that they grew up in. In short, it is within you.

The official motto of Letterkenny is *Ubique Urbem Reminscar* – Latin for *Remember The Town, Wherever You Are* and there is no better maxim to hold onto as our journey together into the past now reaches its final stop and the pages of this history book come to a close. By the people of Letterkenny remembering, no matter where they are in the world, is how the town will continue to survive and thrive. As a 'townie', be proud of where you are from and no matter where you may end up in the world, remember Letterkenny for all the right reasons. Remember the physical of course, but love and cherish the memory of its people – those that made the town what it is. In the future, the architecture and layout of Letterkenny will continue to evolve and change no doubt - every town needs to in order to avoid stagnation. Yet when all has been said and done, despite everything, one thing will always remain constant and ever true; it will always be Our Town - Letterkenny, where the winding Swilly flows.

The official town crest of Letterkenny with its motto – Ubique Urbem Reminscar, Wherever You Are, Remember The Town. Courtesy of Letterkenny Town Council

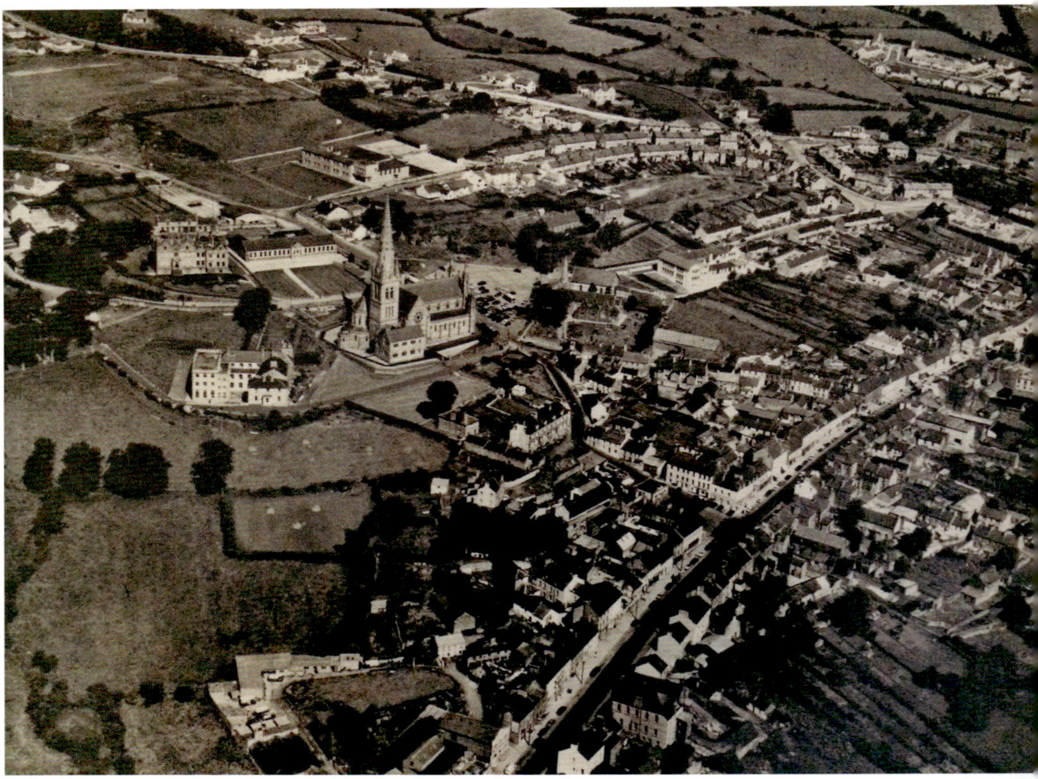

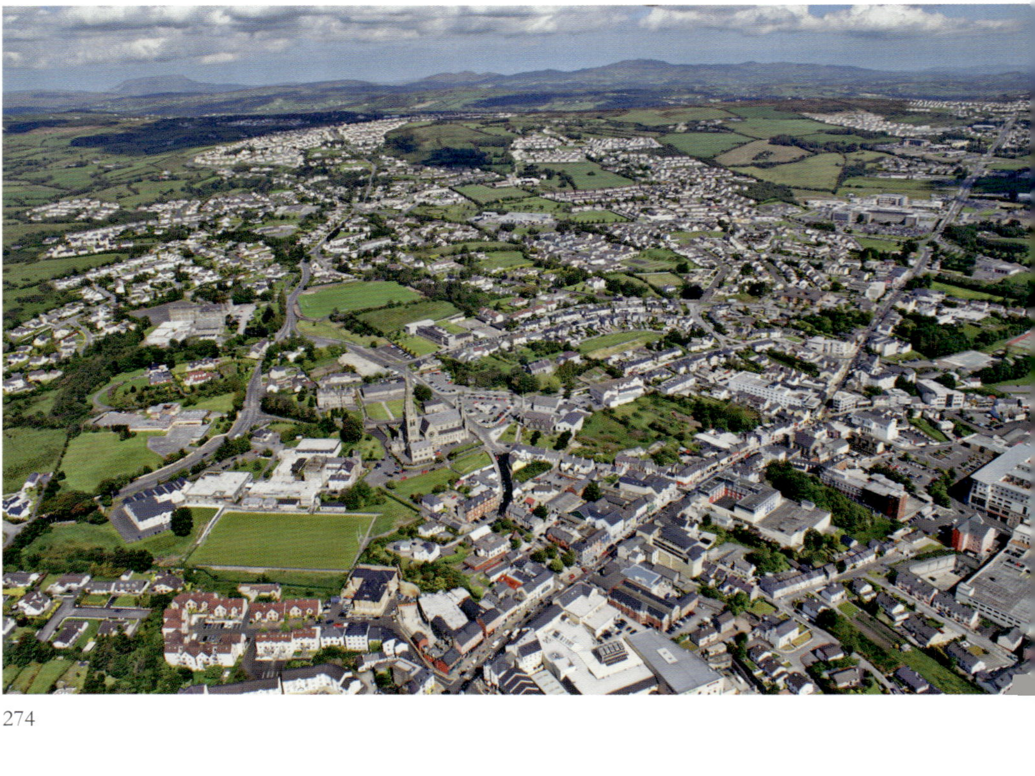

MAIN STREET, LETTERKENNY

The Diamond, Letterkenny, Co. Donegal

CHRONOLOGY

10,000 – 5,000 BC	A hillside valley is carved for the Súileach River flow through
3,500 – 2,000 BC	Neolithic Period – Evidence of Megalthic tom at Lisnanese and Mondooey
600 AD (approx)	Congbhaile monastery founded to the west Leitir Ceanainn by Fiachra, son of Ciarán
615 – 620	Death of Fiachra, son of Ciarán
913	Scannlan, herenach of Congbhaile, dies
1098	Cinéal Chonaill and Cinéal nEoghain meet in battle at Fearsad Mór
1204	Sitric O'Sruithin, herenach of Congbhaile, dies
1248	Gofraidh Ua Domhnaill takes power in Tír Chonaill
1257	Ua Domhnaill victory over Maurice Fitzgerald Credan Kille
1258	Gofraidh Ua Domhnaill defeats Brian O'Neill Battle of Ath – thairsí
1392	Cinéal Chonaill/Cinéal nEoghain troops ma peace at Fearsad Mór
1550	Calvagh Ua Domhnaill builds castle at Scarrifho
1567	Shane O'Neill defeated by Aodh Ua Domhnail in Battle of Farsetmore
1585	Tír Chonaill and Inis Eoghain amalgamated an shired as County Donegal
1594 – 1603	Nine Years' War of Red Hugh O'Donnell and Hugh O'Neill against Elizabeth I
1601	O'Neill and O'Donnell defeated at Battle of Kinsale. O'Donnell flees to Spain and dies
1607	Flight of the Earls
1608	Rebellion of Cahir O'Dochertaigh. Captains Patrick Crawford and William Stewart sent for quell rebellion
1609	Sir Thomas Coach and Sir Maurice Bark granted lands as undertakers south of the Sw in Lismonaghan and Dromore
1610	Phelim O'Doghertie appointed rector of Conw Balliboe of Leitir Ceanainn part of an ini land grant to Hugh McHugh McDubh in Uls Plantation as a deserving Irishman
1610	Captain Patrick Crawford chosen as a servitor receive lands in Kilmacrennan barony

Chronology

1611	1,000 acres including the balliboe of Leitir Ceanainn assigned to Captain Patrick Crawford as part of the Ulster Plantation with the purpose of building a new market town.
1615	Patrick Crawford dies
	Dougall Campbell appointed rector of Conwal
1616	Market patent granted for the new town of Letterkenny
1619	Pynnar's Survey notes the existence of the town of Letterkenny
1636	Conwal Parish Church built
1639	District of Manor Sempill created
1640	Presbytery set up in the town
1650	Battle of Scarrifhollis
1659	Census of Donegal notes 73 people living in Letterkenny
1704	James Dougherty recorded as parish priest of Conwal
1725	Patent granted for a fair at Oldtown
1737	Francis McDevitt recorded as parish priest of Conwal
1775	Ballyraine Port noted
1777	James Harkin recorded as parish priest of Conwal
1782	Bishop Anthony Coyle becomes first Catholic Bishop of Raphoe to live in Letterkenny
1784	First Catholic Church built in Letterkenny on grounds of present St. Eunan's College
1820	Barkhall Church opened and new Catholic church built on site of present Cathedral
1822	The Battle of Sprackburn
1823	Methodist Preaching House built at top of Market Square
1825	School opened on Castle Street
1828	Lighting of Towns Act and first Town Commissioners appointed
1830s	McGoldrick's School opened on College Row
1830	Larger church built on same site
1831	Courthouse built
1835	Belfast Banking Company opened on Main Street (AIB)
1837	Mount Southwell Place built
1838	Poor Law Act passed
1841	Port Road School opened by Bishop McGettigan
1845	Workhouse opened

277

1849	Dr. Crerand's High School opened
1854	St. Patrick's Pro-Cathedral opened
	Loreto Sister arrive to open two new schools
1860	Letterkenny Railway Company formed
1861	Derryveagh evictions
	Woodlands School opened
1866	St. Conal's Hospital built
1870	Tenant Rights meeting at Market Square with te thousand people present
1873	Hibernian Bank opened on Main Street (Bank o Ireland)
1876	Literary Institute opened on Main Street (Coun Library)
1878	Robertson Parochial Hall built on Port Road
1880	Royal Garrison Artillery Barracks opened at Sprackburn
	Dr. Kinnear elected MP for Donegal
	Illistrin School opens
1881	Land League meeting at Market Square with Michael Davitt present
1883	Letterkenny connected to Buncrana/Derry train line
1888	Patrick O'Donnell appointed Bishop of Raphoe
	Trial of Fr. McFadden and Fr. Stephens
1891	Cathedral Building Committee formed
	Letterkenny F.C. formed
	Letterkenny Amateur Dramatic Club formed
1894	Presentation Brothers arrive in Letterkenny
	St. Adamnan's Swifts and Letterkenny Celtic football teams formed
	First recorded game of golf at Rockhill
1895	Gospel Hall built
1896	Presentation Brothers School opened
1898	Local Government of Ireland Act creates Urban District Council
	Aonach Tir Chonaill takes place in Hall Eithne
	St. Columba's Convent National School opened
1901	Cathedral opened
1903	Burtonport Extension built to railway line
1905	Lámh Dearg GAA club formed in Literary Institute
1906	St. Eunan's College opened
1908	Minor crash at Owencarrow Viaduct
1909	County Donegal Railway opened to Strabane

Chronology

1911	Faugh a Ballagh and Tirchonaill GAA clubs formed
1912	Ulster Covenant signed at Letterkenny
1913	Letterkenny Golf Club opened at Crievesmith
1914	Technical School opened on Main Street
1914-1918	World War 1. 91 Letterkenny people died.
1917	Jim Connally Cumann of Sinn Fein formed
	Padraig Pearse's mother, sister and niece visit the town
	Private James Duffy earns Victoria Cross for bravery
1918	DeValera gives a speech at Market Square
	Anti Conscription Rally at Sentry Hill
	Election of E.J. Kelly as Irish Party candidate
1919-1922	War of Independence
1922	Irish Civil War
	Workhouse closes and becomes Lymac's bottling store
1924	Letterkenny Rovers and Geraldines GAA clubs formed
1925	Four people killed in Owencarrow Viaduct Train Crash
1926	Letterkenny Tennis Club
1926-1928	Cinema opened in Recreational Hall on Port Road
1927	Cardinal O'Donnell dies
	Lurgybrack School opens
	Original St. Eunan's Club formed
1900s-1920s	Letterkenny Hearts, Letterkenny United and Letterkenny Rovers football teams noted
1930	Oatfield Sweet Factory opened
	New St. Eunan's GAA Club formed
1931	St. Pat's GAA club formed
1932	First recorded rugby match takes place at Asylum grounds
1933-1935	First 'talking pictures' shown in old Methodist Church
1935	La Scala Cinema opened on Port Road
1937	St. Columba's GAA club formed
	O'Donnell Park opened
1938	Letterkenny Crusaders soccer club formed
1939	Devlin Hall opened at bottom of Main Street
1940	New Technical School opened at Ard O'Donnell
	Ros Suilighe estate built
1946	Letterkenny Boxing Club formed

1947	Letterkenny West End United soccer team formed
	Letterkenny Vocational Players drama club formed
1949	Ard O'Donnell housing estate built
1951-1960	Letterkenny Pantomime Society perform annual shows in the Devlin Hall
1953	Ard Colmcille Estate built
	Londonderry & Lough Swilly Railway closed
1956	Scoil Mhuire gan Smál school opened on Sentry Hill
1957	Letterkenny Crusaders Football Club re-formed
	New Letterkenny Rovers Football Club formed
1959	Extension completed to former girls' school and Presentation Brothers move in opening Scoil Cholmcille.
	County Donegal Railway closed
1962	Fiesta Ballroom opened
	Golden Grill opened on Port Road. Moved across the road to present premises five years later
1965-1974	The Pattersons group tour the world and appear on The Morecambe & Wise Show
1967	Dillon Brothers Supermarket opens on Main Street
1969	Army stationed at Rockhill Barracks after original setting up of Camp Arrow during Battle of the Bogside
	First Letterkenny Folk Festival launched by Gay Byrne
1970s	New housing estates built such as Beechwood, Gartan etc
1970	Arcade Athletic formed, later becoming Bonagee United
1971	Letterkenny Regional Technical College opened
1972	Letterkenny Athletic Club formed
1973	Letterkenny Rugby Club formed
1975	RTÉ documentary televised about Letterkenny called 'Profile of an Irish Town'
	Courtald's factory opens at Kiltoy
1977	Scoil Colmcille opens in new building on Convent Road
1980	Little Angels School opens
	Letterkenny Musical Society formed
1982	Letterkenny & District Christmas

Chronology

	Annual launched
1983	Letterkenny Main Street converted to one way traffic
	Letterkenny Pantomime Society reformed
1984	Unifi Textured Yarns takes over the Courtald's factory
1985	Letterkenny Shopping Centre opened
1987	New Technical School opened at Windyhall
1991	Gaelscoil Adhnamhnáin opened
	Letterkenny Music & Drama Group formed
	First Old Letterkenny Reunion takes place
1993	Courtyard Shopping Centre opens on Main Street
1994	Church of Irish Martyrs opened at Gortlee
1996	Letterkenny Gaels GAA club formed
1999	An Grianán Theatre opened
2000	Coláiste Ailigh opened in former house of the Dunnions
2002	Town Council moves into new Local Area Office on new link road
2006	Educate Together School opened in Ballyraine
2007	Regional Cultural Centre opened on former site of Murrac a Boo
2011	Letterkenny 400 commemorations
2012	Oatfield Sweet Factory closed
	Letterkenny Music & Drama Group win Ulster and All Ireland Drama Finals with 'The 39 Steps'
	Letterkenny Community Heritage Group formed
2014	Letterkenny Town Council closes
	Letterkenny: Where the Winding Swilly Flows book is launched!
The Future	Over to you...

Appendix A

Godfrey O'Donnell's heroic death at Ath-thairsí was recorded through this poem. Sadly, the poet is unknown.

The Bier That Conquered

All worn and wan, and sore with wounds from Credan's bloody fray,
In Donegal for weary months the proud O'Donnell lay;
Around his couch in bitter grief his trusty clansmen wait,
And silent watch, with aching hearts, his faint and feeble state.
The chief asks one evening to be brought into the open air,
that he may gaze once more on the landscape's familiar scenes:
"And see the stag upon the hills, the white clouds drifting by;
And feel upon my wasted cheek God's sunshine ere I die."
Suddenly he starts on his pallet, and exclaims
"A war-steed's tramp is on the heath, and onward cometh fast,
And by the rood! a trumpet sounds! hark! it is the Red Hand's blast!"
And soon a kern all breathless ran, and told a stranger train
Across the heath was spurring fast, and then in sight it came.
"Go, bring me, quick, my father's sword," the noble chieftain said
"My mantle o'er my shoulders fling, place helmet on my head;
And raise me to my feet, for ne'er shall clansman of my foe
Go boasting tell in far Tyrone he saw O'Donnell low.
Go call around Tyrconnell's chief my warriors tried and true;
Send forth a friend to Donal More, a scout to Lisnahue;
Light baal-fires quick on Esker's towers, that all the land may know
O'Donnell needeth help and haste to meet his haughty foe.
Oh, could I but my people head, or wield once more a spear,
Saint Augus! but we'd hunt their hosts like herds of fallow deer.
But vain the wish, since I am now a faint and failing man;
Yet, ye shall bear me to the field, in the centre of my clan.
Right in the midst, and lest, perchance, upon the march I die,
In my coffin ye shall place me, uncovered let me lie;

Appendix A

And swear ye now, my body cold shall never rest in clay,
Until you drive from Donegal O'Neill's host away."
Then sad and stern, with hand on skian, that solemn oath they swore,
And in a coffin placed their chief, and on a litter bore.
Tho' ebbing fast his life-throbs came, yet dauntless in his mood,
He marshaled well Tyrconnell's chiefs, like leader wise and good.
Then rose the roar of battle loud, as clan met clan in fight;
The axe and skian grew red with blood, a sad and woeful sight;
Yet in the midst o'er all, unmoved, that litter black is seen,
Like some dark rock that lifts its head o'er ocean's war serene..
And to his tribes he stretch'd his hands--then pointed to the foe,
When with a shout they rally round, and on Clan Hugh they go;
And back they beat their horsemen fierce, and in a column deep,
With O'Donnell in their foremost rank, in one fierce charge they sweep.
Lough Swilly's banks are thick with spears!--O'Neill's host is there,
But rent and tost like tempest clouds--Clan Donnell in the rere!
Lough Swilly's waves are red with blood, as madly in its tide
O'Neill's horsemen wildly plunge, to reach the other side.
And broken is Tyrowen's pride, and vanquished Clannaboy,
And there is wailing thro' the land, from Bann to Aughnacloy;
The Red Hand's crest is bent in grief, upon its shield a stain,
For its stoutest clans are broken, its stoutest chiefs are slain.
And proud and high Tyrconnell shouts; but blending on the gale,
Upon the ear ascendeth a sad and sullen wail;
For on that field, as back they bore, from chasing of the foe,
The spirit of O'Donnell fled!--oh, woe for Ulster, woe!
Yet died he there all gloriously--a victor in the fight;
A chieftain at his people's head, a warrior in his might;
They dug him there a fitting grave upon that field of pride,
And a lofty cairn they raised above, by fair Lough Swilly's side.

Appendix B

The following is a vivid description of the town of Letterkenny and of Sir George Marbury given by Robert Cartwright in 1625:

A description of Letterkenny in 1625

…on daye I went into a markett towne of Sr. George merburries and cutt about x'en or xii mantles whearof he made a grievous complaint to all the justices of peace, and threatned to indite me for in the Starre Chamber, saying moreover that it was an yll business of your Lop: to make a marshal in his countye, and it is very well knowne that willinglye he will not suffer neither sheriff nor any other officer to exercise any authoritye in that towne, and yet himself a man of so evill government and given to drinking as makes himself a laughing stock and scorne to the countreye, and although I have ever observed him (with too much subiection) to hold friendshippe with him (being near neighbours) yet his disarming firste on of my men, and then the other also, commanding the constable to put him in the stockes without any occasion given, but only to let his towne know that he had power to do any thing thear that pleased him, and at my next meeting with him he told me that he was sending my man to the stockes, I told him that I hoped that he had some other better reason than because he was my man, to which he answeared that if either my man or myself came into his towne to do any thing he would thear disarme us and send us both to they jayle…

…an opinion that was roused, that I neither had power nor durst do any thing thear but by his consent, which appeared to be true, for having formerly acquainted him that divers lewd fellowes frequented his towne and used to playe thear for 4 or five daies together, whearof some of them had formerly broken jayle, yet nothing was done, nor said against them, and when newes was brought me afterwards that thye had been thear from fryday until Tuesday playing all the clothes on their backs, i went thither and apprehended twoo of the gamsters but the two twoo principal men that I looked for wear convaied away, the on throughe a windowe, and the other at a back dore and the party that convaied them away, and the twoo other gamsters I delivered unto the constable with a mittimus to carrye them to the jayle, but Sr. George took them away from him and set them at liberty, saying that he would discharge as many as I should commit.

Robert Cartwright, Donegal Provost Marshall, 28th January 1625

Source: Hunter, Robert "The Settler Population of an Ulster Plantation County", Donegal Annual 1972, pp150- 52

Appendix C

Hearth Money Rolls - 1665 – Donegal

1665, an Act of Parliament decreed that all those with hearths (fireplaces, stoves etc.) would ed to pay a tax and money was collected in the parish of Conwal. Below is a list of the names the heads of families who had fireplaces in their homes in the town of Letterkenny and in the mediate surrounding areas:

Conwall Parish

tterkenny Town
bert Hutcheson
wen Forsyth
bert Porter
exander Ewing
lliam Wigton
lliam Frignall
exander Coningham
n Houston
nes Fuuthy
bert Ewing
an m'Cowall
lliam Bryce
n Bryce
nes Whyte
nes Harper
n Falconer
lliam Carr
nes Russell, younger
trick Ginking
nes Bryce
lliam Thompson
n Miller
bert Mitchell
ander Hunter
bert m'Ilwey
n m'Kessan
lliam Jameson
n Forbes
lter Buchannon
lliam Anderson

Hugh Hay
George Dixon
John Orr
William Orr
John Baxter
John Thomas
Robert Ramsay
Richard Jones
John Boyde

Surrounding Areas
John Stewart of Breachy
John Campble
Robert Bavaird of Airds
James Bavaird
Robert Keminy
James Buchannan
Allexander Gibson
Shan m'Linn of Buragh
Daniell m'Hafferty of Bowhirrill
Owen o'Donnell
John Hunter of Gortnevarne
James Williamson
Thomas Grhame
Allex m'Niaght of Ellistrin
Hugh Liffe
David Mullavill
Drmund m'Cawley
Roory o'Strean
Neale o'Mellan
Robert Dall

Donnagh m'Tegg of Cullboy
Archibald Stewart
Tool m'Cloy
Shan m'Grehan
Remund o'Gallagher of Killelasty
Owen o'Donnell
Manus o'Mulcher of Kilcling
William o'Cahan
Daniel Longe of Glencarr
David Rodger
Robert Boyde
Neale m'Callen
Edmund m'Callen
William Rodger of Gortlee
John Davy
John Ramsey
Robert Ewing of Carnemogagh
Walter Stewart
Walter m'Naire of Lissnennane
Malcome m'Naire
William Ewing of Ballyrehan
William Mitchel
Robert Taylor
James Hare of Salregreane
Gilchreest m'Nicholl
John Glen of Ballim'Cowell
James Wilson
John Wilson
Quantein Black of Conwall
Neale m'Gilhenny
James Frizell

Letterkenny - Where the Winding Swilly Flows

George Mitchell
Adam Wilson of Tullygay
John Wilson, elder
John Wilson, younger
James Rodger
John Wilson
Connor m'Gechan of Downe (Dooen)
Pattrick m'Gechyn
Torlagh m'Mongill
Donagh m'Killaghan of Glenkiragh
Hugh o'Donnell
Pattrick o'Luchary
Dermund m'Ilhenie of Cray & Corr (Rockhill)
Connor m'Ilhenie
Hugh m'Davett
Shan m'Ilhenie
Donnagh m'Ilhenie
Murragh o'Mulfail
Edmund m'Laughlin
William o'Mughan
William m'Ilhenie
Edmund o'Gallogher of Dironan
Manus o'Gallogher
bryan o'Correran
William o'Dougherty
Henry m'Davett of Stakernagh
Neale oige o'Donnell
John Gullyon
Owen bane m'Groerty
Edmund m'Groerty
Donnagh o'Sharky
Mulmurry o'Mullerig of Kileg
Daniel m'Groerty
Connor o'Dougherty of Drumcaveny
Shan m'Cawley
Bryan m'Gillispick of Pollan
Owen o'Gobben
Bryan o'Begley
James o'Gallogher of Carrick
Owen m'Gee
Bryan o'Dougherty of Clonkearny
Dermund o'Murray
William m'Davett of Tryentagh
Thomas Wheaton
Shan o'Gallogher of Drumore
Daniell o'Dougherty
Torlagh o'Donnell

£14 6s for 143 hearths

Conwall is the last parish for Kilmacrenan barony on the Roll which is here signed and sealed b
Cha Hamilton, Rich Perkins, Wm Warren, Geo Cary, John Nibit, An Knox.

Appendix D

Letterkenny in 1824

Gentry & Clergy
Boyd, Alexander, Esq., Gortlee
Boyd, John Esq., Ballymacool
Boyd, Rev. William, Kiltoey
Brooke, Thos. Esq. Castlegrove
Chambers, Dan., Esq. Rockhill
Chambers, Rev. John, Woodville
Gamble, Rev.
Homan, Rev. George, Barnhill
Leyttle, Rev. Joseph
Lighton, W.H.M. Esq., Drumlodge
Mansfield, Francis, Esq., Castlewray
McGettigan, Rev. Patrick
Pratt, Rev. Andrew
Stofford, Rev. Dr. Joseph, Rector Glendoon
Wray, Wm., Esq., Oak Park
Young, Ralph, Esq., Oatlands

Attorneys
Crawford, Charles
Murray, Edward

Surgeons
Hunter, John (and Apothecary)
Patterson, John
Reid, Thos. (to the Dispensary)

Merchants
Allen, Geo. (General)
Gallagher, Jas. (Cloth)
King, David (Cloth)
Leech, Geo. (General)
Moffit, Robt. (General)
Peoples, Jas. (Cloth)
Wilson, Wm. (General)

Shopkeepers, Traders etc.
Allen, Geo. Chandler
Blackwood, Wm., Grocer and Chandler
Buckanan, Alex, Tailor
Caffrey, Hugh, Publican
Carson, John, Parish Clerk
Clarke, Samuel, Publican
Colonhan, William, Publican
Coran, Cornelius, Publican
Coyle, Henry, Publican
Cunningham, Samuel, Saddler
Delap, Wm., Salt Manufacturer
Dobson, John, Grocer
Elliot, John, Baker

Shopkeepers, Traders etc. (continued)
Ferguson, David, Druggist
Fisher, Wm., grocer and Agent to the Dublin Tea Company
Foy, James, Ironmonger
Gaily, Charles, Grocer
Gaily, Robert, Grocer
Greer, George, Grocer
Hall Saml., Painter and Glazier
Henderson, Gustavus, Publican
Hood, Henry, Grocer
Hunter, John & Co., Wholesale and Retail Grocers
Laird, Jane, Innkeeper
Lynch, Hugh, Publican
McAuley, Jn., Painter and Glazier
McCarran, Tim., Woollen Draper
McClintock, Publican
McConney, Thomas, Publican
McCrea, Robert, Saddler,
McCullum, Alexander, Publican
McDevitt, Philip, Publican
McGeehin, James, Publican
McGuily, Neil, Leather Seller
McMullin, Robert, Muslin and Calico Warehouse
Mellen, Andrew, Grocer

Moore, Robert, Publican
Munn, Alexander, Grocer
Patterson, Thomas, Grocer
Ramsey, William, Woollen and Woollen Draper
Ramsey, William, Grocer and Leather Seller
Ramsey, William, Watchmaker
Reid, John, Coppersmith
Scott, Alexander, Publican
Stewart, William, Grocer
Sweeney, Andrew, Publican
Turner, John, Baker
Young, William, Boot Maker

Custom House
Ralph Mansfield, Esq., Collector
William Lighton, Port Surveyor
Robt. Hunter, Esq., Pro-Collector

Linen market
Robt. Cochran, Esq. inspector
Mr. George Russell, Stamper

Stamp Office
Ralph Young, Esq., Distributor for the Coun
H.E. Peoples, Esq., Sub-distributor

Source: "Documents of Local Interest", Donegal County Library papers

Further Reading

Letterkenny & Donegal

Maguire, Canon Edward, "Letterkenny: Past and Present", 1917
Fleming, Sam, "Letterkenny: Past and Present", Donegal Democrat ,1979
Fleming, Sam, "Redmond O'Hanlon", unknown date
NA, "A Local History of Letterkenny", Donegal Printing Co. 1979
McClintock, May, "Seed-Time & Harvest", IFA, 1994
Aoi nGiallach, "Our Town: Letterkenny and hinterland", 1998
Baird, John, "The Port: A Short Illustrated History of Port Ballyraine, Letterkenny", Ian Baird, 2002
Letterkenny Official Guide 1952
Farrell, Noel, "Exploring Family Origins in Letterkenny", 1996
An Tostal Guide 1954
Nolan, W., Ronayne, L and Dunleavy, M, (eds.), "Donegal, History and Society: Interdisciplinary Essays on the History of an Irish County" Geography Publications, Dublin, 1995
Mac Laughlin, Jim (Ed), "Donegal: the Making of a Northern County", Four Courts Press, 2007
Mac Laughlin, Jim and Beattie, Sean (Ed), "An Historical, Environmental and Cultural Atlas of County Donegal", Cork University Press, 2013
Lacy, Brian (ed), "Archaeological Survey of County Donegal – A description of the field antiquities of the County from the Mesolithic Period to the 17th century A.D.", Donegal County Council, Lifford, 1983

The Ua Canannáins and O'Donnells

Cannon, Thomas Gildea, "A History of The O'Cannons of Tir Chonaill", Donegal Annual, 1978
Mc Canann, Thomas, "Carraig an Dúnáin: Probable Ua Canannáin Inauguration Site", JRSAI, 133, 2003
Lacey, Brian," Cenél Conaill and the Donegal Kingdoms: AD 500 – 800", Four Courts Press, 2006
O'Donnell, V (Ed), "O'Donnells of Tír Chonaill: A Concise History of the O'Donnell Clan", Donegal Printing & Stationary Co., 1997
Mc Gallachair, P., "Where was O'Donnell's Island on Lough Beagh?" Donegal Annual 1959, Vol. No. 2,
Kelly, D,H , "The Book of Fenagh in Irish and English, Originally Compiled by St. Cailin", Alexander Thom,1875

Battles of Áth thairsí, Farsetmore & Scarriffhollis

Hayes-McCoy, G.A. "Scots Mercenary Forces in Ireland (1565-1603)", Edmund Burke Publisher, 1996 (first ed 1937)
Hayes-McCoy, G.A. "Irish Battles – A Military History of Ireland", Appletree Press, 1989
Ó Brógáin, Tomás, "The Battle of the Swilly (Farsetmore), 8 May 1567" from History Ireland Vol. No. 3, May/June 2011 pp16-18
McMahon, Sean, "Battles Fought on Irish Soil: A Complete Account", Londubh Books 2010
Ronayne, Liam (Ed), "The Battle of Scariffhollis", Eagráin Dhún na nGall, 2000
Bardon, Jonathan, "A History of Ireland in 250 Episodes", Gill & Macmillan, 2008
McKenny, Kevin, "The Laggan Army in Ireland 1640-1685", Four Courts Press, 2005

<u>Ulster Plantation</u>
Hill, George, "An Historical Account of the Plantation in Ulster at the Commencement of the Seventeenth Century 1608 – 1620", Irish University Press, 1970, First Ed. 1877
Perceval-Maxwell, M., "The Scottish Migration to Ulster in the Reign of James I" Routledge Kegan Paul, 1973
Hunter, R.J., "Towns in the Ulster Plantation", Studia Hibernica, No. 11 (1971)
Simms, J.G., "Donegal in the Ulster Plantation", Geographical Society of Ireland, Dublin, 1972
Hunter, Robert "The Settler Population of an Ulster Plantation County", Donegal Annual 197
McGettigan, Darren "The Donegal Plantation and the Tír Chonaill Irish, 1610-1710", Four Cou Press, 2010
Simms, J.G., "The Ulster Plantation in County Donegal", Donegal Annual 1971
Margey, Annaleigh "Representing plantation landscapes: the mapping of Ulster, c. 1560 – 1640" 140-164, from Lyttleton, James & Rynne, Colin (eds), Plantation Ireland : Settlement and Mate Culture, c.1550-c.1700, Four Courts Press, 2009
<u>Religious Establishments</u>
"An Illustrated Guide to St. Eunan's Cathedral", 1901
"Cathedral of S.S. Eunan and Columba", Conwal and Leck Parish, June 2001
Ó Baoighill, Padraig S., "Cardinal Patrick O'Donnell 1856-1927",
Foilseacháin Chró na mBothán, 2008
Silke, Rev. John J. & Hughes, Mrs. Moira, "Raphoe Miscellany 1", 2012
"Clergy of Derry and Raphoe", the Ulster Historical Foundation, 1999
Seaton Reid, James, "A History of the Presbyterian Church in Ireland" Vol. II, Whitaker & (London, 1853
Weir, A.J., "Letterkenny Congregations, Ministers & People 1615-1960", 1960
"Fragmenta Rapotensiana", Donegal Annual 1956
McClintock, May, "From Dark Troubled Times to an Ecumenical Politician – Early Presbyteriani in Letterkenny (1642 – 1909), Christmas Annual 1992,
<u>Letterkenny Ascendancy</u>
Burke, Sir Bernard, "Vicissitudes of Families", London, 1861
Trench, Charlotte Violet, "The Wrays of Donegal, Londonderry and Antrim", Oxford Univers Press, 1945
MacDonagh, J.C.T, "A Seventeenth Century Letterkenny Manuscript", Donegal Annual 1956
O'Carroll, Col. Declan, "Rockhill House – A History", Defence Forces printing Press,
2nd Edition, 1998
McClintock, May, "Boyd of Ballymacool", Letterkenny Christmas Annual 1991
MacDonagh, J.C.T, "A Seventeenth Century Letterkenny Manuscript", Donegal Annual 1956
<u>Theobald Wolfe Tone</u>
Wolfe Tone, William Theobald (Ed), "Memoirs of Theobald Wolfe Tone", Vol. II, London, 18
Webb, Alfred, "A compendium of Irish biography: comprising sketches of distinguished Irishm and of eminent persons connected with Ireland by office or by their writings", Dublin, 1878
Moody, T.W. et al (Ed), "The Writings of Theobald Wolfe Tone, 1763-98, Vol. III", Oxfc University Press, 2007
Brady, Seamus, "Wolfe Tone and Donegal", Journal of the County Donegal Historical Society, 1948

Hiring Fairs & Workhouse
Gill, P.J., "Some Old Fairs of Co. Donegal", Donegal Annual, 1960
Hanlon, Michael, "Hiring Fairs and Farm Workers in North West Ireland", Guildhall Press, 1992

Derryveagh Evictions
Vaughan, W.E. "*Sin, Sheep and Scotsmen, John George Adair and the Derryveagh Evictions, 1861*", Appletree Press, 1983

Schools
Gilloway, Ken, "George Sigerson Poet, Patriot, Scientist and Scholar", Stair Uladh, 2011
Britt, Marina, "Changed Times: Ballyraine National School, The Background and its History (1976-2007)", 2007
Gill, P.J., "Donegal Schools a Century Ago", Donegal Annual 1956
Carroll, Anne (ed),"Loreto Letterkenny 150: Loreto Convent Letterkenny 1854-2004", 2004
O'Connor, John J., "The Presentation Brothers in Letterkenny", Presentation Studies 11, 2001
Gallagher, Adrian, "A Short Walk, A Long Journey – Woodland National School 1860-1994", Donegal Printing & Stationery, 1994
Buchanan, Sandra (ed), "County Donegal Vocational Educational Committee 1905, 2005", County Donegal Vocational Educational Committee, 2005

World War 1
The County Donegal Book of Honour
Richardson, Neil, "A Coward If I Return, a Hero If I Fall – Stories of Irishmen in World War 1", O'Brien Press, 2010
McFhionnghaile, Niall, "Donegal, Ireland and the First World War", An Crann, 1987
Niallach, Naoi, "Not So Long Ago – World War One", Letterkenny Christmas Annual 1987
Monaghan, Liam, "These Veterans Deserve Remembrance and Gratitude", Letterkenny Christmas Annual 1987

Nationalism, Independence & Civil War
McFhionnghaile, Niall, "Dr. McGinley, His Life and Times", An Crann, 1985
O'Duibhir, Liam, "The Donegal Awakening: Donegal & the War of Independence", Mercier Press, 2009
O'Duibhir, Liam, "Donegal & The Civil War: the Untold Story", Mercier Press, 2011
McMonagle, Col. James, "National activities, Letterkenny, Co. Donegal, 1917-1921", Statement by Witness, courtesy Bureau of Military History, Document Number 1385
Lawson, Anthony "Activities of Letterkenny Company, Letterkenny Battalion, Irish Volunteers, Co. Donegal, 1917-1921" Statement by Witness, courtesy Bureau of Military History, Document Number 1546
O'Connell, Aidan, "The Ulster Covenant in Donegal 1912", Donegal Annual 2011

Sports Clubs
Curran, Conor, "Cricket in Donegal 1865-1914", Donegal Annual 2011
Curran, Conor, "Sport in Donegal: A History", The History Press, 2010
O'Donnell, Ciaran, "Donegal Sporting Greats", Donegal Democrat, 2010
Carroll, Declan, "Letterkenny Golf Club, The Centenary Years 1913-2012", Letterkenny Golf Club, 2012
Duffy, Dick, "The Growth of Soccer in Letterkenny", Letterkenny Christmas Annual 1982
Downey, Lee, "Letterkenny RFC", Letterkenny Christmas Annual 2006

"Twenty Five Years a Growing", Letterkenny Christmas Annual 1997
Delap, Brendan, "The Glenswilly Flyer", Letterkenny Christmas Annual 2004
"A Life Time of Boxing in Letterkenny", Letterkenny Christmas Annual 2001
"The History of Letterkenny Amateur Boxing Club", Letterkenny Christmas Annual 1987
Lynch, Jim, "Row, row, row your boat, gently down the stream", Letterkenny Christmas Annual 2007

Twentieth Century Development
"Letterkenny down the years: Letterkenny in 1824", Letterkenny Christmas Annual 2009
"Footplate man recalls Viaduct Disaster 59 Years ago", Letterkenny Christmas Annual 1984
Watson, Billy, "On the Day of the Crash", Letterkenny Christmas Annual 1992
Curran, Sean, "A Growing Letterkenny With A Bright Future", Letterkenny Christmas Annual, 1982
O'Connor, Leo, "It All Started 66 years ago", Letterkenny Christmas Annual 2001
Prendergast, Charles, "Bacon Factory – The End of an Era", Letterkenny Christmas Annual 19
Dickson, David "A Donegal Revenue Inspection of 1775", Donegal Annual 1972
Kelly. AD, "Port Ballyraine", Letterkenny Christmas Annual 1987
Baird, John, "Remembering the Port Ballyraine", Letterkenny Christmas Annual 1997
Baird, John, "The Thorn: A Look at Letterkenny's Other Port", Letterkenny Christmas Annual 2000
"WM. McKinney & Sons Ltd.", Letterkenny Christmas Annual 1984
Carr, Caroline, "Oatfield – A Short but Sweet History", Letterkenny Christmas Annual 2009
Ball, CT, "Letterkenny 70 Years Ago", Letterkenny Christmas Annual 1984
"Nestle's Factory Letterkenny", Letterkenny Christmas Annual 1991
McGlinchey, Danny, "The Stage Musical in Letterkenny", Letterkenny Christmas Annual 1992
Rainey, Dermot, "The Business and Property scene in Letterkenny 1940s to 1960s", Letterkenny Christmas Annual 1993
Dawson, Pat "Letterkenny Industries Past and Present", Letterkenny Christmas Annual 1995
Mackey, Deace, "The International Folk Festival", Letterkenny Christmas Annual 1995
Duffy, Hugh, "The Story of the IAWS Letterkenny", Letterkenny Christmas Annual 2003
Blake, John, "The Towney's Lament", Letterkenny Christmas Annual 2006
Longwill, Edward, "Donegal and the Outbreak of the Northern Conflict 1968-69", Donegal Annual 2010